Volume 1

DIRECTORY OF WORLD CINEMA
JAPAN

Edited by John Berra

intellect Bristol, UK / Chicago, USA

ALL

First Published in the UK in 2010 by Intellect Books, The Mill, Parnall Road, Fishponds, Bristol, BS16 3JG, UK

First published in the USA in 2010 by Intellect Books, The University of Chicago Press, 1427 E. 60th Street, Chicago, IL 60637, USA

Publisher: May Yao
Publishing Assistant: Jennifer Schivas
Interns: Emily Caulfield, Naomi Warren, Johanna Pittam, Carmen Schaack

Cover Design: Holly Rose
Copy Editor: Heather Owen
Typesetting: Mac Style, Beverley, E. Yorkshire

Directory of World Cinema ISSN 2040-7971
Directory of World Cinema eISSN 2040-798X

Directory of World Cinema: Japan ISBN 978-1-84150-335-6
Directory of World Cinema: Japan eISBN 978-1-84150-356-1

Printed and bound by Gutenberg Press, Malta.

DIRECTORY OF WORLD CINEMA
JAPAN

ACKNOWLEDGEMENTS

This first edition of the *Directory of World Cinema: Japan* is the result of the commitment of a range of contributors from the fields of academia and film journalism. I would like to thank everyone who has contributed to this volume as, although the backgrounds and approaches of the writers who have submitted essays and reviews are quite diverse, their collective enthusiasm for the project has yielded an informed and insightful analysis of a fascinating national cinema. This volume was never intended to be a conventional film guide, as the overall aim was always to discuss Japanese cultural life and history as expressed through the medium of film. As such, I am most grateful to all of the contributors for embracing this brief and fully engaging with Japanese cinema through their preferred method of analysis, whether it be social-political, aesthetic, or genre-based. Through their discussions of such genres as Anime, Monster Movies, Samurai, Yakuza, Pink Films and the Contemporary Blockbuster, they have endeavoured to engage with students, senior academics, and film enthusiasts, and it has been a pleasure to work with each contributor in an editorial capacity.

I would also like to thank the team at Intellect, particularly Masoud Yazdani and May Yao, who have supported this volume through its various stages, making it a truly collaborative process. The commitment which Intellect is making towards the field of Film Studies is exemplified by this Directory, and will continue with other volumes in the *Directory of World Cinema* series. The *Directory of World Cinema: Japan* would also not have been possible without the assistance of David Desser, who was instrumental in bringing together many of contributors to this edition, and the critical network of the Toronto J-Film Pow-Wow, an online community which is dedicated to furthering the discussion of Japanese cinema in the West. A publication with the depth and scope of the *Directory of World Cinema: Japan* cannot come to fruition without such support, and your assistance is greatly appreciated.

John Berra

INTRODUCTION
BY THE EDITOR

The films that have emerged from Japan, from the silent period, to the post-war era, and the present day, represent a historically and culturally important national cinema; this is a cinema that has undergone fascinating transitions as it has responded to shifting political climates, the needs of the domestic audience, and the artistic ambitions of auteur directors. It has been suggested by Gerow in the *Encyclopaedia of Japanese Culture* (Buckley 2009) that the Japanese film industry has consciously modelled itself on Hollywood, with the formation of major studios and a reliance on particular genres and narrative forms, most obviously samurai, yakuza and monster movies, and the development of 'star' identities. However, the post-war Japanese film industry has also been director-orientated, which has allowed auteur filmmakers to develop their distinctive cinematic sensibilities both within the mainstream and on its margins; this has resulted in distinctive bodies of work which effortlessly blend the commercial with the personal, providing rich cultural and social-political insight, whilst also satisfying and subverting audience expectations both nationally and internationally.

Between 1950 and 1958, Japan was producing the largest number of films in the world but, as with its American model, it began to lose audiences due to the advent of television and the rejection of studio-sanctioned cinema by the all-important youth market. The industrial revolution that followed, which resulted in the advent of the Japanese New Wave, independent production, and the emergence of auteur filmmakers who were able to reach the youth audience with their volatile cinematic excursions into the underbelly of contemporary Japanese society, gave rise to a greater diversity in Japanese cinema. This sudden shift provided audiences with films that were experimental and politically-charged alongside more traditional entertainment that revelled in the rich history of the nation, whilst also commenting on modernity through the distance of the period piece. While the cinema of Japan is often appreciated for its aesthetics, with the expertly-staged widescreen-action of Akira Kurosawa and the familial intimacy of Yasujiro Ozu providing two contrasting but equally appropriate examples, it has also chronicled the turbulent history of the nation: the Heian and Edo periods have often served as the backdrop for historical drama, while the positive and negative aspects of the Occupation of Japan and its much-discussed 'bubble economy' have been acutely explored within established genre templates,

Whilst researching the subject of Contemporary World Cinema I had the pleasure of interviewing John Williams, a Welshman who is firmly established in the Japanese film industry since forming his production company 100 Metre Films, through which he has written and directed two fine films in the Japanese language, *Firefly Dreams* (2001) and *Starfish Hotel* (2006). He explained that, upon returning to the UK, he was disappointed to discover that the DVD racks of British retailers only featured titles by specific directors, such as Takeshi Kitano and Takashi Miike, who have been aggressively marketed to overseas audiences due to the 'extreme' nature of their work and that other aspects of Japanese Cinema have been somewhat neglected by global distributors. He also expressed frustration that 'the sexually explicit Japanese cinema that is better known in the West is a very marginal cinema in Japan', and that 'most of what I personally think is the great Japanese cinema of the last ten years has not made it to the UK or even outside Japan at all.' Williams concedes that such distribution issues are a 'market reality', and while this volume also acknowledges that reality by featuring a number of popular titles that are widely accessible outside Japan, it also attempts to readdress the balance by featuring a wide range of films and film-makers from Japan's cinematic past and present.

In the West, the cinema of Japan has recently been associated with cinematic strangeness and extremity, largely due to the J-Horror boom, which is now in decline in the domestic market and has also reached a plateau in the UK and elsewhere, largely due to the demise of the distributor Tartan and its 'Asia Extreme' label. The international success, particularly through the lucrative DVD market, of titles such as *Ring* (1998) and *Dark Water* (2002), both directed by Hideo Nakata, and Takashi Miike's *Audition* (1999), not to mention Kinji Fuka-saku's controversial cinematic swansong *Battle Royale* (2000), have brought contemporary Japanese cinema to an enthusiastic audience that is receptive to innovative genre fare, regardless of its country of origin. However, the popular-ity – and notoriety – of these films have somewhat obscured both the burgeon-ing independent sector of contemporary Japanese cinema and its legacy. Such excellent academic publications as Philips and Stringer's (2006) *Japanese Cinema: Texts and Contexts*, Nolletti and Desser's (2005) *Reframing Japanese Cinema*, and Ritchie's extensive work on the subject, which includes such texts as *Japanese Cinema: An Introduction*(1990) and *Japanese Cinema: Film Style and National Character* (1972), have played a vital role in emphasizing the cinematic identity of Japan, and ensuring that such important auteurs as Kenji Mizoguchi, Kon Ichikawa and Shohei Imamura and have not been neglected due to the popular trends and marketing hooks which often 'reinvent' national cinema, altering perceptions of style and content in pursuit of short-term economic gain.

As with the other volumes in the *Directory of World Cinema* series, the *Direc-tory of World Cinema: Japan* is intended to be informative rather than exhaustive. Instead of providing a general overview of Japanese Cinema, past and present, through a conventional A–Z structure, this volume aims to offer readers both familiar and unfamiliar with this particular national cinema a more culturally-specific insight into the films that have emerged from Japan. Reviews are organized by genre or cinematic movement, each section opening with an introductory essay, which aims to provide cultural and industrial context. Other sections include Industry Spotlight, which focuses on the Art Theatre Guild; a Festival Focus on the annual Nippon Connection event; and Cultural Crossover, which explores the links between Japanese Art and Japanese Cinema. The section on Directors provides the opportunity for more detailed discussion of three fascinating film-makers: Akira Kurosawa, Takeshi Kitano, and Satoshi Kon, with their oeuvres being analysed in relation to their production methodology, thematic concerns, and cinematic lega-cies. It is hoped that, by focusing on a range of significant genres and allowing contributors to adopt their preferred analytical approaches (aesthetic, industrial, social-political, transnational), the *Directory of World Cinema: Japan* provides a unique insight into 'Japaneseness' through the medium of film, and its national evolution as a mode of industrial and cultural production.

John Berra

Akiresu to Kame, 2008. Produced by Bandai/Wowow

FILM OF THE YEAR
ACHILLES AND THE TORTOISE

Achilles and the Tortoise

Akiresu to kame

Studio
Bandai Visual Company, Office Kitano

Director
Takeshi Kitano

Producer
Masayuki Mori, Takio Yoshida

Screenwriter
Takeshi Kitano

Cinematographer
Katsumi Yanagishima

Synopsis

Machisu is an introverted child, immersed in his own world of painting. His father is a wealthy industrialist who believes he is a connoisseur of the arts and has also acted as a patron, sponsoring local artists to study in Paris and find their own style. Indulged, due to his father's money and influence, Machisu has no shortage of art supplies and is able to walk out of a maths lesson to paint instead, or hold up traffic so that he can sketch the vehicles, but his creative comfort comes to an abrupt end when his father's business collapses overnight and his parents commit suicide. He briefly resides with his poor Uncle, who has always resented his brother for not spreading his wealth, but Machisu's ambitions are out of place in this lower-class household and he is soon packed off to the orphanage to which his father once donated money. In his early twenties, Machisu takes on various menial jobs to pay the fees for art school and, while doing so, meets Sachiko, one of the few people who will ever understand his art, and marries her. The naïve Machisu attempts to impress a local art dealer with his paintings but always leaves the gallery disappointed, although the dealer does sell some of his work behind his back. In his later years, Machisu relies on his wife and teenage daughter for financial support but eventually alienates those around him. When his daughter dies and his wife insists on a separation, Machisu's art becomes altogether darker and ultimately self-destructive.

Composers
Yuki Kajiura

Editor
Takeshi Kitano

Duration
199 minutes

Cast
Takeshi Kitano, Kanako Higuchi,
Kumiko Aso, Nao Omori

Year
2008

Critique

It is possible to view Takeshi Kitano's *Achilles and the Tortoise* as the final instalment of a swiftly-realized, semi-autobiographical trilogy about the nature of the artist, as it follows *Takeshis'* (2005) and *Glory to the Filmmaker* (2007). However, *Achilles and the Tortoise* is less self-reflexive than those films, not nearly as divisive, and ultimately more involving in that it revolves around Kitano's great passion – painting – as opposed to his public persona. Kitano's enthusiasm for art has been widely documented, with painterly touches featuring in such films as *Hana-Bi* (1997) and *Dolls* (2002), but the character of Machisu, who Kitano portrays in the final section, is certainly not a self-portrait. Whereas the writer-director-actor-comedian-artist has found success in a variety of fields and guises, and often united multiple facets of his persona within his filmic oeuvre, Machisu repeatedly fails as an artist, rejected by the local art dealer and, eventually, by his own family. The paintings featured in the film are all by Kitano himself but they were obviously created 'in character', with their overt references to modern art reflecting the fact that Machisu is as derivative as he is compulsive.

Although this a more formal work than *Takeshis'* or *Glory to the Filmmaker*, Kitano's absurdist humour is still evident, often suggesting that art can be a tragic folly for those who are not destined for commercial success with a series of throwaway jokes at the expense of the pretentious art students that Machisu falls in with during his college years. In one scene, they try crashing into a wall in order to dramatically spill paint. Initial efforts, achieved by a student riding into the wall on a bicycle, generate striking results but when another student drives his car into the wall, he ends up killing himself. In later life, Machisu's attempt to enter into a state of 'craziness', in order to produce art that is more shocking, almost results in his death as he submerges himself in bath water and asks his wife to hold him under. This only results in Machisu being rushed to the emergency room and his wife being briefly taken into custody, as the police officers who arrive on the scene assume that she has tried to 'murder' her partner by drowning him. Yet beneath the black humour there is also an unflinching honesty to the film, shown through the character of Machisu's daughter, a frustrated teenager who leaves home and becomes a prostitute, later scheduling a brief meeting with her father around a rendezvous with a 'client'. When his daughter dies, Kitano and his now-estranged wife identify the body in the morgue, but what should be a moment of reconciliation at a time of grief becomes a disturbing insight into the depth of Machisu's obsession with art: he takes his wife's lipstick and draws on his daughter's dead body, treating her corpse as an art project. His wife understandably breaks down and leaves in disgust.

As both an artist and a human being, Machisu never really develops and seems to exist in a perpetual state of arrested development. Indulged at a young age, largely due to his father's wealth and prominence in the local community, he stubbornly refuses to accept that there may be things in life more important than art and the pursuit of his dreams. Even experiences which should burst his self-involved bubble, such as living with his working-class uncle, or undertaking menial jobs as a delivery boy or factory machinist, do little for his character and it is only in his later years, when his daughter dies and his wife leaves him, that he begins to consider the ramifications of his devotion to his work. However, even his depression and grief are channelled into the creation of more extreme pieces rather than a re-evaluation of his principles, continuing to paint even when he is caught in a fire.

As an artist, he 'peaks' during childhood and never really evolves, partly because he is 'encouraged' to study other styles as a means of catering to the market for wealthy 'connoisseurs' like his late father, losing any originality by working systematically through the approaches and methods of the most celebrated 'names' in modern art. The early praise he receives is not due to the quality of his work but because nobody dares to offend his father, although unscrupulous dealers are happy to ridicule his lack of taste behind his back. Machisu's main failing as an artist is his desire to sell and his over-eagerness to adopt the style of others as a means of achieving commercial viability. An animated prologue sequence illustrates the Greek philosopher Zeno of Elea's motion paradox of Achilles failing to overtake a tortoise because every time Achilles reaches a certain point, the tortoise has already moved on. Machisu embraces style after style on the insistence of the local art dealer, but always finds that he is a step behind the ever-evolving art world and shifting tastes. A paining that he had produced years earlier does eventually sell, albeit to a commercial enterprise rather than a serious collector, and is seen hanging on the wall of the bar where Machisu meets his estranged daughter to borrow money for art supplies.

The finale, with Machisu released from hospital and reunited with his Sachiko, may seem convenient as the stubborn artist, who has failed to rise above the status of 'amateur', belatedly realizes that 'success' does not always equal 'love' and chooses the latter over the former. Yet he only does this after a final, futile attempt to sell a piece of 'found art', a burnt soda can which he has retrieved from the wreckage of the fire. With its vicious portrayal of gallery owners and agents, *Achilles and the Tortoise* finds Kitano venting his frustration with the hypocrisy of the art world while also questioning the place of art in contemporary society, but it is also an affecting story of a 'misunderstood' artist who all too easily loses what should have been his signature style through critical misdirection.

John Berra

FESTIVAL FOCUS
NIPPON CONNECTION

Nippon Connection is, as of 2009, the largest annual showcase in the world for films from Japan. Staged in April of every year in Frankfurt, Germany, it shows a cross-section of almost the entire audio-visual production of the Japanese media industry. Showcasing around 150 films over five days to an audience of over 16.000, it features a large number of German, European, international and even world premiere screenings. Every year, 30–40 film-makers from Japan attend Nippon Connection in Frankfurt to introduce their films, with past guests including the likes of Shinya Tsukamoto, Ryûichi Hiroki, Kaori Momoi, Toshiaki Toyoda and Koji Wakamatsu. The 2009 festival featured guests such as directors Kazuyoshi Kumakiri, Yuki Tanada, and Ryuichi Honda, anime director Tatsuyuki Tanaka, and Yukie Kito, the producer of the award-winning *Tokyo Sonata* (2008). Aside from its enviable range of screenings, the Frankfurt festival is supplemented by a large number of lectures, exhibitions, workshops, and performances.

Nippon Connection has grown considerably since its inception in the year 2000, when 13 films were screened and two guest film-makers attended, including a young Nobuhiro Yamashita. This expansion coincided with an explosive growth of Japanese feature film production and its increasing success in the international market. Nippon Connection was originally founded by then-students of Theatre, Film and Media from the Goethe University of Frankfurt. With Japanese cinema experiencing a critical resurgence in the late 1990s, such films were, at the time, primarily and very selectively screened at venues such as the Rotterdam International Film Festival or the Cannes Film Festival. The 2000 Nippon Connection Festival was originally conceived as a one-off event but audience attendance was four times the initial expectation, despite the usually lacklustre commercial performance of films from Japan when released in German cinemas. The obvious interest in Japanese film led to the re-conception of the festival as an annually-staged European event on a larger scale. Nippon Connection's considerable success can conceivably be attributed to increased production in Japan, a growing general interest in Japanese popular culture, innovative programming, and the burgeoning of the economy that has led to overall growth and multiplication of film festivals since the early 1980s.

In its present form, the festival consists of four sections. Nippon Cinema shows 35mm productions ranging from every genre and budget level of theatrical releases in Japan. Nippon Digital focuses on a somewhat wider range of predominantly digitally-produced works that include experimental or student films, as well as specials focusing on directors or production initiatives, music videos or commercial feature film productions. By assembling films often difficult to see even for residents of Japan, the Nippon Digital section of the event has developed a reputation as a hunting ground for young talent amongst international critics and programmers. Nippon Retro features an annually-changing retrospective that focuses variably on directors, genres, or other themes. Finally, the Nippon Culture section stages a large variety of additional events that include art exhibitions, lectures, podium discussions, workshops and performances. Nippon Connection 2009 devoted a special focus to the role of women in the Japanese film industry, with a podium discussion on the topic, lectures on gender issues, and special programmes such as *Peaches!* to look specifically at female directors. Often, artists are invited from Japan, and contribute contemporary re-imaginings of film-related arts such as Kami-shibai (paper theatre) and combinations of dance or live-music with film screenings.

Possibly due to its roots in academia, Nippon Connection's programme visibly engages with conceptual problems that accompany the staging of a festival focused exclusively on films produced within a single film industry perceived in a national

framework. These problems become pronounced when the national framework in question is Japan: a country whose national identity has been constructed, both in- and outside of Japan, along the lines of a particularly stubborn cultural essentialism. The tropes of exceptionalism and Japanese uniqueness are easily appropriated by nationalism, and the question remains of how a festival showing films from Japan can complicate such cultural mechanisms. These concerns have, to a certain degree, been exacerbated by the recent interest of the Japanese government in utilizing popular culture as a means for accumulating both economic and political capital through a national brand characterized by 'Japan cool'.

The spectrum of the film selection is thus very broad in an attempt to avoid any possibility of isolating a 'national spirit', instead focusing on the high degree of diversity within the Japanese film industry. Screenings of low-budget films from less-respected popular genres, such as V-Cinema and Pink Film, occur alongside internationally-recognized arthouse films and commercial blockbusters and encourage the rearranging of canon and complicate the construction of a coherent model of film from Japan. The 2009 festival devoted an entire retrospective to pink film, with 78-year old pink film veteran Mamoru Watanabe in attendance, and his presence was accompanied by various lectures and talk events to put this idiosyncratic genre in perspective. Events involving what is labelled as 'traditional' or 'hyper-modern' Japanese culture are, according to the organizers, meant to attract a wider audience that will inevitably have more experience with stereotypical depictions. Attendees are also prompted to spend additional time at the festival centre between screenings, and to see films that counter these very expectancies. Thus, the three-storey festival centre, with its two theatres and large number of events in various spaces of the building, is meant to invite a multitude of experiences.

Side projects further engage the questions of confluence and exchange. From 2003, the Exchanging Tracks project provided composers from all genres and from all over Europe with recordings of urban sounds from Japan as touchstones for new compositions. The resultant musical pieces were then handed over to directors in Japan, who used them to shoot short films which were then screened at the festival in the presence of both the composers and the film-makers. In 2007, the Kinema Club Conference, one of the most important regularly-held international conferences on film and moving images from Japan, was co-hosted by Nippon Connection. In 2009, Nippon Connection featured a 'virtual bar' that connected the bar area at Nippon Connection with a bar in the Shinjuku quarter of Tokyo via video chat. This enabled the audience to interact and share drinks with film-makers assembled at the Tokyo bar whose films had been screened in Frankfurt on the respective day.

The 2009 Nippon Connection once again featured so many sold-out screenings that it is clear that the festival will need to expand beyond the current four screening venues if it wants to increase audience attendance. The 2009 programme assembled the usual broad array of films, ranging from Sion Sono's sensational *Love Exposure* (2008) to indie-animation collective *Animation Soup* and a selection of the best films from the 2009 edition of the legendary Yubari Fantastic Film Festival, while the winner of the audience award for Best Film in the Nippon Cinema section was Toshio Lee's *Detroit Metal City* (2008). A segment of the programme, under the banner of Nippon Connection on Tour, will be screened at various film festivals and arthouse cinema chains in Europe and North and South America, the Barcelona Asian Film Festival and the New York Asian Film Festival among them, making the highlights of the event accessible to appreciative audiences worldwide.

Alexander Zahlten

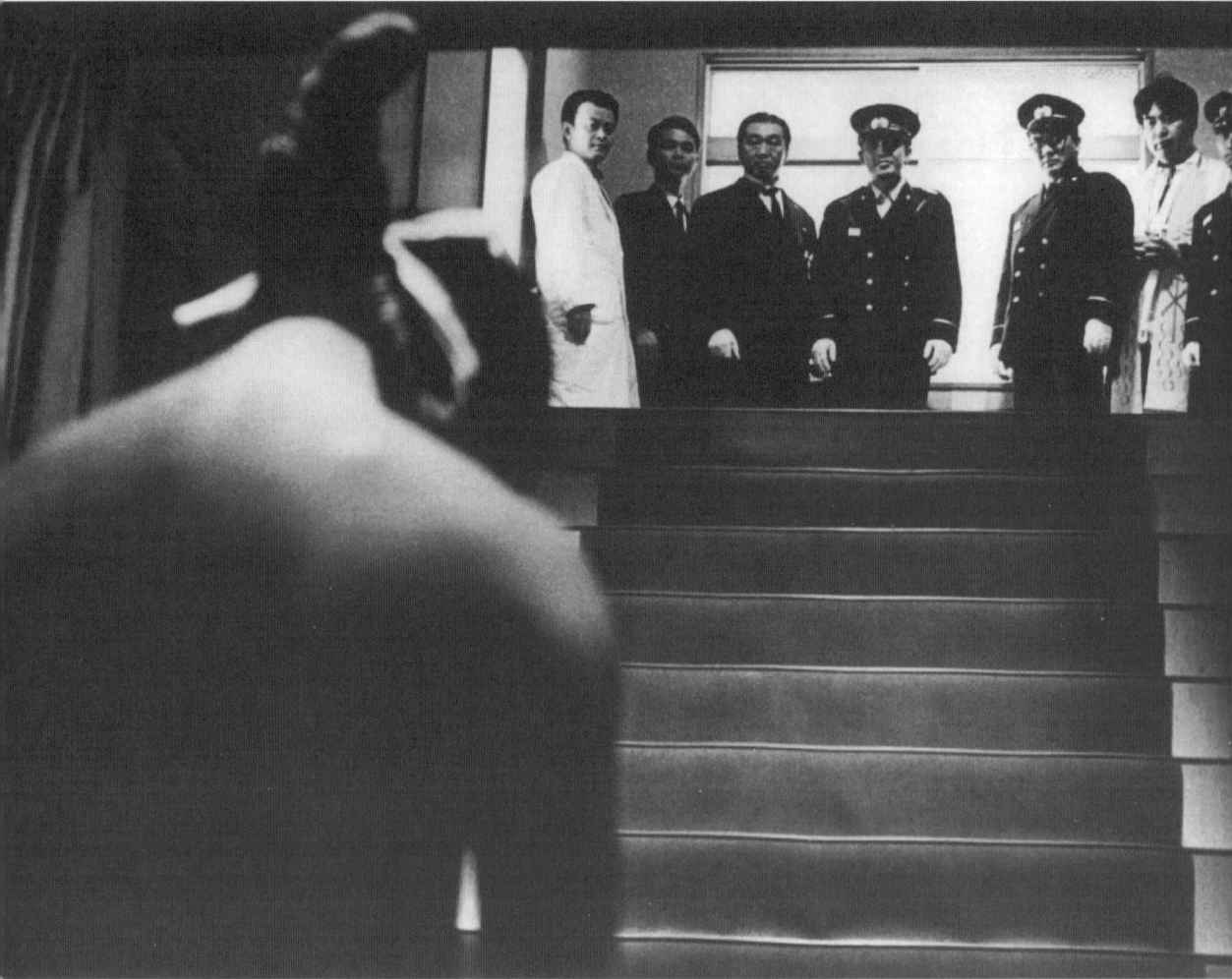

Death By Hanging, 1968. Produced by Sozo-Sha

INDUSTRY SPOTLIGHT
THE ART THEATRE GUILD

1961 saw the birth of the Art Theatre Guild, an independent association dedicated to exploring the artistic possibilities of cinema. ATG quickly achieved its place in film history as the most important producer and distributor of independent films in Japan; their activities led the art cinema scene for many years. As an alternative to the commercial studio products available to the Japanese public, ATG promoted an environment where viewers could immerse themselves in foreign art cinema, and where artists could engage in independent film-making. ATG and their cinemas became the central hub for creativity in the field of the moving image, a meeting point for the nexus of artistic ideas, uniting the network of heterogeneous voices of Japan's underground cinema scene.

Titans of Japanese cinema, such as Nagisa Oshima, Kaneto Shindo, Yasuzo Masumura, Kon Ichikawa, Shohei Imamura, as well as lesser-known artists including Masahiro Shinoda, Hani Susumu, Yoshida Yoshishige and Toshio Matsumoto, were all, for one reason or another, drawn to the institution and were provided with a platform for individual expression uninhibited by commercial constraints. ATG's artistic integrity and flexibility generated a canon of work that resonated with expressive energy and an eagerness to experiment; their corpus perhaps unparalleled in the rest of the world. An attempt to assemble the commonalities within their work meets with complications as their modus operandi entailed individual autonomy, diversity and artistic experimentation. Nevertheless, when we frame the Art Theatre Guild within a socio-historical context, we are provided with a fascinating perspective on the shifting mechanisms of Japanese culture and society, its film history, and a gripping record of the artistic blossoming of many of Japan's key directors.

ATG was first established as a distributor for foreign arthouse films with a commitment to screening a variety of serious art films from around the globe, at this point scarcely available to the general public. Regulation in currency and quota systems on imports meant that local distributors avoided art films, which were unable to guarantee financial revenue. To prevent such a deficiency in the cinema scene, the Art Theatre Guild of Japan was launched in November 1961 with the opening of ten art cinemas across the country. Their programmes were launched in April 1962 with *Mother Joan of the Angels* (Kawalerowicz, 1961) at the Shinjuku Bunka, the main cinema of the ATG chain located on the east side of Shinjuku, which was to become the heart of artistic and political events in Tokyo over the decade. Programming decisions were made by a committee including Japanese film critics, film-makers and Kashiko Kawakita, one of the initiators of the ATG project and a key figure in the cross-pollination of films between Europe and Japan, alongside her husband, Nagamasa, who had founded Towa Trading Company. Devoted to showcasing an array of foreign productions, the films were chosen for their engagement with cinema as an artistic medium. As well as classics never publicly screened before in Japan, including the likes of *Citizen Kane* and *Battleship Potemkin*, ATG distributed films from contemporaries around the world. ATG emerged at an exciting period in film history, where a burst of creativity simultaneously erupted onto the cinematic plateau. Their programme primarily incorporated the New Wave films from Europe, but India's Satyajit Ray, Brazil's Glauber Rocha, and Japanese independents such as Hiroshi Teshigahara also had their work distributed around Japan. ATG established an artistically pensive environment for their audience, with films being screened for at least a month to allow multiple viewings, and their choice of films successfully generated an enthusiasm for international film and advocated an investigation of film history.

Nevertheless, by the late 60s the Art Theatre Guild encountered difficulties when some of their cinemas around the country dropped out of the project, perhaps due to inevitable financial difficulties. In Tokyo, other cinemas recognized the public's interest in foreign art cinema, consequently restricting ATG's selection of films. Furthermore, the government withdrew the quota regulations and relaxed rules on the importation of foreign films and, accordingly, distribution fees for imported films escalated. Amidst these shifting patterns of economic interaction, ATG's aspirations were revitalized in the formation of a production unit. As Kuzui Kinshiro, the manager of the Shinjuku Bunka and a key producer of ATG admitted, '[o]ne could say that, in a way, I benefited from the misfortunes of others'. Young film-makers of the major studios, including Oshima, Shinoda and Yoshida of Shochiku, encountering increasing frustration with the artistic restrictions of their companies, had left their studio occupations to pursue independence. These studio rejects were in search of a place to present their work, and many had been in contact with the cinemas of ATG. Screenings of Oshima's film *Yunbogi's Diary* and Yukio Mishima's *Patriotism* had frequently sold out at the cinemas, encouraging ATG to sponsor independent film-making in their own country. After testing the water by supporting Imamura's *A Man Vanishes* halfway through production in 1967, ATG initiated a plan for 10-million-yen films, where they would provide half the budget of 5 million, and the rest was to be assembled by the film-makers' own production units. Starting with Oshima's seminal film *Death by Hanging*, ATG became the motor that drove the Japanese independent cinema scene for the next thirty years.

Independent film-makers were to discover their perfect partnership with the Art Theatre Guild. Despite the constraints of moderate finance, the artists were given complete artistic autonomy, cinemas for their films to be screened in an appropriate environment, and the possibility of foreign exposure through Kawakita's relationship with film festivals in the West. The planning committee consisted of film critics and Kinshiro Kuzui, who advocated films with artistic energy. This support, along with the social unrest and heated political agitation of the late 1960s in Japan, provided the backdrop for an exciting period of artistic experimentation and political awakening in Japanese cinema. The prospect of the renewal of the Anpo US-Japan Security Treaty at the end of the decade enraged the Japanese public, and led to protests against the continual presence of the US army on Japanese soil. Zengakuren[1] demonstrations became a common occurrence amongst the streets of Shinjuku, which became a platform for interpenetration between art and politics. Student protesters and striving artists freely conversed in the Shinjuku Bunka, encouraging a productive dialogue between politics and art. Bombs exploded on the street where Shinjuku Bunka was located, and the police interrogated Kuzui about his friendship with politically-motivated film-makers-cum-activists like Masao Adachi and Koji Wakamatsu. It was in this environment where politics occupied the forefront of life that the spiral of discontent formed a springboard for the artists, from which ATG productions emerged and were at their prime.

The films of the Art Theatre Guild invigorated the Japanese cinema scene with a thematically and stylistically diverse range of films. Documentarists, studio rejects, TV directors, experimental film-makers, poets and artists were attracted by the prospect of artistic freedom that ATG offered. Projects were initiated for their originality, encouraging film-makers to propose ideas that intentionally subverted the artistic mores of cinema. Although the majority of the productions were original screenplays, theatrical adaptations were not uncommon, with films like *Double Suicide* (Shinoda, 1969) and *Shura* (Matsumoto, 1971) incorporating the aesthetics of traditional Japanese theatre to consciously deconstruct cinematic form. Formal innovation was also encouraged in the ATG and film-makers interrogated cinema as a medium, re-evaluating artistic certainties. The boundaries between reality and fiction were frequently explored through the medium, often disruptively mediating between temporal spaces to generate an immersive experience of confusion and uncertainty. Productions quickly garnered prestige and crewmembers and actors offered to work for low costs, simply for the kudos of taking part. The films courageously tackled subject matter that was deemed socially and politically controversial, such as *Death by Hanging*'s attack on state execution, and the portrayal of such themes were fearless. The films resonated with nihilistic energy and sprightly exuberance, exemplified in Matsumoto's *Funeral Parade of Roses* (1969), Oshima's *The Man Who Left His Will on Film* (1969) and Hani Susumu's *The Inferno of First Love* (1968). Shinjuku Bunka built an underground theatre which featured avant-garde plays by the likes of Yukio Mishima and screened 8mm and 16mm experimental films. It became a meeting point for a constellation of conceptions between the arts, formulating an interdisciplinary network of creativity, which was reflected in the artists' work with the ATG. With the support of the ATG, films like Oshima's *Boy* (1969) and *Ceremony* (1971), Terayama Shuji's *Throw Away the Books, Let's Go into the Streets* (1971), and Koji Wakamatsu's *Ecstasy of the Angels* (1971) emerged out this context and led the forefront of the art cinema scene in Japan.

Although the Art Theatre Guild continued to generate a diverse assortment of inventive cinema, by the mid-70s the films were increasingly geared towards the conventional. After 1972's Asama Cottage Incident, the turbulence of social unrest was no longer a focus of public interest and the radical spirit of the age ceased to exist. With the Shinjuku Bunka shut down in 1974, unable to sustain the high maintenance costs of the building, the New Wave films were no longer screened in such an artistically-interactive environment. ATG's insistence on original scripts was soon abandoned and, after the financial triumph of Yoichi Takabayashi's adaptation of Seishi Yokomizo's *Murder in Honjin Manor House*, a succession of literary adaptations followed. Iseki Taneo retired from his 17-year presidency at ATG to pass the baton to Shiro Sasaki, who ushered in a new era for the Art Theatre Guild. As the major studios curtailed their number of productions to regulate costs, newcomers found it increasingly hard to launch their careers. However, Sasaki's renewed dedication to support newcomers and those from pink cinema backgrounds provided opportunities within ATG. Although there were notable exceptions, these later films no longer demonstrated the impulsive drive and experimental edge that pervaded ATG's earlier productions. As studios continued to downsize their production, independency in film-making became the standard in Japan. Following Sasaki's departure in 1986, ATG activities came to a virtual standstill. After a little action with Shigeo Kusano as president, the cultural initiators have been inactive since the release of Kaneto Shindo's *The Strange Tale of Oyuki* in 1992.

Currently, with the vast majority of Japanese production and distribution organized by independents, and the increasing availability of foreign and local art-house cinema starting with the arrival of video in the 80s, then DVD, and possibly now with downloading, it could be said that ATG accomplished their goals and have no need to remain. Yet, the cinema scene today seems somewhat lacking in comparison; its motivation and energy unparalleled, the Art Theatre Guild is surely missed.[2]

Notes

1. Zengakuren are a socialist federation of university students.
2. Contextual information and ideas are heavily indebted to the inspiring work of Roland Domenig, Go Hirasawa, and Isolde Standish.

Julian Ross

CULTURAL CROSSOVER
ART AND FILM

The close relationship between image and text, or picture and narration, has a long history in Japanese art forms. The first example of this relationship is *emakimono* – narrative scrolls that offered the possibility of following a story in a combination of writing and painting – go back as early as the twelfth century. In certain cases, these were simply illustrated fiction novels, with the most popular being the *Genji monogatari emakimono* (Tales of Genji scroll, c.1130) and those could, to an extent, be compared with illuminated manuscripts. However, versions of storytelling in the form of unreeling images with not a single written word to accompany them were also made, the best known example of these being *Choju Giga* (Scrolls of Frolicking Animals). These were sometimes used in *kamishibai* – picture-story shows, in which they would be presented to help stir the imagination of an audience.

This tradition was to continue in classical painting, often executed on sequential *byobu* panels and popular woodblock prints, where references to literary origins were made via the inclusion of pictures within the pictures in the form of *mitate* (most commonly translated as 'parody' but serving a function of allusion). A practice of illustrated albums where the eye was entertained by a continuous imagery of a similar subject was widespread in the period between the seventeenth and nineteenth centuries, with the most frequently-quoted example being Hokusai's *Manga* series: 15 volumes of varied sketches published over a number of decades after 1814.

The playful spirit of the *Ukiyo-e* world was sometimes expressed in games involving *mawaritoro* – revolving lanterns, resulting in an effect similar to early phantasmagoria shows. Optical devices enabling different or enhanced perspectives were known from the eighteenth century onwards, imported via Holland, and included *oranda megane* ('Dutch glasses') and *nozoki-karakuri* ('peeping automata') box, early forms of entertainment that involved moving pictures. The text-image relationship together with existing interest in and knowledge of methods of image animation were to provide necessary foundation for the twentieth-century developments in crossovers between visual art and film.

The arrival of Western products of the mechanical age – photography and film – were welcomed with curiosity and a willingness for experimentation, with traditional aesthetics and classical theatre fertilizing the ground for their further growth on Japanese soil. At the turn of the century, the spirit of modernism was taking root in Japan with avant-garde artists grouping around *Mavo* magazine and various photography clubs informed by Surrealism, Constructivism and Futurism being established around the country. An active exchange of ideas with European artists and intellectuals and achievements in the visual domain helped bridge the gap between traditional Japanese and the post-war art, which was to embrace transnational heritage of cinematography as an equal visual reference.

The Neo-Dadaist movement that spread in Japan during the early 1960s created a background for experimental photographers, video and film artists, with Hosoe Eikoh, Tomatsu Shomei and Takahiko Imura playing significant roles. This atmosphere informed Nam June Paik while studying aesthetics at the Tokyo University and produced some of the best-known Japanese avant-garde directors.

Multi-media and conceptual movements springing out from the booming New York art scene are the most obvious starting point, and a basis for cross-referencing. Film and visual arts were quick to reach Japan and the first examples of their miscegenation should be looked for in this period. The work of Tadanori Yokoo, an active member of underground Tokyo circles, equally inspired by psychedelic and Pop Art as well as *Edo* period Japanese aesthetics, is particularly important in terms of art-film interaction. Marilyn Monroe and James Dean play as much a part in the visual vocabulary of his posters from the 1970s as the more traditional *Ukiyo-e* iconography. Yokoo not only explored innovative graphic design styles but also announced final inclusion of Japan into international art circles of the postmodern, globalized era.

Aside from more traditional means, in which cinematography and visual art were cross-influencing each other in terms of perspective and time-space representations, Western cinematography informing the work of Japanese visual artists added another layer in interpretation of this type of artworks. The tendency culminated in the 1990s in the oeuvre of Morimura Yasumasa and Shinji Ogawa. Within the domain of photography, Yasumasa's images from the series *M's Self-Portraits* (1993–2000), where he takes on the roles of female Hollywood actresses inspired by Cindy Sherman's *Untitled Film Stills* series, are the best example of the further usage of film imagery in the visual art medium, as previously practiced by Yokoo. Yasumasa appropriated the Western film iconography as a setting of his work, openly quoting his source with a self-portrait as Cindy herself (*To my little sister: Cindy Sherman*, 1998). These are explorations into issues of identity, with the moving image becoming a database of its still counterpart, so photography across different continents was an appropriate vehicle for Yasumasa's cross-cultural, cross-medium and cross-gender experiments. In addition, Shinji Ogawa's *Without You* series, in which he renders still shots from Hollywood movies in oil using photorealistic methodology in order to deploy them on canvas, furthers the question of not only the globalization of the filmic iconography and the ways it is used in the dialogue of different artistic media but the perception of reality and how it becomes signified in the visual domain

The twentieth-century medium that got closest to bringing together visual art and film, however, is video. When discussing the Japanese scene, Mori Mariko is possibly the most apparent representative of this merger. Although her work continued to grow from the initial *Birth of Star* series (1995) towards internationally-acclaimed videos such as *Miko no inori* ('The Shaman's Prayer', 1996) and more demanding installation pieces, especially upon her move to New York, performance and fantasy continued to play a large part. In the construction of a fictional narrative presented in video format, she can be considered similar to another Japanese artist of the medium – Shimabuku. Most recently, Hiraki Sawa practices a particularly filmic style, constructing both miniature settings and narratives for his 'moving collages'.

A component that cannot be omitted in whatever is said about contemporary art in Japan is animation, as its omnipresence in Japanese culture makes it relevant in any discourse, especially the one on cinema. There are a number of artists of the younger generation who use animation as the medium of their expression and Ayako Tabata, aka Tabaimo, and her installation pieces based on animated hand drawings are probably the finest example. With a general tone that is reminiscent of traditional Japan, drawing on classic *Ukiyo-e* iconography (*Japanese Bathhouse*, 2000) she is demonstrating the latest achievements of multi-media and is equally recognized in Japan and on the international stage. Animation is maybe the most interesting medium when thinking about different crossovers between cinema and art – in Panofsky's sense that 'comic strip is the most important root of cinema' – as there are a number of cross-pollinations in Japanese context that can be looked at.

The process, which combines visual narration of *emakimono* as an origin of manga comics and anime films with cinematic technology, goes back to becoming a formal art form outside of its studio production, with production stills being considered works of art in themselves. Because most of the animated productions have become computer-generated during the 1990s, animation cels as original artworks are now established as the latest collectibles, with those from Studio Ghibli being on special demand. However, classical *Ukiyo-e* iconography continues to be a recurrent visual reference in the work of contemporary Japanese artists, and, as such, has found its way to the film as well – through *Ukiyo-e projections*, series of photographs by Eikoh Hosoe made in 2002 most notably to the 2006 film *Sakuran* directed by the photographer Mika Ninagawa.

Examples of visual art inspiring the work of film directors include some of the Japan's most prolific authors, such as Akira Kurosawa and Takeshi Kitano. Kurosawa is known to have failed an entrance exam to art school, thus abandoning early aspirations of becoming a painter. His passion for visual art was to manifest in frequent visits to gallery spaces and the talent he had is obviously expressed in the sketches he made for his films, *Kagamusha* (1980) in particular. A life-long admiration for the work of Van Gogh (who was himself inspired by Japanese woodcut print artists, especially Hiroshige Ando) was to be expressed in the *Dreams* (1990). Van Gogh has also been inspiration for a series of paintings by Takeshi Kitano, who first ventured into artistic practice after a motorbike accident in 1994. Colourful and playful canvases that he continued to create in the following years have been included in some of his films – *Hanabi* (1997), *Kikujiro* (1999) and most notably *Achilles and the Tortoise* (2008). The lives of artists have also proved inspirational for film-makers in cases such as Kenji Mizoguchi's *Utamaro and his Five Women* (1946) and Seijun Suzuki's *Yumeji* (1991).

The border territory between art and film provides a field for constant exploration, and for the continuous evolution of the relationships between text and image, representation and reality, space and perception. Within the Japanese context, referencing traditional art history and media, as well as the appropriation of globalized film imagery, plays an additional role. As a result, the field can be seen as an open domain for transnational dialogue, allowing the reassessment of understanding the many issues surrounding the always-relevant issues of identity, artistic practice and taxonomy of contemporary art.

Jelena Stojkovic

Kikujiro No Natsu, 1999, Sony Pictures Classics. Photographed by Tsuranuku Kumagai

DIRECTORS
TAKESHI KITANO

'Everyone's crazy', comments the cool-headed assassin in the finale of Takeshi Kitano's directorial debut *Violent Cop* (1989), having just off-loaded Azuma (Kitano), the violent cop of the title. It is a comment that could easily apply to nearly all the major protagonists across Kitano's fourteen films to date. Madness, and the suicide that can often follow, is a consistent preoccupation for Kitano, just as death and disability haunts his films like a spectre.

In the case of *Violent Cop*, it is illness, mental or otherwise, that drives the plot. Azuma's colleague Iwaki, already sick with terminal cancer, has been selling confiscated drugs to make enough money to support his family – though when killed by the yakuza, his death is made to look like suicide. Meanwhile, Azuma's sister Akari, the only character he treats with kindness, has been recently released from a psychiatric hospital, leaving her virtually catatonic. She is later kidnapped, drugged and raped in an act that sends her brother on a suicidal revenge mission. Indeed, *Violent Cop* sets the pattern for many a Kitano film to come, with the almost casual juxtaposition of extreme brutality (notably, the unforgettable moment when Azuma kicks a gun away from an assailant, only for it to blow off an innocent bystander's head) and physical comedy. Like a mix of Dirty Harry and Charlie Chaplin, as he comically kicks a young man down the street after he catches him enjoying 'relations' with his sister, Azuma may well be the craziest of all. The finale, which sees him kill his sister along with her kidnappers, proves just how close to madness he is.

Such themes have long been a part of Kitano's work, even before his near-fatal motorbike crash in August 1994, which left him with an open skull fracture, brain contusions and a fractured cheekbone, causing partial paralysis to the right side of his face. Accident or otherwise – Kitano had ridden, drunk, into a barrier without a helmet – it came at a time when he was at his lowest ebb. *Sontaine* (1993), his masterly third film about a yakuza who decides to quit the life of crime, had failed to find an audience in Japan. Already, Kitano was well aware that those reared on his outrageous television appearances as in game shows like *Takeshi's Castle* (1986–1999) were unwilling to accept him as a serious actor-director. Little wonder, then, that *Sonatine* brims with an unerring pessimism as its lead character Murakawa (Kitano) contemplates the futility of existence. 'When you're scared all the time, you reach a point when you wish you were dead', he claims. By the end, he will be – putting a gun to his head after slaying his rival gangsters.

As Kitano's regular composer Joe Hisaishi later reflected of his director, 'I feel that *Sonatine* showed that he was tired of living.' He followed it with *Getting Any?* (1994), a sex comedy that symbolized his self-destructive streak. Later dubbed 'artistic suicide' by Kitano, this absurdist story of a lad who just wants to get laid is a riotous piece of self-mockery. If this does not sound like the work of a man contemplating the end of his life, his long-time producer Mori Masayuki noted on the shoot that '[w]e began to be concerned that Kitano was beginning to lose his mental balance.'

The subsequent accident changed all that – yet Kitano's fascination with death did not diminish. Perhaps it is no coincidence that the high point of his career came shortly afterwards. After completing his comeback with *Kids Return* (1996), his amiable autobiographical account of his schooldays, he made *Hana-Bi* (1997), the film that went on to win the Golden Lion at the Venice Film Festival. This story of the near-silent unstable cop Nishi (Kitano) represented something of a catharsis for the writer-director-star. Curiously, the film almost feels like a sequel to *Violent Cop*. In both, Kitano is a renegade police officer; in both, he follows acts of savagery with tender feelings towards a loved one. In the case of *Hana-Bi*, these are towards his wife, who is dying of leukaemia – a tragic fact that inspires him to take her on one final road trip, winding up at the beach (echoing Azuma's outing with his sister). Similarly, Nishi demonstrates the suicidal tendencies of Azuma: 'Go on, shoot me punk!' he cries to a debt-chasing hoodlum. The film turns on the fact that Nishi's former partner Horibe (Ren Osugi) has been confined to a wheelchair following a shoot-out in a shopping mall. Distraught and depressed, Horibe attempts suicide by swallowing sleeping pills. When he survives, he turns to painting – using materials secretly paid for by Nishi. Featuring real paintings by Kitano, made during his recuperation from his accident, these bizarre but beautiful works (an owl with sunflower eyes, penguins with orchid heads and so on) suggest the redemptive power of art.

Strangely, in Kitano's later film *Achilles and the Tortoise* (2008), he questioned the very usefulness of art. Once again, suicide is prominent – as the young artist-wannabe Machisu (played later as a grown-up by Kitano) is orphaned after his parents' business crumbles and they kill themselves. He then spends his life trying to make his fortune through painting, convinced that, if it sells, it is great art. The more obsessed (another key Kitano theme) Machisu becomes, the more he risks losing his family, friends and, above all, health. Art can be cruel – particularly to those who do not recognize their own limitations. *Achilles and the Tortoise* arrived as the third of a self-reflective trilogy, following *Takeshis'* (2005) and *Glory to the Filmmaker!* (2007), an examination of his own status as a director. *Takeshis'*, meanwhile, examines his 'Beat' Takeshi persona and how it has impacted upon his life. Seen by some as a sequel of sorts to *Getting Any?*, it represents a second 'artistic suicide', quite literally as the title can be read as read as *Takeshi* and *Shis* ('shisu' means 'to die' in Japanese), suggesting *Takeshi Dies*.

Likewise, *Dolls* (2002), Kitano's most deliberately artificial and highly symbolic film shows that we are never far from tipping over the edge. Three separate but intertwining stories about the uncompromising and obsessive nature of love, the most potent is the story of the bound beggars. Matsumoto (Hidetoshi Nishijim) and Sawako (Miho Kanno) are engaged to be married – until the former's parents beg him to marry his boss's daughter instead. Reluctantly agreeing, his decision causes Sawako to attempt suicide. She fails, but loses her sanity. Not unlike *Hana-Bi*'s Nishi, Matsumoto is guilt-ridden by his actions – and walks out of his wedding ceremony to find his former lover. When he encounters her, she is damaged and fragile – like so many of the women in Kitano's films. To ensure that he does not lose her, he connects them with a red cord – a literal example of the ties that bind. Dressed in sumptuous costumes by Yohij Yamamoto and surrounded by the vibrant colours of the changing seasons, they are destined to walk the earth as he seeks forgiveness and she her sanity. While mental illness is a Kitano staple, so is physical disability. In *Dolls*, we encounter road worker Nukui (Tsutomu Takeshig), a devoted fan of teen pop star Haruna (Kyôko Fukada). When she loses her left eye in a car accident, and withdraws from public life because she feels ashamed of her disfigurement, he blinds himself so he can meet her without being able to look upon her and cause embarrassment. The ultimate form of worship and devotion, it truly proves that love is blind.

Blindness is also a key theme in *Zatôichi* (2003), Kitano's exuberant spin on the tale of a sightless swordsman made famous by the 26 films starring Shintaro Katsu. As he wanders the countryside, playing dice, helping old ladies and slicing foes with a sword hidden in his cane, Ichi (Kitano) appears to dispense a primitive form of justice – like many of Kitano's characters. Being blind, he has no reason to stare his opponents down and lose his nerve; meanwhile, being able to see is as much an impairment, it seems, for it causes one to judge by appearance. As Ichi says in the final scene, when it is revealed that his blindness was a ruse to put others off-guard, 'even with my eyes wide open, I can't see a thing'. If he is suggesting that being able-bodied is no guarantee of being a good person, Kitano is not above mining humour from disability – a trait that stems right back to his days as a stand-up comic when he used to mock the elderly, the handicapped and the infirm in his act. In *Zatôichi*, for example, a running gag features the neighbouring 'certified idiot' racing around in costume pretending to be a samurai.

His earlier work *A Scene at the Sea* (1991), the film he made to help establish his Office Kitano production company, following his troubled sophomore film *Boiling Point* (1990), also finds humour in physical impairment – this time deafness. Prefiguring the blind couple in *Dolls*, the film sets out to tell a simple love story. Shigeru (Maki Kuroudo) is a deaf-mute sanitation worker hooked on surfing. His girlfriend Takako (Oshima Hiroko) is also deaf – meaning that when the announcement for the surfing competition is made, neither hear it and Shigeru is disqualified.

It all adds up to a consistent thread in the work of Takeshi Kitano that shows no signs of abating. Just as violence can strike the innocent at any moment, so can mental or physical illness. In Kitano's world, humans – even those belonging to the yakuza – are vulnerable creatures, teetering on the brink. But for all this, his work is also tempered by hope – at least since his bike accident. Recalling the closing words of *Kids Return*, however difficult life gets, in Kitano's mind, 'we haven't even started yet.'

James Mottram

Paprika, 2006. Produced
by Madhouse/Sony

DIRECTORS
SATOSHI KON

Satoshi Kon's opening credit sequences exemplify the tendency towards thematic condensation and narrative economy that is inherent within anime. Encapsulating both the respective film and Kon's entire oeuvre, these sequences thrive on surprising and disorienting editing, visually spectacular ideas and exuberant cinematic speed. They are typically Kon in that they are deliberately visceral, always setting the viewer's sights just abreast of his intellectual and social concerns. This emphasis shifts on second and third viewing, and it is clear that Kon is one of the great calculating minds of anime, a field already full of obsessive, micromanaging artists. His directorial output is, for the field, quite limited. However, Kon's debut film *Perfect Blue* (1998), the follow-ups *Millennium Actress* (2001), *Tokyo Godfathers* (2003) and *Paprika* (2006), and the television series *Paranoia Agent* (2004), have built a reputation and a thematic consistency that have made him an international brand name. He thus follows the path of so many Japanese directors – live action and anime – in being a complete exception within Japan but seen as being representative of his country by overseas critics and audiences.

Kon's versatility in aligning complex cinematic montage techniques with equally dense themes to spellbinding, if initially confusing, effect is not obviously explained by his background. Trained as a painter at Musashino Art University – a breeding ground for many well-known artists in cinema and animation – Kon won the Chiba Tetsuya Newcomer Award for Manga while still a student in 1984. He began work as assistant to Katsuhiro Otomo, manga artist and later the director of the seminal *Akira* (1988), shortly thereafter and wrote *World Apartment Horror* (1991), which would become Otomo's first live-action film as a director. While mainly working in manga, Kon occasionally did design the layout for various anime projects throughout the early 1990s, among them the *Patlabor: The Movie 2* (1993). In 1995, he wrote his first anime script, *Magnetic Rose*, a Madam Butterfly-deconstructing episode in another Otomo project, the anime omnibus *Memories* (1995). The story of several space travellers that follow a distress signal and stumble into a holographic simulation of a long-dead opera singer's fantasy world already featured many of the themes central to later Kon projects: the centrality of memory for the – often illusory – construction of identity, a plot revolving around a woman whose degree of reality is in question, and the inability to distinguish subjective 'reality' from so-called objective 'reality'.

It was, however, unusual in terms of its science-fiction setting. Kon would later prove himself a master of utilizing contemporary urban locations – always within Tokyo – as environments that perfectly described the embedded protagonists. Beginning with the singer-turned-actress Mima and her room in *Perfect Blue*, and reaching a pinnacle in *Tokyo Godfathers*, Kon carefully orchestrates the context his characters live in, making them inseparable from their environment and, therefore, making the surrounding 'reality' as tenuous as their own identity.

In *Perfect Blue*, 'Who are you?' is the first line that Mima must speak in her acting debut, and her frantic repetition of the question is programmatic for Kon's entire work. His worlds are characterized by doubling, by the vibrant but disconcerting space that exists between the image and the 'original', between the virtual and the 'real'. As Mima must come to terms with her own position between public image and private volition, so the homeless outcasts of *Tokyo Godfathers* reveal glimpses of hidden stories and other lives. *Paranoia Agent* deftly supplies each of its protagonists with a double life often bordering on schizophrenia, and *Paprika*'s dream-tapping device most overtly poses the question of what identity might mean when disembodiment and the surfacing of subconscious alterity become a technological possibility. 'I want to portray truth, not facts', Kon states in an interview on his website. The portrayal of an ever-ongoing slippage of identity and a multitude of subjectivities within every individual becomes the starting point for this project. This affects his status as an auteur as well. Although his footprint is highly visible, Kon's collaborators have strongly helped shape what has become identified with him. All of his animation projects have been realized with involvement by Madhouse, one of the most creative anime production outfits in Japan. His frequent work with electro-pop legend Susumu Hirasawa is conceptually relevant as well: Hirasawa has frequently engaged with questions of virtual identity, both existential and gender-related, in his long career.

Fiction is thus both a topic and a conceptual tool in Kon's output. Brimming with film quotes from such varied sources as Akira Kurosawa, Dario Argento, Terry Gilliam or David Lynch, Kon is all too easily subsumed under the label of a postmodern auteur. Yet, as perfectly constructed and coherent as Kon's fictional worlds are, they cannot be reduced to hermetic, playful philosophical musings. Kon is aware of a social and political reality and he takes great pains to inject it into his work, even as he vigorously balances it with generous amounts of visual excess and sheer entertainment value. As Mima is caught in a delirious identity and career crisis, the newscasts in the background report on global warming and the political efforts to combat it. The three bums in *Tokyo Godfathers* are, despite the heavy doses of comedy, highly unusual heroes for anime, and the portrayal of their destitution and discrimination connects to the very real swelling of Tokyo's homeless population. Nonetheless, Kon paradoxically remains committed to the group that most represents a retreat from politics in the public sphere. Otaku (a Japanese term for those with an obsessive interest in such things as anime, manga, and video games) rarely appear as positive figures in his work, although common themes of otaku culture figure heavily in his oeuvre. The dangerous psycho-fan in *Perfect Blue* is close to the most blatant otaku stereotypes circulating in early 1990s' Japan and, in *Paranoia Agent*, the otaku-ish character designer Tsukiko Sagi brings Japan to the brink of destruction with a cute-dog character and an imaginary baseball bat-wielding youth that develop destructive lives of their own. Fantasy and insecurity bond with potentially disastrous consequences, a scenario Kon, despite his international success and transnational references, strangely never takes beyond Japanese concerns – at least within his own reasoning.

Alexander Zahlten

DIRECTORS
AKIRA KUROSAWA

The six wide-screen (Tohoscope) films of Akira Kurosawa represent the director at the height of his international reputation, operating during the most autonomous period of his career. There is symmetry worth noting with regards to the order of the six films. Beginning and ending with jidaigeki films and with two gendaigeki films, surrounding the duet of *Yojimbo* (1961) and *Sanjuro* (1962), this is a cadence of the six films: samurai (action), modern (morality), samurai-samurai (action/morality), modern (morality/action), ending with period film *Red Beard* (1965) a morality piece, and a summation.

Prior to making *The Hidden Fortress* (1958), Kurosawa had completed three films that were derived from Western sources: *Throne of Blood* (1957), from Shakespeare's *Macbeth*, an adaptation of Maxim Gorky's *The Lower Depths* (1957) and Dostoevsky's *The Idiot* in (1951). *The Hidden Fortress* is a rousing adventure, the most unabashed entertainment of the group. Much has been written about its influence on George Lucas and *Star Wars* (1977), including structuring the story around the viewpoints of the lowest figures in the story in terms of class hierarchy, not to mention the vast horizontal landscapes, a morally-ambiguous action hero, and the crossing of a hostile border by a young sheltered princess – the latter element actually a re-visiting of Kurosawa's early film *Those Who Step on the Tiger's Tail* (1945) from historically-based kabuki.

Less acknowledged but equally exacting is the influence that *The Bad Sleep Well* (1960), the first film that Kurosawa produced independently of Toho, exerted on Francis Ford Coppola, who has said: 'The first thirty minutes of *The Bad Sleep Well* seem to me as perfect as any film I have ever seen.' He, in fact, uses it as a template for the opening sequences in all three of his *Godfather* films, and this influence is particularly evident in the first film as both *The Godfather* (1972) and *The Bad Sleep Well* open with wedding sequences, stylishly delineating a great deal of plot and character information while a celebratory public ceremony serves to counterpoint a darker reality. Although it is scarcely a direct adaptation, in the manner that *Macbeth* was to *Throne of Blood*, there are clearly calculated similarities to *Hamlet* in the characters, plot and theme. The hero, played by Toshiro Mifune, has plotted a measured revenge that takes us through a corrupt corporation. Rather than Shakespeare, however, it is the indigenous Japanese tradition of tales of vengeance that were more relevant sources for Kurosawa. The avenging hero shares with Ôishi Kuranosuke, the head of the Akô league of revenge in the Chûshingura story, a great deal of ingenuity and seemingly endless patience. The primary interest is with the elemental ethical issues of good and evil, basic to all revenge tragedies, and with the inevitable moral price that must be paid in order to exact revenge, no matter how justified.

Kurosawa said that, in *The Bad Sleep Well*, he wanted to make a film of social significance. This represents something of a return to the type of contemporarily-set film that first established his reputation, in such works as *Drunken Angel* (1948) and *Stray Dog* (1949). The film was made in 1960, during the early stages of that Japanese 'economic miracle' that signalled recovery from the devastation of the war. It was an era of growing prosperity that would, in time, evolve into the opulence of the 'bubble economy' of the 1980s. In this early phase, however, the chief preoccupations were corporate survival and ruthless expansion by highly competitive businessmen. Kurosawa would revisit this corrupting mindset in *High and Low* (1963), only the second film that he had made in the wide-screen format. An unusually large number of scenes feature three people, such as the three principal 'bad guys', the police in their office, Nishi with his two confederates, or the trio of Nishi, his wife, and her brother. These are shot either on a flat plane to form a triptych composition, or with one or two people in the foreground to create a triangular formation. Throughout the film doors are constantly opened and shut, seeming to symbolize a border between the public and private personas and serve as passageways into the true nature of the characters. We see elevator doors that open and close like stage curtains, setting off contrasting groups of passengers. Another door is slammed in the faces of the reporters. A series of bank doors create a labyrinth for access to laundered money. Shoji screens are opened to reveal a married couple's true relationship. The door between a company president and his personal aide provides both proximity and separation. And a heavy vault door in a bombed-out munitions factory is used to imprison and taunt.

Many elements make *Yojimbo* (1961) just as rewarding today as it was the nearly fifty years ago: the irreverent morals and black humour, the artistry of cinematographer Kazuo Miyagawa and the contemporary-sounding score of Masaru Sato. Similar to the realism that *Rashomon* (1950) and *Seven Samurai* (1954) brought to jidai-geki film-making, *Yojimbo* had a direct influence on depictions of heightened graphic violence on screen. While *Rashômon* and *Seven Samurai* were early and accurate renderings of how physically difficult it is to actually wield a sword, it is in *Yojimbo* and *Sanjuro* that the residual effects that swordplay has on human flesh – such as the depiction of severed limbs and arterial spurts – are shown graphically for the first time. The unforgettable climax to *Sanjuro* takes the arterial spurt to its limit and adds an unearthly sound effect to the stand-off in a quick draw method called *iaijutsu*, in which no thrusts or parrying of blows take place. This abbreviated, close-quartered, lethal duel is more like a gunfight. Kurosawa makes full use of all cinematic components. The static composition, the long single take (by comparison, Sergio Leone may have had as many as fifteen extreme close-ups in his rendition of a similar scene), the sound effects of wind, swoosh of sword and gurgling of the cut (not to mention the minimizing of sound), the technology in the spurting of blood and, most of all, the unprecedented patience to allow the dramatic tension to build, all make this an unforgettable scene. It is still impressive today, even after years of spectacular, largely gratuitous, screen violence.

In *Yojimbo*, as in most Kurosawa films, nature's elements become characters within the story. An untimely visit by officials is prolonged by heavy rain. The dust and wind that travel down the main street, the stage for the showdown, are among the many cross- references to American Western films that *Yojimbo* became known for. The first screen meeting between Toshiro Mifune and a gun-toting Tatsuya Nakadai is most memorable. The introduction of the gun, a new weapon, implies a new set of rules and morals. The sword, the eternal symbolic soul of Japan, has been quickly outdated and, by implication, a code, a morality, a way of life ends with it. Therefore this battle between sword and gun might also be viewed as a struggle between East and West, or perhaps maintaining the East against the oncoming West: a last stand for the traditional against the technical. But mostly it is a struggle between good and bad. The character that Toshiro Mifune plays in this film is often referred to (even in later non-Kurosawa films) as Yojimbo, which means 'bodyguard', and he is one of the actor's most original and engaging characters. Mixing in both broad and subtle reactions, the first ten minutes of *Yojimbo* are virtually silent as he becomes accustomed to his environment and the people in it. Unshaven and unconventional, it is his wit and superior sword skills that get him out of the dangerous situations that he himself orchestrates. Survival is based upon dealing with an imperfect, bad, world by making his own rules and being detached from alliances of any kind.

In the sequel, *Sanjuro* (1962), Mifune reprises his role, with the differences being the situation and the environment. *Yojimbo* took place in a small town in its own world of bad and worse characters and morals and Mifune fits right in the fringes among the gamblers, yakuza and outlaws; *Sanjuro* takes place within a more formal, more refined world where bad deeds are done less in the open. Because the ronin has long been free from the constrictions of reserved samurai behavior, *Sanjuro* is something of a comedy of manners with 'fish-out-of-water' elements. Much of the humour in this very funny film comes from his disregard for, or impatience with, traditional conventions and protocol.

The structure of the next film, *High and Low* (1963), is most unusual as the first part of the film is confined to a single set: the luxury high-rise apartment. While the set itself may be limiting, the action is not. The staging is remarkable, with character movements, plot delineation and developments all played out in the claustrophobic setting of the high-rise, air-conditioned apartment overlooking the low, sweltering city. The middle section of the narrative, the train sequence, seems even faster-paced following the confinement of the previous section. It plays in 'real time' and the split-second timing in the narrative is largely due to the split-second timing in the staging and actual filming. Even more so than the beginning, the final section of the film, the manhunt, is about procedure. The concept of finding a single individual in a huge metropolis recalls the early Kurosawa motif of *Stray Dog* (1949).

Revisited in *Red Beard* is the relationship between teacher and reluctant pupil, found many times in Kurosawa's work, from his first directorial effort, *Sanshiro Sugata* (1943), through to *Drunken Angel* (1948), *Stray Dog*, *Seven Samurai* and even *Sanjuro*. The story takes place during a period of transition in Japanese history: the end of the Edo/Tokugawa period when the age of the samurai is about to end and Western influences are to become more prevalent. *Red Beard* also marks the end of many aspects of Kurosawa's career. Not only is it his last 'scope'-formatted film, it is his last black-and-white effort. After replacing Fumiyo Hayasaka, whose death was untimely, composer Masaru Sato wrote every score for Kurosawa beginning with *Throne of Blood* in 1957. *Red Beard* was his last film with Kurosawa. Yet nothing exemplifies the era's closure more sadly than the fact that the great collaboration, spanning sixteen films in seventeen years, between director Kurosawa and actor Toshiro Mifune ended with *Red Beard*. It is also the end of the prolific bulk of Kurosawa's career in which he made twenty-three films in twenty-five years. After making *Red Beard*, it would take five years for his next film, *Dodeskaden* (1970), to reach the screen and the following twenty-eight years would yield but seven films.

If, as it is sometimes suggested, the films under discussion here fall short of the masterworks that preceded them – *Rashômon*, *Ikiru* (1952), and *Seven Samurai* – they fall short by only a small margin. Along with *Stray Dog*, *Throne of Blood*, *Ran* (1985), they represent the next tier of Kurosawa classics, depending on personal preference, ranging from very good to great. It would be challenging indeed to try to find another run of six consecutive films in any director's filmography as impressive as these. If they had been his only films, Akira Kurosawa would still be considered a timeless and influential master film-maker.

Fred Shimizu

ALTERNATIVE JAPAN

There is no shortage of alternative Japanese cinema for those who wish to experience Japanese national cinema in its less overtly commercial form. The current interest in Japanese art cinema has much to do with its presence and success at major film festivals. After Naomi Kawase's *Mourning Forest* was awarded the Grand Prix at the Cannes Film Festival in 2007, Kiyoshi Kurosawa's *Tokyo Sonata* won the Best Director prize at the 2008 Mar Del Plata and Takeshi Kitano's *Achilles and the Tortoise* was nominated for Golden Lion at the Venice Film Festival in the same year. Judging by the constant flow and continuous success of Japanese titles at the international film festivals, there has not been this much activity since the much-discussed outbreak of the second New Wave in the 1990s.

The term 'New Wave' usually refers to a 'movement' of film-makers who emerged in the Heisei era, braking away from the traditional studio system and responding to the issues of social concern, unclear identity and blurred future resulting from the crash of the Japanese economy. With Takeshi Kitano and Takashi Miike at its forefront, it was to include a new generation of independent Japanese post-bubble directors, with the success of the two creating ample opportunity for the likes of Shunji Iwai, Shinji Aoyama, Kiyoshi Kurosawa, Naomi Kawase and Hirokazu Koreeda.

Aside from exploring the topics different from the standard studio productions, a significant characteristic of the directors of the new generation was that they came into the film-making from other media – a path which was until that point unprecedented in Japanese film history. Naomi Kawase and Hirokazu Koreada used to be documentary-makers and Shunji Iwai directed music videos and television productions in the past.

Tokyo Sonata, 2008.
Produced by Django Film

Such contemplative, socially-engaging and visually-gripping, films such as Aoyama's *Eureka* (2000), Iwai's *All About Lily Chou Chou* (2001) or Ichikawa's *Tony Takitani* (2004) all came out of the 1990s' independent film-making scene, affirming the promise that there is a definite quality and maturity to independent Japanese film-making, despite the concerns that, although initially avant-garde and innovative, these directors would soon succumb to the market demand for more commercially-orientated cinema. Alongside the focus on problems of communication and alienation, social degradation and its impact on family values remains very important in the 2000s, as seen in Koreada's *Nobody Knows* (2003) or Kurosawa's *Tokyo Sonata* (2008).

The year 1997 seems to have been a turning point in signalling the final crumbling of the studio system: as Masayuki Suyo's *Shall We Dance?* broke the box office records for Japanese cinema in the US market, Hayao Miyazaki's *Princess Mononoke* became the most popular theatre release in Japan; Shohei Imamura's *The Eel* and Naomi Kawase's *Moe no suzaku* collected awards at the Cannes while Takeshi Kitano's *Hana-bi* received the Golden Lion in Venice. Although the studios have been involved with early Kitano and Imamura productions, those courses were soon abandoned, and the largest box-office hits recorded in the year 1997, both in Japan and abroad, came from independent productions.

The border line between the mainstream and alternative cinema was, up to that point, very difficult to draw, especially since some of the authors considered as 'independent' had been supported or came out of the studios themselves, as in the case of Jun Ichikawa, whose debut *Tokyo Lulluby* (1997) was produced by Shochiku, or Juzo Itami, who has enjoyed a close and productive relationship with Toho. As the most common mainstream genres in Japan could be broadly listed as yakuza, samurai, monster, romantic drama and comedy, the territory of the alternative scene, before independent film-making reappeared in the 1990s, comprised marginal genres such as J-Horror, soft porn or, arguably, even adult animation. The wave of J-Horror, rising as a result of the worldwide success of Hideo Nakata's *Ringu* (1998) and Takashi Miike's *Audition* (1999), followed by the American remakes, *The Ring* (2002) and *The Grudge* (2004) settled in a peaceful bay of multi-million sell-outs. Although this had a positive outcome in spreading the cinematic legacy of the 1990s outside of Japan, and has brought international directors to Japan, most notably to shoot such conceptually-ambitious films as *Babel* (2006) and *Tokyo!* (2008), the popularization of the J-Horror genre created exactly the contra-effect of becoming not only the Japanese mainstream but also the Hollywood mainstream.

The latest Hollywood acquisitions are to include live action remakes of Katsuhiro Otomo's animated feature *Akira* (1988), produced for the US market by Leonardo Di Caprio, and the cult animation series *Cowboy Bebop* (with a film already made in 1998), scheduled for 20th Century Fox release with Keanu Reaves in the leading role of intergalactic bounty hunter Spike. This undoubtedly signals how the (commercial) success story of J-Horror has been further applied to the genre of live-action animation productions, as the newest and the latest trend springing out at the borderline between mainstream and alternative film-making. Starting from Katsuhito Ishii's *Shark Skin Man and Peach Hip Girl* (1998), there was a number of prominent manga: animation-originated sources remade for the big screen in their live action versions over the last decade. Ai Yazawa's best selling *Nana* series had its two sequels released in 2005 and 2006, Tsugumi Ohba's *Death Note* informed three films: *Death Note* and *Death Note: The Last Name* made in 2006 and a spin-off *L: Change the World* directed by Hideo Nakata in 2008 with *Akira's* Otomo Katsuhiro himself behind an adaptation of

Mushishi series in 2006. Takashi Miike's *Ichi the Killer* (2001), Higuchinsky's *Spiral* (2000), Kazuaki Kiriya's *Casshern* (2004) and Tetsuya Nakashima's *Kamikaze Girls* (2004) are just another few examples.

As the films are staying true to the original material on different levels, encompassing a wide variety of genres – drama, horror, fantasy, comedy and sci-fi –and are all fairly recent, it is hard not to group them under the same umbrella, and it is impossible to dismiss them as simply targeting the existing fans of the stories that they convey. These films also openly use computer technology in order to create hybrid substitutes for the more traditional anime, and have therefore become a substantial part of annual film production in Japan. With such new developments in popular entertainment, and taking into consideration the many issues even mainstream production centred around the major studios of Toho, Toei and Shochiku have with regards to attracting audiences (due to strong competition not only from foreign films but also from other forms of entertainment, especially video and television) independent or alternative films face challenges both industrially and commercially. They have to not only find a means of financing but also have to reach a significant body of viewers in order to ensure significant returns on investment, while still aiming at critical acclaim rather than compromising with stereotypical depictions of Japanese life and society. At times, these challenges make the collective aim of sustaining an independent production sector in Japan seem almost impossible as a number of smaller production companies, and an occasional industry commission, are hardly providing enough resources in the absence of governmental support.

Also, although managing to maintain the opposition to the Japanese mainstream and possibly remaining the only alternative films with any critical value, even the majority of the 'independent' films are still hard to grasp without a wider knowledge of the socio-political circumstances in Japan itself, making some of the sector's output difficult to export. As 'Japaneseness' is a label that is easily sold, an objective position of determining whether those films are intended to represent Japan for the international audience, or whether they are the only true voice coming out from the country, has to be achieved, especially when the distributional lag is considered. Also, it is very hard to tell whether the constant flow of Japanese titles at the festivals truly represents the existence of a productive scene or if the films are the only internationally-valuable productions to be emerging from the independent sector.

However, the works of Hirokazu Koreada, such as *Maborosi* (1995), and especially *After life* (1998), exhibit a universal appeal and deliberate avoidance of the trappings of commercial cinema, serving to reflect the issues that are particular only to Japan. They stand out as rare examples in which engaging stories and cleverly composed camera work prove to be sufficient film-making tools for innovative Japanese film-makers, and yet leave space for the possibility that such practice could be developed on a wider scale, within a new generation that might be able to benefit from the support of hopefully then-improved governmental policies.

Jelena Stojkovic

Afterlife

Wandâfuru raifu

Studio:
TV Man Union

Director:
Hirokazu Kore-eda

Producers:
Masayuki Akieda
Shiho Sato
Yutaka Shigenobu

Screenwriter:
Hirokazu Kore-eda

Cinematographer:
Masayoshi Sukita
Yutaka Yamasaki

Composer:
Yasuhiro Kasamatsu

Editor:
Hirokazu Kor-eda

Duration:
120 minutes

Cast:
Arata
Erika Oda
Susumu Terajima
Yakashi Naito

Year:
1998

Synopsis

After they have died, but before they go to Heaven, the recently-departed find themselves in a spacious but ramshackle office building, where case workers help them to select a memory from their life to take with them to the next stage. After this memory has been selected, the case workers recreate it on film and, once the scene has been viewed, the dead are able to move on. The case workers must deal with a variety of individuals, some of whom believe that their lives yielded no significant memories and others who cannot decide which to select, while others simply refuse to choose.

Critique

Afterlife is a unique vision of the hereafter, one which benefits from a clear, systematic structure that explores ideas before revealing its low-key emotional core. Much of the first half of the film involves the interviews that the case workers conduct in order to establish which memories to recreate. These interviews, which form much of the two-hour running time, are so naturalistic that they suggest improvisation. Yet the similarities and differences in the collective reminiscences, and the manner in which the various perspectives on, and attitudes towards, life and its moments of pleasure and pain tie together and ultimately inform the cathartic closure, reveal Hirokazu Kore-eda to be a writer, director and editor of subtle skill and genuine depth. Many of the recollections, although eventually scripted, were actually thoroughly researched, with 500 people being interviewed. Kore-eda also cast the film as delicately as he selected memories from his research process, balancing non-actors with professionals to achieve the quality of a documentary within a fiction narrative, while these scenes are shot by Yutaka Yamazaki, an experienced documentary cinematographer, on 16mm film stock.

The recreation of memories also serves as an affectionate commentary on the nature of shoestring communal film-making, as events are recreated by using whatever limited sets, props and simple visual effects are available. Unlike Hollywood depictions of the afterlife, such as Vincent Ward's visually sumptuous but overly indulgent *What Dreams May Come* (1998), Kore-eda's film is an aesthetically sparse experience, with the comparative lack of onscreen clutter enhancing the director's themes and philosophical musings. As with other examples of Japanese art (calligraphy, dance, poetry), the film pares everything down so that the elements which remain are those which are essential to the experience. This is also what the counsellors ask the recently deceased to do: select one profoundly affecting memory to take with them to afterlife, leaving all others behind.

The second half of the film becomes more dramatically conventional, but is no less affecting for it, as Kore-eda explores the 'lives' of the case workers and their reasons for not choosing a memory but remaining in limbo, helping others while dealing with their attachments to their earlier, mortal existence. As these case workers never age beyond their natural death, it is interesting to observe how a seemingly-young man such as Mochizuki deals with the tentative romantic advances of a young woman such as Shiori, his attractive trainee. He died at the age of twenty-two, she at the age of eighteen, making them seem compatible, but Muchizuki's passing occurred five decades before that of Shiori, meaning that they come from entirely different eras, explaining Mochizuki's comparatively reserved and traditional manner. These are people who remain in limbo because they still have something to learn, or accept, as suggested by Mochizuki's initially frustrating but ultimately fulfilling sessions with an elderly client, and Shiori's eventual promotion from assistant to fully-fledged case worker. The original Japanese title translates as *Wonderful Life* and, for all the regrets expressed by his characters, Kore-eda's fanciful film succeeds as a celebration of existence and experience, and the importance of retrospective memory in finding meaning long after the moment has passed.

John Berra

All about Lily Chou-Chou

Ririi Shushu no subete

Studio:
Rockwell Eyes Inc.

Director:
Shunji Iwai

Producer:
Koko Maeda

Screenwriter:
Shunji Iwai

Cinematographer:
Noboru Shinoda

Art Director:
Noboru Ishida

Composer:
Takeshi Kobayashi

Editor:
Yoshiharu Nakagami

Duration:
146 minutes

Synopsis

All about Lily Chou-Chou charts the relationship between 14-year-old boys Hasumi and Hoshino as they become tentative friends on entering high school, only for the relationship to break down completely when Hoshino changes after a near-death experience. As Hoshino goes from class president to class bully, Hasumi is made an unwilling participant in the escalating acts of violence and violation: forced to make one girl prostitute herself, and also made complicit in the harassment of a childhood friend. He takes comfort in the music of Lily Chou-Chou, a singer-songwriter whose fans are deeply affected by her music. An online bulletin board becomes Hasumi's sanctuary, a place for him to express his profound feelings towards Lily and develop the kind of emotional bonds with like-minded fans that he is denied in his daily life.

Critique

'Kids today are scary', says one character, but, much like the film, does not offer either reasons or solutions. In *All about Lily Chou-Chou* there are no causes, only effects. Why does Hoshino's personality shift so suddenly and dramatically? How did he get hold of the video he uses to blackmail his classmate into prostitution? Why blackmail her in the first place? No explanations are given, making the abuse even more indiscriminate, yet Hoshino is not an unsympathetic villain. It is one of the strengths of the film that their young characters are neither excused nor vilified for their outrageous behaviour.

Shunji Iwai provides a very human view of Japanese youth, scattering moments of naïvety and uncertainty to balance out the stream of calculated bullying that is based on seemingly-random shifts of opinion. At one point, the leader of the school's girl gang turns to Hasumi and asks 'I'm not a bad person, am I?' right outside the building where a

Cast:
Hayato Ichihara
Shugo Oshinari
Aoi Yu

Year:
2001

female classmate is, on her insistence, being punished for her popularity with the boys. It is a question that could easily be asked by Hasumi, whose own behaviour clearly appalls and upsets him even as he is directly involved in the suffering of people he cares about, and whose own motivations are every bit as mysterious as Hoshino's.

Divorce, unemployment, prostitution, rape and suicide are amongst a variety of issues affecting contemporary Japanese youth, and these problems are softened by the lush cinematography and the soothing soundtrack of Lily Chou-Chou (singer Salyu). Her constant, God-like presence adds a layer of innocence and intensity to the film, with the children viewing her as the last source of purity and harmony in their corrupted, isolated lives. The youth in *All about Lily Chou-Chou* may be viewed as representing the breakdown of society, but this is not a story, or a society, that is entirely without beauty or hope.

Amelia Cook

Bright Future

Akarui mirai

Studio:
UPLINK Co., Digital Site Corporation

Director:
Kiyoshi Kurosawa

Producer:
Takashi Asai

Screenwriter:
Kiyoshi Kurosawa

Cinematographer:
Takahide Shibanushi

Art Director:
Yasuaki Harada

Composers:
Shigeomi Hasumi
Takemasa Miyake

Editor:
Kiyoshi Kurosawa

Duration:
115 minutes

Synopsis

Two socially-alienated young men, Yuji and Mamoru, live lives of quiet desperation working at a hand-towel factory. When not at work, Yuji and Mamoru hang out together devising secret hand signals and spending time with Mamoru's poisonous jellyfish, which he has slowly been acclimatizing to fresh water. But one day the mindless routine of their lives is irrevocably altered when Mamoru murders their boss and his wife. Mamoru is arrested and subsequently sentenced to death. Yuji inherits the jellyfish and continues his friend's experiment to adapt the creature to a new way of life. Eventually, Yuji begins a cautious friendship with Mamoru's estranged father, Shin'ichiro, who desperately wants to understand his son through Yuji but, like the poisonous jellyfish – which has accidentally been released into the Tokyo waterway and is now breeding – that understanding may forever be simultaneously translucent and unfathomable.

Critique

It should be no surprise to anyone who has been following the career of Kiyoshi Kurosawa that *Bright Future* is a weird one. The film is also multi-layered, deeply obscure, and quietly riveting in ways that will be immediately expected from a film-maker who thrives on the unexpected. *Bright Future*, a title only partly ironic, is a significant move away from the genre transmutations of films like *Cure* (1997) and *Charisma* (1999). Although the slow doom of individual annihilation is ever-present, exuding an atmosphere of malice that would not be out of place in one of Kurosawa's more genre-oriented experiments, *Bright Future* does offer up the *possibility* for a positive new beginning for its characters. That is not to suggest that Kurosawa is offering up an easy, tidy Hollywood sense of 'closure', i.e. phony and unrealistic, for his troubled characters or that the film lacks a biting satirical edge – the youth gang that Yuji leads for a brief time is portrayed as both liberating and completely ridiculous.

Akarui Mirai, 2003. Produced by Digital Site Corp/Klock Worx Co.

Cast:

Joe Ogadiri
Tadanobu Asano
Tatsuya Fuji

Year:

2003

But certain destruction for Yuji is not ... well, certain. Kurosawa expresses great sympathy for his lost souls – even the dopey rebels without a cause are not entirely viewed with jaundiced eyes – and their actions are arguably the only proper responses for individuals dangling over an abyss. And that is perhaps the biggest difference with this film compared to Kurosawa's earlier efforts – an emotional attachment, however slight, to his characters. In no way could Kurosawa – thankfully – be accused of slathering on sentiment. But as much as there is a creeping dread permeating the film, a gradual and subtle emotional sting – much like the poisonous sting of the jellyfish in the film – surprises us, enriching this otherwise ambiguous and slippery film.

The performances from former teen idol Joe Ogadiri and the always-dependable Tadanobu Asano are excellent, suitably low-key and at times impenetrable, perfectly capturing the howl of psychic pain that moves through them. Kurosawa, though, does not revel in Mamoru's brutal act of violence despite sympathizing with his turmoil. This is no simple exercise in glamorously anaesthetized savagery as in David Fincher's *Fight Club* (1999), a film that shares many of the same themes as *Bright Future*, which makes Mamoru's crime even more upsetting and inexplicable. Neither does Kurosawa offer up easy answers when Yuji joins up with the gang of youths. The world of the older generation, as represented by Mamoru's father and others, is obviously falling apart and in ruins, offering nothing to Yuji other than a context and justification for his rebellion. Likewise, the youth gang is a dead-end as well. By the end, though, we do sense that the otherwise-passive Yuji has finally made a vital and conscientious act determining his fate, inserting a tendril of hope into a film where hope seems so rare.

Derek Hill

Fine, Totally Fine

Zenzen daijobu

Studio:
Tohokunshinsha Film

Director:
Yosuke Fujita

Producer:
Yosuke Fujita

Screenwriter:
Yosuke Fujita

Cinematographer:
Yoshihiro Ikeuchi

Production Designer:
China Hayashi

Composer:
E. Komo Mai

Editor:
Zenuske Hori

Duration:
118 minutes

Cast:
YosiYosi Arakawa
Yoshino Kimura
Yoshinori Okada

Year:
2007

Synopsis

Hironabu and Teruo are friends living in a small town. Hironabu is the more responsible of the two and has a job as a manager at a medical facility. He is outwardly nice but, as a senior manager observes, this likeable disposition stems more from his fears that other people will not accept him than it does from a genuine desire to be helpful. By comparison, Teruo is professionally aimless, holding on to a dream of opening his own spooky theme park, but unable to realize it due to a lack of finance and proper planning. Things begin to change when Akari, an attractive young woman who, unfortunately, is something of a walking disaster, stumbles into their lives, initially working at the medical facility with Hironabu, and then in a second-hand book store with Teruo, who is the son of the shop owner. As they juggle professional commitments and personal ambitions with helping some friends complete a low-budget horror movie, both Hironabu and Teruo fall for Akari and rivalry ensues.

Critique

Fine, Totally Fine is an offbeat comedy which owes some debt to the character-based humour of American independent cinema, particularly the deadpan charms of the cinema of Jim Jarmusch and the more overtly commercial film-makers that have appropriated his style. However, first-time director Yosuke Fujita understands the neurosis which underpins his characters and has a genuine empathy for them, regardless of their professional or personal failings, enabling his debut feature to become a celebration of friendship and the importance of helping others whilst still serving up a series of hilarious scenes which sit comfortably aside the more contemplative moments. Observations about friendship and the frustrations of small-town life are nicely balanced with laugh-out-loud comedy, with the gruesome, horror-themed pranks of Teruo providing many amusing moments, not to mention a sequence in which he tries to research his spooky theme park project by staying in a 'haunted' hotel room. Araki's clumsiness also provides numerous opportunities for some slapstick comedy as her job as a lowly orderly causes chaos in the medical facility and there is a painfully funny scene in the second-hand book store involving the wrapping of a pornographic magazine. Much of this seemingly-relaxed, yet perfectly-timed, humour is the result of Fujita spending many years working with the Otona Keikaku comedy troupe, but his deft skill as a screenwriter ensures that such scenes are as revealing of character as they are fitfully amusing.

Ultimately, the sensitive heart of Araki is captured by a local artist who frequents the second-hand book store, leaving both Hironabu and Teruo unlucky in love, yet the experience strengthens their friendship and makes them aware of the their individual states of arrested development. Minor embarrassments and awkward moments abound: Hironabu rejecting the advances of a co-worker, who has asked him to come to her flat to fix her VCR but also believes the buttoned-down manager to be the ideal candidate for a quick fling; Teruo's father wandering around his house in search of a pen when the magic marker he is using to write a 'Shop Closed' sign dries up; Araki's attempts to overcome her shyness and interact the world around her. There are no conventional 'life lessons' in *Fine, Totally Fine*, a film which leaves its characters simply getting on with living rather than achieving, and it is this delicate balance between absurd comedy and nuanced observation which makes such a seemingly slight tale such a consistently engaging, and quietly rewarding, experience.

John Berra

Getting Any?

Minna yatteru ka?

Studio:
Office Kitano and Bandai Visual

Director:
Takeshi Kitano

Screenwriter:
Takeshi Kitano

Exective producer:
Masato Hara

Producers:
Masayuki Mori
Hisao Nabeshima
Yasushi Tsuge
Takio Yoshida

Cinematographer:
Katsumi Yanagishima

Art Director:
Norihiro Isoda

Composers:
Senji Horiuchi
Hidehiko Koike

Editors:
Takeshi Kitano
Yoshinori Oota

Duration:
110 minutes

Cast:
Duncan
Takeshi Kitano

Year:
1995

Synopsis

Asao is an amiable half-wit whose only ambition in life is to get laid. One morning, he has a revelation: to get a girl, he needs a car. In the next scene, we see him in the showroom, asking the blandly-smiling salesman if he has anything that would be suitable for kaasekkusu ('car sex'). The salesman is eager to oblige and Asao is soon driving out of the lot and trying to pick up the first girl he sees, but realizes that it is going to be harder than he thought. Asao's quest continues, leading him down one wacky blind alley after another. By the end, poor Asao has run through the entire catalogue of male illusions about what women really want and is nowhere nearer his goal. Finally he tries to become an invisible man – in short, a voyeur. He gets his wish – and more than he bargained for.

Critique

Takeshi Kitano had released six feature films prior to *Getting Any?*, starting in 1989 with *Violent Cop*. None, however, featured much of the raucous, raunchy and frankly silly comedy that had long been his forte on Japanese television. In *Getting Any?* Kitano finally brought this side of his comic mind out of hiding. Much of the movie's humour is of the numbskull school, with gags so lame-brained that one has to laugh at the sheer brass of Kitano's putting them on the screen and charging admission. Structurally, it is a grab-bag, with nothing holding it together but attitude. But there is also a method – and a message – behind the madness. Kitano, whose television act was often the opposite of PC, has made a film that has a strong, if absurd, feminist subtext.

In telling this black comic tale, Kitano throws in a raft of movie references, including the *Waka Daisho* series, the *Zatoichi* series, yakuzu flicks, monster movies, and porno, while filling the soundtrack with *enka* (Japanese ballad) numbers, minyo (Japanese folk songs), and even *taiko* (Japanese drumming). He is seemingly emptying his mental attic of all the pop culture junk he stored there over the years, while working out various obsessions, sexual and otherwise on the screen. *Getting Any?* is thus a personal, as well as playful, film, in which Kitano takes off the masks of intellectuality and unwinds with a simplicity and directness that is disarming. It's easy to groan at *Getting Any?*, but it's also hard to hate it.

Mark Schilling

The Happiness of the Katakuris

Katakuri-ke no kofuku

Studio:
Shochiku Company, Katakuri-ke
no Kôfuku Seisaku Iinkai

Director:
Takashi Miike

Producer:
Hirotsogu Yoshida

Screenwriter:
Kikumi Yamagishi

Cinematographer:
Hideo Yamamoto

Art Director:
Tetsuo Harada

Composers:
Koji Endo
Koji Makaino

Editor:
Yasushi Shimamura

Duration:
113 minutes

Cast:
Kenji Sawada
Keiko Matsuzaka
Shinji Takeda

Year:
2001

Synopsis

The Katakuri family run a small bed-and-breakfast deep in the mountains. Their entire savings and lives have been sunk into it since they were convinced that a highway was being built in the area and assumed it would bring in many visitors. Unfortunately, they have not had a single one yet. Masao, the patriarch of the family, is almost at breaking point when a guest actually shows up at their door. They welcome him with open arms and have a new sense of optimism – until he kills himself later that night. Instead of informing the police, they bury him to avoid the bad publicity. Things turn from bad to worse as other new guests arrive and also end up dying.

Critique

'What's the deal with these dead bodies?' Considering the fact that people keep dying in his guest house, Masao's question is a fair one. All he has ever wanted is to live and work with his loving family, and he has he bought the guest house to allow his whole family – his wife, troubled son, single parent daughter and aging father – the chance to work together to build something of their own. It is just unfortunate that everyone who stays at the guest house keeps dying on him. Takashi Miike pulls off an amazing feat with *The Happiness of the Katakuris* by mixing black comedy, zombies, fantastical images, claymation and song-and-dance numbers to tell a sweet story of one family's love for each other. Of course, they have their own problems too. Masayuki has a history of stealing and not being able to hold down jobs, so his rebellious nature is always at odds with his father, Masao. Shizue for her part has had a bit of a wild youth, and perhaps not chosen her boyfriends with the greatest of care. As a single mother to little Yurie, she is still seeking her own true love. All these family traits and characteristics are further fleshed out in the musical numbers. Whether they crop up during the story, such as the sudden burst into frenzied dancing and singing as the family finds the dead body of the first guest, or as flashbacks, the musical portions of the film are simply great fun.

All the actors find the perfect ground between serious and camp, with Kenji Sawada as Masao and Keiko Matsuzaka as his wife Terue excelling in these scenes. One of the best musical numbers is when Shizue meets and falls in love with a British Royal Navy serviceman, who claims to be a secret agent. It is pure, goofy fun, complete with people flying in the air and flowers popping up in the background. That is the kind of film it is – sometimes surreal, sometimes sweet and sometimes just loony. The special effects that Miike chooses to use are appropriate for the film: the choppy editing, the sparkling stardust and the silly superimpositions all contribute to the almost giddy feeling. Then there are the stop-motion claymation sections of the film, which are all funnier and more grotesque than they have any right to be. The connections to reality are occasionally tenuous, and the comedic aspects may be very black at times, but the sweetness remains. As Masao's father says, 'Let's all laugh together. That's happiness.'

Bob Turnbull

Kikujiro

Kikujiro-no natsu

Studio:
Bandai Visual Company

Director:
Takeshi Kitano

Producers:
Shinji Komiya
Masayuki Mori
Takio Yoshida

Screenwriter:
Takeshi Kitano

Cinematographer:
Katsumi Yanagishima

Art Director:
Norihiro Isoda

Composer:
Joe Hisaishi

Editors:
Takeshi Kitano
Yoshinori Ota

Production Design:
Tatsuo Ozeki

Duration:
121 minutes

Cast:
Takeshi Kitano
Yusuke Sekiguchi
Kayoko Kishimoto
Great Gidayu

Year:
1999

Synopsis

It is summer vacation and nine-year-old Masao has no plans for a holiday as he is living with his grandmother. He believes that his father has died in a car accident, and he has never met his mother. A neighbour who hears his story assigns her unemployed and shady-looking husband to accompany him on his quest, and his newly-appointed guardian immediately takes advantage of the opportunity to spend the travel money provided on bicycle racing and hostesses. After days of hitchhiking and generally getting into trouble, they reach their destination only to discover that the woman from the picture has another family, so they head back home without even speaking to her. This leads to an improvised camping site with a trio of other travellers that they met on the road, all of whom are happy to distract the heartbroken Masao with a series of games, constructing for him an illusion of a real school-break.

Critique

A Japanese road movie, *Kikujiro* was inspired by Takashi Kitano's memories of his own father and was widely acclaimed at film festivals both in Japan and abroad. The deep sadness of the story is leavened by a cheerful soundtrack and the beauty of the landscape, with the narrative being divided into chapters of a diary that Masao is writing during their journey. These open with funny pictures and titles in a child's handwriting, to suggest that he is having fun, despite his setbacks. Masao's character is by no means portrayed as distressed and we see him trying to escape his loneliness, looking for other children to play with, but his fears and anxieties unravel in the depictions of the dreams that he is having, staged as dance performances that follow the main events of the story. In his devotion to his mother, and in the manner in which he makes friends along the way, Masao resembles Tetsuro, a hero of Leiji Matsumoto's *Star Galaxy 999* manga series from the 1970s, except for the fact that his companion cannot be more of the opposite to Maetel.

Kikujiro's character develops gradually from a careless, self-centred man, picking fights on any occasion and not hesitating to expose the boy to gambling, stealing and fighting, to a harmless drifter, not the smartest tool in a box, as we witness him not being able to swim, or carry out any of his cons. This transformation is achieved through Kitano's comedic performance, as Kikujiro is more of a parody of a criminal then a real yakuza. Even a full back tattoo that can be seen when he takes Masao to a hotel swimming pool does not seem to suit him, especially as he trips over in the same scene. As he grows genuinely attached to Masao his vulnerable nature that is hiding beneath the rough surface shows through, and this culminates in the admission that he is an abandoned child himself.

The camera work plays a role in building up the multi-layered meanings of the film: Masao's fragile situation is highlighted as we see him alone in the large bare surface of a playground field or a beach, even smaller in the midst of the large open spaces, and the bonding between the two characters is suggested in shots of them walking

Kikujiro No Natsu, 1999, Sony Pictures Classics. Photographed by Tsuranuku Kumagai

down the road or standing at the end of a tunnel. Visuals of a sup-posedly innocent and safe Japanese setting are especially successful when contrasted with their inhabitants, such as school bullies, child molesters or child-abandoning mothers. The story is made complete with excellent casting, with supporting roles played by a host of famil-iar Japanese actors.

Jelena Stojkovic

Love & Pop

Rabu & Poppu

Director:
Hideaki Anno

Producer:
Toshimichi Otsuki

Screenwriter:
Akio Satsukawa

Cinematographer:
Takahide Shibanushi

Synopsis

Hiromi is a high school girl who lives a seemingly-normal middle-class life in Tokyo. One weekend, Hiromi and her friends venture out to the consumer mecca of Shibuya in order to buy new swimsuits for their upcoming beach trip. While shopping, Hiromi becomes entranced by a topaz ring and decides that she must have it that day. To make some quick money, she and her friends end up singing karaoke with a mid-dle-aged man. He then asks them to gently chew some grapes, which he neatly collects and labels. Her friends try to get Hiromi to take all of the money, which is enough to buy the ring, but she refuses, predicting that such an action would cause a rift in their friendships. She is still intent on buying the ring, though, so she must resort to enjo kousai (or 'compensated dating') in order to make the required amount of money before the store closes for the day.

Composer:

Shinkichi Mitsumune

Duration:

110 minutes

Cast:

Asumi Miwa
Kirari
Hirono Kudo
Yukie Nakama
Tadanobu Asano

Year:

1998

Critique

In the late-1990s, director Hideaki Anno became famous for his work on the animated *Neon Genesis Evangelion* television series (1995–1996), which was a hit with both anime fans and the general public. Anno's tale of giant robots fighting invading 'angels' in a post-apocalyptic world also delved into the psychologies of the characters via experimental film-making techniques, unique not only to anime but to popular television. *Love & Pop* showed the beginning of Anno's move away from years spent with the *Evangelion* franchise and the otaku-oriented anime and science fiction that had established him as a film-maker. In addition to the television series, two *Evangelion* films came out in the late-1990s. Not coincidentally the date given of the main action in *Love & Pop* was the date of the premiere of the second *Evangelion* film called *The End of Evangelion* (1997).

The setting and content of the film is rather ordinary, with high school girls dealing with such issues as friends, fashion, and fitting-in. However, the theme of trying to figure out how one fits into the world and society in general is a constant issue throughout Anno's works. The most striking thing about the film is Anno's innovative use of camera angles and shot composition. Anno used multiple digital video cameras, which enabled him to achieve unique shots that he pieces together into a whole that is full of interesting seams. Sometimes, Anno uses such shots to depict a character's point-of-view while at other times they are used to fit into spaces not usually filmed, such as from below a bowl of soup, inside a microwave, or under a piece of clothing. Such shots could be thought of as an animator's approach to film-making, using the camera as a stylus in order to sketch necessary distortions of mundane life. In this way, the viewer is provided with angles on the characters that are intimate but not prurient – Anno carefully constrains his camerawork so as to not provide the titillating images that someone watching a film about girls engaging in enjo kousai might expect.

Through these images, Anno breaks modern life in Tokyo into distinct pieces and images, perhaps meditating on the contemporary fracturing and reassembly of self. This film-making also points to how the characters are able to separate from aspects of our selves when we need to – in Hiromi's case, she is able to put certain pieces aside and focus on what she needs to do in order to obtain the ring she wants. However, this ability is questioned in the end with Hiromi's encounter with a young man who goes by the pseudonym Captain XX (Tadanobu Asano). Her encounter is frightening, but in the end provides her with insight into her own actions.

Brian Ruh

Moonlight Whispers

Gekkô no sasayaki

Studio:
Nikkatsu

Director:
Akihiko Shiota

Producer:
Nobuyuki Kajikawa

Screenwriter:
Akihiko Shiota
Yôichi Nishikawa

Cinematographer:
Shigeru Komatsubara

Art Director:
Norifumi Ataka

Composer:
Shinsuke Honda

Editor:
Yoshio Sugano

Duration:
100 minutes

Cast:
Kenji Mizuhashi
Harumi Inoue
Kôta Kusano

Year:
1999

Synopsis

In a quiet countryside town, unobtrusive Takuya and the pretty Satsuki are regular Kendo partners in their high school gym. Takuya is embarrassed but happy when the much more direct Satsuki reveals that she has feelings for him. However, between the first kiss and probing, clumsy sexual exploration Takuya seems strangely disengaged, although he obviously adores his new girlfriend. When Satsuki discovers he has been taping her toilet sessions and stealing her chapstick and underwear, she cuts off the relationship. Takuya, in emotional turmoil, confesses his fantasies of being dominated by her, which plunges Satsuki into anguished confusion.

Critique

Akihiko Shiota later became known for the popular fantasy love story *Yomigaeri* (2002) and the magic-and-swords spectacle *Dororo* (2007), but in 1999 he wrote and directed two much-lauded subtle gems of the youth genre, *Don't Look Back* and *Moonlight Whispers*. In the early 1980s, Shiota was part of a group of film-crazed students at Rikkyô University from which directors such as Kiyoshi Kurosawa, Kunitoshi Manda and Shinji Aoyama were to emerge. He began his career as the assistant director on Kurosawa s first commercial release, a pink film called *Kandagawa Wars* (1983), and went on to write screenplays for straight-to-video films. He used his pupils at the Film School of Tokyo as staff to shoot *Don't Look Back*, and *Moonlight Whispers* became his first theatrically-released commercial work as a director.

Although the narrative arc – an increasingly sadomasochistic emotional journey for two high school students – sounds sensationalist on paper, the film impresses with the respectful intricacy of its observations, and avoids lurid voyeurism. When the scenes become more emotionally intense and the characters become painfully vulnerable, the camera consistently keeps its distance. The Rikkyô directors are all known for their manipulation of genre conventions, especially Kurosawa. Shiota is no exception, yet he avoids parody in subverting the sub-genre of sweet high school romance set in a rural town and instead aims for honesty through simple direction and impressive performances from the main actors. Takuya and Satsuki s confusion as to what they may or may not want, and its contradiction with what they are supposed to want, is so universal a theme that the intricate power-play of emotional sadomasochism becomes, at once, completely believable and touchingly universal. Here, Shiota is less interested in wider social questions than he would be later in the film festival favourite *Harmful Insect* (2001) and his sights are set squarely on the trials of growing up, the pressure to conform, and the inevitable clash of emotions and urges that are not yet fully comprehended. Since *Moonlight Whispers* was showered with awards in Japan, Shiota has since divided his time between commercially-successful star vehicles and more experimental works such as *Kanaria* (2005).

Alexander Zahlten

Noriko's Dinner Table

Noriko no shokutaku

Production Company:
Mother Ark Co.

Director:
Sion Sono

Producer:
Takeshi Suzuki

Screenwriter:
Sion Sono

Cinematographer:
Sohei Tanikawa

Art Director:
Toru Fujita

Composer:
Tomoki Hasegawa

Editor:
Junichi Ito

Duration:
159 minutes

Cast:
Kazue Fukiishi
Ken Mitsuishi
Yoriko Yoshitaka

Year:
2005

Synopsis

Seventeen-year-old Noriko, runs away from her suburban home in the Aichi prefecture in the hope of finding the administrator-guru of haikyo. com. In Tokyo, Noriko, who now goes by her screen-name of Mitsuko, meets her web-pal Ueno54, who goes by her presumably real name, Kumiko. She manages The Family Circle, a bizarre gang of 'actors' who rent themselves out to men whose wives and children have left them, grandmothers whose offspring do not properly appreciate them, and psychotics who want the ultimate revenge on their cheating girlfriends. After Noriko's sister Yuka follows her to Tokyo, Noriko's father, a journalist for a local publication, afraid that his daughters might be part of a suicide craze, tracks the girls to the big city and contrives to hire them.

Critique

Noriko's Dinner Table was poet-provocateur Sion Sono's follow-up to his Dionysian stream-of-content shocker-cum-cop-drama-cum-JPop-musical *Suicide Club* (2002), and it was awarded the Don Quijote Prize at the 2005 Karlovy Vary Film Festival. While, for anyone who has seen the earlier film, the spectre of the events narrated in *Suicide Club* hang over *Noriko's Dinner Table* like an ominous cloud, the storyline is only tangentially related to its precursor. *Noriko's Dinner Table*, though less formally radical than *Suicide Club*, is still decidedly non-linear, recursive, and digressive, structured as five segments, each with a focal character, each of whom contributes an idiosyncratic voiceover. But *Noriko's Dinner Table* is also more nuanced, more aesthetically assured, and lighter than its antecedent – even in its grisly, blood-soaked climax.

Thematically, Sono's film feels more akin to his *Strange Circus* and *Yume no naka e*, both of which, like *Noriko's Dinner Table*, premiered in 2005. While *Suicide Club* concerns itself with the broad philosophical problems of 'the nature of being' in a world full of others, the trio of films from 2005 is focused on more specific questions about the relation of that 'being' to literature (*Strange Circus*) or to acting (*Yume no naka e*, *Noriko's Dinner Table*). In *Noriko's Dinner Table*, for example, Kumiko collects keepsakes in the Ueno station left-luggage locker in which she claims to have been abandoned as a newborn – an allusion, perhaps, to Ryu Murakami's brilliant and Sono-esque 1995 novel *Coin Locker Babies*. But her souvenirs are phony, and the alternatively poignant and cutesy stories that she invents for them seem contrived to mimic the most manipulative moments of mainstream cinema. She, like her charges in The Family Circle, creates a 'role' for herself and then plays it. She becomes, as she tells Noriko/Mitsuko 'the person I always wanted to be', the star of her own self-scripted J-Drama.

The production of the project echoed the volatility and precariousness of Noriko's journey. Sono and Tanikawa shot the logistically-complex feature with mini-DV cameras and a tiny crew, on a micro-budget, in only two weeks. The resulting film, nonetheless, feels more tonally unified than *Suicide Club*. Surely one of the wonders of the film-making here is that Sono and his team were able to combine the vapidity of the high school girl's diary and the excess of the gore-fest into such a perfectly-modulated lyrical poem.

Bob Davis

A Scene at the Sea

Ano natsu, ichiban shizukana umi

Production Company:
Office Kitano

Director:
Takeshi Kitano

Producers:
Masayuki Mori
Takio Yoshida

Screenwriter:
Takeshi Kitano

Cinematographer:
Katsumi Yanagishima

Art Director:
Osamu Sasaki

Composer:
Joe Hisaishi

Editor:
Takeshi Kitano

Duration:
101 minutes

Cast:
Claude Maki
Hiroko Oshima
Sabu Kawahara

Year:
1991

Synopsis

While working as a part-time garbage collector, deaf-mute Shigeru finds a broken surfboard, the Blue Bunny, among the trash left out for pickup. He mends the board with foam core and electrical tape but, much to the amusement of the local surf crowd, is unable to make much headway in the water. Nonetheless, Shigeru returns to the sea day after day, his deaf girlfriend Takako in tow. When the Blue Bunny snaps in two during a ride, Shigeru and Takako use what little money they have saved to buy him a proper board from a surf shop. Impressed by the young man's determination, the shop owner, a former professional surfer, offers him a wet suit and some coaching, gratis. Shigeru improves enough to enter a surfing contest but is disqualified when he does not hear his group called into the water. Never discouraged, however, Shigeru enters a second surfing competition and captures fourth place. The summer ends, but he continues his daily trek to the beach despite the cold weather and the rain. When Takako arrives late one day, she finds Shigeru's surfboard washed up on the beach.

Critique

After only two features, Kitano claimed to have become bored with the yakuza genre and, if he had continued to work in that vein, he would have been forced to top himself with increasing levels of violence. Therefore, he decided to select a subject matter for his third film that nobody would ever expect from him. *A Scene at the Sea* also includes the first major female role in the work of a director whose attitude towards women, at least as reflected by his films, is anything but feminist. Takako fulfils a traditional function here as Shigeru's 'helper'. She negotiates a price for his surf board, dutifully folds his clothes, sits for hours on the beach smiling at his sometimes ludicrous attempts to master the waves, corrects his calligraphy on a competition application, and, in a show of loyalty to a boyfriend who has been banned from boarding a crowed bus because his surfboard takes up too much space, refuses to take a seat herself even after almost everyone has disembarked. When Takako no longer walks several feet behind Shigeru, this scene marks, by the standards of a Kitano film, the big step forward in their relationship.

Despite Kitano's desire to abandon the style of his two previous films, *A Scene at the Sea* develops the aesthetic the director had been working towards in his crime dramas in that his third film is protracted, distant, deadpan, and mute. Lengthy static wide shots and lateral tracks emphasize the masks that the principal performers present to the camera. Dialogue is characteristically minimal and consecutive shots are most often 'separations' in that nothing in a prior shot is seen in the subsequent one, a fact that allows the editor – Kitano himself – to exercise maximum control of the rhythm of the film and create the modern equivalent of action/reaction or shot/reverse shot, as seen in silent comedy. Frontal and dorsal views of the characters – shots are rarely more than 10 degrees off axis – suggest a presentational proscenium also reminiscent of early cinema.

Classical comedy tropes lighten this tragic romance as they did in Kitano's genre films. Laughs often come from variations on a theme, with Kitano repeatedly showing Takako folding Shigeru's clothes on the beach. Then, one day when she arrives late, she folds a pile of clothes that turn out to belong to someone else. There is also a pair of goofy young men, precursors to the *manzai* duos in Kitano's *Kids Return* (1996), who repeat virtually everything that Shigeru does, but do so in their own wacky way. They eagerly buy a surfboard that he rejected; they too are presented with a free wet suit, but they fight over who will get to wear it first, with the winner then putting it on backwards; and they carry their board in tandem, like Shigeru and Takako did, past the same field, in the same set-up, a repetition that forces the audience and even the characters themselves to identify the young man in the rear as 'the girlfriend'. For all his supposed efforts to distance himself from himself, Kitano seems to have fortunately failed here from being Kitano.

Bob Davis

Starfish Hotel

Studio:
100M Films

Director:
John Williams

Screenwriter:
John Williams

Producers:
Misako Furukawa
Brian Hulse
Yumiko Miwa
Tsuyoshi Toyama
Martin B.Z. Rycroft

Cinematographer:
Benito Strangio

Composers:
Shoko Nagai, Satoshi Takeishi

Editor:
Yusuke Yafune

Duration:
98 minutes

Cast:
Kiki
Tae Kimura
Kazuyoshi Kushida

Year:
2006

Synopsis

Arisu is a bored salaryman who lives a humdrum existence, alternating between the bland surroundings of his corporate office and designer apartment. When his wife Chisato mysteriously disappears, her sudden vanishing act may be due to her discovery of his affair with Kayoko, an alluring younger woman whom Arisu met at a hotel whilst out of town on business, or she may have fallen victim to something more sinister. Arisu enlists the help of the Tokyo police department, but also conducts his own investigation, coming into contact with Mr. Trickster, a volatile alcoholic who wanders the streets in a rabbit suit in order to promote the new novel by a popular mystery writer, and ventures into Wonderland, a new erotic nightclub in the downtown area of the city. Fact and fiction begin to blur as Arisu's experiences take on the form of a mystery story, and he recalls his affair with Kayoko at the Starfish Hotel.

Critique

The literary fiction of the celebrated Japanese novelist Haruki Murakami presents a strangely intoxicating world in which characters searching for something intangible that seems to be missing from their lives; these protagonists wander around major cities, and sometimes their outskirts, experiencing chance encounters and unusual events, whilst feeling adrift from the society to which they belong. Although his stories are vividly told and entirely contemporary, Murakami's fiction has resisted the transition to the big screen, with Jun Ichikawa's quietly haunting adaptation of his short story *Tony Takitani* (2004) being the only official cinematic realization of his work to date. *Starfish Hotel* takes its inspiration from Murakmi's fiction, often playing as a filmic tribute to his literary universe, most notably the companion pieces of *A Wild Sheep Chase* and *Dance, Dance, Dance* and also *Hard Boiled Wonderland at the End of the World*, although the loose-limbed narrative assembled by writer-director John Williams explores his own thematic concerns as much as it takes its cues from Murakami's novels.

At times uneasily pitched between mystery thriller and character study, and ultimately too ambiguous for those viewers who prefer easy resolutions, *Starfish Hotel* utilizes its salaryman protagonist to take the audience on an excursion into the darker side of contemporary Tokyo. In his quest to find his missing wife, Arisu (Koichi Sato) visits a garishly designed erotic club called Wonderland, and comes into contact with Mr. Trickster (Akira Emoto), a middle-aged failure who has been deserted by his family and makes his living wandering around in a rabbit suit to promote the latest novel by a popular genre writer. In a parallel story-strand, Williams relocates to the outskirts of Tokyo, and the hotel of the title, which stands in a snow-covered town which may really exist, or be contained within the dreams of the beleaguered hero. Such transitions are occasionally jarring but prevent the film from slipping into the over-used template of 'modern noir' and add to the literary themes that Williams wishes to discuss. Arisu is an avid fan of the mystery novels of Jo Kuroda, whose latest best-seller is keeping Mr. Trickster in cheap liquor, and Arisu himself once wanted to be a writer but failed to follow through on his ambitions due to a lack of imagination. These characters also stray from their conventional roles within genre, as Mr. Trickster displays a destructive temperament yet is more of a darkly comic tragic figure than a violent antagonist, while Kayoko is certainly an enticing *femme* but more vulnerable than she is *fatale*.

Starfish Hotel was shot on digital video, which enabled Williams to complete a logistically-complex film with relatively limited resources, and cinematographer Benito Strangio expertly alternates between the anonymous commercial sheen of Arisu's office and apartment, and the sleazy grime of downtown Tokyo. The scenes outside the city, particularly Arisu's encounters with Kayoko at the titular hotel and his climactic walk into an abandoned mine, have an otherworldly quality which is nicely complemented by an atmospheric score courtesy of Shoko Nagai and Satoshi Takeishi. Through interweaving the influence of Murakami with his own vision of mid-life crisis and sexual desire, Williams has created a multi-layered cinematic puzzle that unravels in a manner which is often as fascinating and it is unexpected.

John Berra

Tokyo Fist

Tokyo ken

Studio:
Kaiju Theater

Director:
Shinya Tsukamoto

Screenwriter:
Shinya Tsukamoto

Producers:
Kiyo Joo
Shinya Tsukamoto

Cinematographer:
Shinya Tsukamoto

Art Director:
Shinya Tsukamoto

Composer:
Chu Ishikawa

Editor:
Shinya Tsukamoto

Duration:
87 minutes

Cast:
Shinya Tsukamoto
Kaori Fujii
Koji Tsukamoto

Year:
1995

Synopsis

Yoshiharu is a nerdy salaryman living contentedly with his willowy girl-friend Hizuru in a Tokyo high-rise. One day, their lives are invaded by Yoshiharu's high-school classmate, a boxer named Kojima. Attracted by Kojima's smoky aura, repelled by Yoshiharu's insane jealousy, Hizuru moves into the boxer's run-down rooming house. Enraged by what he considers to be Kojima and Hizuru's betrayal, Yoshiharu begins to train at Kojima's boxing gym. Gradually the flabby wimp transforms himself into a mean fighting machine. A showdown of apocalyptic proportions is in the making.

Critique

If there is such a thing as a born film-maker, Shinya Tsukamoto is it. By the age of nineteen, when most film students of his generation were sitting in classrooms, his work had been screened at a festival sponsored by the NTV network, featured three times on the TBS network, and shown in a portable theatre at various sites around Tokyo. His first film, *Tetsuo: The Iron Man* (1989), was an ultra-violent, ultra-erotic fantasy about a man who transforms into a metallic monster. Using thousands of cuts flashing by like images out of a bad speed trip, Tsukamoto created a world of chaotic, primal impulse that may have been surreal and grotesquely funny (the morphed Tetsuo resembled an ambulant metal junk pile) but had a raw emotional punch. No one had distilled the extremes of violence and lust on the screen with such obsessive detail and unbridled directness.

Tsukamoto gives further evidence that he is reaching out for a wider audience with *Tokyo Fist* while continuing to work out his obsessions. Once again we have shots of Tokyo office buildings, high-rises and freeways in all their totalitarian splendour, juxtaposed with shots of factory furnaces, industrial scrap-heaps and dark forests of freeway pylons in all their hellish glory, while in the background, Chu Ishikawa's score pounds away with its spiky, hypnotic rhythms. Having set a familiar stage, Tsukamoto tells a story of a love triangle that stirs the base passions of its principals in exotically-violent ways. As in Tsukamoto's previous films, this story is pulp-simple, the forces driving the characters, elemental. His way of telling his story, however, is anything but primitive. Again working with a minimal budget, Tsukamoto creates a fanatically-complex, maniacally-insistent visual mosaic. If his film descends into the most wretched of violent excess, with gouts of blood spraying skyward and faces dissolving into masses of bruised flesh, its sincerity is so naked, its fantasies so vivid and its artistry so original that one has to grin with admiration.

In *Tokyo Fist*, however, he also constructs, for the first time, characters of more than primary colours. Kaori Fujii's Hizuru is not a passive pawn in a macho sexual game, but a strong-willed type who, through the tattoo artist's needle and her own experiments in body piercing, explores the erotic ecstasy of pain. Sharing the hero's fascination with violence, she begins to inflict it herself. The film's most intriguing character, she is, in some ways, the most frightening. But it is Tsukamoto, as Yoshiharu, who stands at the centre of *Tokyo Fist*. Compared

Tokyo Fist, 1995. Produced by Kaiju Theatre Production

with the mugging nerds Tomoro Taguchi portrays in the *Tetsuo* films, Tsukamoto is less comic, more ferociously sincere. His fiery-eyed little salaryman burns with a high, arid, ultimately absurd flame, while exposing the inner machinery of the mad, bad, original talent that is Tsukamoto himself.

Mark Schilling

Tokyo Sonata

Tôkyô sonata

Studio:
Django Film, Entertainment Farm (EF), Fortissimo Films

Director:
Kiyoshi Kurosawa

Producers:
Wouter Barendrecht
Yukie Kito

Synopsis

Salaryman Ryuhei Sasaki has lost his job as Director of Administration for a large firm. The company has decided to outsource a great deal of its work to China since they can now get three people working for the price of one in Japan. The shame is overpowering for Ryuhei and he decides not to tell his wife while he searches for another position. He discovers that he is not alone in this kind of deception as many other white collar workers are keeping similar same secrets from their families while they line up at soup kitchens. Meanwhile, Ryuhei tries to retain some semblance of control at home – especially with his sons. He forbids just about everyone pursuing activities that would make them happy without providing any reasons. This insistence on attempting to regain some form of control further distances himself from his sons and his wife. What he has not noticed, however, is that the whole family has already started shutting each other out.

Screenwriters:
Kiyoshi Kurosawa
Sachiko Tanaka

Cinematographer:
Akiko Ashizawa

Art Director:
Tomoyuki Maruo
Tomoe Matsumoto
(Production Design)

Composer:
Kazumasa Hashimoto

Editor:
Koichi Takahashi

Duration:
119 minutes

Cast:
Teruyuki Kagawa
Kyôko Koizumi
Yû Koyanagi

Year:
2008

Critique

Most articles about Kiyoshi Kurosawa's Tokyo Sonata take great pains to point out that it is not a horror picture. As the film-maker behind some of the best J-Horror films, it made sense to separate Kurosawa's first straight drama from the type of film for which he is best known. Covering basic themes like hypocrisy, loneliness, Japan's patriarchal society and the consequences of borders, the film avoids standard genre form conventions, and yet it is still horrifying at times.

Ryuhei's family does not so much talk to each other as *at* each other. They have pretty much sealed themselves off in their own worlds. It is in this environment that Ryuhei tries to exert further control in order to regain his stature as head of the household. He tries to stop the eldest son from joining the US Army and forbids his youngest from studying piano. He gives no reasons – he just needs to have the control. He rationalizes to his wife that once he has said 'no', he cannot change his mind for fear of losing authority over his children. His position within society has been taken from him, so he desperately needs to retain his traditional role in the family. There seems to be an abundance of hypocrisy, however, since youngest son, Kenji, is chided by both teacher and father for doing things that they themselves do. It is behaviour that appears to be commonplace.

Kurosawa sets up most of his interior shots to have layers of different frames: windows, arches, shelves and just about anything else that can divide and separate his characters from each other. It is incredibly effective in depicting a family that has shut themselves off. In addition, the occasional dropping out of all sound helps us to focus on a single person's feelings – yet another way of having a character isolated from what is around them. Of course, that is not the only way Kurosawa uses sound. Low ominous rumbles, blowing winds and echoing trains signal the continued slide of the family's fate.

As each member of the family begins to get more desperate for not only a way out but a way to start over, the tone of the film seems to lose its way a bit. First, it attempts to mirror some of the issues of the family as well as the societal structure of Japan with US involvement in Iraq, but it feels a bit forced within the context of the film. In addition, the late appearance of another character, a thief played by Koji Yakusho, brings some strangely comedic scenes into the story – not only due to the thief's bumbling attempts but also because of Yakusho's broad and almost over-the-top performance. Again, it feels like this section was shoehorned into the story. Overall, however, there are some beautifully-realized moments in *Tokyo Sonata*. The film makes a strong case for rejecting societal roles that box people into specific behaviours. Perhaps there may even be some hope lingering outside those limiting conventions.

Bob Turnbull

Tony Takitani

Production Company:
Breath

Director:
Jun Ichikawa

Producer:
Motoki Ishida

Screenwriter:
Jun Ichikawa

Cinematographer:
Taishi Hirokawa

Art Director:
Yoshikazu Ichida

Editor:
Tomoh Sanjo

Composer:
Ryuichi Sakamoto

Duration:
76 minutes

Cast:
Issei Ogata
Rie Miyazawa
Shinohara Takahumi

Year:
2004

Synopsis

A talented but socially-detached illustrator Tony Takitani is the son of a saxophone-playing drifter. As his mother died in childbirth, Tony spent much of his childhood alone, immersed in his sketches, and this continues into his adult life as by his mid-30s he is still a bachelor, dedicated to his work and resigned to his solitude. This changes when Eiko, a young editorial assistant, steps into his office and leaves him breathless. He asks Eiko to leave her boyfriend and marry him. Their life together is harmonious but Eiko continues to indulge her uncontrollable passion for designer clothes, a vice rooted in her pre-married life, and she stores her expensive purchases in a specially-designed room in their house. Concerned for the mental health of his wife, Tony asks her to try and restrain herself. In an attempt to do so she returns some items but, on her way home from the boutique, she decides to go back – tragically dying in the accident caused by her U-turn. Tony continues with his life but, haunted by his late wife's wardrobe, advertises for an assistant to wear her clothing whilst working in his office.

Critique

Director Jun Ichikawa employs unconventional camera angles to visually render the melancholy atmosphere of Haruki Murakami's short story – one of his many commentaries on the lonely landscape of urban life. As Murakami's work is usually rich with autobiographical references and echoes of the author's personal life, in *Tony Takitani* we find Murakami represented by the character of Tony's father, Shozaburo Takitani, a self-centered jazz musician who is completely immersed in his art. The love story that develops between Tony and Eiko is somewhat peculiar, with their ultimate inability to completely connect to each other or the world around them being rich with allusions to the spiritual emptiness of Japan's post-war economic revolution. The very choice of Tony's name comes from his father's belief that a Westernized moniker could be useful on the eve of occupation, and his own political ignorance and emotional loss after his wife's death result in the lack of a conventional upbringing for his son that would make Tony a self-sufficient person and also liberates him from succumbing to any prescribed model of existence.

However, although Tony is largely free to do whatever he wants with his life, after achieving professional success and settling into his daily routine, it is the chance to share his existence with somebody similar that means everything to him. Unfortunately, his beautiful younger wife compensates for her inability to find a meaningful goal by wrapping herself in luxurious and exquisite materials, with these designer items becoming her only means of expression. This leads to an addiction that she is simply not capable of fighting – putting it before her marriage and even her own life. The only living thing in their home is a cactus that she and Tony admire together and, in pursuing the latest fashions rather than making an effort to raise a family, she demonstrates her essentially escapist nature. The film only departs from Murakami's text towards the end when Tony makes an attempt to re reconnect with Hisako, reaching out from his solitude, but his phone call remains unanswered. Ichikawa leaves us thinking that it is not only our deliberate choices but the circumstances that we are living in that play a part in determining our destiny.

Jelena Stojkovic

ANIME / ANIMATION

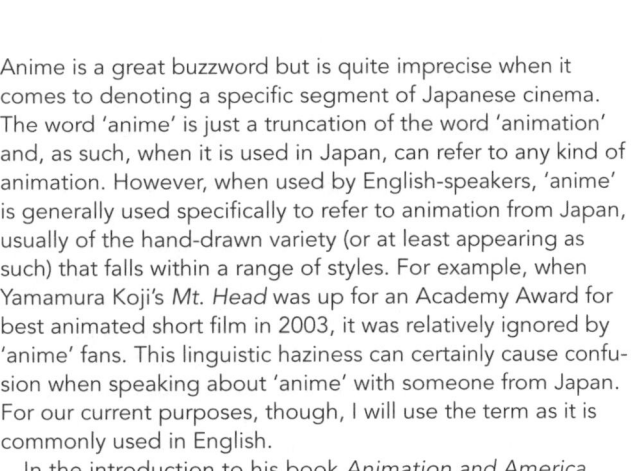

Anime is a great buzzword but is quite imprecise when it comes to denoting a specific segment of Japanese cinema. The word 'anime' is just a truncation of the word 'animation' and, as such, when it is used in Japan, can refer to any kind of animation. However, when used by English-speakers, 'anime' is generally used specifically to refer to animation from Japan, usually of the hand-drawn variety (or at least appearing as such) that falls within a range of styles. For example, when Yamamura Koji's *Mt. Head* was up for an Academy Award for best animated short film in 2003, it was relatively ignored by 'anime' fans. This linguistic haziness can certainly cause confusion when speaking about 'anime' with someone from Japan. For our current purposes, though, I will use the term as it is commonly used in English.

In the introduction to his book *Animation and America* (2002), animation scholar Paul Wells identifies the 'animated cartoon' as one of America's 'four major indigenous art forms'. Although animation of course exists in many countries other than the United States, it was in the US that some of the earliest advances in the medium were made. The works of major American animators, especially those of Disney and the Fleischer brothers, have often been cited as formative and stylistic influences on the creators of Japanese comics and animation. Anime expert Helen McCarthy (2003) states that '[t]he American animated films of the period [before WWII] were not so far removed from the traditions of Japanese folk art, with their sense of the ridiculous, their gross exaggeration of physical characteristics for dramatic or comic purpose, their anthropomorphic animals and clean, simple lines, and their influences were readily absorbed.' Japanese animation as a whole can be seen as the work of globalization in action – animators from Japan took ideas and styles from abroad and created a product that reflects their own lifestyles and culture.

Japan is one of the world's leading producers of film and television animation. According to one source, anime accounts for over half of the animated films shown worldwide and in 2004 the anime market was estimated to be worth $4.2 billion in the United States alone. Part of the reason for anime turning to global markets has been out of sheer necessity. Japanese animation production companies that used to be able to cover the majority of the costs of producing an animated television series through fees from broadcasters now generally recoup less than half of their costs in this way; companies generally rely on selling branded merchandise and overseas sales to compensate for this. Toei Animation president Tsutomu Tomari has said that his company, which is Japan's largest animation producer, 'gets almost 40% of its revenues from abroad, and the percentage is growing every year'. Japanese television programmes are increasingly being seen on television systems around the globe and such products are increasingly available for download on the internet as well. In particular, Japanese television is very popular throughout much of East and Southeast Asia.

The tension between the 'Japanese' and 'global' elements of anime have been with the form since its inception in the early part of the twentieth century. Daisuke Miyao's 2002 *Japan Forum* article, 'Before Anime: Animation and the Pure Film Movement in Pre-war Japan', gives a brief account of the early antecedents of anime, which are located in the Pure Film Movement: a trend in Japan in the 1910s that tried to establish film as its own medium, as distinct from live theatrical drama. This move was a rejection of previous methods of Japanese cinematic communication in favour of American and European techniques. Imported animation was first shown in Japan in 1909, much of which was from France and served as models for subsequent Japanese experiments. Since efforts in animation were inherently non-theatrical, Miyao suggests that the early Japanese animators may have fulfilled the goals of the Pure Film Movement better than many of the live-action film-makers. However, there were debates over form and content of animation among some in the Movement due to the fact that one of its intended results was to bring Japanese film into line with other, global cinema. Miyao writes that, although some in the Movement 'insisted on the necessity of Japanese stories and landscapes in order to differentiate the Japanese product for the foreign market, many opted nonetheless for subjects and stories that would be comprehensible to audiences accustomed to Western films.' One can see in Japan, even at this early stage of animation, the tension between making a recognizably Japanese product and an easily-exportable global one.

Since that time, anime has gone back and forth between being made solely for a domestic audience and being made with international export in mind. In the late 1950s and early 1960s, Japanese anime films like *Saiyuki* (1960, released in English as *Alakazam the Great* a year later) made their way outside of the country with animation studio Toei Douga's goal of becoming 'the Disney of the East', and television anime like *Astro Boy* only cemented this trend. However, the late sixties and seventies saw less anime being exported until the 1980s, when Japanese studios began creating more work-for-hire shows for overseas products like *Care Bears* and *Spider Man* as well as having their original works exported with shows like *Voltron* (1985) and *Robotech* (1985).

Even so, there were still segments of the Japanese anime industry that did not realize that there was a market for Japanese animation outside of Japan until the 1990s or 2000s. One possible reason for this (or perhaps an outgrowth of it) is the common misperception that exists to this day that anime is either light fare for little kids or contains ultraviolence and sadistic sex. Both types of anime certainly do exist, although the innocuous shows and films for children greatly outnumber the sex-and-violence ones. The fact that both types of anime exist is a testament to the breadth that anime encompasses and anime has a wide demographic of viewers and fans. There exists sports anime, cooking anime, mahjong anime, domestic romance anime, and all styles in between (although some genres of anime shows and films tend to be exported more readily than others.)

Anime is also a remarkable medium in which a director can develop his style (there are still, unfortunately, few female anime directors). One of the benefits of working in animation is that the form provides one with a kind of control that is unprecedented in live-action film-making. Since whole worlds are created from scratch in anime, even the smallest included detail must be intentional to a greater or lesser degree. This provides the opportunity for auteur anime directors like Hayao Miyazaki, Mamoru Oshii, and Satoshi Kon to create unified bodies of work.

Of these directors, Miyazaki and his Studio Ghibli are certainly the most renowned of the bunch. Perhaps due to the fact that 'anime' has become an international buzzword for a style of animated cinema and has even been actively promoted by the Japanese government, Miyazaki tends to shy away from the 'anime' label in Japan. He has famously called his work 'manga eiga', ('comics films') a term that places his films in the continuity of the earlier animated films that were around before the term anime became the term of choice. Miyazaki's approach to film-making is very much grounded in the artistry of animation, which makes sense given Miyazaki's background as an animator who has worked his way up through the ranks. A film-maker like Oshii, on the other hand, is much more of a traditional director in that he himself is not an animator. Such approaches to their respective oeuvres could explain why Miyazaki has produced mostly animated films and some manga, while Oshii's body of work contains both animated and live-action films, documentaries, novels, manga (which he has written but not drawn), and a stage play. With advances in technology, the anime film is becoming a more auteur-oriented art form since more work can be done by fewer people. One particular case in point is a director like Makoto Shinkai, whose films like *Voices of a Distant Star* (2002), *The Place Promised in Our Early Days* (2004), and *5 Centimeters per Second* (2007) were acts of individual creative expression as Shinkai performed much of the direction, writing, editing and animation by himself.

Animation has been a part of the Japanese cinema for nearly one hundred years, and will probably become a greater part of the global cultural landscape. At this writing, anime has hit something of a peak and is starting to show a decreased presence on television and on store shelves. However, this seems more like a market correction than an abandonment of the animated form. Increasingly, mainstream Hollywood films have found anime to be a rich source of themes and visual cues for their own films. Many Hollywood remakes of anime films are currently planned or are in production, for better or for worse. Regardless of the quality of these films, how they perform at the box office, or if they are even produced, anime (and animation in general) will always be a part of the global conversation about cinema.

Brian Ruh

Akira

Studio:
Toho

Director:
Katsuhiro Otomo

Producer:
Ryohei Suzuki
Shunzo Kato

Screenwriter:
Katsuhiro Otomo
Izo Hashimoto

Cinematographer:
Katsuji Misawa

Art Director:
Toshiharu Mizutani

Composer:
Shoji Yamashiro

Editor:
Takeshi Seyama

Duration:
125 Minutes

Cast:
Mitsuo Iwata
Nozomu Sasaki
Mami Koyama

Year:
1988

Synopsis

Thirty-one years after World War III has destroyed much of Tokyo, the island metropolis of Neo-Tokyo is threatened by political strife and gang violence. Teenagers Kaneda and Tetsuo are members of a biker gang. One night, while fighting a rival gang, Tetsuo encounters a strange child with psychic powers, only to be apprehended by military forces and forced to become part of a secret project under the authority of the Colonel. The project involves developing psychic powers and Tetsuo meets three other psychic children, learning from them that another psychic, Akira, triggered the war, and that this child now sleeps in a cryogenic chamber beneath the half-built Olympic stadium. Meanwhile, Kaneda tries to learn what happened to his friend and comes into contact with a revolutionary political group.

Critique

Akira is based on Katsuhiro Otomo's own two-thousand-plus-page *manga* series of the same name and the storyline has been vastly altered to fit within the length of a feature film. However, despite some confusion caused by packing such a dense story into such a narrow time frame, *Akira* manages to be simultaneously compelling and philosophical. It is also beautiful to look at. At a time when most anime films were notorious for cutting corners in terms of production value, *Akira*'s animation style was groundbreaking and highly detailed, and it heralded a renaissance within the industry and the genre, which remains visible to this day. From the opening frames, the audience is immersed in a future world of biker gangs, skyscrapers, and neon lights. The story jumps at first between the large number of characters, and from one conflict to the other as we see the gangs duelling, the revolutionaries on the run, and the Colonel and his forces in pursuit. Kaneda and Tetsuo's friendship is clearly defined, as Kaneda, the gang leader, exudes confidence and cool, a stark contrast to the sullen and brooding Tetsuo. As his powers emerge, Tetsuo's rebellious nature sets him in conflict with those around him.

Akira, 1988. Produced by Akira

There are stunning scenes throughout. The psychic children live inside a nursery and use their toys to attack Tetsuo when he first encounters them. There is a chase through subterranean tunnels on flying platforms and a showdown between Kaneda and Tetsuo that is truly impressive to watch as Tetsuo's power grows beyond the limits of his body. Mention should also be made of the soundtrack conducted by Shoji Yamashiro as the music provides a haunting tempo to the film and complements the visuals by being rich and textured. Whether seen as a metaphor for Japan's post-war economic revival or an allegory on the nature of human development, *Akira* does not shy away from exploring big questions and, at least in the West, the film served to elevate anime to a level of art form that it had previously only hinted at.

Justin Howe

Biohunter

Studio:
Madhouse

Director:
Yuzo Sato

Producers:
Naoko Takahashi
Masao Maruyama

Screenwriter:
Yoshiaki Kawajiri
Fujihiko Hosono (manga)

Cinematographer:
Hitoshi Yamaguchi

Art Director:
Masayoshi Banno

Composer:
Masamichi Amano

Editor:
Harutoshi Ogata

Duration:
58 minutes

Cast:
Toshihiko Seki
Kazuhiko Inoue
Yuko Minaguchi

Year:
1995

Synopsis

Komada and Koshigaya are university professors specializing in genetics and biology, but they also have another job: hunting down demons. By means of the 'Demon Virus', these creatures invade the human body, allowing them to take over their host and use them him to attack other human beings. Through their genetic research, Komada and Koshigaya have managed to produce an antidote to the virus, and they spend their nights tracking down the victims. Unfortunately Komada has also been infected but the antidote does not seem to work for him. He is able to control the creature within him to a certain extent, however, using his strength to fight the demons they come across. His time is limited though, and Komada can feel himself slowly losing control.

Critique

The creator of violent, stylish films like *Ninja Scroll* (1993), *Vampire Hunter D: Bloodlust* (2000) and *Highlander: The Search for Vengeance* (2007), Yoshiaki Kawajiri is one of the most popular and respected anime directors in Japan. His 1987 film *Wicked City* helped to establish the pattern for demonic sex-and-splatter movies that dominated anime horror for years to come. One of the many works it influenced was Yuzo Sato's *Biohunter*, which Kawajiri himself scripted from the Fujihiko Hosono manga. An OVA or 'original video anime', the anime equivalent of direct-to-video, *Biohunter* is in many respects a typical, if better than average, example of mid-1990s' anime horror. As you might expect, there are obvious similarities with *Wicked City* – both films begin with a sexual encounter that quickly spirals out of control, for example (neatly suggesting a connection between demonic possession and female sexual excitement).

Like Kawajiri's own directorial efforts, *Biohunter* is smart, well-paced and punctuated by eye-catching, imaginative action-horror sequences: a twisted face appears in a woman's chest and bites off her lover's hand at the wrist; a multitude of demonic faces writhe and squirm beneath a young girl's skin. As well as the bloody horror, *Biohunter* also benefits from a couple of interesting central characters and a strong plot that often feels like an occult-themed political thriller. With their comparatively short running times of 45–55 minutes, many OVA attempt to compensate by providing too much information, and the results can be ludicrously over-plotted, but mercifully *Biohunter* does not suffer from this problem, thanks equally to Sato's energetic direction and Kawajiri's concise, sharply-written script. Although not suitable for all tastes, *Biohunter* is a superior example of an under-appreciated genre.

Jim Harper

Black Jack

Burakku Jakku

Studio:
Shochiku, Tezuka Productions

Director:
Osamu Dezaki

Producers:
Takayuki Matsutani
Kotoku Minoru
Kazuyoshi Okuyama
Yoshihiro Shimizu
Ishida Yasuo

Screenwriters:
Eto Mori
Osamu Dezaki

Cinematographer:
Hajime Noguchi
Hirokata Takahashi

Art Director:
Jiro Kono

Composer:
Isao Tomita

Editor:
Morita Seiji

Duration:
93 minutes

Cast:
Akio Ohtsuka
Mayo Suzukaze
Yuko Mizutani

Year:
1996

Synopsis

Kuro Hazama, known as Dr. Black Jack, is an unlicensed but exceptionally gifted surgeon who charges extortionate fees to carry out particularly difficult operations, supported only by his young assistant Pinoko. Contactable only by telephone, he repeatedly ignores the calls of a woman named Jo Carol, who eventually confronts him with the fact that she has hidden Pinoko away, and will only return her if he agrees to help her. Black Jack is furious, but has no choice but to agree. A small group of people breaking world records and establishing new levels of achievement in the arts, sports and sciences have been called super-humans but, only a couple of years after the peak of their achievements, they lie in Jo Carol's hospital, wasting away as their internal organs rapidly age inside their bodies. Black Jack is assigned a team of world-class doctors to diagnose the problem, and lead them to a cure.

Critique

Black Jack is based on the manga by Osamu Tezuka, who is often referred to as the 'father of manga', but is also a graduate of medicine. It is Tezuka's background that adds weight to the medical procedures on which *Black Jack* hinges, and which are consistently animated in precise detail. Japanese animation is often accused of ignoring the human anatomy in its character designs but this is not so in *Black Jack*. When carrying out their impressive feats, the super-humans' bones, muscles and tendons are shown working beneath their skin, incorporating accurate human anatomy into character designs that, Pinoko aside, are more lifelike than usual. This inclination towards realism lays the groundwork for the scenario of sudden, dramatic human evolution, and paves the way for the suspension of disbelief required for the more incredible assertions later in the film.

A running theme of *Black Jack*, which was written at a time of great hardship in Tezuka's life, is of how humans cope when they must face extraordinary difficulty. This theme is approached with both the withering super-humans, and the doctors working on them, and director Osamu Dezaki tackles this is by including flashbacks that attempt to flesh out some of the characters, but which unfortunately detract from the large scale of the story. The result is that the extremely strong opening is undermined by the implausible characterization of the villains and some tacked-on sentimentality, often feeling more like a plot arc from a manga that has been compressed rather than a story designed for film. Dezaki's adaptation may have been more successful if he had focused on the complexity of the concept and the character of Black Jack, who is at his most interesting when enraged or facing a setback. However, it is a decent introduction to the character, with a number of other animated versions and the original Tezuka manga for suitably intrigued audiences to turn to for further investigation.

Amelia Cook

The Castle of Cagliostro

Rupan sansei: Kariosutoro no shiro

Studio:
Tokyo Movie Shinsha (TMS)

Director:
Hayao Miyazaki

Producer:
Tetsuo Katayama

Writer:
Hayao Miyazaki
Tadashi Yamazaki/Harauya Yamazaki
Monkey Punch/Kazuhiko Kat
(original graphic novel series)

Cinematographer:
Hirokata Takahashi

Art Director:
Shichiro Kobayashi

Composer:
Hirokata Takahashi

Editor:
Mitsutoshi Tsurubuchi

Duration:
100 minutes

Cast:
Yasuo Yamada
Kiyoshi Kobayashi
Taro Ishida

Year:
1979

Synopsis

The famous international gentleman thief Arsène Lupin III and his closest friend and companion Daisuke Jigen trace the high quality counterfeit money that they stole in a casino heist in Monaco to the fictitious tiny European country of Cagliostro, home of a vast counterfeiting organization which has caused economic turmoil all over the world during the past 400 years. There, they discover that the menacing ruler of the country, The Count, is attempting to marry the unwitting young Lady Clarisse, the surviving daughter of the deceased Duke of Cagliostro, in order to unite the ruling families and claim the country's mysterious treasure. A series of daring escapades and action-packed high jinks follow as, with the help of some friends, Lupin attempts to foil The Count, reveal the counterfeiting operation to the world, and rescue Clarisse.

Critique

Lupin III is an enduring character in Japanese popular fiction who has featured in a number of mangas, anime television series and feature films. Originally the creation of manga author Monkey Punch in the late-1960s, Lupin III was conceived as the grandson of the French fictional character Arsène Lupin, the gentleman thief of Maurice Leblanc's stories from the early twentieth century. *The Castle of Cagliostro* is the second animated film based on the Lupin III character, and was the first feature to be written and directed by Hayao Miyazaki prior to his formation of Studio Ghibli. Miyazaki was already familiar with the character as he had previously directed a number of episodes in the first Lupin III television series.

The Castle of Cagliostro is to some extent tied to the conventions of the Lupin III mythos and characters, and features more mature characters in a more realistic fictional setting then the later films of Miyazaki, but also has less narrative depth and does not involve themes that have since become part of his directorial signature. In terms of animation, *The Castle of Cagliostro* lacks the detail and refinement of the Studio Ghibli anime, although the skill of Miyazaki as a director/animator who is known for personally checking and redrawing individual unsatisfactory sketches by his staff, is evident in the artwork in that it is of a particularly high standard for an animated film, most of which were created on lower budgets prior to the 1980s.

Although the film shows a number of elements of his signature animation style that he later honed in his Studio Ghibli films, *The Castle of Cagliostro* should primarily be viewed as part of the Lupin III franchise. Lupin and his friends have had some of the more adult aspects of their personality toned down from the original manga, but they remain uncharacteristic of protagonists in family films due to their duplicitous occupations. Still, their actions are motivated for justice and it is difficult not to be charmed by the suave, yet comical, behaviour of Lupin and to become absorbed by the spectacle of his daring adventure. The action is exciting and many of the events of the film are amusing enough to make most viewers laugh out loud. *The Castle* of Cagliostro lacks real depth and is unlikely to fervently engage a mature audience on an intellectual basis, but it is a thoroughly entertaining film and one that the whole family can enjoy.

Matthew Holland

Fist of the North Star

Hokuto no ken

Studio:
Toei

Director:
Tooo Ashida

Producer:
Shoji Kishimoto

Screenwriter:
Susumu Takaku
Tetsuo Hara
Buronson

Composer:
Katsuhisa Hattori

Editor:
Masaaki Hanai

Duration:
110 minutes

Cast:
Akira Kamiya
Yuriko Yamamoto
Kenji Utsumi

Year:
1986

Synopsis

In the aftermath of a global nuclear conflict, the Earth has become a barren wasteland, where a handful of survivors fight for the control of uncontaminated food and water. While travelling with his fiancée Yuria, Kenshiro – master of the martial art known as Hokuto Shinken – runs into his former friend Shin, who attacks him and leaves him for dead, taking Yuria with him. A year later, Kenshiro returns – fully recovered and eager to find Shin and rescue Yuria. With the help of some unlikely allies – among them two orphans, Bat and Rin, and Rei, a Nanto Seiken master looking for his long lost sister – Kenshiro travels to the city of Southern Cross, Shin's base of operations.

Critique

Fist of the North Star is the feature-length adaptation of the animated television series of the same title, which in turn was based on the sprawling manga by Tetsuo Hara and Buronson. The film is the work of the same creative team responsible for the television series and was in fact developed and produced alongside the series itself as a simplified retelling of the original story for theatrical audiences, rather than as an extension of the series itself. Indeed, from a canonical standpoint, Fist of the North Star only covers the basic storyline detailed in the first fifty episodes of the television series and, by the time of its release in March 1986, it inevitably lagged far behind the plot developments presented in the twenty or so episodes that had since hit the airwaves.

What makes Fist of the North Star quite unusual is the unorthodox strategy it adopts in abridging the narrative material from the series into a cogent, autonomous feature. Rather than simply summarizing the existing storyline, the film not only takes obvious liberties with the story's chronology but it also changes events and characters. The effect is all the more unsettling as the film follows the television series in terms of character design and animation style, suggesting an adherence to the source material that is ostensibly contradicted by the multiple departures from the original storyline. For instance, in the television series Kenshiro reaches Southern Cross, where he confronts and defeats Shin, only to learn that Yuria has already taken her own life rather than submitting to Shin's advances (he will learn later that Yuria is actually still alive). In the film version, upon arriving to Southern Cross, Kenshiro finds Shin already dying from the wounds suffered during an earlier battle with Raoh, and learns that Yuria managed to escape from the city but was eventually captured by Raoh, who is now holding her captive.

Overall, the substantive streamlining and conflation of plot points and characters result in an abrupt, erratic storyline where the lack of narrative breathing space confers an aura of contrivance to most events and encounters. In particular, the film-makers drop most references to the clash between irreconcilable fighting philosophies that functioned as the structural backbone of the original storyline. Thus severed from the existential core of the television series, and lacking its breadth and sprawling scope, the film eventually finds an aesthetic compass in the protagonist himself. More Clint Eastwood than Bruce Lee, Kenshiro wanders the wastelands with expressionless resolve, validating the narrative not as the intended rehash of the original elaborate storyline but as a bone-dry, quasi Shakespearian tragedy unravelling in a ravaged land straight out of John Ford's nightmares.

Ricardo de Los Rios

Ghost in the Shell

Kokaku kidotai

Studio:
Shochiku

Director:
Mamoru Oshii

Producer:
Yoshimasa Mizuo
Ken Matsumoto
Ken Iyadomi
Mitsuhisa Ishikawa

Screenwriter:
Kazunori Ito

Cinematographer:
Hisao Shirai

Art Director:
Hiromasa Ogura

Composer:
Kenji Kawai

Editor:
Shuichi Kakesu

Duration:
82 minutes

Cast:
Atsuko Tanaka
Akio Otsuka
Koichi Yamadera

Year:
1995

Synopsis

Major Motoko Kusanagi is a cyborg agent who works for a Section 9, a government agency dedicated to fighting crime and cyber-terrorism through sometimes-questionable means. In their most recent case, Kusanagi, her teammates Batou and Togusa, and the rest of Section 9 are assigned to the case of the Puppet Master, a mysterious, internationally-known hacker. After a few false leads, a damaged cyborg body manufactured under mysterious circumstances makes its way to Section 9. Within the body is the Puppet Master, originally a secret government artificial intelligence but which has gained sentience. It is trying to seek asylum but another branch of the government manages to steal it. However, Kusanagi is able to track the Puppet Master and reclaim it. It then proposes to her that they should merge to create a new form of life that would be a melding of their unique faculties and would live within the world's networks. After thinking it over, she agrees to the merger, in part because it will free her from control of the government. Other government snipers try to destroy Kusanagi and the Puppet Master, but Batou manages to save Kusanagi. He takes her back to his safe house, puts her into a new body and, from there, the newly freed amalgam of Kusanagi and the Puppet Master venture into the uncharted territory of the net.

Ghost in the Shell: Innocence

Inosensu

Studio:
Toho

Director:
Mamoru Oshii

Producer:
Mitsuhisa Ishikawa
Toshio Suzuki

Screenwriter:
Mamoru Oshii

Cinematographer:
Miki Sakuma

Art Director:
Shuichi Hirata

Composer:
Kenji Kawai

Editor:
Sachiko Miki
Chihiro Nakano
Junichi Uematsu

Duration:
100 minutes

Cast:
Atsuko Tanaka
Akio Otsuka
Koichi Yamadera

Year:
2004

Synopsis

Batou is still reeling from Kusanagi's absence. He knows that she is 'out there' somewhere, perhaps watching over him, but he is constantly beset with feelings of loneliness and unease. He is partnered with Togusa to try to solve the case of a series of murders committed by sex robots against their masters. In the process, they come across the gruesome murder of an employee of Locus Solus, the manufacturer of the robots. Batou and Togusa decide to visit Kim, an electronic warfare specialist acquaintance of Batou. When they get there, Kim traps Batou and Togusa in a repeating maze within their heads and they cannot distinguish reality from imposed hallucination. However, Batou is given a clue from someone who looks much like Kusanagi did at the end of the original film, and he subsequently manages to find their way out and apprehend Kim. When he raids the Locus Solus factory, Batou has to fight humanoid security robots and is helped by Kusanagi, who takes command of one of the robots and fights alongside him. They discover that Locus Solus was trying to infuse their sex robots with certain qualities by dubbing them with the minds and spirits of kidnapped young girls. With the case solved and Locus Solus on its way to prosecution, Kusanagi leaves Batou again.

Critique

Both of Mamoru Oshii's *Ghost in the Shell* films are based on stories that originally appeared in Masamune Shirow's original manga. Although Shirow's characters were fun, sexy, and violent, Oshii's take on the world is much more sombre and contemplative. Many of Oshii's previous films dealt with the fuzzy border between dreams and reality, and how technology affects the perception of the two, making him the appropriate director to adopt the manga. It was the first *Ghost in the Shell* film that cemented Oshii's reputation as a director outside Japan, becoming both a critical and relatively-commercial success. Presaging contemporary discussions about privacy and piracy, one of the key concepts explored in the film is how the nature of ownership will change as digital technology becomes more prevalent throughout society. Although the agents of Section 9 are powerful, they are the property of the government and are locked into perpetual servitude. If one ever wanted to leave, they would be able to do so but they would have to return their bodies and cyberbrains, leaving one to wonder what would be left. Other characters encountered in the film have had their memories and experiences overwritten, leading to questions of how much our past contributes to our self, and the extent to which we can be in possession and control of our mental histories.

Although the first *Ghost in the Shell* became well known abroad (particularly after *The Matrix*, which drew heavily upon the film, was released in 1999), within Japan the name was seen as something of a liability, so the second film was released simply as *Innocence*, without any reference to *Ghost in the Shell*. Even more so than the first film, its use of visual imagery was striking and its use of computer graphics was phenomenal, although, stylistically, *Innocence* looked different from its predecessor and was more like *Avalon* (2001), Oshii's previous live-action film. However, many viewers were confused by the film's constant allusions and use of quotations, with references including Milton's *Paradise Lost*, Villiers de l'Isle-Adam's *Tomorrow's Eve*, Raymond Roussel's *Locus Solus*, and feminist scholar and cyborg theorist Donna Haraway. Although Oshii rarely constructs naturalistic dialogue between his characters, this was taking such conversations to a new level. Part of this was probably due to the fact that, for the first time in many years, Oshii was not working with Kazunori Itoh, who had been his regular scriptwriter and may have kept Oshii's solipsistic tendencies in check.

In addition to these films, other *Ghost in the Shell* anime have been created. To date, there are two seasons of a television series, a film-length compilation of each, and an original direct-to-video feature, all of which were directed by Kenji Kamiyama. Released under the banner *Ghost in the Shell: Stand Alone Complex* (2002–2004), these animes are somewhat closer in tone to Shirow's original manga, and take place in a different conceptual universe from Oshii's films, although they still owe a great deal to Oshii's version. Oshii had very little involvement with *Stand Alone Complex*, although he was credited with the story concept for the second season of the series. In 2008, Oshii released a revamped version of the first film, calling it *Ghost in the Shell 2.0*. Although some cynics thought that this endeavour was just an attempt to gain attention for Oshii's new film *The Sky Crawlers* (2008), the new version of *Ghost in the Shell* is actually a reimagining of the world. One of the key differences is that Oshii makes the world of the earlier anime look more like that of *Innocence*, providing a more cohesive aesthetic across the two films.

Brian Ruh

Grave of the Fireflies

Hotaru no haka

Studio:
Studio Ghibli

Director:
Isao Takahata

Producer:
Toru Hara

Writer:
Isao Takahata

Cinematographer:
Nobuo Koyama

Synopsis

In Kobe, Japan, after the end of World War II, fourteen-year-old Seita recounts the last few weeks of his life, which have been spent caring for his four-year-old sister Setsuko. In a US military air raid on Kobe towards the end of the war, the children's house is destroyed and their mother is killed. With their father serving in the Imperial Japanese Navy, they are forced to go and live with their aunt. Both children become increasingly aggravated by their aunt's selfish behaviour and negative attitude towards their presence in her home and, unable to contact their father or other members of their family, they decide to leave and live independently in an abandoned air raid shelter on the outskirts of the city.

Critique

Isao Takahata is the second chief director at Studio Ghibli, which he co-founded with Hayao Miyazaki in 1985. The pair have worked together on many projects during their careers, but their individual

Art Director:
Nizou Yamamoto

Composer:
Michio Mamiya

Editor:
Takeshi Seyama

Duration:
88 minutes

Cast:
Ayano Shiraishi
Tsutomu Tatsumi

Year:
1988

styles differ greatly. Whilst the more prolific and internationally-famous Miyazaki is known for creating fantastic worlds and characters, Takahata's films are more focused on creating a sense of realism and any fantastic elements are usually grounded in reality. *Grave of the Fireflies* is perhaps his most realistic study in that it is based on the novel of the same title by Akiyuki Nosaka and much of the story is taken from Nosaka's own recollections of being a fifteen-year-old in Kobe at the end of the war. In addition, some of the imagery is drawn from the experiences of Takahata, who was 10 years-old during the period depicted in his film, and he captures a sense of time and place, achieving a realism that makes the characters and their predicament more affecting. Made in a relatively short time-frame, the animation in *Grave of the Fireflies* sometimes seems a little rougher than in other Ghibli films. However, the rural location of the children's bomb-shelter home and the houses in the city are drawn in superb detail, and the watercolour-like landscapes and skylines depicting the desolation after the bombings are particularly memorable. The narrative effectively balances sweeter and lighter moments in which the children play, with darker sequences where they struggle to survive, and the complex portrayal of the characters is handled with care as the child actress voicing Setsuko brings a feeling of honesty to the role that truly engages the audience.

  Grave of the Fireflies is not an easy film to watch. It is realistic reflection on a particularly dark period of contemporary Japanese and world history, focusing on a human dilemma and more immediate personal consequences. The film presents a complex situation in relatively simple terms and, while there is a definite anti-war sentiment, it is not weighed down by melodrama or pretence, and does not seek to lay blame or present a polemic lecture. Harrowing and beautiful, *Grave of the Fireflies* is an exceptional work with real emotional depth.

Matthew Holland

Howl's Moving Castle

Hauru no ugoku shiro

Studio:
Studio Ghibli

Director:
Hayao Miyazaki

Producer:
Toshio Suzuki

Synopsis

Sophie is a quiet, hat-shop assistant who has a spell cast over her by the jealous Witch of the Waste; when Sophie discovers that she has been turned into an old woman, she seeks help from the infamous Howl, a handsome wizard who is said to devour the hearts of beautiful, young girls. Believing that she is safe in her 90-year-old form, Sophie becomes a live-in maid at Howl's castle, where she gets more and more involved in the lives of its inhabitants: Howl, Markl the apprentice, and Calcifer the fire demon. Soon war breaks out and the King of the land orders all the royal wizards to join the military. Not wanting to use his magic for combat, Howl and his makeshift family go on the run.

Screenwriter:
Hayao Miyazaki

Cinematographer:
Atsushi Okui

Art Directors:
Yoji Takeshige
Noboru Yoshida

Composer:
Joe Hisaishi

Editor:
Takeshi Seyama

Duration:
119 minutes

Cast:
Kimura Takuya
Cheiko Baisho
Akihiro Miwa

Year:
2004

Critique

Following the international success of *Spirited Away* (2001), the highly-anticipated release of *Howl's Moving Castle* could have been the greatest Japanese animated anticlimax of the 2004 if it had not been followed by *Steamboy*, but while Katsuhiro Otomo's first film since the timeless *Akira* (1988) had the excuse of failing to live up to the expectations of an audience who had waited a decade, *Howl's Moving Castle* had no such excuse. Instead, it appeared to owe its tragic failure to the over-confidence of its creators. Some credit is due to studio Ghibli for attempting to adapt Diana Wynne Jones' multi-layered children's novel into a single feature-length film, but it is a shame the Miyazaki lacked the foresight to see that it could not be done. The original plot is simply too complex and, although *Howl's Moving Castle* is able to carry off much of it, in the end it fails to deliver those things that ensure a smooth conclusion.

Featuring a notable soundtrack, the voices of some star names like Kimura Takuya, as well as an impressive English voice cast for its international release, a great deal of effort was invested in this film. Despite its eventual shortcomings, it begins as a sumptuous journey full of rich, lovable characters, breathtaking animation and the signature attention to detail which gives Miyazaki films their warmth. It is unfortunate, then, that these elements soon become the film-makers' hubris. The creators seem to waste a fair deal of valuable running-time indulging in the animation and attention to detail, which are praiseworthy but ultimately unable to make up for a badly-developed plot. In its final twenty minutes, *Howl's Moving Castle* struggles to tie together the story's many loose ends as new characters emerge out of nowhere while others do and say atypical things and villains turn less than villainous. Miyazaki has previously demonstrated his ability to work magic with very simple stories. Perhaps if it was not so ambitious, *Howl's Moving Castle* would have disappointed less.

Elest Ali

Howl's Moving Castle, 2004. Produced by Tohokushinsha Film Corp/Ntv/Tokuma Shoten

Millennium Actress

Sennen joyuu

Studio:
Kadokawa Shoten Publishing
Co., WoWoW, Chiyoko
Committee, Bandai Visual,
Genco

Director:
Satoshi Kon

Producer:
Taro Maki

Screenwriter:
Satoshi Kon
Sadayuki Murai

Cinematographer:
Hisao Shirai
Art Director:
Nobutaka Ike

Composer:
Susumu Hirasawa

Editor:
Satoshi Terauchi

Duration:
87 minutes

Cast:
Miyoko Shoji
Mami Koyama
Fumiko Orikasa

Year:
2002

Synopsis

While the famous Ginei Studios is being demolished, Genya Tachibana is determined to film a documentary on its biggest star, Chiyoko Fujiwara. Offering only a key in a box, Tachibana and his cameraman ask Chiyoko, now a charming woman in her seventies, to tell the story of her life. She does better than that, taking them into her history as a young actress living through World War II, and into the history of her characters, who, over a thousand years from feudal Japan to the space age, have all been searching for one man, tied to Chiyoko by the mysterious key that Tachibana has just returned.

Critique

Millennium Actress seems to have three goals. The first is to replicate the director Satoshi Kon's artistic and commercial success with his previous work, *Perfect Blue* (1997). The second is to sweep through a thousand years of Japanese history without losing interest or coherence. The third is to write a love letter to Japanese cinema. What is impressive is that it achieves these goals, and provides an example of effective and creative storytelling through animation. The narrative framework of Tachibana and his cameraman being pulled through various time periods is not impossible in live action, but undoubtedly works better with the suspension of disbelief that is more easily achieved through animation. When Tachibana starts taking on roles himself, the changes are not jarring but comedic, with his intensity playing off the cameraman's frustration with his boss, and Chiyoko's confusion over his presence.

Millennium Actress is a busy and complicated web of stories, with several strands twisting together and then snapping apart on a regular basis, but the sheer range of historical periods it covers means that, through her costume, hair, make-up, Chiyoko's characters are easily distinguished from one other. The historical periods are also evoked by the detailed settings and, in one particularly attractive montage sequence, the art of Japanese woodblock prints. The types of films that Chiyoko is shown to have starred in are another indicator, and the journey she takes will be nostalgic for those familiar with the studio system of Japan, its genres and narrative tropes.

The weakness of *Millennium Actress* is actually what gives it consistency: Chiyoko's unrequited love for the man with the key, whom she initially meets only briefly. She is single-minded in her pursuit of him, even taking her first film role in order to follow him and, after the first few years, the strength of the motivation becomes unconvincing. Much more convincing – and more interesting – is Tachibana's relationship with Chiyoko, starting as idolization and deepening to genuine affection as he learns more about her, providing much needed emotion to the film. *Millennium Actress* is an ambitious film, but it meets its ambitions and, in so doing, exceeds typical viewer expectations.

Amelia Cook

Momotarô's Sea Eagle

Momotarô no umiwashi

Studio:
Geijutsu Eigasha

Director:
Mitsuyo Seo

Cinematographer:
Mitsuyo Seo

Producer:
Einosuke Omura

Screenwriter:
Shigeru Kurihara

Duration:
37 minutes

Year:
1942

Synopsis

Silhouettes of soldiers diligently working on fighter planes atop a wave-shaken aircraft carrier are etched into the morning sky. The troops – comprised of pheasants, monkeys and dogs – assemble for their commander Momotarô to instruct them about their mission: to attack and destroy the demon island Onigashima. Underneath the Japanese flag, the troops scramble into their aircrafts and fly off into the dark, cloudy sky only for one of the planes to find that a baby eagle has landed on their wing. After handing the baby over to its parent, Hawaiian music indicates that the target is near, and the attack on Onigashima commences. Momotarô's forces succeed in almost completely destroying the enemy aircrafts and naval fleet, reducing the oversized enemy soldiers to wailing babies. When, however, the troops return to the aircraft carrier and a proud Momotarô, one plane is still missing. It has been badly hit and is in danger of crashing into the sea.

Critique

Momotarô's Sea Eagle is an attempt at propaganda on several levels. It lifts the attack on Pearl Harbor to a mythical level, incorporating the famous legend of Momotarô, a boy born from a peach who led pheasants, monkeys and dogs into a fight against evil demons. However, it also functioned as a symbol of combat on a greater filmic and technological level and *Momotarô's Sea Eagle* was touted as Japan's first feature-length animation, demonstrating the nation's technical prowess. The film employed an impressive depth-creating multi-planar image technique with a camera especially developed by Tadahito Mochinaga. The enemy soldiers were copies of Bluto from the *Popeye* serial, right down to voices dubbed from an actual *Popeye* episode.

The film was made possible by funding from the Ministry of the Navy, just as government funding became very important for the entire animation industry of the period, and it is without question an impressive feat of work for a total staff of twelve to complete over six months. A very limited number of cels were available for the production, and they had to be washed and reused for drawing after being photographed (cels were made of celluloid, which was also used for explosives, so they were rare commodities in wartime Japan). The film became a box-office hit and was deemed a great success by the Navy officials and Prince Takamatsu, leading to a kind of sequel, *Momotarô – Divine Troops of the Ocean* in 1945. It was the latter film that might more legitimately have been called 'feature length' at 74 minutes, and it was also directed by Seo.

Yet the film may sport some oddities for contemporary viewers. Momotarô is the only human character on the Japanese side, portrayed as a stern and bellicose figure. His cute animal troops – dehumanization was often enough reserved for the enemy in many other propaganda films – experience several comical interludes, somewhat incongruous to the ominously-rising tension of the first scenes. The 'demons', on the other hand, are all human, or rather Bluto, and their evil character is assumed more than it is displayed. The creators themselves do not seem to fit easily into the militaristic propaganda of *Momotarô*: Seo was a former member of the leftist film-making organization Prokino, who previously had experienced problems with the military police, while Mochinaga emigrated to Manchuria after the war and helped establish Shanghai Animation Studios for the communist government, and producer Omura later became an executive of the Japanese Communist Party. But the considerable technical achievement of *Momotarô* is what they are usually remembered for – a film that, according to legend, made Osamu Tezuka, the creator of *Astroboy*, want to become an animator when he saw it as a child.

Alexander Zahlten

Nausicaä of the Valley of the Wind

Kaze no tani no Naushika

Studio:
Toei

Director:
Hayao Miyazaki

Producer:
Isao Takahata

Screenwriter:
Hayao Miyazaki

Cinematographer:
Hideshi Kyonen

Composer:
Joe Hisaishi

Editor:
Naoki Kaneko
Tomoko Kida
Shiyoji Sakai

Duration:
116 minutes

Cast:
Sumi Shimamoto
Goro Naya
Yoshiko Sakakibara

Year:
1984

Synopsis

One thousand years after The Seven Days of Fire nearly destroyed human civilization, various outposts of humanity have emerged, isolated from each other by the ravaged remains of the Earth's eco-system: the Sea of Decay. Nausicaä is the young princess of the peaceful Valley of the Wind. Here, people have adapted to the new world by mixing post- and pre-industrial technologies, and Nausicaä has earned the respect of her people. One day, an airship from another kingdom crashes in their valley, and soon Nausicaä is caught in the middle of a new war that threatens to further destroy the Earth.

Critique

Often considered to be the founding film of Hayeo Miyazaki's Studio Ghibli, *Nausicaä of the Valley of the Wind* possesses a complex story that it succeeds in telling with elegance. From the start, the viewer is immersed into a fascinating future world that fits together seamlessly. The giant insects, the world's feuding kingdoms, and the various technologies built out of the remains of our own recognizable world, add up to give the setting its strong appeal, and the fact that Miyazaki is capable of telling a story with genuine depth only makes events more compelling. *Nausicaä of the Valley of the Wind* is very much a film with a message. There are messianic undertones as Lord Yupa, Nausicaä's mentor, is searching for a man in blue who will appear out of a field of gold and redeem the world. Princess Nausicaä herself typifies the charismatic, compassionate leader in touch with the spirit realm, and one could read an element of Joan of Arc into her. In her adventures, she is assisted and hindered by a host of companions and part of what makes the story so rich is that no one is entirely good or evil. The villains are merely people with priorities at odds with the heroes', yet they are no less human and Miyazaki, much like Akira Kurosawa, treats every character with compassion.

This depth of subtlety is further applied to the film's environmental message. When first released in 1984, the film was presented by the World Wide Fund for Nature and the environmentalist message states that we should live in harmony and balance with the Earth, but that the system is larger than that. Much of what mankind fears in the Sea of Decay are the results of the natural processes necessary for the rehabilitation of the planet; it is only that needless power struggles have blinded the human kingdoms, making them incapable of withstanding the forces of nature because they cling too tightly to dominance and the glories of the past. *Nausicaä of the Valley of the Wind* is a near-perfect science fiction film, and one that will even warrant the appreciation of audiences who are not anime fans.

Justin Howe

Paprika

Papurika

Studio:
Madhouse, Sony

Director:
Satoshi Kon

Producers:
Masao Takiyama
Jungo Maruta

Screenwriter:
Satoshi Kon
Seishi Minakami

Cinematographer:
Michiya Katou

Art Director:
Nobutaka Ike

Composer:
Susumu Hirasawa

Editor:
Takeshi Seyama

Duration:
90 minutes

Cast:
Megumi Hayashibara
Akio Otsuka, Koichi Yamadera
Toru Furuya

Year:
2006

Synopsis

Police detective Konakawa is undergoing experimental treatment for anxiety using the DC Mini, a newly-created device that allows therapists to become part of the dreams of their patients. He is guided through his experiences by a woman named Paprika, who is the dream alter-ego of Dr. Chiba, one of the chief researchers on the DC Mini project. However, when a DC Mini is stolen from the lab, the project is jeopardized. The thief is able to use the device to invade the consciousnesses of people who are not even attached to a psychotherapy machine, which makes them act erratically and eventually lapse into a coma. Chiba and her colleagues, Drs. Tokita and Shima, team up with Konakawa to try to discover who is behind the theft of the machine.

Critique

Paprika (based on a science-fiction novel by Yasutaka Tsutsui, whom critic Takayuki Tatsumi has dubbed 'the guru of Japanese metafiction') presents an engaging pop-psychological world that resembles our own, aside from the presence of a fantastical device that allows people to see and enter into the dreams of others. The visuals by animation studio Madhouse are able to convey a sense of vibrancy and fluidity in the movements of the characters. The fact that the film so handily engages the eye plasters over some of the defects in the storytelling. The theft of the DC Mini is really a MacGuffin in the film – it is not really a detective story, so the identity of the culprits does not require a lot of serious investigative work. Still, the fact that the workings of the DC Mini and the 'psychotherapy machines' are never explained are likely to baffle viewers who care about such things. In a film like *Ghost in the Shell* (1995), the crossover between reality and dream/virtual worlds occurs due to the advent of high technology implanted in people's heads. The same may be the case in *Paprika* but, since the majority of the world appears to be contemporary Japan, save for a few technological innovations, this kind of crossover can appear haphazard and sloppy. However, if one suspends such disbelief, the visuals might be sufficient for a thought-provoking ride.

It is intriguing that, as a science-fiction film, *Paprika* displays a strong bias against geeks, or otaku. This is mainly directed at the morbidly-overweight Dr. Tokita. The creator of the DC Mini, he is still a child at heart, giving very little thought to his social responsibilities or the implications of what he creates. In contrast to other depictions of geeks in Japanese film and television that range from the lauditory to the cautionary, the depiction of Tokita comes across simply as mean. However, *Paprika* does have an important, albeit trite and simplistic, call for engagement with morals and social responsibilities for the technophiles who may make a significant portion of the film's audience.

Brian Ruh

Perfect Blue

Pafekuto Buruu

Studio:
Rex Entertainment, Madhouse

Director:
Satoshi Kon

Producer:
Hiroaki Inoue

Screenwriter:
Sadayuki Murai

Cinematographer:
Hisao Shirai

Art Director:
Nobutaka Ike

Composer:
Masahiro Ikumi

Editor:
Harutoshi Ogata

Duration:
80 minutes

Cast:
Junko Iwao
Rica Matsumoto

Year:
1997

Synopsis

Mima is a pop idol, albeit a rather low-ranking one. She wants to move on and try something new, so she decides to quit her pop group and become an actress. Her first role is a minor one in a television drama. However, some of her previous fans seem to be upset that she has turned her back on them and is trying out a role that is less clean-cut than her previous image. At the same time, Mima's perception of reality begins to blur and she finds it more difficult to distinguish between her real life and the onscreen role she is playing. When people around Mima begin to be attacked and killed, her world becomes even more claustrophobic. Mima begins to wonder if these things are really happening to her or if they are just events that have been written into the drama. As she becomes increasingly unsure of herself, Mima is forced to navigate the line between delusion and reality in order to survive.

Critique

Although *Perfect Blue* was the first film directed by Satoshi Kon, some of his previous work had involved collaboration with both Mamoru Oshii and Katsuhiro Otomo on anime projects. Kon's fortuitous involvement with some of contemporary anime's most original creators seems to have paid off as his promotion to the role of director was rather rapid, considering that his anime resume was rather small at the time. Like many good directors, though, Kon was able to take a project he was assigned and make it his own or, as he explained, 'I was given the three keywords of "idol", "horror" and "fan", and was completely free as a director as long as I stuck to those overarching themes.' Although certain things about the film had been decided in advance, Kon was able to impart his own particular take on the material and begin to develop as one of the most acclaimed anime directors working today.

One of the first questions people often ask when presented with a film like *Perfect Blue* is why it was animated. It seems that animation finds popular acceptance when there are talking animals, or other

Perfect Blue, 1997. Produced by Rex Entertainment

aspects that are difficult to pull off in a live-action film, but when it comes to a film that could have been filmed using live actors, the question arises as if live-action film is the default mode of film-making and animation is some kind of special case or aberration. In fact, animation came about before live-action cinema, and therefore has a longer history; one way to think of live-action cinema is simply as a form of animation that uses photorealistic elements as its raw materials. However, the common assumption is that if a film can be made as a live-action film, then it should be, although the more interesting part of the *Perfect Blue* is not necessarily the narrative, but how it plays out onscreen.

As Mima gets more involved in the acting world, she seems to lose her grip on reality and becomes unable to tell which parts of her life are truth and which parts are fiction. Kon seems to want to impart this feeling of uncertainty to the audience as well and it is for this reason that *Perfect Blue* is particularly suited for animation. As animation critic and historian Fred Patten writes: 'The use of animation rather than live-action enhances *Perfect Blue*'s surrealistic elements. It is harder to tell how much of "what the camera shows" is real and how much is Mima's imagination, or what someone is trying to convince Mima is her imagination—or whether the camera is showing both.' In other words, since the audience is willing to accept animated figures onscreen as 'real' people, there is already a degree of suspension of disbelief occurring. With this in mind, it perhaps becomes a little easier for a director of animated films than for a director of live-action films to play with the filmic 'reality' he or she has created.

Brian Ruh

Spirited Away

Sen to Chihiro no
kamikakushi

Studio:
Studio Ghibli

Director:
Hayao Miyazaki

Producer:
Toshio Suzuki

Writer:
Hayao Miyazaki

Cinematographer:
Atsushi Okui

Art Director:
Yoji Takeshige

Composer:
Joe Hisaishi

Editor:
Takeshi Seyama

Duration:
120 minutes

Cast:
Rumi Hîragi
Miyu Irino
Bunta Sugawara

Year:
2001

Synopsis

Whilst a young girl named Chihiro is moving to a new town with her family, her father decides to take a shortcut and the family stumble across what they assume is an abandoned theme park. Exploring the park, her parents seem drawn to a food stall and, with no one around, they begin to gorge themselves. Wandering off alone, Chihiro meets a boy named Haku, who warns her to flee the area before nightfall. However, when she tries to get away she discovers her parents have transformed into pigs and her escape is cut off. What they mistook as a theme park is in fact a small town built around a huge bath house and, as night falls, Chihiro finds that its patrons are a colourful array of spirits, monsters and gods. With the help of Haku, Chihiro hopes to save her parents and return to the real world, and that the only way for her to survive is to find inner strength she never knew she had.

Critique

The great charm of Miyazaki's work is that he is able to create feelings of childlike fascination in audiences of any age and, as with the films of all great film-makers, watching them becomes an experience rather then just spectacle or entertainment. *Spirited Away* is widely considered to be his finest achievement precisely because it has a sense of magic that appeals universally. It is a strange yet enchanting film that often seems dreamlike, filled with moments of ambiguity, and the shifting pace of narrative flow can be a little disconcerting. After only a few minutes, Chihiro is abruptly transferred into a land of whimsy and, while the main body of the film relays a staggered series of unusual events over the course of just a couple of days, it leads to a strangely rushed anticlimactic dénouement. This complicated mode of narration is particularly unusual in a family film, but is effective in absorbing the audience in to the alternate reality of the films fantasy world.

Production work on the film is impeccable, with sound effects, voice dubbing and music fitting superbly. The animation in particular is of an unprecedented beauty and, like much of Miyazaki's artwork, it has depth based on reality, as many of the characters, events and fictional landscapes are influenced by real-life observations of people, situations and locations. Something as simple and obscure as the wallpaper designs in Yubaba's inner chambers, which Chihiro flies by in an early scene, are drawn with remarkable attention to detail that gives the fantasy an almost tangible quality. Miyazaki's guiding influence over nearly all aspects of production is evident in the symbiosis that helps bring such an imaginative work as *Spirited Away* to life on the big screen.

Although it is somewhat lost amongst the beautifully-realized creations, and in the unusual telling of the story, the core of the narrative remains the theme of youth finding inner strength and succeeding through hard work, a theme echoed in other Ghibli films, notably *Kiki's Delivery Service* (1989). There is little introduction to the character of Chihiro before the magical situation develops, although

Spirited Away, 2001. Produced by Studio Ghibli

she initially appears somewhat whiney and lazy, and a little cowardly: common negative aspects of modern youth. Chihiro only spends a short amount of time at the bath house, although it seems that she perseveres and works hard to complete jobs, despite struggling. In the final quarter of the film she faces dangerous situations without fear, proving that, in a short period of time, she was able to find the strength she needed in herself to face her problems.

Spirited Away is the highest-grossing Japanese film of all time; it has won several prestigious awards and is widely regarded by both critics and international audiences as one of best animated films ever made. By mixing a magical story, intriguing characters, incredible animation, and a truly enchanting fantasy world, a sense of wonderment at extraordinary things is captured for the audience. While all of Miyazaki's films are of a high standard, a couple of them exceed and can only be regarded as masterpieces. *Spirited Away* is definitely in this category.

Matthew Holland

Steamboy

Suchimuboi

Studio:
Toho

Director:
Katsuhiro Otomo

Producers:
Shinji Komori
Hideyuki Tomioka

Screenwriters:
Sadayuki Murai
Katsuhiro Otomo

Cinematographer:
Mitsuhiro Sato

Art Director:
Shinji Kimura

Composer:
Steve Jablonsky

Editor:
Takeshi Seyama

Duration:
130 minutes

Cast:
Anne Suzuki
Manami Konishi
Masane Tsukayama

Year:
2004

Synopsis

In 1866 in Manchester, a precocious teenage boy named James Ray Steam receives a package containing blueprints and a mysterious metal orb from Lloyd Steam, his inventor grandfather. Almost immediately afterwards, two men from the O'Hara Foundation, which had previously employed Lloyd and Ray's father Edward, arrive and try to take the orb back. Ray takes it and leads them on a fantastic motorized chase that ends with Ray being taken back to the O'Hara foundation in London to work with his father on his massive Steam Tower. This is a scientific marvel and powerful new weapon powered by three steam balls, one of which was the orb Ray had received from Lloyd, who had taken it and sent it away because he did not want to see his work being used in such a destructive manner. The Steam Tower is put to use in the Great Exhibition, where it is displayed to a visiting congregation of international arms buyers. By engaging with the English military and destroying the exhibition grounds, Ray takes it upon himself to try to stop his father's work.

Critique

In many ways 1998's *Akira* was both a blessing and a curse for director Katsuhiro Otomo. Its success would have been enough to catapult him into the pantheon of great anime directors if he had continued to direct with much regularity. Although he was still active in comics and animation after *Akira*, *Steamboy* was Otomo's first full-length film since his striking debut. In many ways, it is hard to take the film seriously. The names of the protagonists set the tone – a family of engineers who work with mechanics and pneumatics with the name of Steam. Throw in the equally unlikely assortment of Scarlett O'Hara, Robert Stevenson, and a pair of thugs named Alfred (Freddie) and Jason, and the result is an odd pastiche of monikers plastered onto one-dimensional characters.

Equally unlikely is the film's discourse on the goals and reasons behind science. Like *Akira*, *Steamboy* seems like it wants to say something about the state of scientific progress in the world, and the evil uses to which science can be put if left to its own devices. But in reality, the trope of science gone wrong is just an excuse for showing things falling apart and exploding spectacularly. For all pretence at meaningfulness and characterization, which takes up far too much of the film's lengthy running time, this is where *Steamboy* excels. The steampunk world of the film is fantastically detailed, and the movement of people and machines across the screen is where the majority of the emphasis lies. In the end, *Steamboy* is a film about technology, but not in the way it thinks it is – it is about how advancing animation techniques are able to create and destroy worlds at a whim.

Brian Ruh

Tokyo Godfathers

Tôkyô Goddofâzâzu

Studio:
Madhouse / Tokyo Godfathers
Production Committee

Director:
Satoshi Kon (Co-director: Shôgo
Furuya)

Producer:
Takiyama Masao
Shinichi Kobayashi

Screenwriter:
Satoshi Kon
Keiko Nobumoto

Cinematographer:
Katsutoshi Sugai

Art Director:
Nobutaka Ike

Composer:
Keiichi Suzuki

Editor:
Takeshi Seyama

Duration:
90 min

Cast:
Aya Okamoto
Toru Emori
Yoshiaki Umegaki

Year:
2003

Synopsis

On Christmas Eve, three homeless denizens of Tokyo stumble upon an abandoned baby in a mound of trash and embark on a madcap urban journey, determined to hand the child over to its parents and not to a foster home. Each has a personal reason for this quest: Gin is an alcoholic who long ago abandoned his own family due to debts and now toils away his days in guilt; Teary-eyed Hana is an oversized transvestite with a temper and first-hand experience of foster-home life; Miyuki is a runaway teenager with a big mouth and a torn conscience. As clues and coincidences chase them across the checkerboard cityscape of Tokyo, they stumble, baby in hand, through yakuza weddings, immigrant housing, graveyards, and the gay quarter of Shinjuku ni-chôme and, as they circle in on the real parents, one last shocking revelation awaits the down-and-out trio.

Critique

Tokyo Godfathers is Satoshi Kon's third feature-length anime and was widely regarded as his first attempt at full-blown comedy but, as the choice of protagonists suggests, this generalization falls somewhat short. The story is partially inspired by the John Ford's *Three Godfathers* (1948), itself based on a much-filmed novel by Peter B. Kyne, and Kon also picks up Ford's skill in mixing various emotional shades. In fact, much of *Tokyo Godfathers* relies on threading contrasts together; the tragedy of Gin, Hana and Miyuki's lives are deftly interwoven with slapstick and spectacular chase sequences, which prompt Gin to complain that 'we are homeless, not action heroes!' The multifaceted Tokyo cityscape, a character in itself, is rendered in imaginative detail, setting new standards for anime while stopping just short of photographic realism, while the narrative is at pains to show the degree of abuse and discrimination that the destitute protagonists suffer at the hands of an indifferent society.

Kon constantly plays with the idea of deus-ex-machina miracles, angel imagery, and a Christian theme of redemption. The latter, starting with the sermon held at a soup kitchen's nativity play, is never really more than a playful element and possibly inserted to give the film additional appeal in the American market. But Kon does take another theme more seriously – that of family. *Tokyo Godfathers* carries the theme of non-blood-related family in its title, but 'real' family always hovers in the background in the form of dreams and regrets. It is never clear how naïvely this message is intended as the film plasters the urban environment with ad-campaign images of family bliss, so obviously at odds with the experiences of its heroes, yet family becomes a very real route to their salvation.

Tokyo Godfathers is an extraordinary technical achievement and repeat viewings reveal new levels of plot, character, and loving design. However, the playful lightness of tone that *Tokyo Godfathers* strikes with regard to heavy themes may not sit well with everyone, especially with regard to his near-farcical treatment of Hana and her sexuality. More than a postmodern diversion, and yet never quite a serious social critique, Kon has succeeded in creating an enchanting hybrid that showcases the sheer magic of anime.

Alexander Zahlten

CHAMBARA /
SAMURAI
CINEMA

Yojimbo, 1961.
Produced by Toho

In the years that followed World War II, the Japanese histori-cal film shifted away from the pure costume dramas (*jidaigeki*) of the pre-war era and instead focused upon the significance of swordfights. To some extent, the presence of feudalism and a warrior caste guaranteed that, at least in part, *jidaigeki* films would be in some way action-oriented. Most entries in the genre are set during the Tokugawa era (1603–1868), an era of strong local authority, increasing civil unrest and national isolationism. Along with these films, the past half-century has seen the rise of a new genre: the 'swordfight' film referred to as *chambara*, or samurai cinema. Both genres are historical in setting and scope with attention to period detail and politics. They investigate the lives of the varying social classes from the samurai and merchants down to the craftspeople and undesirables. Of the two, *jidaigeki* strived to be more serious in tone and ambitious in scope often touch-ing upon key thematic concepts typical of the era such as that between *giri* and *ninjo:* the tension between one's personal compassion (*ninjo*) and the social obligation (*giri*) due to one's clan or lord. As time passed, the focus shifted away from drama and instead gravitated towards the action elements of the genre. These became *chambara*, the swordfight film, and they focused on the underclass of ronin, drifters, and yakuza, disassociating themselves from the subtle thematic of drama and centring their stories upon simple motives such as the pursuit of justice or vengeance for past wrongs.

Chambara has proved a fertile source of material, and directors of nearly every type have worked within the genre: from action specialists, to realists, to directors with a political message. Imagine that nearly every single film-maker in the United States had made a Western at some point in his or her career, and that would provide some idea as to the variety and scope of the *chambara* genre and its appeal to Japanese directors. At the top of the scale of great film-makers who have worked within both the *chambara* and the *jidaigeki* genres is Japan's most world-renowned director, Akira Kurosawa. Kurosawa started making films in the years before the Second World War and proved to be a master of many genres. His well-drawn characters, his devotion to realism, and an attention to simple human qualities marked him as the transitional figure between the *jidaigeki* and the *chambara* film. From the 1950s onwards, Kurosawa would make some of the most internationally successful and accessible examples of both *jidaigeki* and *chambara* films. *Seven Samurai* (1954), *Yojimbo* (1961), and *Hidden Fortress* (1958) would be his three must-see films in these genres, each of them becoming a classic in their own right.

Much of Kurosawa's appeal comes from his attention to detail and depiction of action. He employed telephoto lenses, allowing the picture frame to be layered with action and details. He also employed multiple cameras filming at a distance in order to give his action sequences a dynamic quality. As anyone who has watched *Seven Samurai* can testify, a battle scene by Kurosawa is an awe-inspiring spectacle with swirling action and unwavering devotion to realism. However, while Kurosawa is probably the most popularly-celebrated director to have tackled the *jidaigeki* and *chambara* genres, the works of Masaki Kobayashi and Hideo Gosha are easily as exciting and entertaining, and both are film-makers who deserve to be better-known outside of Japan. Kobayashi's work is intensely formal, yet also visually exciting. He retains the dramatic element of the *jidaigeki* and his films *Harakiri* (1962), *Samurai Rebellion* (1967), and *Kwaidan* (1964) are phenomenal cinematic experiences, and possibly even more haunting than Kurosawa's entries. Hideo Gosha might lack some of the formalism of Kurosawa and Kobayashi but he makes up for it with his devotion to realism and his desire to undermine the world of the samurai. Gosha began his career as a reporter and rarely saw violence as a heroic deed. The action in his films occurs in sudden bursts, more often than not the result of panic as opposed to premeditated purpose. These films are nearer to black comedies or crime dramas in that they often involve political cover-ups. Both his films, *Sword of the Beast* (1965) and *Goyokin* (1969), portray the feudal system as a hollow edifice where those in power readily make use of and manipulate any character devoted to clan honour for their own personal gain and satisfaction.

All of the aforementioned films can be called *jidaigeki*, with varying degrees of the elements of *chambara*. Of course, one could choose not to start with them but, instead, begin at the other end of the spectrum and dive directly into the world of pure *chambara*. This is the realm of the Baby-Cart Assassin, the Crimson Bat, Zatôichi, and the Sleepy Eyes of Death amongst many others. These films have an almost primal appeal, and it is near-impossible to describe the delight one feels when watching the star swordfighter mow his or her way through a host of opponents. These characters often went on to star in multiple sequels, some of which ran into dozens of instalments. More often than not they chose to deal with the world of commoners and those outsiders on the edge of society. Zatôichi, played initially by the unforgettable Shintaro Katsu, is not a samurai but a yakuza and a gambler. He is also blind, an example of a common element in the pure *chambara* film: the main character has some type of quirk in his or her character that serves as a trademark. Sleepy Eyes of Death was a nihilist and half-breed; Lady Snowblood kept her blade hidden in an umbrella. There are two other common features in pure *chambara*. First, the story will somehow intersect with a festival of some kind as a nod towards traditional Japanese folk culture and its appreciation for nature. In almost all of these films there is an attention to the landscape and rural life that gives even the most ludicrous plots a touch of realism.

Secondly, the films will end with a swordfight featuring the lone hero taking on a host of assailants one at a time. For some reason, the bad guys never choose to attack the hero at once, but each politely waits his or her turn to be cut down.

By the last decade of the twentieth century, the *chambara* genre had become absurd as the 'swordfight' had been elaborated on to the point where it had become a tired cliché. However, in recent years there has been a shift in the genre. Films such as the remakes of *Roningai* (1990) and *Zatôichi* (2003), as well the original film *The Twilight Samurai* (2002) have begun toying with *chambara* conventions and imbuing them with new life. They have often done this by anchoring themselves once more in the realm of *jidaigeki*. The story of *Roningai* traces its roots back to the beginning of Japanese cinema when, in 1928, Masahiro Makino filmed the first of what would become a three-film series. The title translates as 'Ronin town', and the film provided an opportunity to make use of an ensemble cast without relying on any one star. As portrayed in the remake, the story focuses on a group of poverty-stricken ronin who have taken up residence in and around a roadside inn. The director Kazuo Kuroki depicts the emptiness of their lives and the petty struggles they face day-to-day with almost clinical precision and clarity. He also casts recognizable *chambara* actors such as Shintaro Katsu and Yoshio Harada as characters, allowing them to reinvestigate the tropes of the genre. This allows him to indulge audience expectations while devoting his own attention to realism and detail. *The Twilight Samurai*, directed by Yoji Yamada, takes this even further. This film depicts the life of Seibei Iguchi (played by Hiroyuki Sanada), a low-ranking samurai near the end of the Tokugawa era. Yamada, best known for the long-running, melodramatic *Tora-San* series, spends much of the film depicting the non-militaristic aspect of samurai and their role as bureaucrats and accountants during times of peace. These moments only serve to heighten the drama as Seibei is swept along by clan politics towards a final duel that is stunning in its tension and character implications. Both of these films are easily accessible to the foreign viewer, and blend both the drama and the action that are inherent within the *jidaigeki* and *chambara* genres.

The remake of *Zatôichi* on the other hand remains pure *chambara*. Helmed by the renowned Takeshi Kitano, *Zatôichi* gives us the classic *chambara* storyline of a village being torn apart by the exorbitant demands of a ruthless gang of yakuza. Into this scenario walks the blind swordsman Zatôichi, played by Kitano himself who has updated the classic costume somewhat by replacing Zatôichi's shaved head with a close-cropped peroxide-blond hairstyle. As usual, our hero comes to the aid of several of the most-wronged innocents and, working together, they defeat the villains, but not before the audience gets to witness several spectacular swordfights (with computer-generated gouts of blood) and, most surprising of all, a tap-dancing musical number. In the end, the film nods to the original series while allowing Kitano to manipulate the audience's expectations and provide enough surprises to reinvestigate the storyline.

With the spread of Japanese popular culture, it has only become easier for these films and others to be found and enjoyed by a wider audience. In a way, we live in a resurgent time where it is now possible to explore the history of the genres while being able to find contemporary films that satisfy both our desire for realistic drama and action-packed swordfights. Even outside of Japan, films such as Quentin Tarantino's *Kill Bill* (2003/2004) make no secret of the debt they owe to the *chambara* genre and, as more years pass, it can only be expected that the *jidaigeki* and *chambara* genres will continue to have an impact on world cinema.

Justin Howe

Azumi, 2003. Produced by Toho

Azumi

Studio:
Toho

Director:
Ryuhei Kitamura

Producers:
Toshiaki Nakazawa
Mataichiro Yamamoto

Screenwriters:
Isao Kiriyama
Rikiya Mizushima

Cinematographer:
Takumi Furuya

Art Director:
Yuji Hayashida

Composer:
Taro Iwashiro

Editor:
Shuichi Kakesu

Synopsis

A young orphan girl, Azumi, is trained by a samurai master to become a lethal assassin. But Azumi is not the only one. Master Gessai is also training nine other teenagers, all boys, to overthrow three villainous warlords who have plunged the country into war. Azumi must undergo a series of trials before she is sent out on her mission, which includes killing her best friend. Eventually, Azumi and her comrades in arms are sent out to destroy the warlords and face much calamity and bloodshed. With sword in hand and retribution in her head, Azumi and her family of killers wage a war for peace against the warlords, including a fey though wily rose-sniffing master killer, Bijomaru.

Critique

This is not your grandfather's samurai *chambara*. While *Azumi* does contain a stately, refined, and even reverent tone underneath its post-millennial pixilated sheen and revisionist gloss, its fast-and-loose sense of historical detail and its teenybopper lead assassins (many of the cast, including Ueto and Odagiri, are/were huge teen idols) are light years away from the films of Akira Kurosawa, Hideo Goshi, or even relative newcomer Yoji Yamada. Nevertheless, this epic tale of good, evil and honour among killers-with-hearts-of-gold is rentertainment, due to director Kitamura's keen visual sense and his weakness for the grand emotional gesture. It may be slight work and perhaps

Duration:
142 minutes

Cast:
Aya Ueto
Yoshio Harada
Jo Odagiri

Year:
2003

not the giant step forward that many expected after his delirious yet overstuffed action/zombie film *Versus* (2000), but Kitamura's obvious affection for his lead anti-heroine is infectious.

As a mix between television's favourite vampire slayer Buffy and everyone's favourite blind swordsman/masseur Zatôichi, pop idol Ueto is perfectly fine as the petite assassin just as long as you do not expect much nuance or depth. The blame for this cannot be put solely on her slender shoulders, though, as Kiriyama's and Mizushima's screenplay refuses to deal with any of the moral paradoxes it so casually tosses up. So those looking for a serious meditation on the role of a trained killer to preserve the peace should probably look elsewhere. *Azumi*, on the other hand, never sinks into pseudo-serious stasis despite its slender weight. Although sombre and explicitly violent, this is still pure escapist joy, and an imaginatively kinetic one at that.

Derek Hill

The 47 Ronin

Genroku chushingura

Studio:
Shochiku

Director:
Kenji Mizoguchi

Screenwriters:
Yoshikata Yoda
Kenichiro Hara, based on Seika Mayama's play

Cinematographer:
Kohei Sugiyama

Art Director:
Hiroshi Mizutani

Composer:
Shiro Fukai

Duration:
241 minutes

Cast:
Yoshizaburo Arashi
Utaemon Ichikawa
Daisuke Kato

Year:
1941 (part 1), 1942 (part 2)

Synopsis

In 1701, Lord Asano assaults the unctuous Kira, a veteran courtier of forty years, for criticizing his execution of official protocol. But because he dared to draw his sword in an Imperial Palace, Asano is ordered to retire to Tamura castle and commit *seppuku*. His mansions are confiscated and his retainers dismissed. Asano's chief steward, Kuranosuke Oishi, and the eponymous ronin vow their revenge. As months pass, the vengeance-obsessed samurai begins to doubt the motives of an Oishi who, now in the comfortable employ of Lord Konoe, has petitioned the shogunate to restore Lord Asano's clan and thereby deny the ronin of any opportunity to strike against Kira without violating the samurai code.

Critique

Mizoguchi's adaptation is surely, despite its nearly four-hour running time and two-part structure, the most elliptical of the more than two-dozen filmed versions of this famous tale. The only 'action' that viewers, expecting a traditional samurai movie, are treated to here is a brief, and somewhat comical, skirmish between Lord Asano and Kira in the opening scene, and a wide shot of a stylized clash between renegade ronin Sukeyemon and Tsunatoyo Tokugawa, which occurs more than two hours into the film. Asano's *seppuku*, the 47's siege on Kira's estate, Kira's assassination, and execution of the death sentences of the film's heroes, all take place off-screen. This film, the budget for which was the biggest of Mizoguchi's career, proved to be a commercial disaster.

In lieu of swordplay and scheming, Mizoguchi emphasized protocol, accounting, reporting, and ceremony. Yoda and Hara's screenplay includes protracted scenes elaborating the rules of who may request an audience of whom, and Oishi's revenge is perpetually delayed by a procedural miscalculation. Over a minute is taken up with working out silver and gold exchange rates. The assembled ronin are treated, in a single scene, to readings not only of the verdict that condemns their master to death but also of his last words and his last poem. Lady Asano, and Mizoguchi's audience, find out about the ronin's successful revenge when her maidservant reads the account from a lengthy letter. Tea ceremonies, hair-shearing rites, and preparations for ritual suicides, but not the suicides themselves, are all foregrounded here.

Mizoguchi's long-take, wide-shot aesthetics and the deliberate, sombre performances of his actors, affect an overall pace for *The 47 Ronin*. Shots sometimes last for over five minutes and any movement within them tends to be muted. Lord Asano approaches a gate in a wide shot and gradually recedes into the background when he enters the grounds in which he is to die. The shot continues as the camera slowly cranes up over the arena wall, granting an extremely wide high-angle view of the grounds, including the screens behind which Asano disappears and the noblemen have assembled for the event. Similarly, a sequence begins when, outside their home, Oishi's wife and children board sedan chairs and are carried off towards her father's residence so that Asano's chief steward can effect his revenge; Oishi's elder son and then Oishi himself enter the extreme wide view and watch the travellers withdraw into the woods, with father and son continuing to stare off towards the trees long after the sedans have disappeared, their backs to the camera, motionless. This kind of understated, but emotionally-intense pathos reflects the philosophical conflict at the heart of Mizoguchi's adaptation: the conflict between individual, personal loyalties and national, political duties, a conflict that had particular relevance to the film's original wartime audience.

Bob Davis

The Hidden Fortress

Kakushi toride no san-akunin

Studio:
Toho

Director:
Akira Kurosawa

Producers:
Masumi Fujimoto
Akira Kurosawa

Screenwriters:
Shinobu Hashimoto
Ryuzo Kikushima

Synopsis

In the sixteenth century, two conniving peasants, Tahei and Matashichi, find themselves caught in the middle of a samurai clan war. They are taken captive, only to escape and discover the treasure of the defeated clan. However, a loyal swordsman, the General Rokurota Makabe protects the treasure, and must escort it and the clan's surviving princess across enemy territory. He takes the peasants captive and manipulates their greed in order to gain their assistance.

Critique

There are similarities between *The Hidden Fortress* and the earlier Kurosawa film *They Who Step on the Tiger's Tail* (1945) in that both films share character types and a similar plot structure, and also make use of traditional Japanese music as employed in the Noh theater. But *The Hidden Fortress* goes even further. Kurosawa has returned to the same story, now adding more sets, more music, and displays a generally greater control of the camera than he possessed a decade earlier. On one level, *The Hidden Fortress* is Kurosawa's love letter to the glorified heroics of the entire *chambara* genre. He gives the audience what it expects: the disguises, the swordplay, and the climax during the fire festival, but from the start Kurosawa plays with these conventions.

The Hidden Fortress, 1958. Produced by Toho/Albex

Hideo Oguni
Akira Kurosawa

Cinematographer:
Kazuo Yamasaki

Art Director:
Yoshiro Muracki

Composer:
Masaru Sato

Editor:
Akira Kurosawa

Duration:
139 minutes

Cast:
Toshiro Mifune
Misa Uehara
Minoru Chiaki

Year:
1958

Instead of an army on the march, we begin with peasants and farmers. Two emerge from this mass, bickering with each other: Tahei and Matashichi. They are not good men. They are cowardly, greedy, sly, and petty, the very antithesis of heroes. In other films of the genre, they would have remained as mere comic relief but, here, Kurosawa makes us watch their story. He also attacks the heroics of the overly-loyal retainer. For if the farmers are considered bad for being all-too human, then the General is considered just as bad for being inhuman. He has sacrificed his own sister in order to save the princess, and Yuki knows this and mocks him for it, recognizing that his decision has made him something of a monster. Of all the characters, Princess Yuki (Misa Uehara) is the one who is the most consistently down-to-earth and sensible. She is not blinded by her sense of loyalty and can adapt to her changed status with ease. In fact, she finds the adventure to be insightful and finds a freedom on the road that she would never have gained if she had simply remained inside a peaceful castle.

The Hidden Fortress holds a particular reputation in the west as it is the basis for George Lucas' *Star Wars* (1977) and the similarities between the two plots are apparent on first viewing, with a courageous princess fleeing from her destroyed home, assisted by a brave warrior and two bickering retainers. However, on its own terms, *The Hidden Fortress* warrants its high reputation.

Justin Howe

Lady Snowblood

Shurayukihime

Studio:
Toho Film (Eiga) Co. Ltd.

Director:
Toshiya Fujita

Producer:
Kikumaru Okuda

Screenwriter:
Norio Osada

Cinematographer:
Masaki Tamura

Art Director:
Kazuo Matsuya

Composer:
Masaaki Hirao

Editor:
Osamu Inoue

Duration:
97 minutes

Cast:
Meiko Kaji
Toshio Kurosawa
Masaaki Daimon

Year:
1973

Synopsis

Lady Snowblood begins with the cries of a newborn baby from within a women's prison in 1874 Japan. Her mother, on the brink of death, explains to her cellmates how, a year previously, her family was brutally destroyed at the hands of four villains who murdered her husband and son and took her captive, after being raped and beaten for days on end. She breathes her last and, with her final breath, dubs her newborn a child of the netherworld, meant to fulfill one purpose in life: revenge. After many years, this daughter finally sets out to find the remaining villains and claim her vengeance. As she carries out her travels, she remains an eternal outsider, her very existence defined by the tragic events that took place before she was even born. Even though she is destined to walk a lonely path, she is aided in her quest by the fatherly priest, a resourceful clan chieftain and an eager young journalist. With their help, she tracks down her prey, one by one, fully intent on claiming her long-due justice.

Critique

Easily one of the most memorable elements of this 1970's revenge classic is its star, Meiko Kaji, the queen of Japanese exploitation cinema. As Shurayuki, she gives a strong performance as the literal embodiment of revenge, bringing to the character a blend of cool determination and thinly-veiled sadness. *Lady Snowblood* contains a fair amount of informative historical content: the story hinges on Japan's transition between the tradition-bound Tokugawa era and the Meiji Restoration which introduced Western values and ideas to Japanese society. The four villains commit their heinous crime as part of a scam they pull on a village which involves them posing as protectors against imposed conscription and government agents, thereby using to their advantage the distrust that the peasants have towards the new practices of the country. Shurayuki wanders through this world of turbulent change as an almost other-worldly entity, her pre-destined purpose presented as a spiritual counterpoint to the country's fixation with modernity and progress, perhaps most strikingly illustrated when she pursues one of her targets through a Western-style charity ball, her focused gaze cutting through a crowded room of masked guests dressed in foreign fashions while an orchestra performs classical music. With her traditional white kimono and razor-sharp katana sheathed within her umbrella, she is viewed as a romantic heroine from a different era altogether, even portrayed as such by the journalist when he writes about her for his paper.

Along with its cultural critique, Shurayuki's story raises interesting questions concerning purpose and how righteous or necessary revenge truly is, and there are the villains and other supporting players to consider as well, with each major character being invested with an admirable degree of depth and personality. Topping everything off are the Fujita's beautifully-composed visuals, as the director presents his tale in a stylish package of falling snow, pastel-coloured lighting

and, of course, streams of crimson blood. One of the biggest influences on Quentin Tarantino's *Kill Bill Vol. 1 & 2* (2003/2004), which
specifically borrowed the wintery set pieces and the song 'The Flower
of Carnage', *Lady Snowblood* is a rewarding genre gem, offering up a
primer on Japanese history, plenty of vicious 1970's violence and one
of the most iconic female warriors to wield a sword onscreen.

Marc Saint-Cyr

Samurai Spy

Ibun Sarutobi Sasuke

Studio:
Shochiku Co., Ltd.

Director:
Masahiro Shinoda

Producer:
Shizuo Yamauchi

Screenwriter:
Yoshiyuki Fukuda, based on the
novel by Koji Nakada

Cinematographer:
Masao Kosugi

Art Director:
Junichi Ozumi

Composer:
Toru Takemitsu

Duration:
100 minutes

Cast:
Koji Takahashi
Mutsuhiro Toura
Jitsuko Yoshimura

Year:
1965

Synopsis

Set in the early decades of the seventeenth century during the
Tokugawa era, *Samurai Spy* tells the story of Sasuke Sarutobi, a spy
for the Sanada clan, which has maintained its neutrality despite the
ongoing intrigue between the Tokugawa shogunate and the Toyotomi
clan. It is an era of peace but, with hostilities simmering below the
surface, Sasuke finds himself drawn into this struggle when he assists
Toyotomi spy Mitsuaki Inamura, enabling him to escape from a local
magistrate. Mitsuaki knows the whereabouts of a top-level Tokugawa
spy who hopes to change sides and join the Toyotomi and he asks for
Sasuke's assistance, but Sasuke refuses, believing that such activities
will only destroy the fragile peace and lead once more to open civil
war. However, he cannot remain neutral for long, and eventually must
choose a side in the struggle.

Critique

On first viewing, *Samurai Spy* is a confusing film with many characters
and multiple levels of double-cross. It deals with episodes in Japanese
history that would be common knowledge to the domestic audience
but which will probably be unfamiliar to many outside Japan. Despite,
or even because of, this, *Samurai Spy* is worth the time and effort.
Director Masahiro Shinoda sought to make a film to counter the direct
confrontations portrayed in other samurai films set in the Tokugawa
era. He believed in the element of intrigue and espionage that was
inherent to that era, but which had been neglected by genre film-
makers in favour of depicting heroic battles, and intended to show the
role of spies and even ninjas within the feudal system.

Sasuke's main foil for much of the film is Sakon Takatani, the spy-
master for the Tokugawa Shogunate. He is a white-clad samurai, in
stark contrast to the dark-clad men around him, and his confrontations
with Sasuke are almost entirely silent and quite dance-like. When they
duel within the back alleys of the village, Shinoda punctuates their
battle with the passage of a child captivated with a rotating pin-
wheel – a traditional symbol of life's duality and the passage of light
into darkness and back again. Touches such as these are examples
of a directorial talent which, like that of Hideo Gosha, has remained
unknown for far too long in the West.

Samurai Spy is visually stunning. Masao Kosugi's cinematography is at home in urban and rural environments, and the characters inhabit the shadows in a world of black and white. There are some of the standard *jidaigeki* set pieces, in particular a festival scene, but these are all backdrops for the factions moving within them. While confrontations are as violent and deadly as those portrayed in any *chambara* film, *Samurai Spy* death does not confront its opponents openly but hides and strikes from the shadows. Shinoda's film might not impress viewers who are seeking pure *chambara* thrills but it certainly succeeds as a spy thriller set during a historical period, and can also be appreciated as an exploration of Japan's role in the world of Cold-War-era espionage.

Justin Howe

Sanjuro
Tsubaki Sanjuro

Studio:
Toho

Director:
Akira Kurosawa

Producers:
Ryuzo Kikushima
Tomoyuki Tanaka

Screenwriters:
Ryuzo Kikushima
Akira Kurosawa

Cinematographers:
Fukuzo Koizumi
Takao Saito

Composer:
Masaru Sato

Editor:
Akira Kurosawa

Duration:
96 minutes

Cast:
Toshiro Mifune
Tatsuya Nakadai
Keiju Kobayashi

Year:
1962

Synopsis

Sanjuro is a ronin who becomes embroiled in clan politics when he wakes up to find a secret meeting of nine young samurai taking place at the shrine where he is squatting. The young men, driven by the desire to rid their clan of corruption, have misjudged the Chamberlain and appealed to the support of the Superintendant. This man promptly shows his true colours by betraying them, and arresting the Chamberlain. After saving their lives, and ascertaining that they are utterly useless, Sanjuro volunteers to help the young samurai and they venture into a rescue mission. However, Sanjuro's plans are constantly fouled by the restless young samurai who mistrust his unorthodox behavior, and insist on getting involved.

Critique

Sanjuro is another of Kurosawa's critiques on the flowery glamorization of violence in the Chambara Jidaigeki (swordplay period dramas) which were so popular both before and after World War II. Speaking volumes in this regard is the juxtaposition of Sanjuro in all his ragged, uncouth glory, against the preened, mannered samurai of the court. The cowardly, deluded gangsters of the small town in *Yojimbo* (1961) have here been traded for city clansmen in their effeminate, patterned kimonos, with a naïvely-zealous attitude towards killing and dying for the samurai code of honour. Ultimately, the concept is the same in that these people are clueless about the consequences of leading the life of a swordsman.

Amongst the most comic scenes are those which involve the nine young samurai keenly hitching up their trousers and tying back their sleeves in preparation for combat, only to be told by Sanjuro that they are not allowed to use their swords because he would not put it past their stupidity to accidently injure him. Indeed, while they are quick to pledge that they will live or die together, as a show of bravery in the face of danger and difficulty, such a statement is promptly followed by a yawning Sanjuro finding a solution to their predicament single-handedly, either by concocting an intelligent plan or by fighting his way through small armies.

The gruff, unruly warrior is arguably the character that Toshiro Mifune does best, and such parts are certainly amongst his most memorable roles. His performance here is excellent, especially when the unshakeable Sanjuro is thrown-off by the most unlikely individual: the Chamberlain's old wife. The two, though polar opposites, are more similar than Sanjuro would like to admit. Just as he baffles his company with his tactless behaviour and unconventional approach, she with her gentle admonitions and devotion to aestheticism at the most inappropriate of times, is disregarded as a mere woman. In the end, it is Sanjuro who takes her most seriously. Her naïvetée, sage-like calm and incessant politeness, even in the face of danger, at first daunts and eventually confronts him with the realities of his own flaws. Though considerably more light-hearted, this sequel to Kurosawa's legendary *Yojimbo*, is no less of a cinematic success in terms of making a strong, humanist statement.

Elest Ali

Sanshiro Sugata

Sugata Sanshiro

Studio:
Toho Company

Director:
Akira Kurosawa

Producer:
Keiji Matsuzaki

Screenwriters:
Akira Kurosawa
Tsuneo Tomita

Cinematographer:
Akira Mimura

Composer:
Seiichi Suzuki

Editors:
Toshio Gota
Akira Kurosawa

Duration:
80 minutes (97 minutes original Japanese version)

Synopsis

In the late nineteenth century, Sanshiro Sugata, an aimless traveller with no real direction in life, arrives in a bustling town, eager to learn jujitsu from the master of the local Shimmei School. They are a rough-looking group of martial artists, who spend less time training and more time sitting around or getting into pointless brawls. Sugata fits in but quickly experiences a revelation one night when he witnesses a man defeat his entire jujitsu school, tossing them all into the river. This stranger uses a style that Sugata is unfamiliar with – judo. Sugata quickly abandons his school and joins up with Shogoro Yano of the Shudokan School. Through a series of fateful events, Sugata soon finds himself defending his school in a series of bouts in local tournaments, ultimately leading to a climactic showdown with the best student that the Shimmei School has to offer.

Critique

Sanshiro Sugata was Akira Kurosawa's proper debut film after directing some scenes of *Uma* (1941). Released at the height of World War II, the film became a huge success, spawning a sequel two years later. It was based upon a popular novel of the same name by Tsuneo Tomita, marking the first time that Kurosawa would adapt a work of literature for the silver screen. This was the first, in a long line of firsts, which make up the cinematic extravaganza that is *Sanshiro Sugata*.

The plot of *Sanshiro Sugata* would become the template for many of the martial-arts films to follow in its path: rival martial-arts schools, a quick-tempered student who must learn discipline and focus, and an old rival bent on the destruction of the protagonist. But what sets the film apart from the many films to follow it is its unique cinematic style. It is

Cast:
Susumu Fujita
Denjiro Okochi
Yukiko Todoroki

Year:
1943

apparent that, even with his first film, Kurosawa was a natural cinematic storyteller. The fight scenes are tense, and expertly crafted. Long takes build the suspense until the final moment, when Kurosawa blasts away with a series of beautiful quick shots. It is one of the first films to utilize slow motion for dramatic emphasis during an action sequence: a hanging from a dojo falls from its perch gracefully after a judo master is thrown into it. It is beautiful and painful all in the same moment. Kurosawa seemed to have the flexibility to experiment with various cinematic techniques, some of which would become hallmarks of his style. The film utilizes a great many wipes and has some amazing montages used to depict the passage of time. It repeatedly uses the staggered cutting in from wide shot to medium shot to close up. And while there is much cinematic flair evident in the film, Kurosawa also shows restraint, waiting to cut to his perfectly-composed close-ups until just the right moment – when the impact will be that much more effective.

Sanshiro Sugata is also a propaganda film, but Kurosawa manages to keep nationalism to a minimum. The winner of one of the tournaments wins the honour of training with the city police force, and Sugata, after falling in love with his aging rival's daughter, is forced to fight the old man for the good of the system, rising above his individuality and doing what is 'right'. Fortunately, Kurosawa crafts such a vibrant cinematic experience from a film which might have otherwise been a derivative exercise in nationalist fervour that one cannot help but be amazed by what the master accomplished.

Matthew Hardstaff

Seven Samurai

Shichinin no samurai

Studio:
Toho

Director:
Akira Kurosawa

Producer:
Sojiro Motoki

Screenwriters:
Akira Kurosawa
Shinobu Hashimoto
Hidero Oguni

Cinematographer:
Asakazu Nakai

Art Director:
So Matsuyama

Synopsis

During the Warring States period, a village threatened by bandits turns to a group of penniless ronin for protection. However, tensions arise between the two groups and it is only their decision to face a common enemy that unites them.

Critique

Seven Samurai is the quintessential samurai film. It has been adapted countless times and single-handedly succeeded in focusing the world's attention upon both the genre and Kurosawa. Here, and seven years later in *Yojimbo* (1961), Kurosawa elevated the chambara film into a means of making social commentary and took the world of the samurai and turned it on its head. The cast features many Kurosawa regulars and each actor does a masterful job bringing his character to life as a nuanced individual. Takashi Shimura stands out as Kambei, the leader of the ronin, an intelligent and compassionate man who has survived many a losing battle. He is in search of one final cause to justify his existence and draws together a fascinating bunch of samurai to serve with him. There is the young idealist, Katushiro (Isao Kimura), the wild one, Kikuchiyo (Toshiro Mifune), jolly Gorobei (Yoshio Inaba), Heihachi (Minoru Chiaki) the laid-back Shichiroji (Daisuke Kato) an old

Composer:
Fumio Hayasaka

Editor:
Akira Kurosawa

Duration:
207 minutes

Cast:
Takashi Shimura
Toshiro Mifune
Yoshio Inaba

Year:
1954

friend of Kambei's, and the master swordsman Kyuzo (Seiji Miyaguchi). The farmers are no less well drawn. The intense Rikichi (Yoshio Tsuchiya) is fuelled by a secret shame. The cruel Manzo (Kamatari Fujiwara) is unhealthily fixated on the chastity of his daughter Shino (Keiko Tsushima, and Yohei (Bokuzen Hidari) is a bumbler.

Kurosawa takes all of these characters and sets them within a pressure cooker. He has no intention of painting a picture of purely heroic samurai or simple innocent peasants. These are people of vastly-different classes brought together almost against their will by poverty. The samurai, if they wish to save the village, must overcome their prejudices just as much as the peasants must overcome theirs. Kurosawa maintains this tension by keeping the events on screen in a constant state of motion. His use of editing is phenomenal, as there are few moments of quiet or rest in the film. The samurai are heroic, yet their fight is against men much like themselves. They, too, are like the bandits: men of violence, potential marauders. So the heroics they exhibit are almost suicidal. The crucial difference is that these ronin have redeemed their deaths and made themselves honourable through their actions.

Kurosawa shies away from little in this film. His fascination with humanity is evident in every scene and every interaction Very little is caricature and even throwaway moments add up to make the story fascinating and compelling. When Kurosawa delivers the action, he does so without overly glorifying the violence. The final battle scene is a heart-wrenching masterpiece of explosive action and human drama as the samurai and bandits fight during a torrential downpour. The sequence entirely strips the illusions from the chambara genre, as heroism and ideals have no place in the ensuing wasteland of mud, while honour and glory are nullified. There is only death and, to those ronin who survive, there is no victory as their way of life is ending and their own days are numbered.

Justin Howe

Shogun Assassin

Kozure Okami

Studio:
Toho Company

Director:
Robert Houston

Producers:
Robert Houston
Shintaro Katsu

Synopsis

Shogun Assassin follows the quest for revenge of the shogun's assassin, Ogami Itto. He is the only person of whom the Shogun is truly afraid and, in order to curb his fear, he decrees that Itto be killed. However, when assassins for the Shogun attempt to kill Itto, he fights them off and, unfortunately, his wife is killed in the process. Ogami Itto flees with his young son, Daigoro, and decides to travel the 'road to hell', seeking revenge against the Shogun. As Itto travels, he is hired to kill one of the sons of the shogun. However, he is confronted with the task of surmounting the son's bodyguards: the Masters of Death.

Critique

Based on the original manga by Kazuo Koike and Goseki Kajima, *Shogun Assassin* actually consists of the splicing together of the first two of the six *Lone Wolf and Cub* films (both 1972), altered for the

Screenwriters:
Robert Houston
Kazuo Koike
Goseki Kajima
David Weisman

Cinematographer:
Chishi Makiura

Art Director:
Akira Kaijo

Composers:
W. Michael Lewis
Mark Lindsay
Kunihiko Murai
Hideaki Sakurai

Editors:
Lee Percy
Toshio Taniguchi

Duration:
86 minutes

Cast:
Tomisaburo Wakayama
Kayo Matsuo
Akihiro Tomikawa

Year:
1980

English-speaking market. This intensely visceral film is centred heavily on the relationships between father and son. With regards to the relationship between Ogami Itto and his son Daigoro, the son becomes the narrator of his father's exploits and provides the commentary on not only his father's actions but how they affect the psychological makeup of the young Daigoro. The two engage in a seemingly-religious quest for vengeance following the trauma of the death of Daigoro's mother, declaring that they will walk the 'road to hell': the assassin's road, a purgatory of sorts between former life and inevitable death.

However, this is not simply a tale of a father dragging his young son along on his own personal quest for vengeance. Daigoro becomes the central figure of this tale, and it is less a saga of vengeance than an exploration of kinship and duty between father and son. At the beginning of the quest, when Daigoro is a toddler, Itto offers his son the choice of the blade or to join his mother in death. Even at this precarious young age, Daigoro is drawn to the blade, and thereby the three elements become united: Ogami Itto, the Blade, and Daigoro. There is an unspoken intensity between Itto and Daigoro that finds its outpouring in one particularly powerful scene. Following a near-fatal injury from which Itto must recover, Daigoro takes it upon himself to nurse his father back to health. No words are shared between father and son, yet that is precisely what makes this particular scene remarkable. Daigoro struggles valiantly to bring his father water from the nearby lake, only to have it slip through his hands until he realizes that he can carry it in his mouth. What follows is the deeply intimate sharing of life between father and son, as Daigoro slowly delivers his father the much-needed water. There is an unspoken reciprocal relationship between the two: Itto protects and helps develop Daigoro and vice versa. In this manner, the father-son relationship between Itto and Daigoro is built upon a solid foundation of kinship.

The other paternal relationship that is explored is the one that exists between the Shogun and Ogami Itto. The Shogun acts as a patriarch to his subjects and, thereby, Itto is his chosen son and his personal assassin. The quest for vengeance that Itto takes against the Shogun occurs when the reciprocal relationship between father and son is broken; kinship and duty become meaningless. The Shogun enacts as a variation of the Oedipus theme. As Itto serves the Shogun, and in turn rises in prominence and power, the Shogun-father fears that the power of Itto-son, whom he projects in his paranoia, may in turn kill the Shogun-father, and claim the Japan-mother. This traditional oedipal triangle is not present between Itto and Daigoro because they have been forced out of it due to the death of Daigoro's mother at the hands of the Shogun. Yet this triangle is shifted for Daigoro, as the Shogun takes the place of the father and Ogami Itto the place of the mother. This shift is allowed to take place not only because of the death of Daigoro's biological mother but because Itto and Daigoro have opted into an existence which is beyond the traditional Oedipal triangle. They entered the realm of the religious quest, the 'road to hell', which enables them to travel together in the purgatory between life and death, and between the distinctive traditional Oedipal framework which is at the heart of the relationship between the Shogun and Itto.

Angus McBlane

The Sword of the Beast

Kedamono no ken

Studio:
Shochiku

Director:
Hideo Gosha

Screenwriter:
Hideo Gosha, Eizaburo Shiba

Cinematographer:
Toshitada Tsuchiya

Art Director:
Mamoru Abe

Composer:
Toshiaki Tsushima

Duration:
85 minutes

Cast:
Mikijiro Hara
Go Kato
Takeshi Kato

Year:
1965

Synopsis

A young samurai, Gennosuke, forsakes his honour and must flee for his life after being manipulated into killing one of his clan's counsellors. The samurai now turns ronin and seeks refuge in the wilderness where he joins forces with a poor farmer and encounters various outlaws, including another ronin, Jurata, and his wife, Taka. They are illegally prospecting for gold on the Shogun's mountain and, at first, Jurata and Gennosuke fight against each other. Eventually, in the face of other opponents, the pair joins forces. Meanwhile, the son and daughter of the man that Gennosuke murdered pursue him.

Critique

Hideo Gosha deserves to be better known in the West than he currently is. His films *Goyokin* (1969) and *Hunter in the Dark* (1979) are landmarks within the *chambara* genre and his entries generally have a faster pace than those of Kurosawa, while Gosha also brings a renewed sense of realism to the genre. Gosha started his career by working in television as a reporter and went on to become a producer and director for Fuji Television, creating successful *chambara* shows throughout the 1950s, and this small-screen work honed his dramatic skills, while his cinematic use of violence is explosive and shocking and it often takes the viewer by surprise, as would such an outburst in real life.

All of this is evident in the early scenes of *Sword of the Beast*. When we first encounter Gennosuke (Mikijiro Hira), he has been fleeing for some time and is resting in a field of grass, where he sleeps like an animal and is startled by every sound. This is not the down-on-his-luck serene swordsman as portrayed in *Seven Samurai* (1954) as Gennosuke is a hunted animal, prey to those who no longer have a need for him. Several of the swordfights take place inside buildings, and these action scenes have a desperate, almost frenzied, quality as Gennosuke has long shed his innocence and is now only concerned with his survival. Taking a room in an isolated inn, he prepares for a confrontation by practising with his sword inside the confined space. It is a matter-of-fact moment, showing a man who has grown immune to the emotions that should come with the act of killing. Like other *chambara* films of the period, *Sword of the Beast* skewers the world of the samurai and their conformity to clan and honour. Clan elders routinely manipulate the naïve for their own purposes and take advantage of those with higher principles, while the noble are always at the mercy of the corrupt. Gennosuke has learned this, and it is a lesson repeated to those samurai that he encounters on his journey.

Another striking feature of the film is the setting. The mountainous forest is a welcome change from the towns and villages that usually populate the genre, and the rugged terrain highlights the desperation of the characters. This is the wilderness, a place that is separate from the civilized world. Clan honour may exist for a time here, but it cannot remain static as it must change in order to survive. To resist change is to die, and even those who do survive must live outside the system once they have seen the hollowness it hides. *Sword of the Beast* is well worth seeking out, not only as a great film, but as an ideal introduction to a great director who is little known outside of Japan.

Justin Howe

The Twilight Samurai

Tasogare Seibei

Studio:
Shochiku

Director:
Yoji Yamada

Producesr:
Hiroshi Fukazawa
Shigehiro Nakagawa
Ichiro Yamamoto

Screenwriters:
Yoji Yamada
Yoshitaka Asama

Cinematographer:
Mutsuo Naganuma

Art Director:
Yoshinobu Nishioka

Composer:
Isao Tomita

Editor:
Iwao Ishii

Duration:
128 minutes

Cast:
Hiroyuki Sanada
Rie Miyazawa
Nenji Kobayashi

Year:
2002

Synopsis

Iguchi Seibei is a samurai nicknamed Tasogare (meaning twilight) because he has always had to go home at dusk right after work and never drinks with the other samurai. This is due to Iguchi's familial duties – he has two young children, a mother aging into senility, and his wife has passed away. He is heavily in debt, dresses shabbily, and even has no time to bathe properly because he not only works during the day but also tries to maintain the household and planting duties. As a consequence he feels that he cannot take another wife and subject her to a life of poverty, even though he has long been in love with Tomoe, the sister of a friend. Seibei is a capable swordsman, though, so when a renegade samurai barricades himself in his house, the clan decides to send Seibei in to kill him.

Critique

After making films for over forty years, it is interesting that director Yoji Yamada's first foray into period samurai films would also mark the first time that any his films have been properly released in English-speaking countries. Yamada is probably most famous for his long-running *Tora-san* series of films (48 were released between 1969 and 1995) that depict the travels and loves of wandering salesman Torajiro Kuruma. In addition to his contributions to such a popular franchise, Yamada is an acclaimed director, having won four Best Picture awards from the Japanese Academy, including one for *The Twilight Samurai*.

Yamada manages to make the everyday lives of samurai interesting and relevant to a contemporary audience. Although there is some sword fighting in the film, such action is not its primary emphasis. By the time of the late Tokugawa period, when the film takes place, the samurai no longer devoted their days to the martial arts. In fact, the recordkeeping duties of Seibei and his co-workers are more in line with what one might expect of civil servants rather than the stereotypical samurai. As in his previous films, Yamada is interested in depicting the relationships between people and the strength of families. He also seems to want to deflate the cinematic myth of the samurai. Indeed, Seibei does not in the least cut a dashing figure. He is poor, unkempt, and works the Tokugawa equivalent of a stuffy office job. His family even has to do manual labour, like making wooden insect cages, to try to make more money. More importantly, though, he is a well-meaning father who tries hard and encourages his eldest daughter to learn the Confucian classics. He loves his daughters and watching them grow, and refuses to be as miserable, as many would think his circumstances would dictate, and hence turns down an offer of an arranged marriage.

Although Seibei and Tomoe are of the samurai class, the film shows how they, too, were constrained by the class system. Even though Seibei was supposedly on the top, the film demonstrates that this does not necessarily translate into material well-being. The film evidences a social conscience as well: Seibei's eldest daughter, in voice-over, mentions that Tomoe said that the reason they could live as samurai was due to the hard work of the peasants. In some ways, Seibei would

Tasogare Seibei / Twilight Samurai, 2002. Produced by Hakuhodo Inc/Nippon TV Network

much rather be a peasant – he says that if possible he would leave the samurai life to become a farmer. However, even though Seibei and his family are poor, they are not in imminent danger of starvation – unlike some of the corpses that sometimes appear floating down the river. Yamada plays with audience expectations as well. After overcoming so much, Seibei's daughter tells the audience in voice-over that there was no happy ending for the family. A few years after Seibei married Tomoe, Seibei was shot and killed during the Boshin War (which led to the Meiji Restoration). Tomoe took the two daughters to Tokyo, where they lived and she supported them. It is concluded that in spite of everything that happened they were happy as a family and that she is proud to have had such a strong, loving father.

Brian Ruh

Yojimbo

Studio:
Kurosawa Films

Director:
Akira Kurosawa

Synopsis

A lone ronin comes to a desolate town that has been torn apart by duelling criminal gangs. Caught inbetween are the helpless towns-people so the ronin offers his services as a bodyguard (*yojimbo*) to both of the bosses, and soon he has them set to destroy each other. By careful manoeuvring and desperate swordplay, the ronin attempts to force a mutually-destructive showdown.

Producers:
Ryuzo Kikushima
Akira Kurosawa
Tomoyuki Tanaka

Screenwriters:
Ryuzo Kikushima
Akira Kurosawa

Cinematographer:
Kazuo Miyagawa

Art Director:
Yoshiro Muracki

Composer:
Masaru Sato

Editor:
Akira Kurosawa

Duration:
110 minutes

Cast:
Toshiro Mifune
Tatsuya Nakadai
Yoko Tsukasa

Year:
1961

Critique

After the contemporary drama of *The Bad Sleep Well* (1960), Kurosawa returned to the *chambara* genre with *Yojimbo*. In many ways, it was a return to form and, once again, he crafted a film that went on to become not only a worldwide success but an inspiration to countless other films. Sergio Leone's 'Man with No Name' series is the closest example, and the character of Toshiro Mifune's ronin is readily present in Clint Eastwood's equally iconic cowboy drifter. Like Eastwood, Mifune would go on to play the same character in at least two other pictures: *Sanjuro* (1962) and *Incident at Blood Pass* (1970), and he would also appear in an altered version of this persona in *Zatoichi Meets Yojimbo* (1970).

Drawing his own inspiration from the work of crime novelist Dashiell Hammett, whose *The Glass Key* and *Red Harvest* have been cited as the underlying foundations of the film, Kurosawa crafted a story along the lines of the classic Hollywood Western. It is easy to draw parallels between *Yojimbo* and *Shane* (1953) and also the films of John Ford. A stranger enters a god-forsaken town locked in conflict between two factions, where both sides are equally bad and repugnant, and the audience welcomes the swathe of destruction that the hero creates as he exacts justice. There is something inherently appealing about this scenario. It speaks to a desire latent within all of us: that some agency will come and clean up the mess that we have made of our society. Kurosawa's film eschews tragedy and melodrama and strikes out to create a wry action-packed black comedy. Where the heroes of the Western stood for some higher moral authority, Mifune's ronin is an amoral opportunist. He may fight for what is 'right' but does not do so out of any great sense of purpose and acts merely because the bad should be punished, and he might be able to profit from it.

The opening shot of *Yojimbo* establishes the locale as a dog strides across the screen carrying a severed hand in its mouth. The grotesque aspects build from there and the various gangsters and thugs show themselves to be an assortment of monsters made flesh. There are giants and craven cowards, men and women who are thirsty for blood and violence. The townsfolk, like the farmers of *Seven Samurai* (1954), are not idealized portraits as they, too, suffer from the malaise of their environment. However, they are not prone to violence and whatever wrong they do is minor in comparison to the rapacious nature of the thugs. Amongst these is Tatsuya Nakadai, who plays the only man with a firearm in the town. He has a clear advantage over the sword-wielding Mifune and their showdown is a tense standoff, with Nakadai at his villainous best. In these duelling gangs it is also possible to see aspects of the Cold War conflict. One side can be read as the Soviet Union and the other as the United States, with Mifune standing in for post-war Japan. Kurosawa points at the nuclear proliferation and the policy of assured mutual destruction and exposes them as absurd pursuits. That he chooses as his hero a man who is as bad as any of the villains shows the director to once more be at the top of his form.

Justin Howe

Zatôichi

Studio:
Bandai Visual, Tokyo FM,
Dentsu, TV Asahi, Saito
Entertainment & Office Kitano

Director:
Takeshi Kitano

Producer:
Chieko Saito

Screenwriters:
Takeshi Kitano
Kan Shimosawa (original novels)

Cinematographer:
Katsumi Yanagishima

Art Director:
Norihiro Isoda

Composer:
Keiichi Suzuki

Editor:
Takeshi Kitano

Duration:
116 minutes

Cast:
Takeshi Kitano
Tadanobu Asano
Michiyo Ookusu

Year:
2003

Synopsis

In seventeenth-century Japan, a wandering blind masseur arrives in a mountain village; but he is Zatôichi, no ordinary masseur, and an expert swordsman, his weapon concealed in his walking stick. He takes up lodgings with a kindly spinster, who describes to him how the villagers are being terrorized by a gang of crooks led by a man named Ozi. Meanwhile, two parallel narratives unfold: one of an unhappy samurai who must work as Ozi's bodyguard in order to buy medicine for his dying wife, and the other of two geisha on a mission to avenge their family's murder. Zatôichi ultimately comes to rescue the two geisha and the narrative threads come together when he must defeat Ozi's bodyguard in order to end the gang's reign of terror.

Critique

Zatôichi is Kitano's most commercially successful film, but one that he was reluctant to make. For 30 years the character had been portrayed on film and television by the hugely-popular actor Shintaro Katsu, and Kitano understandably did not want to compete with Katsu or imitate him. When Katsu's friend and patron Madame Saito entreated Kitano to make the film, he eventually agreed on the condition that, physically and psychologically, he could make the character his own. The result is a film with a hero who is an eccentric outsider with inexplicably bleached-blonde hair and a blood-red cane and a villain who, according to Kitano, is a killing machine. While Katsu's Zatôichi was sympathetic and kindly and had morality firmly on his side, Kitano's incarnation is aloof and detached; when he helps the geisha it is for the same reason he fixes a fallen scarecrow that almost trips him up – because they are obstacles in his path. We learn nothing of his past – he mumbles and chuckles his way through the film, with his eyes closed and head bowed down throughout – but this impenetrability is compelling, and Kitano's subdued performance is arguably the best element of the film.

According to Kitano, 'the spectacle in *Zatôichi* was as important as the central intrigue of the protagonist', and the spectacle consists of dazzlingly-fast sword play with lashings of CGI blood, broad knockabout comedy, and charming musical interludes, culminating in the final scene when the entire cast break into an impressive tap-dancing routine. In the original script, the camera was supposed to pull back at this point to reveal the crew and cameras; this originally-intended touch clearly indicates a director very much at play, and in this sense it is easy to believe Kitano, who came to fame as a stand-up comedian, when he insists that he still considers himself to be a comic before anything else. Problems arise when *Zatôichi* takes itself too seriously. Perhaps it is because the protagonist does not care about anyone around him that it is difficult for the audience to do so; the depressing histories of the geisha and the bodyguard unfold at length in elaborate flashbacks and yet carry no emotional weight, making the film desperately slow at times. The script was rewritten at Madame Saito's behest to include the geisha plot and it is perhaps a plot too many, with its deadly seriousness wholly out of place in what is essentially a light-hearted and playful film.

Alanna Donaldson

CONTEMPORARY BLOCKBUSTERS

In 2006, Japanese films finally overturned the dominance of Hollywood productions to capture over 50 per cent of the local box office. This was the first time that local productions had reached such a figure in twenty years and, by 2008, Japanese films had extended their market-share to almost 60 per cent. Whilst, in the preceding years, anime such as Studio Ghibli's *Princess Mononoke* (1997) and *Spirited Away* (2001) had broken Japanese box office records, the main force behind this more recent trend was not so much animation as a wave of successful Japanese live-action films. Although individual films may still not have the audience appeal of Miyazaki's summer hits, in 2008 over two dozen live-action productions were able to achieve 'hit' status, grossing in excess of 10 billion yen. Whilst not all of these are special-effects-driven spectaculars, Japanese films have undoubtedly benefitted from higher budgets, a renewed interest in local stars and wider changes in distribution and exhibition. Therefore, it is necessary to examine the re-emergence of the blockbuster in Japan and its industrial and aesthetic contexts.

Since the post-war development of colour and widescreen technology, the Japanese film industry has found itself struggling to compete with the appeal of big-budget Hollywood spectaculars. In the 1950s innovative local producers quickly tried to duplicate the aesthetics of Hollywood epics. But whilst films such as *Emperor Meiji and the Great Russo-Japanese War* (1957) were an enormous success in the domestic market, exporting such local spectaculars, particularly outside of Asia, proved to be a far more difficult proposition. Here, the attempts of producer Masaichi Nagata to win over global audiences with 70mm productions such as *Buddha* (1961) and *The Great Wall* (1962) also ended in failure. After the difficulties major film-producing countries suffered with the migration

The Bullet Train, 1975. Produced by Toei

of audiences to television, Hollywood's fortunes were revived in the 1970s, thanks in part to the emergence of the must-see summer 'blockbuster'. Again, Japanese producers tried to respond, with films such as *The Bullet Train* (1975) duplicating elements of the disaster film and Kinji Fukusaku's *Message from Space* (1979) attempting to draw on the success of science-fiction films such as *Star Wars* (1977). Without the equivalent financial resources of Hollywood, however, Japanese blockbusters from the 1970s again struggled to match their rivals, this time even in the local market.

Without the budgets to match Hollywood productions, or the same kind of international appeal, the major Japanese studios gradually moved towards focusing on anime as the best means to safeguard their domestic interests. Whilst during the 1980s and 90s, Hollywood films gradually established a dominant position in Japan, regular instalments of sure-fire hits such as the *Doraemon* or *Detective Conan* series at least offered the local studios a more stable stream of income than the hit-or-miss risks of live-action film. This strategy, of course, also worked to the advantage of Toho partner Studio Ghibli, but whilst the record-breaking feats of *Princess Mononoke* and *Spirited Away* may appear as the culmination of the decision to focus on anime, the success of these particular films was also indicative of industrial changes that could ultimately assist with the resurgence of live-action blockbusters. Here one of the forces behind Ghibli's two record-breakers was the role of the multiplex cinema. As in some other countries such as South Korea, the multiplex was slower to arrive in Asian territories than in Europe and North America. Together with its modern, comfortable surroundings, an improved ticketing system and the possibility of a wider release on multiple screens, the multiplex was highly effective in drawing Japanese audiences back to the cinema.

What also improved the potential for local live-action films, however, were the links between multiplexes and further structural changes in the organization of the industry. One important factor has been the way in which the Japanese studios, and in particular Toho, have strengthened the vertical integration of distribution and exhibition through multiplex ownership. Indeed much of Toho's market dominance has been achieved through its position as the largest multiplex chain in Japan. This has taken place in a context in which, like the Hollywood majors, the Japanese studios have divested the most risky part of the film business, production, to independent companies. Whilst Toho was involved as distributor of the two breakout live-action hits *Bayside Shakedown* (1998), and *Bayside Shakedown 2* (2003), the driving force behind these films was one of Japan's five major commercial broadcasters, Fuji Television. Although some broadcasters have previously supported film production (see the relation between Ghibli and NTV), with the terrestrial television sector a largely saturated market, all five national broadcasters (also including TBS, TV Asahi and TV Tokyo) have increased their involvement with film. While the funding from such wealthy companies has helped facilitate larger budgets, the Japanese film industry has also benefited from smaller companies with a strong experience in using special effects. In this context, Robot, a Japanese CM (television commercial) company, has also emerged as an important player in the production sector, involved in films such as the *Bayside Shakedown* franchise, *Always – Sunset on Third Street* (2005), and *Umizaru 2* (2006).

The links to broadcasters have also provided valuable synergies for the film industry. Not only are the broadcasters useful for helping to promote films across their media outlets (including television, magazines and radio) but a number of hit films have been adaptations or spin-offs from popular television series. This includes Fuji Television's *Bayside Shakedown* series and the highest-grossing local film of 2007, *Hero*, starring SMAP member Kimura Takuya. In trying to capitalize on media synergies, one trend has been to develop film projects through film committees (*iinkai*). Whilst there can be a number of committee partners, these will invariably include a distributor, a broadcasting company and a book or manga publisher who, as investors, all work together to decide how a project can be developed to complement their individual commercial interests. This is one of the reasons why contemporary blockbuster films will often only form one part in a media 'chain' based on the same franchise. The *Death Note* films (2006/2008), for instance, are part of a range of franchise products including manga, a television anime series, video games and a novel. Japanese advertising giant Dentsu has also often acted as a member of film committees. Aside from any merchandising tie-ins, Dentsu also works as a leading talent agency and their involvement allows films to draw on popular clients from across the worlds of film, music and television.

The strategic nature of these film committees has led some Japanese critics such as Morihiko Saito to condemn this system as inherently conformist through avoiding risk and restricting creativity. This is in addition to long-standing complaints about the conservative values of the commercial broadcasters. Whilst special effects driven films have incorporated a variety of different subject matters and genres, it perhaps requires a greater precision to assess whether this is only a surface diversity that echoes Hollywood practices in which studios are linked to a 'portfolio' of different projects in the expectation that, in an unpredictable market, at least something is likely to attract audiences. There have, however, been some more concrete changes in audience demographics and one feature of the Japanese multiplex has been the ability to attract more young women to the cinema. Drawing on television drama or *shojo manga*, many film blockbusters, such as *Umizaru 2*, contain romantic elements that might prove too sentimental or melodramatic to European and American audiences. However, other recent films have moved closer to incorporating Hollywood romantic conventions. Whilst this may seem a step closer to global homogenization, blockbuster films with more independent female leads, such as *K-20: Legend of the Mask* (2008), can nevertheless offer a challenge to Japan's entrenched sexual inequalities. The importance of this trend is reflected in the star images of a new generation of popular film actresses, including Aoi Miyazaki, Ko Shibusawa, Takako Matsu and Anna Tsuchiya.

There are, however, other ways in which we must consider the place of Japanese blockbusters within the nexus of the global and the local. Despite impressive box-office results in Japan, most blockbuster films have not received any kind of theatrical or DVD release in Europe or America, and even those that have, such as the *Death Note* series, still made the vast majority of their revenue in the domestic market. As the popularity of South Korean blockbusters in Asia has started to wane, Japanese films have been gradually making inroads into some other East and South East Asian markets. These still, however, remain far smaller territories, with low ticket prices. Thus, as I would also argue was the case with the majority of South Korean blockbusters, Japanese blockbusters have so far predominantly been directed towards a national rather than 'transnational' audience. Whilst the business infrastructure of Toho and the commercial broadcasters is primarily orientated towards Japan, the increasing global circulation of Japanese media such as games, television anime and manga may forge a greater overseas interest in Japanese blockbusters. With the entrenched position of Hollywood films, however, there nevertheless appear to be almost insurmountable boundaries for Japanese live-action blockbusters to win a wide release in European or North American multiplexes.

Despite the trend for Hollywood remakes of successful Asian films, the power of local films in the Japanese market (and to a limited extent in other Asian countries) has evidently been such as to persuade the Hollywood major Warner Brothers to start investing in local productions. This is also indicative of Warner's wider strategy in other international territories and their position as the second-largest multiplex owner in Japan. With the vast majority of Japanese blockbusters released in conjunction with Toho, there has also been increasing concern as to whether the company is heading towards a monopolistic position in the Japanese market. Whilst the repercussions of the 2008 global economic crisis are still unclear, if the Japanese majors (Toho, Toei, Shochiku) are able to retain a position of health this might also see local blockbusters further eroding the possibilities for the release of more creative films made outside the *iinkai* system. One effect of industrial changes has been to see some directors moving out of the independent sector and into studio productions. This includes the notorious pink film director Zeze Takahasa with his thriller, *Pandemic* (2009), and the various big budget projects directed by Takashi Miike. Whilst it will be a challenge for Miike to reduplicate the creative heights of *Audition* (1999) while operating in the studio sector, his continued presence might further complicate any simple attempt to divide the local from the global and the mainstream from a spirit of independence.

Christopher Howard

Avalon

Avaron

Studio:
Bandai Visual Company, Deiz
Production, Nippon Herald
Films

Director:
Mamoru Oshii

Producers:
Tetsu Kayama
Shigeru Watanabe

Screenwriter:
Kazunori Ito

Cinematographer:
Grzegorz Kedzierski

Composer:
Kenji Kawai

Editor:
Hiroshi Okuda

Duration:
106 minutes

Cast:
Malgorzata Foremniak
Wladyslaw Kowalski
Jerzy Gudejko

Year:
2001

Synopsis

Ash is an expert at the immersive virtual-reality computer game Avalon, so skilled that she actually earns her living by playing it. However, outside of the game her life is shown to be rather empty – the only thing that ties her to the physical world is her basset hound, which she lovingly cares for and feeds even better than herself. Ash used to be a member of a legendary band of players but the team dissolved when her teammate Murphy tried to go too far in the game: to a mysterious region called Class Real. Outside of the game, he is a vegetable, cared for in an institution, but his consciousness may still be inside the game. Ash is determined to figure out exactly what happened to him, and begins by deducing what she needs to do in order to get to Class Real.

Critique

In 1995, Mamoru Oshii directed *Ghost in the Shell*, which became phenomenally successful around the world and was a formative influence on *The Matrix* (1999). The two films shared common themes, aesthetics, and some scenes from *The Matrix* directly reference scenes from *Ghost in the Shell*. However, Oshii was reportedly not terribly impressed with the Hollywood interpretation of his film. In many ways, *Avalon* can be seen as a direct response to the themes and the aesthetics of *The Matrix*. Where *The Matrix* was action-packed, *Avalon* takes a much more methodical approach to telling a story that blurs the lines between 'real' and 'virtual' worlds. This confusion about the nature of reality is something that Oshii has carried across the majority of his films from the very start of his career. As computers (and, perhaps not coincidentally, computer-based animation) became more powerful and prevalent, Oshii began to switch from the blurring of dreams and reality, as in *Urusei Yatsura 2* (1984), to the confusion of an external, 'real' world and a mediated computer world. In most of his films, the line is pretty clear in the end. *Avalon*, however, is perhaps Oshii most ambiguous film in this regard.

Avalon is notable because it was the first live-action film directed by Oshii that seemed to be on a par with his animated work. Throughout his career, Oshii has directed live-action films, including *The Red Spectacles* (1987), *Stray Dog* (1991), and *Talking Head* (1992). Although all of these films had themes and styles common to Oshii's oeuvre, they were all obviously low-budget affairs, and Oshii was able to save on production costs by shooting *Avalon* in Poland with local actors and crew members. With *Avalon*, Oshii was able to build on the foundation he had set with *Ghost in the Shell* in order to create a story of virtual reality that was very much of-the-moment at the turn of the millennium.

Brian Ruh

Battlefield Baseball

Jigoku kôshien

Studio:
The Klockworx, Media Suits,
Napalm films

Director:
Yudai Yamaguchi

Producer:
Ryuhei Kitamura

Screenwriters:
Yudai Yamaguchi
Isao Kiriyama

Cinematographer:
Takumi Furuya

Art Director:
Susumu Nakaya (SFX Make-up)

Composer:
Daisuke Yano

Editor:
Shûichi Kakesu

Duration:
87 minutes

Cast:
Tak Sakaguchi
Atsushi Ito
Hideo Sakaki

Year:
2002

Synopsis

The talented baseball team of Seido High School is gearing up for the legendary Koshien high-school tournament – every Japanese schoolboy's dream – when devastating news arrives: Gedo High School is back from baseball retirement, and they are Seido's first opponents. Seido's principal knows what this means, having watched other teams be, literally, destroyed by Gedo, who deign to kill their opponents legally on the field by decapitation and other unusual baseball techniques. Luckily, transfer student Jubeh proves exceptionally skilled both in baseball and in battle. On the day of the match, Jubeh arrives late and finds the entire team massacred by the monstrous, green-skinned Gedo crew. Guilt-wracked, Jubeh embarks on a quest to assemble a new team with the help of bionics, reincarnation, and his dead father.

Critique

Battlefield Baseball's narrative speeds along with the same high velocity as main actor Tak Sakaguchi's spin kicks, leaving the viewer similarly stunned. In a blur of outrageous twists and absurd characters, the basic framework is that of all sports films, with the underdogs finding their inner strength in order to prevail. However, neither the manga the film is based on by Gatarô Man nor the film itself take this structure seriously for even a single frame, while Director Yudai Yamaguchi was assistant director and scriptwriter for Ryuhei Kitamura on the cult hit *Versus* (2000), with which *Battlefield Baseball* shares the same star and a penchant for hyper-kinetic action. Since *Battlefield Baseball*, Yûdai has been heavily involved in attempts to transfer the irreverence and meta-absurdist drama of boy's manga to film with such offerings as *Cromartie High School* (2003) and *Elite Yankee Saburo* (2009).

Like those later adaptations, *Battlefield Baseball* is less a film in the classic sense than an experiment in translating storytelling across media and, therefore, his work has been able to attract little more than a small but loyal audience. However, here Yamaguchi also attempts to transfer the inherent self-reflexivity of manga to the film version, framing the story between a speech by two actors, both claiming to be Gatarô Man and elaborating on the story, and there is a wonderfully inventive final voice-over narration by a surprise character. *Battlefield Baseball* established Yamaguchi as one of the most inventive and dynamic young directors of his generation, so it is no surprise he has since then been able to produce a steady flow of films with slowly-but-surely rising production budgets.

Alexander Zahlten

Battle Royale

Batoru rowaiaru

Studio:
Toei

Director:
Kinji Fukasaku

Producers:
Masao Sato
Masumi Okada
Teruo Kamaya
Tetsu Kayama

Screenwriters:
Kenta Fukasaku
Koshun Takami (novel)

Cinematographer:
Katsumi Yanagijima

Art Director:
Kyoko Heya

Composer:
Masamichi Amano

Editor:
Hirohide Abe

Duration:
109 minutes

Cast:
Tatsuya Fujiwara
Chiaki Kuriyama
Beat Takeshi

Year:
2000

Synopsis

A class of 14-year-old schoolchildren find themselves forced to participate in the Battle Royale Programme, a government-enforced 'game'
in which the contestants must fight each other to the death. Armed
with a variety of weapons and tools, the contestants are confined to
a deserted island for the duration of the game, with only one person
allowed to win and leave the island. If there is more than one player
left after three days, all of them will be executed. In order to keep
track of their activities the contestants have been fitted with electronic collars that also serve as a means of controlling them: should
any players attempt to escape from the island or attack the government forces, a tiny explosive charge in the collars can be remotely
detonated, killing the wearer immediately. When his class is selected,
Shuya Nanahara and his friend Noriko must take on the psychopathic
game controller Kitano and the government forces in order to survive.

Battle Royale II: Requiem

Batoru rawaiaru II: Chinkonka

Studio:
Toei

Directors:
Kinji Fukasaku
Kenta Fukasaku

Producers:
Masumi Okada
Kimio Kataoka
Hikaru Kawase

Screenwriters:
Kenta Fukasaku
Norio Kida

Cinematographer:
Yuta Morokaji

Art Director:
Toshihiro Isomi

Composer:
Masamichi Amano

Duration:
133 minutes

Cast:
Tatsuya Fujiwara
Ai Maeda
Sonny Chiba

Year:
2003

Synopsis

Having disrupted and successfully escaped from the Battle Royale Programme, Shuya Nanahara has since been a fugitive and rebel fighter, waging a guerrilla war against the Japanese government. In order to crush Shuya's rebellion, the government have altered the Battle Royale Programme. Now the contestants will be given military arms and equipment and sent against the rebels, forcing a confrontation between Shuya and the people he claims to be fighting for. However, when both sides realize what is happening they join forces for a last-ditch stand against the tyrannical government.

Critique

Along with Hideo Nakata's *Ring* (1998) and Takashi Miike's *Audition* (2000), Kinji Fukasaku's *Battle Royale* (2000) is one of the most-well-known Japanese films of recent years. Controversy has accompanied *Battle Royale* ever since its inception, with Kôshun Takami's novel heavily criticized for its graphic violence and provocative story. Needless to say, the book was a best-seller, with Toei picking up the film rights and appointing Kinji Fukasaku – a respected elder states-man of the Japanese film industry and no stranger to controversy – as director. When the film arrived, it stirred up the controversy once more, thanks to Fukasaku's unflinching depiction of teenagers slaughtering each other in a desperate and bloody struggle for survival. The subject was raised in the Japanese parliament, accompanied by outraged protests, and the director was invited to screen the film for a group of politicians and government staff. In the end they decided not to block the release, although cuts were made to ensure the film received the R–15 rating Fukasaku was seeking. Although it arrived on DVD in the United Kingdom to great acclaim, it did not receive a full release in the US until 2004, possibly because Toei were wary of exciting even more controversy.

   Although certainly violent and graphic, *Battle Royale* is not just a blood-drenched attempt at offending conservative audiences. Informed by his own wartime experiences – where government policy resulted in needless slaughter and children were indoctrinated with a survival-at-any-cost viewpoint – Fukasaku created an incisive, intelligent film that delivers a potent emotional impact, even though little time is devoted to character development (more depth is present in the extended edition, but it weakens rather than improves the film). Instead, the two-dimensional outlines of the schoolchildren serve as a blank canvas that allows the viewer to impose a picture of themselves on it, tying the film into their own school experiences and inviting them to wonder how their own friends would have reacted in this hellish scenario. Despite the seemingly pessimistic and nihilistic attitude, *Battle Royale* carries a strong message of hope: through their struggles the director maintains that love, loyalty and friendship are worth fighting for and, although they are forced to kill in self-defence, they manage to survive without ever compromising their morality. As the final film from a 70-year-old director whose life had been characterized by one struggle after

Battle Royale / Batoru Rowaiaru, 2000. Produced by Toei

another – whether with politicians, studio executives, hostile audiences or the cancer that finally killed him in 2003 – *Battle Royale* is perhaps the finest cinematic swansong ever conceived.

After the box-office success of *Battle Royale*, the release of a sequel was almost guaranteed. This time the director and his son Kenta – who had adapted Takami's novel for the screen – developed their own script that followed Shuya and Noriko's continued struggles. Having delayed medical treatment for his cancer to begin work on *Battle Royale II*, Fukasaku collapsed shortly after shooting began, later dying in hospital on 12 January 2003. With only one day of shooting completed, Toei decided to push ahead with the film, handing the director's chair over to Kenta Fukasaku. Unfortunately the finished article is heavily flawed, although it could be argued that even Kinji Fukasaku might have had difficulty following a landmark film like *Battle Royale*. Too much of the sequel comes across as a heavy-handed attempt to reproduce the first film; for example, instead of Beat Takeshi's chuckling menace we have Riki Takeuchi's ridiculous scenery-chewing antics. Whereas Kinji Fukasaku's message was intended to be almost universal, *Battle Royale II* is very firmly anchored to a specific time – the years immediately following the US invasion of Iraq and the escalation of the 'war on terror'. Throughout the film Kenta Fukasaku uses real-life media and contemporary events to underline his opposition to the United States: Shuya's men carry out an attack that closely resembles the World Trade Centre attacks, while footage of smiling Afghan children is used on a couple of occasions. Not only does this compromise the film's internal logic (*Battle Royale* collapses if you try to fit it into an actual historical framework) but it seriously undermines its moral attitude. By aligning his heroes with Al-Qaeda – their intentions and methods are largely the same – Fukasaku makes it very difficult to see Shuya as anything other than a terrorist.

Battle Royale II is not without interest, however. The film's standout scene is the beachhead invasion, a chaotic blood-and-fire episode shot on hand-held camera in an obvious tribute to the elder Fukasaku. (In a further nod to the director's father, iconic Japanese action hero Sonny Chiba appears as one character's revolutionary uncle). It is also the most harrowing moment in the film, as teenagers in military gear are cut down in droves by Shuya's men, unaware that their opponents are the next generation of Battle Royale Programme contestants. Even this sequence, as powerful as it is, does not fully live up to its potential. The school uniforms of *Battle Royale*'s lucky contestants served as a reminder that they were still just children; the camouflaged combat gear of their successors transforms them into the faceless soldiers visible in every news bulletin. After the explosive beach invasion, *Battle Royale II* becomes bogged down in discussion and rhetoric as the morose Shuya debates the political, sociological and philosophical implications of his actions, and the film never quite manages to recover. Despite memorable moments, *Battle Royale II* is ultimately a confused and uninspired attempt at producing a sequel to a pop-culture milestone that never needed one. Kenta Fukasaku has since shown himself to be a capable director, but his debut was not an auspicious one.

Jim Harper

Battles without Honour and Humanity (Series)

Jingi naki tatakai

Company:
Toei

Director:
Kinji Fukasaku

Producer:
Kazuo Kasahara

Synopsis

In the first film in the series, the US military drops the atomic bombs on Hiroshima and Nagasaki to end four years of unprecedented bloodshed and suffering. But bloodshed and suffering follow the horrendous devastation. Everyday citizens of Japan are turned into criminals, buying and selling in the thriving black markets, all conducted under the watchful eye of the US-led occupation. Ex-soldier Shozo Hirano is trying to stay alive in post-war Hiroshima, but he is quickly sucked down into a world of criminality when he kills a local gangster. Shozo is arrested and sent to jail, where he makes connections with a yakuza member who becomes his blood brother. Upon release, Shozo joins up with a yakuza clan and enters a serpentine underworld of gangsters trying to live up to their 'honourable' criminal code, though more often than not failing to do so in spectacularly lurid and violent fashion. Then war breaks out among the yakuza gangs. In episode two, *Deadly Fight in Hiroshima*, Shozo is back on the streets after

Screenwriters:
Koichi Iiboshi
Kazuo Kasahara

Cinematographer:
Sadaji Yoshida

Art Director:
Takatoshi Suzuki

Composer:
Toshiaki Tsushima

Duration (series):
500 minutes

Cast:
Bunta Sugawara
Hiroki Matsukata
Kunie Tanaka
Eiko Nakamura
Tsunehiko Watase
Goro Ibuki

Years:
1973, 1974, 1975, 1976

serving a term for murder and gets in with the Muraoka clan. But a young, wild-eyed thug from a rival family stirs things up and plunges the clans into war once again. Episode three, *Proxy War*, finds Shozo in the middle of another gang war, trying to maintain his neutrality especially when tensions increase as a rival yakuza gang from Kobe dives into the fray. Shozo gets sucked into the violence once again. In the fourth episode, *Police Tactics*, the Tokyo Olympics are about to start and, with growing public unease over the senseless gang blood-shed, pressure is on for the police to quell the chaos. While the gangs and their leaders are rounded up, Shozo makes his move against a rival gangster who crossed him years earlier. *Final Episode* revolves around the gangs trying to legitimize themselves by entering politics, but that decision does not go down well with certain gangsters, such as Otomo, who want the carnage to continue.

Critique

Although director Kinji Fukasaku had already caused a sensation with his gritty, fiercely unromantic yakuza films *Sympathy for the Underdog* (1971) and *Street Mobster* (1972), the multi-part saga *Battles Without Honour and Humanity* revolutionized the genre and became a box-office smash. Unlike the earlier *ninkyo eiga* (chivalry films) which proved highly successful despite repetitive plot lines involving stoic, heroic criminals – more often than not played by Nikkatsu Studios' most popular stars, Akira Kobayashi, Yujiro Ishihara, Keiichiro Akagi, and Tetsuya Watari – Fukasaku's take on the genre was brutally honest, savagely ironic, and visually combustible due to a heavy (though skilful) use of hand-held camera shots. In complete opposition to the predictable, escapist storylines that permeated the genre, *Battles without Honour and Humanity*'s plots were unwieldy, complex, and aggressively political as the series steamrolled on. There was also the vibrant rage at the core of it all. Stylized violence and brutality have always been the crimson-stained hallmark of the genre, but with Fukasaku's films the violence and anarchy perpetuated by this new criminal class was spectacularly stripped of its heroic, honour-bound traditions, revealing only the ugly brutality and stupidity underneath the tacky hipness.

In many ways, these rough-and-tumble films are the antithesis of Francis Ford Coppola's more widely known *Godfather* films (the first one being released the year before Fukasaku's first instalment). Both series are epic in scope with large casts and complex plots but, where Coppola cannot help but indulge in romanticizing his Italian mobsters to Shakespearean proportions, Fukasaku always maintains that these sharks in suit and ties are still sharks. Based on a series of newspaper articles written by a retired yakuza member, Fukasaku and his screen-writers diligently document the lives of the criminal class, showing us in excruciating detail how completely boring and repetitive all of the backroom squabbling, gambling, and vendetta-making truly is, though without ever boring *us*. Although it is Fukasaku's approach to violence which immediately captures our attention, heightened by cinematographer Sadaji Yoshida's jittery camera work replicating the spontaneity of street violence in all its gritty, uncalculated glory, upon subsequent viewings it becomes apparent that the camera work, widescreen compositions, and superbly-orchestrated frenetic action scenes are more calculated than initially thought. Almost forty years since these films exploded on screens, the rage contained within them is still overwhelming.

But despite the immediacy and brilliance of these moments, it is the carefully drawn-out and admittedly confusing multi-layered story and central performance by the coolly magnetic Bunta Sugawa that remain the series' strong points. Fukasaku's series has frequently been compared to Coppola's *Godfather* films and the comparison is not as reckless as it initially seems. Both are complex, dense, and stylish dissections of their subject matter. But whereas Coppola's epics are self-consciously artistic and infuse his cast of gangsters with moral depth, equating the Corleone family with something far more noble and mythic than they arguably deserve, Fukasaku never deviates from portraying his killers as killers, although actor Bunta Sugawara's character does have his own tarnished badge of honour to defend. Coppola's films, despite their virtuosic artistry, are removed from the reality of accurate mob life – a condemnation that could never be hurled at Fukasaku's loser wolves. And because of that, Fukasaku's series is the harder to digest at the end of it all, and the harder to shake. Despite the overall thematic complexities of the two series, Fukasaku's films are closer in spirit to William Friedkin's police procedural *The French Connection* (1971) and Martin Scorsese's own demythologized gangster epic *Goodfellas* (1990). Perhaps if he had clouded up his vision with romantic subplots, pop psychology, and grandiose violent set-pieces, Fukasaku's thugs would be spoken of with reverence the world over as well. Thankfully, there is still something threatening and unwholesome underlying it all. Even underneath the larger-than-life swagger and anti-authoritarianism, these cinematic predators still have the ability to startle.

Derek Hill

Bayside Shakedown

Oduru daisosasen

Studio:
Fuji Television

Director:
Katsuyuki Morihito

Producer:
Chihiro Komiyama

Synopsis

Aoshima works as a detective for the Wangan Police Service in the bay area of Tokyo. After the precinct's commissioner is kidnapped outside his home, Aoshima and his local colleagues are supplanted from the case by the more senior Special Investigations service. One of the main investigators is Aoshima's friend and former Wangan colleague, Muroi. After a failed ransom exchange, however, the sophisticated techniques of Special Investigations fail to produce any substantial leads. In the meantime Inspector Waku has also been kidnapped after trailing a suspicious character returning to the kidnapping scene. Although consigned to traffic duty, Aoshima takes it upon himself to question Hyuga, a brilliant but sociopathic criminal recently captured by the Wangan police, and to track down the kidnapper.

Screenwriter:
Ryoichi Kimizuka

Cinematographer:
Osamu Fujiishi

Composer:
Akihiko Matsumoto

Duration:
119 minutes

Cast:
Yuji Oda
Toshiro Yanigiba
Kyoko Koizumi

Year:
1998

Critique

Bayside Shakedown is the big screen spin-off from the popular Fuji Television Series that was screened in Japan in early 1997. At a time in which virtually all Japanese box-office hits were animations, the film marked the beginning of a new trend in successful live-action films. In the light of its $100 million returns, the brand spawned an even more successful sequel, *Bayside Shakedown 2: Save the Rainbow Bridge* (2003) and two spin-offs based on individual characters from the series, *The Suspect: Muroi Shinji* (2005) and *The Negotiator: Mashita Masayoshi* (2005). These successes coincided with the tie-up between Fuji Television and distributor Toho, who have continued to capitalize on their position as Japan's dominant multiplex exhibitor.

Whilst more recent Japanese live-action hits have tried to incorporate blockbuster effects, *Bayside Shakedown* generally opts for recreating a glossier version of its television aesthetic. While the film employs superior sound technology and the odd extravagant aerial shot of Tokyo's urban landscape, its primary appeal relies on the strengths of the television series. As in the television incarnation, Aoyama and his fellow detectives continue to struggle against police bureaucracy, but there is always a camaraderie and light-heartedness that stops the film descending into world-weariness. The character interactions are particularly skilful and, despite his pin-up looks, Oda adds endearing depths to the idiosyncratic Aoshima. Even when the film shifts to moments of high tension, light comedy usually returns to defuse any dramatic posturing. There are, nevertheless, several problems with the film and the visual referencing of *The Silence of the Lambs* (1991) and *High and Low* (1963) are rather perfunctory, while inviting comparison with Akira Kurosawa's film also exposes problems with the film's politics. Whilst Aoyama remains committed to everyday grafting and the importance of local police knowledge, he forms an agreement with Muroi, who will continue to climb the bureaucratic ladder in order to one day make changes at the top that will help those working at the bottom. Interestingly, the focus on police work seems to ignore the motives for crime, with the main kidnapper stereotyped as an anti-social, effete otaku with an over-protective mother. Through the figure of Aoyama, the film thus seems to be a rather passive and conservative validation of the importance of hard work rather than criminal idleness, whilst waiting, perhaps indefinitely, for a more senior figure to magically change the conditions of working life.

Christopher Howard

The Bullet Train

Shinkansen daibakuha

Studio:
Toei

Director:
Junya Sato

Producers:
Kanji Amao
Suano Sakagami

Screenwriters:
Junya Sato
Ryunosuke Ono

Cinematographer:
Masahiko Iimura

Art Director:
Shuichiro Nakamura

Composer:
Hachiro Aoyama

Editor:
Osamu Tanaka

Duration:
153 minutes

Cast:
Ken Takakura
Akira Oda
Kei Yamamoto

Year:
1975

Synopsis

After his company goes bankrupt and his wife leaves him, Okita enlists the help of two young accomplices, Oshiro and Koga, to commit the 'perfect crime'. Together they plan to extort US$5,000,000 by planting a bomb on the Japanese bullet train, Hikari 109, which will detonate should its speed fall below 80km an hour. When they demonstrate their intentions by detonating a similar device on an empty steam train, the police try to capture the culprits in a ransom exchange.

Critique

One of Toei's aims in producing *The Bullet Train* was to respond to the popularity of the American disaster cycle of the 1970s. Rival studio Toho had already tried to produce its own disaster films but, due to their limited budgets, these features struggled to compete with the special effects extravaganzas offered by Hollywood. *The Bullet Train*, attempts to circumvent some of these budgetary restraints by effectively being a thriller that also contains some elements of the disaster film. Here, the pending destruction of the shinkansen is palpable after the production used a real steam train in the opening explosion but while the film contains a near train collision, a passenger's stillborn delivery and a tense conclusion in which it is unclear whether all explosives have been disarmed, these set pieces share screen time with the crime elements of the story.

Problems with the Japanese rail authorities meant that the production schedule increased by two months, enough to also spoil the film's box-office chances by pitting it against *The Towering Inferno* (1974). However, after being released on home video in 1980, *The Bullet Train* has been re-evaluated as a classic of the 1970s. Many of Toei's big names take on cameo roles, and there are also appearances by the likes of Takashi Shimizu and Sonny Chiba, while the film is based on the prize-winning popular novel by Arei Kato, and the thriller aspects are expertly captured by renowned blockbuster director Junya Sato. But what is also of interest is the film's attitude towards its three 'criminals'. Through its flashback structure, the film lends much sympathy to Oshiro, a migrant worker from Okinawa, forced to sell his blood out of poverty, and Koga, a former student radical struggling to fit in to society. The problems of Okita also appear to tie in with the economic slump caused by Japan's 1973 oil shock. In one of his best performances, Ken Takakura captures the otherwise stoic Okita's paternal feelings for his accomplices, and his reluctant turn to crime as a way of making sense of his deteriorating world. The critique of Japanese society is also evident in the way that the police ignore the rail chief's entreaty to publicly announce the eventual safety of the passengers in favour of using misinformation to trap Okita. Rather than simply being the inspiration for Jan De Bont's *Speed* (1994), the film thus offers some pointed social criticism as well as being a thoughtful and well-crafted thriller.

Christopher Howard

Chaos

Kaosu

Studio:
Taki Corp.

Director:
Hideo Nakata

Screenwriter:
Hisashi Sato

Cinematographer:
Tokusho Kikumura

Composer:
Kenji Kawai

Editor:
Junichi Kikuchi

Duration:
104 minutes

Cast:
Jun Kunimura
Ken Mitsuishi
Masato Hagiwara

Year:
1999

Synopsis

A handyman becomes involved in a blackmail scam when he meets the unhappy wife of a successful businessman who is convinced that her husband is having an affair. He agrees to stage her kidnapping, and ties her up in a flat to add authenticity to their plan. When her husband receives the ransom demand he contacts the police, who begin to investigate. Upon returning to the flat, the handyman discovers that the wife has been murdered and that someone is framing him for the crime. When he sees the 'dead' woman on the street, the handyman becomes aware that he is a pawn in a dangerous game and tries to turn the tables and clear his conscience.

Critique

During the Hollywood craze for remaking Asian films that followed the success of the American transfer of Hideo Nakata's *Ringu* (1998), a remake of *Chaos* was mooted, with Robert De Niro and Benicio Del Torro suggested for the roles of the businessman and the blackmailer respectively. Although this was one proposed remake which did not make it into production, it may have been a more appropriate choice for an American make-over than Nakata's *Dark Water* (2002), which was transplanted from Tokyo to New York in 2005. This is because *Chaos* is a taut neo-noir in the tradition of James M. Cain or Dashiell Hammett which takes some of its cinematic cues (intricate flashbacks, a leading lady in 'dual' roles) from the implausible yet enjoyable early thrillers of Brian De Palma, and toys with such motifs as pouring rain and the archetype of the femme fatale, while adopting the multiple perspective structure that Akira Kurosawa arguably pioneered with *Rashômon* (1950), but was popularized much later by such American independent film-makers as Quentin Tarantino and Bryan Singer. However, the pared-down stylistic sensibility adopted by Nakata, which recalls Kurosawa's *High and Low* (1963) in its methodical treatment of its kidnapping device, ensures that *Chaos* is much more than a classy genre pastiche.

The title refers not only to the state that the principal characters (the businessman, the wife, the blackmailer) find themselves in as the kidnapping scheme escalates beyond their control but to the manner in which Nakata arranges his story, with flashback and alternative perspectives causing some confusion for the viewer but ultimately revealing the twists and turns of the story and the motivations of its main players at the appropriate junctures. *Chaos* moves at a pace that is steady rather than hurried, with the fine performances emphasizing panic and anxiety, and Nakata building tension from what could otherwise have been a routine thriller. A drawn-out scene in which the blackmailer adds 'reality' to the staged kidnapping by tying up and harassing the wife is all the more uncomfortable for the matter-of-fact manner in which it is performed and edited. The unusual, percussion-based score by regular Nakata composer Kenji Kawai adds to the ambience and enhances the intensity of the finale as the blackmailer and the femme fatale confront the fact that they cannot trust one another. As with any thriller that relies on twists to maintain interest, there are contrivances and inconsistencies, but *Chaos* weaves such a complex web of amoral activity that it is easy to suspend disbelief and become immersed in its labyrinth of cross and double-cross.

John Berra

Crows: Episode Zero

Kurozu zero

Studio:
Toho

Director:
Takashi Miike

Producer:
Mataichiro Yamamoto

Screenwriters:
Shogo Muto
Hiroshi Takahashi

Cinematographer:
Takumi Furuya

Composer:
Naoki Otsubo

Editor:
Shuichi Kakesu
Tomoki Nagasaka
Duration 129 minutes

Production Designer:
Yuji Hayashida

Cast:
Shun Oguri
Kyosuke Yabe
Meisa Kuroki

Year:
2007

Synopsis

The Suzuran Senior High School for Boys, nicknamed 'The School of Crows', is the lowest-scoring, most violent school in the country. The students band together in factions, battling each other for influence and power. They all share a common ambition: to unify the school under one rule. Genji, the brooding son of powerful yakuza Takitani, makes a deal with his father: if he can conquer the school, he will be allowed to succeed him as the head of his crime syndicate.

Critique

With *Crows: Episode Zero* – a cinematic prequel to the best-selling manga, *Crows* – Takashi Miike playfully reconciles many of his vastly divergent creative impulses and ultimately conjures a film that reeks of box-office-friendly teenage angst as much as it belies the director's own idiosyncratic inclinations. Miike imagines Suzuran High – a run-down wasteland of stylishly-dilapidated classrooms, hallways and courtyards – as a working model of feudal Japan: a broken land carved into separate turfs and ruled by feuding factions whose power is constantly threatened by scheming rivals. In the complete absence of teachers and administrators, Suzuran's teenagers engage in a constant struggle for supremacy that directly echoes the endless clashes of medieval daimyos. What holds this volatile microcosm together is the common set of values shared by all characters; traditional virtues such as loyalty, perseverance, or honour intersect to define the boundaries of a deeply-moral universe, where friendship between males is the ultimate bond.

Brash and energetic, *Crows: Episode Zero* celebrates a playful violence whose skin-deep brutality reads rather like the choreographed ritual of a high-school-prom dance. Far from adopting brawls and scuffles as an extreme form of testosterone-induced conflict resolution, the boys in the film crave each fight as a proof of life, driven as they are by an overriding urge to experience their own existence in a world that has all but forgotten them. This need also accounts for the more melodramatic aspects of the film, where the tough guys' softer nature comes to light. Rather than eschewing such moments to preserve the characters' tough personas, Miike fully embraces them, partly in pursuit of his own brand of poignant quirkiness, partly as a reflection of his interest in conflicted inner lives that stems from his personal struggles as a child in Osaka, and is more obviously echoed in his *Young Thugs* films. It is all the more appropriate, then, that the entire film revolves around the character of Ken – the third-rate yakuza-henchman-turned-mentor. As Miike's heartfelt alter ego, he provides most of the opportunities for offbeat digressions, but by facing the ultimate sacrifice for Genji's sake he also gives the Suzuran boys the validation they had been craving all along.

Ricardo de Los Rios

Detroit Metal City

Detoroito metaru shiti

Studio:
Toho Company

Director:
Toshio Lee

Producer:
Yuka Higuchi, Genki Kawamura

Screenwriters:
Kiminori Wakasugi (manga)
Mika Omori (adaptation)

Cinematographer:
Koichi Nakayama

Art Director:
Norifumi Nakayama

Composer:
Takayuki Hattori

Editor:
Takuya Taguchi

Duration:
104 minutes

Cast:
Ken'ichi Matsuyama
Rosa Kato
Gene Simmons

Year:
2008

Synopsis

Detroit Metal City follows the rise of DMC aka Detroit Metal City, a death metal band fronted by Johannes Krauser II. He spews songs of hate, murder, rape, filth and depravity. DMC's army of fans chant the lyrics ritualistically, believing Krauser is the true god of evil, who spends his time raping ten women in one minute, ingesting any available drugs, and killing his friends and family. But behind all the make-up and demon armour hides Soichi Negishi, a timid country boy with a mushroom hair cut who has aspirations of becoming a trendy pop star, singing songs that inspire people to dream, and living a happy life in Tokyo.

Critique

In the 1980s, Takeshi Kitano was hard at work making Japanese audiences laugh. From time to time, he still does but those early years saw Kitano and his comedic genius in its prime. Or was it really his comedic genius? There was a man – the man-behind-the-man, so to speak – who helped create some of the absurdist humour that we know only too well from that period. That man, Toshio Lee, finally made his leap into motion pictures almost two decades later. But could Toshio Lee, a man known for such insane comedic humour, translate his particular form of comedy to the silver screen? And could he take an incredibly popular manga and please its legion of fans and newcomers alike?

Detroit Metal City is based on a rather simple idea and, in the wrong director's hands, could have quickly become a redundant and repetitive film, spoofing contemporary pop culture and the death metal music scene. But in Lee's hands, the film becomes an inspired piece of madcap cinema. Structured rather like a comedy variety show, something Lee is obviously familiar with, DMC is built around a series of utterly insane comedic set pieces, the climax of which is a showdown between Jack and Krauser. The always egotistical Gene Simmons plays Jack II Dark, who travels with a demon bull and plays an electric guitar designed by Yoshihiro Nishimura, the special effects genius behind *Tokyo Gore Police* (2008). Needless to say, even if the climax did not feature a plethora of explosions every time Gene Simmons moved his lips, it would still be a sight not soon forgotten.

Because *Detroit Metal City* is structured in a format that Lee is so familiar with, it still manages to flow beautifully, behaving less than a series of set pieces and more like a unified film. It also helps that he brings more to the film than just his comedic sensibility, instilling it with a message, albeit a cheesy one, about inspiring people to dream. This, along with Ken'ichi Matsuyama's performance, helps ground the film, and gives it cohesion and unity. However, it is Ken'ichi Matsuyama's performance that is the real heart of the film. Not only does he switch with such ease between foul-mouthed showmanship and extreme social awkwardness, sometimes in the same scene, but he is a master of physical comedy, and you will not laugh harder than when seeing Negishi run, dance or play the guitar.

Matthew Hardstaff

Hula Garu, 2006. Produced by Black Diamonds/Cine Quanon

Hula Girls

Hula gâru

Studio:
Black Diamonds, Cine Quanon

Director:
Sang-Il Lee

Producer:
Hitomi Ishihara

Screenwriters:
Sang-Il Lee
Daisuke Habara

Cinematographer:
Hideo Yamamoto

Art Director:
Yohei Taneda (Production
Design)

Synopsis

In the mid-1960s, a small mining town in Northern Japan is facing crisis. The mine will soon be closing and the town is desperate to figure out how it will survive. Amongst the many ideas the towns-people offer up is a suggestion to build a new Hawaiian Centre – complete with stores, palm trees and hula dancers – to attract tourists. Even though Hawaiian culture is popular in Japan, the concept is not exactly embraced by the locals. Facing resistance, a group of young women decide to train to become hula dancers, and enlist the help of an ex-professional dancer from Tokyo. Against all odds, they work towards their dream of finding something outside of the cold desolate mining village whilst still hoping to save their town.

Critique

The first act of the film plays out like *The Full Monty* (1997), though with young Japanese women, less nudity, and more grass skirts. Things start out a bit slowly but there is some semblance of a story and scenes of hula dancing, which provide relevance and meaning through the different gestures of the dances. Unfortunately, when the second act kicks in *Hula Girls* collapses upon itself. Things take a darker turn and, aside from weeping, the characters do not get a

Composer:
Jake Shimabukuro

Editor:
Tsuyoshi Imai

Duration:
108 minutes

Cast:
Yasuko Matsuyuki
Etsushi Toyokawa
Yû Aoi

Year:
2006

chance to do anything interesting for long periods of time, while every emotional scene is stretched to its breaking point. A prime example is a scene in which two of the original dancers say goodbye to each other. One is running along the top of a ridge chasing the truck carrying the other and for what seems like ages they yell 'See you!' to each other until the camera holds interminably on the remaining friend waving frantically while the music swells. Another major issue is the music score, which desperately tries to pull at the heartstrings, but tinkling piano and delicate acoustic guitar are not enough to warrant an emotional response from an audience.

Aside from the climactic dance, which is the best part of the movie by far, the film loses its early sense of fun. Even the expected montages, showing dancers slowly improving, getting to know each other better and starting to help one another, are overly clichéd and fall flat. With so many interesting ingredients – the possible impact of different cultures, economic implications of failing industries within blue collar communities, women in grass skirts – it is a shame that the film-makers found nothing interesting to say. Somehow, the film actually won a number of awards within Japan, including four Japanese Academy awards, one of which was for Best Film, and was submitted as the Japanese entry for the 2007 Academy Award for Best Foreign Language Film.

Bob Turnbull

Maborosi
Maboroshi no hikari

Studio:
TV Man Union

Director:
Hirokazu Kore-eda

Producer:
Naoe Gozu

Screenwriter:
Yoshihisa Ogita, from the novel by Teru Miyamoto

Cinematographer:
Masao Nakabori

Art Director:
Kyôko Heya

Composer:
Ming Chang Chen

Synopsis

In Osaka, an elderly woman walks determinedly across a bridge busy with traffic. When stopped momentarily by Yumiko, her young granddaughter, she simply explains that she wants to die in her hometown, and then continues on her way. Years later, Yumiko is a young woman living happily with Ikuo, her husband, and their infant son. She is content with her life until one night when she is told that Ikuo was killed by a train while walking along a bend in the tracks, seemingly ignoring all warnings of the approaching danger. After this confounding tragedy, Yumiko meets a man named Tamio through a matchmaker friend of hers, marries him and moves with her son to their new home in a small coastal village. However, she remains haunted by her memories of Ikuo and attempts to find a sense of peace and resolution regarding the events of the past.

Critique

The first feature film from director Hirokazu Kore-eda, *Maborosi* is a sublimely-rendered consideration of life and loss. Its style is gentle and contemplative, achieving a poetic beauty strongly reminiscent of such masters as Ozu or Mizoguchi. Impeccable framing, excellent use of natural lighting and many beautiful still-life compositions and portrait-like shots give the film a clear painterly essence. Its strong

Editor:

Tomoyo Oshima

Duration:

110 minutes

Cast:

Makiko Esumi
Takashi Naito
Tadanobu Asano

Year:

1997

emotions and serious themes are communicated in a reserved, minimalist fashion, not concerned with telling a story so much as relaying a tableau of personal experiences and everyday observations to the audience. Through its subtle methods, *Maborosi* reveals the power of memories long after the moments that initially planted them have passed: there is the bicycle that Ikuo steals and paints green with Yumiko, and the small bell he gives to her and, after his death, these seemingly mundane objects become aching reminders of his deeply-felt absence. Death is something that continually returns to Yumiko throughout her life, starting with her grandmother's departure, then later with Ikuo's. Tragedy threatens to strike yet again when a feisty old woman sets off in her fishing boat during a cruel winter storm. The image of her resolutely walking away from Yumiko is an all-too-clear reminder of the previous losses that still weigh heavily in her memory.

Among *Maborosi*'s most pleasurable features are the many eloquent passages that show life ceaselessly passing. The calm of the Osaka neighbourhood is repeatedly punctuated by passing commuter trains, sometimes accompanied by blinking crossing gates. The fishing village's inhabitants are shown through various sequences as they talk, fish, work and rest amid the relentless rhythm of the crashing sea. One sequence is solely devoted to the two children as they run and play throughout the hilly coastal setting, discovering both its natural and man-made delights. While many of these brilliantly reflective moments serve a descriptive purpose, they also complement Yumiko's ongoing healing. She achieves some happiness with Tamio, yet there is an underlying feeling of melancholy that quietly torments her. Near the end of the film, a number of long shots capture a funeral procession from afar with Yumiko following behind, the small, dark figures making their way through falling snow flurries and across a flat plain underneath an overcast blue sky. Without the use of dialogue, this scene clearly communicates the two central concerns of the film: Yumiko's inability to completely let go of the past and the perpetual influence death imparts upon the living. Ingrained with such rare wisdom and insight, *Maborosi* is a profoundly moving experience.

Marc Saint-Cyr

Shall We Dance?

Shall we dansu?

Studio:
Daiei

Director:
Masayuki Suo

Producer:
Kazuhiro Igarashi
Hiroyuki Kato
Shigeru Ohno
Yasuyoshi Tokuma
Seiji Urushido

Screenwriter:
Masayuki Suo

Cinematographer:
Naoki Kayano

Art Director:
Kyoko Heya

Composer:
Yoshikazu Suo

Editor:
Jun'ichi Kikuchi

Duration:
136 minutes

Cast:
Koji Yakusho
Tamiyo Kusakari
Naoto Takenaka

Year:
1996

Synopsis

Sugiyama is an accountant in his forties with a loving wife, an affectionate daughter and a house of his own. He has everything he thought he wanted but something is missing. Looking out of the window on the train journey home, he catches sight of a young woman in a dance studio not far from the station. He begins to look out for her every day until he works up the courage to jump off the train, run to the studio and ask nervously for lessons in ballroom dancing. What begins as a way to get to know Mai, the sad, severe young woman he glimpsed from the train, slowly becomes a passion, but one that he must keep from his family and workmates or risk unbearable humiliation.

Critique

Sugiyama is the embodiment of the hard-working Japanese everyman, reaching the ultimate goal of owning a home for his family only to discover that he has sold his soul to his company in order to pay for it. In Japan, most young people must start work in a company as soon as they finish university, with few opportunities for gap years or extended holidays once they start their career. The ideology that work itself should bring satisfaction, whether you enjoy your job or not, is a cultural hangover from post-war Japan, when motivating large numbers of people to enter and stay in the workforce without complaint was crucial to the economy. However, this ideology had become questionable by 1996, just a few years after Japan's booming economy collapsed and many workers were made redundant from jobs they had no love for but had assumed to be secure. Those who kept their jobs, like Sugiyama, would not consider leaving their positions, especially while being committed to buying a family home in Tokyo's over-priced and over-crowded housing market.

Sugiyama is likable, decent and non-descript – until he meets Mai. Had this been a love story between the two central characters, it might have been off-putting, but instead their relationship is only a catalyst for them to rediscover a love for their own lives through dance. However, the quirky supporting characters and self-deprecating physical humour offset this sentimentality. Sugiyama's beginner's class of three men also consists of the acquaintance who puts on a curly wig and becomes Latin dancer 'Donny', and the loud, obnoxious dancer Toyoko, who is looking for a new partner but insults anyone within reach, and getting to know these characters and witness their growing confidence and trust in other people adds layers of interest and depth without sacrificing the comedy that made this film such a popular success. *Shall We Dance* is a film with much to say about quality of life, gender roles, and pride in Japanese society, but always makes such observations with a sense of humour.

Amelia Cook

Sukiyaki Western Django, 2007.
Produced by Dentsu/Sony Pictures

Sukiyaki Western Django

Sukiyaki uesutan jango

Studio:
First Look Studios

Director:
Takashi Miike

Producers:
Toshiaki Nakazawa
Nobuyuki Tohya
Hirotsugu Yoshida
Toshinori Yamaguchi
Masato Osaki

Screenplay:
Takashi Miike
Masa Nakamura

Cinematographer:
Toyomichi Kurita

Art Director:
Nao Sasaki

Composer:
Koji Endo

Editor:
Taiji Shimamura

Duration:
98 min. (International release);
121 min. (Japanese uncut
version)

Cast:
Hideaki Ito
Koichi Sato
Yusuke Iseya

Year:
2007

Synopsis

A lone gunman arrives in a town laid waste by two warring clans and offers his services to the highest bidder. The Heikei and Genji clans are both after the town treasure and neither of the two proves to be more appealing than the other. The town's innkeeper, Ruriko, steps in to suggest that the gunman does not need to side with either clan since he is so skilled with his weapon. She advises him to get some rest at her inn and think it over before making his choice. There, the gunman meets Heihachi, the Heikei-Genji 'half-breed' grandson of Ruriko. Boss Kiyomori, leader of the Heikei clan has murdered his father and boss Yoshitsune of the Genji clan has pushed the boy's revenge-seeking mother, Shizuka, into prostitution. The Gunman sympathizes with the plight of mother and child and decides to play both clans against each other in order to avenge them.

Critique

Sukiyaki Western Django is a deliberate play on reclaiming the genre that was effectively hijacked from Japanese cinema when Sergio Leone remade Akira Kurosawa's *Yojimbo* (1961) as *A Fistful of Dollars (1964)*. Leone's film was a shameless imitation, even in its novel, unromantic depiction of the Wild West – an element that Kurasawa had created in *Yojimbo* to deglamorize the popular *chambara* films. There is no single consistent element stringing together Takashi Miike's work, except perhaps his penchant for the shock factor, derived from gory sadism to twisted comedy and often a disturbing combination of the two. So it is not surprising that *Sukiyaki Western Djnago* is another oddball creation which could only have been pulled off by Miike. Do not expect to find character depth or an engrossing and beautifully-developed story. Do expect to find stock characters, and a conventional plot riddled with sometimes predictable but often deliciously-random references to clichés of Western and Japanese cinema.

Miike's biggest misjudgement was perhaps his decision to shoot this film in phonetically-pronounced English. The dialogue is dubbed, creating a lack of synchrony between discourse and its visual expression. Furthermore, for the predominantly Japanese-speaking cast, the challenge of having to deliver their lines hinders their performances altogether, with the actors' laboured delivery and erratic pronunciation often making the result embarrassing. On a positive note, the crowning glory of the film is its visuals, with costumes alone being worthy of mention. Clan members, in their elaborate neo-Kabuki cum Cowboy attire, tattoos and body Jewellery, look like something between Visual Kei J-rock bands and Bosozoku biker gang youth.

Something of a parody, but without the silliness of a spoof, *Sukiyaki Western Django*'s skilful merging of transnational themes is not merely restricted to Westerns and Samurai films but is a statement on the reciprocal borrowing between Japanese and Western culture in general. Look out for a laugh-out-loud moment where Quentin

Tarantino admits to being an 'anime Otaku' – a term used to describe fan-boys of anime and manga, similar to a comic-book nerd. Needless to say, the viewer's ability to pick up on such cultural reference points will add to an appreciation of the film, and not being aware of them will simply make one wonder why Takashi Miike needed to further exhaust the genre with such an unremarkable reworking.

Elest Ali

Tampopo

Dandelion

Studio:
Itami Productions

Director:
Juzo Itami

Producers:
Seigo Hosogoe
Juzo Itami
Yasushi Tamaoki

Screenwriter:
Juzo Itami

Cinematographer:
Masaki Tamura

Art Director:
Takeo Kimura

Composer:
Kunihiko Murai

Editor:
Akira Suzuki

Duration:
114 minutes

Cast:
Tsutomu Yamazaki
Nobuko Miyamoto
Ken Watanabe

Year:
1985

Synopsis

When truckers Goro and Gun stop at a noodle restaurant, one tasteless bowl of ramen and a fight with the local customers leads to Tampopo, owner of the restaurant since her husband died, begging Goro to teach her how to make the perfect bowl of ramen. Touched by her determination to provide for her young son without being forced to remarry, Goro agrees, and Tampopo becomes his disciple. While Goro sternly puts Tampopo through a number of seemingly-silly training exercises and gathers a ragtag group for assistance including a tramp, chauffeur and the local bully, their feelings for each other begin to develop.

Critique

Juzo Itami has called *Tampopo* a 'noodle western'. It is an apt name but in this western the girl is a widow and business owner, and the cowboys leave town frequently but are committed to coming back to continue her training. *Tampopo* not only plays with the genre conventions of the spaghetti western but pokes fun at many other genres and references as well, from yakuza films to erotica to training scenes à la *Rocky* (1976). The vignettes, however, establish *Tampopo* as a comedy of manners, going beyond parody to satire as they highlight various absurdities of social roles and customs.

On a more obvious level, *Tampopo* is an ode to the love of food. From the very start, the preparation and consumption of food are viewed philosophically, as more than simple nourishment. This is in itself a parody of contemporary Japan where food is a central part of the society, most clearly seen on television, in which food is incorporated into talk shows, game shows and even reality TV. In *Tampopo* it is taken to extremes: food becomes the equivalent to love and sex, and women are a conduit for this.

Whether or not *Tampopo* could be called a feminist film is up for discussion. Tampopo is the only major female character and she is by no means helpless but she does rely almost completely on a large number of men to teach her how to improve her product, customer service, business environment and even her appearance. She is treated well by these men, and specifically requests their help, but their self-congratulation when the business becomes more successful is reminiscent of a similar scene in *My Fair Lady* (1964). In that film,

Tampopo, 1986. Produced by Itami

however, the lady in question is angered and upset; Tampopo merely agrees. However, *Tampopo* is a fluffy satire, all the more appealing because it does not have much bite. The many layers mean you can take from it what you wish, and the entertaining cast and whimsical execution ensure that viewers are likely to enjoy the film, and consider its political implications in retrospect.

Amelia Cook

The Taste of Tea

Cha no aji

Studio:
Grasshoppa

Director:
Katsuhito Ishii

Producers:
Kazuto Takida
Kazutoshi Wadakura

Screenwriter:
Katsuhito Ishii

Cinematographer:
Kosuke Matushima

Composer:
Tempo Little

Editor:
Katsuhito Ishii

Duration:
143 minutes

Cast:
Maya Banno
Takahiro Sato
Tadanobu Asano

Year:
2004

Synopsis

Young teenage boy Hajime is somewhat scared of women and girls but he falls in love with Aoi Suzushi, the new girl in his class. Young girl Sachiko sees a giant version of herself constantly watching everything that she does. Because of a story she once overheard her uncle Ayano telling, she wonders whether, if she can do a flip around a horizontal playground bar, the vision will go away. Grandfather Akira Todoroki is an eccentric man who gives his daughter-in-law Yoshiko tips on poses since she is an animator who works from home. The rest of the family each has their own small adventures and quirks. Towards the end of the film, the grandfather dies. When the family goes into his room on the day of the funeral, they discover flipbooks of sketches of each of them. Sachiko's shows her finally doing a backflip around the horizontal bar.

Critique

Before *The Taste of Tea*, Katsuhito Ishii directed the features *Sharkskin Man and Peach Hip Girl* (1999) as well as *Party 7* (2000). Although both films showed promise, the most interesting things about each of them were the introductory credit sequences. With *The Taste of Tea*, Ishii manages to step back from his cinematic influences and begin to further explore his own voice. If the earlier films fizzled out too quickly, *The Taste of Tea* manages to maintain a slow burn throughout to the very end. Instead of gangsters, this time Ishii tackles the contemporary Japanese family like a postmodern Ozu. Through his use of CGI and cel animation, Ishii is able to showcase his comfort with the animated medium as well as live-action films. His methods range from the fantastically frenetic yet internationally understandable (as in the short animated sequence designed by frequent Ishii collaborator Takeshi Koike) to the very simple yet quite Japanese (the communication to the audience that the grandfather has died by juxtaposing a scene of Sachiko looking down upon his supine form and smoke emerging from a smokestack, indicating a crematorium and hence his death)

Luckily, Ishii is able to rein in his flashier side in this film to the benefit of the characters and the overall mood. The plot synopsis really does not adequately describe how the film meanders and goes in and out of the lives of the family members, going backwards and forwards in time as well. It is true that very little happens with regard to the narrative. Yoshiko succeeds in getting back into the anime business, which we can infer she left years previously to start a family. Hajime begins getting better acquainted with the girl he likes, although their relationship is still in the very beginning stages when the film ends. Sachiko does a backflip, the grandfather passes away, and nothing much happens to the father or Ayano. The film will take a digression for over five minutes while Ayano tells a seemingly-random and inconsequential story, and then later it clears up some mysterious points in a scene that involves none of the main characters. The film is an assembly of occasionally odd shots, long takes, and scenes that do not seem to add up to an overarching story. Ishii is more interested in exploring the moments of beauty and comedy that occur throughout than he is in telling a single coherent story. In a way, the film is a series of small, often comedic, vignettes that tie together and build to a greater whole.

Brian Ruh

JIDAIGEKI & GENDAIGEKI / PERIOD & CONTEMPORARY DRAMA

Floating Weeds / Ukigusa, 1959. Produced by Daiei

Drama within the Japanese cinema occurs on both an epic scale and in miniature, and yet also somewhere in between, as Eastern film-makers have embraced the epic and the intimate while also taking to the streets of major cities to document urbanization and the social-economic shifts of the post-war era. In broad terms, dramatic Japanese cinema can be divided into two categories: *jidaigeki* (period pieces) and *gendaigeki* (films set in contemporary or modern times), both of which reveal much about Japan's past and present, even when working within the confines of genre, or serving as government-endorsed propaganda pieces, or painting a nostalgic portraits of 'lost' eras. Many directors have alternated between both categories of film, depending on both their own interests and the changing taste of the domestic audience, with the *jidaigeki* and *gendaigeki* leading to sub-genres such as *chambara* or *yakuza*, both of which are now firmly established as narrative forms in their own right within Japanese cinema.

The period drama often takes place in the Edo period of Japanese history (1603–1868), with the stories focusing on such protagonists as samurais, lords, craftsmen, merchants, and peasants. However, some film-makers, such as Kenji Mizoguchi, have explored the Heian period (794–1185), while others, such as Horoshi Inagaki, have located their stories within the Meiji era (1868–1912). Akira Kurosawa actually made his directorial debut with a Meiji-era picture, *Sanshiro Sugata* (1943), a film which captured the spirit of judo and became something of a template for martial arts film in general. The formation of modern Japan started in the Edo period with the nation's exposure to Western imperialism, although this did not immediately affect the lives or livelihoods of the masses, as many were not able to reject older methods of living and working, however much they may have wanted to. The palpable tension caused from the transition between two eras is explored in the *jidai-geki* genre, as directors have utilized the narrative form to discuss modernization and shifting social roles within an evolving economy.

Many period pieces involve samurai, although this has led to the *chambara* film, a sub-genre of the *jidaigeki* that has its own characteristics and conventions. The *chambara* genre often has more of an emphasis on action and places thematic importance on the code of honour, although some entries into the cycle, such as Masahiro Shonoda's *Samurai Spy* (1965) and Hideo Gosha's *Hitokiri* (1969) also reflect the politics of the period through stories that mix the excepted action with genuine intrigue, and emphasize the status of the samurai as an exceptionally skilled 'hired hand' rather than portraying such warriors as romantic figures. Yoji Yamada's more recent trilogy of *The Twilight Samurai* (2002), *The Hidden Blade* (2004) and *Love and Honour* (2006) take a realistic look at the daily responsibilities – and occasional drudgery – of samurai life, examining the economic hardship which can come with such rigid nobility.

As Sybil Thornton has argued, the *jidaigeki* has always been inherently anachronistic in that the genre has been adopted by directors not as a means of recapturing Japan's past but as a vehicle to critique its present, with the trappings of the period piece actually enabling film-makers to be more overtly critical of the Japanese government and various national institutions.[1] This is certainly true of the work of Kenji Mizoguchi, who frequently dealt with the issue of the role of women in society, either in fiercely-realist contemporary dramas such as *Osaka Elegy* (1936) or period pieces like *Ugetsu Monogatari* (1953) and *The Life of Oharu* (1952). The events and themes within Mizoguchi's work were heavily influenced by his own childhood, during which his sister was sold to a geisha house and his mother passed away prematurely. In many of his films, the female characters make great sacrifices to help their families or to potentially better their own standing in society, only for their efforts to be ultimately futile. After being forced by the government to make propaganda pieces within the *jidaigeki* genre during the war, such as *The 47 Ronin* (1941), Mizoguchi became perhaps Japan's first feminist director, balancing period and contemporary films that were as emotionally engaging as they were aesthetically ravishing. Widely acknowledged as a master of the period piece, Mizoguchi completed 94 films in a career which spanned four decades, with his most celebrated cinematic achievement being *Ugestu Monogatari*, an account of two peasant couples whose lives are uprooted when Shibata Katsuie's army rampages through their rural farming community. *Sansho the Bailiff* (1954) is based on a short story by Mori Ogai and follows the fate of two children who are sold into a life of slavery, while *The Life of Oharu* deals with the misfortunes of the titular prostitute in seventeenth-century society.

Akira Kurosawa also worked within the *jidaigeki* genre, although many of his masterpieces, such as *Yojimbo* (1961), are more associated with *chambara* cycle. His work is also distinctly different from that of Mizoguchi, less episodic in structure and with an emphasis on heroism and vividly-realized battles, not to mention a grander scale of tragedy in such epics as *Throne of Blood* (1957) and the later *Ran* (1985), with Kurosawa exploring the archetypes of the genre as opposed to Mizoguchi's victims of the social condition. However, his *gendaigeki* films have no qualms about tackling the darker side of Japanese society. *Drunken Angel* (1948) is set in a squalid slum that is largely ruled by the local yakuza, and the director utilizes this milieu to represent the moral decay of postwar Japan, observing that moral standards have not survived the conflict, and selfishness and opportunism have emerged: negative attributes which are here exemplified by the presence of the yakuza and their own internal power struggles. Kurosawa provided another tour of the seedy side of Tokyo just one year later with *Stray Dog* (1949), an uncompromising police drama about a homicide detective who loses his gun, leading to a series of crimes and an excursion into the underbelly of society to retrieve his missing weapon.

Both these film exemplify the influence of American *film noir* on the Japanese cinema, yet while they adhere to a certain genre template in their use of shadows, flashbacks, narration and urban locations, they also examine the social fabric of post-war Tokyo through the interactions of characters with defined roles (the doctor in *Drunken Angel*, the detectives and their superiors in *Stray Dog*) with criminals and other individuals who occupy the social margins. *Stray Dog* in particular offers an unflinching insight into a world where women will steal pistols for criminals just so they can secure rice-ration cards, and the uneasy shift from one era to another is suggested by the climactic pursuit through vegetation territory, where the city and the countryside meet. The pessimism of Kurosawa's contemporary films would perhaps reach its peak with *I Live in Fear* (1955), a film which dealt with the issue of nuclear power just one year after Honda's *Godzilla* (1954) by focusing on an elderly foundry-owner who tries to persuade his family to flee Japan for South America to avoid nuclear fallout, with his relatives perceiving his fears as a sign of instability.

The comparatively-calm oeuvre of Yasujiro Ozu has excited scholars of Japanese cinema for a variety of reasons. Bordwell and Thompson have frequently focused on his film-making technique; placing academic emphasis on the trademark long takes.[2] They have also commented on Ozu's preference for low angles and the prominent positioning of such seemingly mundane, everyday objects as teapots, laundry baskets and kitchen appliances within the frame, sometimes at the expense of the actual protagonists of his slight, but socially-revealing, narratives. *Tokyo Story* (1953), perhaps Ozu's best known film in the West, is a fascinating study of generational differences which focuses on an elderly couple who make the long journey from the countryside to the big city to spend time with their children, only to find that their career-oriented offspring have little time for them. Ozu invented the 'tatami shot', where the camera was placed at a low height, as if one were kneeling on a *tatami* mat, which provided his films with a great sense of intimacy, involving the audience in the gradually-unfolding, often understated, family drama. In conjunction with his preference for purely diegetic sound and lack of regard for the 180-degree, this signature style sets Ozu apart from his contemporaries and influenced later international film-makers as diverse as Wim Wenders, Jim Jarmusch, Aki Kaurismaki, and Hou Hsiao-Hsien, the last of which would direct the Shochiku-financed *Café Lumiere* (2003) on location in Tokyo to celebrate the centenary of Ozu's birth.

The output of these film-makers, and others not discussed here, is incredibly varied in terms of subject and style, and it should be stated once again that 'drama' is a general category which encompasses a wide range of films that focus on multiple time periods. As Japanese cinema spans more than one hundred years, and is both the oldest and largest film industry within Asia, the genres of *jidaigeki* and *gendaigeki* offer remarkable insight with regard to the history of the nation, and its post-war evolution.

Notes

1. Sybil Thornton (2007)*The Japanese Period Film: A Critical Analysis*, Jefferson, NC: McFarland & Co.
2. David Bordwell & Kristen Thompson (2006) *Film Art: An Introduction*, 8th edition, New York: McGraw-Hill.

John Berra

An Autumn Afternoon

Sanma no aji

Studio:
Shochiku

Director:
Yasujiro Ozu

Producer:
Shizuo Yamanouchi

Screenwriters:
Kogo Noda
Yasujiro Ozu

Cinematographer:
Yuharu Atsuta

Art Director:
Tatsuo Hamada

Composer:
Kojun Saito

Editor:
Yoshiyasu Hamamura

Duration:
112 minutes

Cast:
Chishu Ryu
Shima Iwashita
Keiji Sada

Year:
1963

Synopsis

Widower Hirayama lives with his 24-year-old daughter Michiko and younger son Kazuo. His older son, Koichi, is now married and lives in a small apartment with his wife Akiko. Hirayama's friend and colleague, Kawai, proposes an omiai (arranged introduction) to find Michiko a prospective husband. Whilst Hirayama hesitantly raises the issue with Michiko, she seems content to remain at home looking after her father. Meanwhile Kawai and Hirayama, together with another old friend, Horie, have organized a class reunion with former teacher Sakuma. When the pair escorts the drunken teacher home, they find that he has been reduced to running a cheap noodle bar with his unmarried daughter. After seeing the desperation of the middle-aged daughter, Hirayama becomes more determined to find Michiko a husband.

Critique

An Autumn Afternoon was Ozu's final film before his unexpected death at the age of 60. As with many of the director's works, the film uses story lines and characters with echoes of earlier films, particularly in this case the father-daughter relationship from *Late Spring* (1949). In this film, however, the focus is less on the 'springtime' of the daughter and more on the 'autumnal' perspective of the aging father. This is also why the literal translation of the Japanese title is 'a taste of sanma', a type of fish in season during the autumn months. As with other Ozu films, narrative drive typically gives way to an emphasis on everyday conversations, whether day-to-day exchanges in Hirayama's home, the married bickering of Akiko and Koichi, or the alcohol-laced dinner meetings of the three old school friends. Indeed, in this film, important narrative events such as Miura's engagement and Michiko's marriage ceremony receive no onscreen representation. There is even an authorial self-consciousness about such an approach in the way Hirayama, Kawai and Horie reveal or conceal information when playing jokes on each other. Whilst there are also other familiar Ozu 'games', such as the inconsistent positioning of objects, this concealing and revealing can have profound as well as comic effects. It is particularly effective, for instance, when the rather shallow characters of Horie and Kawai suddenly demonstrate far greater depth when, in their final conversation, they stop joking and instead reminisce about their own children leaving home.

Just as the film is engaged in a process of repetition and difference from *Late Spring*, repetition and difference also form part of the internal structure of the film, particularly in the comparisons between Hirayama and his eldest son, Koichi, even down to the different ways they take off their ties at the end of the day. The marriage plot works alongside another logic that builds a picture of the life of Hirayama. Whilst the death of his wife remains almost entirely undiscussed, there are other striking disclosures such as about Hirayama's days as a captain during the Pacific War – a role more important, of course, than a mid-level salaryman. It may now seem incongruous to see Shima

Iwashita playing the role of an Ozu OL (office lady) when soon after, she became the wife and muse of radical director Masahiro Shinoda. The film also seems guilty of many of the criticisms that have been raised against Ozu by younger directors, particularly the way in which the characters appear so passive, waiting for things to happen rather than taking action themselves. But with some memorable characters and Ozu's most successful use of colour cinematography, it actually functions as a fitting (if unintentional) final film, and one of the most underrated works within Ozu's oeuvre.

Christopher Howard

The Bad Sleep Well

Warui yatsu hodo yoku nemuru

Studio:
A Kurosawa Films Production

Director:
Akira Kurosawa

Producers:
Akira Kurosawa
Tomoyuki Tanaka

Screenwriters:
Shinobu Hashimoto
Hideo Oguni
Akira Kurosawa

Cinematographer:
Yuzuru Aizawa

Art Director:
Yoshiro Muracki

Composer:
Masaru Sato

Editor:
Akira Kurosawa

Duration:
151 minutes

Synopsis

A young executive, Koichi Nishi, seeks revenge upon those responsible for his father's death five years earlier. He becomes the assistant to one of them, a businessman named Iwabuchi, and through a blackmail scheme, Koichi begins to exact his revenge. The post-war housing corporation that Koichi and Iwabuchi work for is a mirror to contemporary Tokyo society in that it is rife with potential scandal, and there have been investigations and cover-ups. Koichi knows who is responsible for his father's death and lets nothing sway him from his quest. The fact that his wife and his friend are the daughter and son of those responsible holds little weight with him. Soon, the old are pitted against the young, and the idealism of youth finds itself in conflict with the ingrained evil of the truly corrupt.

Critique

The first film Kurosawa made after parting ways with Toho, *The Bad Sleep Well* exhibits both deft craftsmanship and heavy-handed plotting. Kurosawa set himself the task of making a socially-relevant picture, and he chose public corruption as his subject matter as it existed within businesses at the time. The film opens with the wedding of Koichi (Toshiro Mifune) and Kieko (Kyoko Kagawa). This scene introduces all of the major characters and Kurosawa sets the stage for the ensuing tragedy by a masterful use of editing, dialogue, and establishing shots. Newspaper reporters stand in for a chorus and give the audience the relevant facts about each character. The final touch is a wedding cake in the shape of an office building. One black rose has been placed in a window. This is the window Koichi's father jumped out of and the sight of it makes those guilty of the death react sharply. It is a captivating sequence, and one that provides a lot of background information without being straight exposition. After this compact moment of storytelling the narrative slows. Too much of the film remains latent and unfulfilled, while the characters are too remote and the performances of the leading plays perhaps too subtle, forcing the audience to pay close attention to both dialogue and action to avoid becoming become lost.

Cast:
Toshiro Mifune
Takeshi Kato
Masayuki Mori

Year:
1960

One reason for this is that *The Bad Sleep Well* was intended to be Kurosawa's *Hamlet*. Kurosawa proved to be capable of handling Shakespeare with *Throne of Blood* (1975) but *The Bad Sleep Well* lacks *Hamlet*'s focus and Kurosawa has allowed his ambition to cloud his creative judgment. He had not yet mastered the boardroom, as he already had the police precinct and the post-war slum, and fails to establish the corporate world as an appropriate environment to capture human drama. It would not be for another three years, until the contemporary crime film *High and Low* (1963), that he would once more be able to deftly tell such a story, set in the modern world. Despite this, there are enough moments in the film to please the avid Kurosawa aficionado.

Justin Howe

Dodes'ka-den

Clickety-Clack

Studio:
Toho Company, Yonki-no-Kai productions

Director:
Akira Kurosawa

Producers:
Akira Kurosawa
Yoichi Matsue

Screenwriters:
Shinobu Hashimoto
Akira Kurosawa
Hideo Oguni, from the novel
A Town without Seasons by
Shugoro Yamamoto

Cinematographers:
Yasumichi Fukuzawa
Takao Saito

Art Director:
Shinobu Muraki
Yoshiro Muraki

Composer:
Toru Takemitsu

Editor:
Reiko Kaneko

Synopsis

Dodes'ka-den gathers together the stories of several people living amidst squalid conditions in a Tokyo slum. Rokuchan is a simple-minded boy who spends his days driving an imaginary trolley through the streets. An elderly man generously offers his assistance to those in need. A father and son, who live in an abandoned car, beg for food while envisioning their dream home. Two drinking buddies swap their wives while remaining the best of friends. A young woman, who exhaustingly assembles artificial flowers at home, is tormented by her selfish uncle and offered friendship by a sake delivery boy. A man lives his day-to-day life all but sapped of willpower, paralysed by a painful past. The kind Mr. Shima, who possesses a facial tic, earns the respect of those around him while remaining loyal to his rude, much-feared wife. Around the sole water faucet available to the community, a group of women perpetually gossip while washing their dishes and vegetables.

Critique

Dodes'ka-den is an extremely important film in Akira Kurosawa's life and career. After the lengthy production of *Red Beard* (1965), he became involved with 20th Century Fox for the making of the World War II epic *Tora! Tora! Tora!* (1970); he was to direct the segments that would portray the Japanese side of the conflict but his relationship with Fox soon soured and Kurosawa was eventually fired from the project. In response, he sought to re-establish himself in the Japanese film industry and formed a new production company called the Club of the Four Knights, which also included Kon Ichikawa, Keisuke Kinoshita and Masaki Kobayashi. Their maiden film was *Dodes'ka-den* – which was also to be their last. Even though it was nominated for an Academy Award for Best Foreign Language Film, it fared poorly both critically and commercially in Japan, leading to the company's dismantlement and partially contributing to Kurosawa's 1971 suicide attempt.

Many years later, *Dodes'ka-den* deserves reconsideration as it served as the testing ground for a variety of new stylistic techniques

Duration:
140 minutes

Cast:
Yoshitaka Zushi
Shinsuke Minami
Tomoko Yamazaki

Year:
1970

and marks the beginning of a new chapter in his career. Most significantly, it was his first colour film, which allowed him to draw upon his painting background and further explore his creative potential. Using a fantastically-vivid palette, he transforms the trash-filled wasteland in which the film is set into a place of wondrous, recycled beauty, decorating it with brightly coloured plastic, clothing, painted surfaces and, covering the walls of Rokuchan's home, hand-drawn illustrations. At some moments, the sky is depicted using Impressionistic backdrops, and lighting and makeup is used to similarly unnatural yet bold effect. With its wildly-inventive craftsmanship, *Dodes'ka-den* is one of Kurosawa's most visually-impressive films.

The many characters that populate *Dodes'ka-den* face the challenges in their lives in different ways. Some choose to carry on with their daily chores and uphold neighbourly bonds in a constantly sociable manner. Others rely more closely on the illusions of their desires with varying consequences. Rokuchan almost achieves innocent bliss in his trolley rides through the slum, oblivious to the calls of derision that are hurled at him by children. In a more serious story strand, the father and son continue to make their dream house more lavish and elaborate as their conditions in the real world grow increasingly grim. Kurosawa highlights the redeeming qualities of his characters through their various quirks, antics, and displays of kindness, skillfully balancing the darker moments with uplifting humour. Bravely executed and emotionally stirring, *Dodes'ka-den* is a solid testament to Kurosawa's artistic integrity. The lives of his subjects are presented in an imaginative, often surreal blend of fantasy and reality, composing a film which unflinchingly reveals the hardships inherent in poverty, as well as the enduring strength of the human spirit.

Marc Saint-Cyr

Dreams

Yume

Studio:
Warner Bros. Pictures, Akira Kurosawa USA

Director:
Akira Kurosawa, Ishiro Honda (segments 'The Tunnel', 'Mount Fuji in Red' and prologue and epilogue for 'The Weeping Demon'; uncredited)

Synopsis

Dreams is divided into eight separate segments based on actual dreams experienced by Akira Kurosawa himself. In most of them, a stand-in character for Kurosawa appears as an observer: sometimes a small child, and sometimes a young man wearing the director's trademark hat. The film begins with two dreams that reveal fantastic sights: *Sunshine through the Rain* follows the boy as he witnesses a secret wedding procession of foxes, while in *The Peach Orchard* he encounters the spirits of fallen peach trees. In *The Blizzard*, a lost party of mountain climbers struggle for survival against the elements. *The Tunnel* dwells on the tolls of war, as a veteran is revisited by his perished platoon. In *Crows*, the dreamer wanders through the paintings of Vincent Van Gogh in pursuit of the artist himself. *Mount Fuji in Red* and *The Weeping Demon* comprise two loosely-successive takes on nuclear devastation and the stupidity of man before *The Village of the Watermills* ends the film with an optimistic vision of utopia.

Producers:
Mike Y. Inoue
Hisao Kurosawa

Screenwriter:
Akira Kurosawa

Cinematographer:
Takao Saito
Masaharu Ueda

Art Director:
Yoshiro Muraki
Akira Sakuragi

Composer:
Shinichiro Ikebe

Editor:
Tome Minami

Duration:
119 minutes

Cast:
Akiro Terao
Mitsuko Baisho
Meiko Harada

Year:
1990

Critique

Dreams is Kurosawa's most painterly film. Extremely simplistic in terms of story and character, the vignettes act more as an assortment of cinematic paintings than anything else, with each one providing a vivid sensory experience of image, sound, unfettered emotions and ideas, while Kurosawa still voices his concern for humanity and shares his views on a variety of subjects. *Crows* openly puts forth many ideas surrounding art and pays tribute to Van Gogh's legacy. Also evoking painting through its title, *Mount Fuji in Red* envisions the volcano awakened from its dormant state by exploding nuclear reactors, sending crowds of people into a frenzy as a small group of onlookers laments mankind's foolishness. *The Weeping Demon* continues this theme with the dreamer walking through a barren wasteland of black soil and mutated dandelions. He meets the titular creature, who describes the damage done by humans to the Earth with the same tone of anger and despair felt in the previous episode. *The Tunnel* does the same with a specific focus on war, but Kurosawa also offers a positive worldview in *The Village of the Watermills*, in which the oldest inhabitant of an idyllic community describes its way of living in harmony with nature.

Dreams primarily functions as an experimental film, presenting a diverse mosaic of light, colour, texture, and natural elements such as shadows, fog and, Kurosawa's trademark, rain. Much of *The Blizzard* concentrates solely on the colossal efforts of the climbers to keep marching towards their camp, the film seeming to slow down to capture their tired breaths and slow, strenuous passage through the snow. In *The Peach Orchard*, even before the boy happens upon the richly-dressed tree spirits, one's eyes cannot help but be drawn towards a blossoming tree in his house, its petals bathing the room in soft pink light. *Mount Fuji in Red*'s disaster scene portrays an angry sky, blooming fireballs and swirling clouds of radioactive pollutants. There is much to see and savour in *Dreams*, not only because of Kurosawa's vision but also the artistry of the cinematography, art direction and the sumptuous costumes.

Dreams can be seen as a film by an 'old master', one that Kurosawa could only have made after amassing a considerable amount of renown and experience in the film-making community. Amongst those who assisted the production were the special effects wizards at Industrial Light and Magic, and executive producers Steven Spielberg and Martin Scorsese – the latter also acting as Van Gogh. This outflow of support from such prominent admirers of his work allowed him the freedom which is present in every frame. *Dreams* is clearly a film made for the sheer joy that comes with creating a work of art; an exploration of the aesthetics of cinema that only Kurosawa could accomplish.

Marc Saint-Cyr

Yoidore Tenshi, 1948. Produced by Toho

Drunken Angel

Yoidore tenshi

Studio:
Toho Company

Director:
Akira Kurosawa

Producer:
Sojiro Motoki

Screenwriter:
Akira Kurosawa
Keinosuke Uegusa

Cinematographer:
Takeo Ito

Art Director:
Yoshiro Muraki

Synoposis:

In the slums of postwar Tokyo, where prostitutes line the streets that are ruled by the yakuza, the drunken angel of the title is an alcoholic doctor trying to cure the city of its ills: just as he shoos children away from the contaminated swamp that is their playground, so he tries to rescue the yakuza from the debauched lifestyle that consumes them. When a young yakuza named Matsunaga comes to his surgery to have a bullet removed from his hand, the doctor diagnoses him with tuberculosis. Terrified of dying, Matsunaga begins to hate the doctor as a harbinger of death and refuses to heed his advice, but the doctor intends to be his saviour and will not leave him alone until he has abandoned his toxic lifestyle.

Critique

Drunken Angel was Kurosawa's seventh film, but the first where he had complete directorial control. His intention was 'to take a scalpel and dissect the yakuza', and his portrayal of them, Matsunaga included, is almost entirely unsympathetic. At that time, it was illegal to criticize the American occupation of Japan in film but Kurosawa

Composer:
Fumio Hayasaka

Editor:
Akira Kurosawa

Duration:
98 minutes

Cast:
Takashi Shimura
Toshiro Mifune
Reisaburo Yamamoto

Year:
1948

managed to do so indirectly in his damning portrayal of the western-ized yakuza, who imitated American gangsters in their hairstyles, clothing and general manner. The director's distaste for their lifestyle is nowhere more evident than in the salacious dance-hall sequence, in which Matsunaga jitterbugs wildly to the wailing of a cabaret singer. A sudden screenwipe transports us to the surgery where the doctor slaps him sharply across the face. The matching of the wipe with the slap tells us that the film-maker's sympathy lies firmly with the doctor, and the humour of this moment, like many others associated with the doctor, endears him further to the audience.

The collaboration between Kurosawa and leading man Toshiro Mifune began with this film and would prove to be one of the most successful and prolific in cinema history. As ever, Mifune's performance is captivating in its theatricality, and he brings repulsive attitude to Matsunaga, who skulks and snarls his way through the film like a sickly cat. There are some memorable sequences, such as the protracted fight sequence that would be echoed in *Rashômon* (1950) but, overall, the film is too ponderous and didactic to be truly great. The symbolism of the swamp is overused and there are some uncomfortable shifts in tone, such as the overblown dream sequence and the unnecessary and mawkish coda, suggesting a director who had not yet achieved the height of his powers.

Alanna Donaldson

Fighting Elegy

Kenka erejii

Company:
Nikkatsu

Director:
Seijun Suzuki

Producer:
Kazu Otsuka

Screenwriter:
Kaneto Shindo

Cinematographer:
Kenji Hagiwara

Art Director:
Takeo Kimura

Synopsis

Bizen, Okayama, Japan, 1935. A rebellious teenager, Kiroku Nanbu, spirals into lustful turmoil when he falls in love with a young pretty Catholic girl, Michiko, with whose family he boards. Unable to express his desires to Michiko, Kiroku sublimates his sexual urges through frenzied masturbation and equally crazed violence. Kiroku is sent to a military school in the country and finds a new outlet for his lust in the guise of strict, disciplined military training. Kiroku falls under the spell of a writer named Ikka Kita, who has rebellion on the brain, and subsequently finds himself fit and ready for a surprising act of violent action against the government.

Critique

Deviating from the wild and woolly yakuza films that made his name, and would eventually become his downfall at Nikkatsu with the release of *Branded to Kill* (1967), director Seijun Suzuki turned his anarchic satirist's scalpel to Japanese militarism leading up to the events of 26 February 1936. It was that infamous night in which over one thousand soldiers, led by right-wing extremists, assassinated several of Tokyo's civilian government officials in an attempt to reconfigure Japan into a fully-fledged military dictatorship. The coup failed and the key conspirators, including the writer and fascist ideologue

Composer:

Naozumi Yamamoto

Editor:

Masami Tanji

Duration:

86 minutes

Cast:

Hideki Takahashi

Junko Asano

Mitsuo Kataoka

Year:

1966

Ikki Kita (played in the film by Hiroshi Midorigawa), were executed. Suzuki's film is not a dramatic examination of the event, though there is plenty of foreshadowing of that fateful day as well as of Japan's eventual plunge into World War II, but an astute lampoon of macho aggression, sexual repression, and blind nationalism – elements that make for a volatile mix for any militant-minded youth.

As if Suzuki was already sensing his eventual termination from Nikkatsu, the director-cum-provocateur does not pull any satirical punches, making this one of his finest works. While Suzuki's absurdist tendencies helped fuel this subversion, firebrand screenwriter Kaneto Shindo, director of the classic allegorical horror film *Onibaba* (1964) and known for his outspoken leftist sympathies, also contributed significantly to the film's subversive tendencies. But while the film's satire is ruthless (though, to his credit, Suzuki *does* fill his story with plenty of action and manly fisticuffs), there is a poignancy to the proceedings as we creep toward the finale. Kiroku and the rest of the restless youth head to Tokyo to do their part for the new cause, and we know full well what his fate will be. Even if he survives the coup itself, there is still the inevitable war in China and against the US to come. *Fighting Elegy* was to be only the first film of a two-part series – the sequel dealing with Kiroku's enlistment in the army and eventual death in China. But the film ends at the precise moment, with Kiroku boarding a train headed for the new bloody dawn in Tokyo, as the rebellion kicks in – his fate inextricably locked into something far more powerful than one man.

Derek Hill

Fires on the Plain

Nobi

Company:

Daiei

Director:

Kon Ichikawa

Producer:

Masaichi Nagata

Screenwriter:

Nato Wada (based on a novel by Shohei Ooka)

Cinematographer:

Setsuo Kobayashi

Synopsis

1945; the final days of World War Two. Stationed on the island of Leyte in the Philippines, a tuberculosis-stricken Japanese soldier, Private Tamura, is ordered by his commander to hike through the jungle and seek treatment at a poorly-equipped and under-staffed military field hospital. But, when he arrives at the hospital, the doctor informs Tamura that he is not sick enough to treat. Too sick to fight yet too healthy to care for, Tamura wanders deeper into the jungle and encounters a number of other soldiers also desperately trying to survive for a little while longer. Tamura exists in a state of macabre limbo wandering the bleak and desolate terrain in search of a way out, descending deeper into madness and eventually partaking in one of the ultimate taboos known to man in order to survive.

Critique

How entertaining should an anti-war film be? There are countless Hollywood film-makers (great and lesser ones alike) who have aspired to utilize the archetypal canvas of the war film as a means to explore one's ability to show great reserves of courage and honour under the

Art Director:

Tokuji Shibata

Composer:

Yasushi Akutagawa

Editor:

Tatsuji Nakashizu

Duration:

104 minutes

Cast:

Eiji Funakoshi
Osamu Takizawa
Mickey Curtis

Year:

1959

pressures of almost unimaginable stress and suffering, as well as our almost limitless capacity to inflict cruelty and unthinkable violence upon another human being. Most serious commercial film-makers in the post-Vietnam War years, i.e. those not working in the exploitation marketplace, would regard their films as being anti-war or espousing some sort of anti-war sentiment – e.g. having a cynical view of authority, a jaundiced view of phoney heroism and blind nationalism – despite the fact that many of them were also filled with exhilarating action scenes, confused morals, and no discernible anti-war politics whatsoever. For every Robert Altman, Hal Ashby, and Oliver Stone – directors sometimes capable of astute and savage political complexity – there is a Michael Cimino, Francis Ford Coppola, and, again, an Oliver Stone – film-makers who have anti-war pretentions but who lack the intellectual and political clarity to follow through with their pessimistic views of war and human nature. In the years since Steven Spielberg revamped the previously-mothballed World War II genre for a tougher, bloodier, modern cinema age with *Saving Private Ryan* (1998), pretty much all contrary notions to war-as-character-building have been successfully excised from the multiplexes.

It is difficult to imagine a film like Kon Ichikawa's *Fires on the Plain* ever being made in Hollywood; it is difficult to imagine it being made at all. Bleak, caustic, and fiercely unflinching in its depictions of human suffering, Ichikawa's film is a rare bird indeed – an unequivocal anti-war statement and one that, despite moments of black humour, is sometimes difficult to sit through. Along with Dalton Trumbo's *Johnny Got His Gun* (1971), Elem Klimov's *Come and See* (1985), Kinji Fukasaku's *Under the Flag of the Rising Sun* (1972) – a film that is thematically closely linked to this one – and the Japanese anime *Grave of the Fireflies* (1988), Ichikawa's tale of souls at zero is an unforgettable excursion into psychological and physical hell. But despite the film's harsh subject matter, Ichikawa does manage to inject a surprising amount of suspense into of the story's inevitable trajectory, and the black-and-white scope cinematography by Setsuo Kobayashi is occasionally stunning in its clarity and use of space. No doubt, Ichikawa's film is a dark journey and one that a modern viewer bred on more glorious and rousing war films might find difficult to stomach. But is not that the point?

Derek Hill

Floating Weeds

Ukogusa

Studio:
Daiei Studios

Director:
Yasujiro Ozu

Producer:
Masaichi Nagata

Screenwriter:
Kogo Noda
Yasujiro Ozu

Cinematographer:
Kazuo Miyagawa

Art Director:
Tomoo Shimogawara

Composer:
Kojun Saito

Editor:
Toyo Suzuki

Duration:
119 min

Cast:
Ganjiro Nakamura
Machiko Kyo
Ayako Wakao

Year:
1959

Synopsis

One glorious summer, a boisterous Kabuki-theatre troupe pays a visit to a tranquil fishing village. Each day, the troupe's aging leader, Komajuro, sneaks out to visit his former lover Oyoshi and their teen-age son Kiyoshi, who live in the village. Ashamed of being a lowly actor, he has never told Kiyoshi that he is his father and has, instead, pretended to be his uncle. One day, his girlfriend Sumiko discovers his secret and confronts him. Furious, he tells her that he never wants to see her again. Seeking revenge, she pays pretty young actress Aiko to seduce Kiyoshi and break his heart. Aiko goes along with her plan, but soon the young 'couple' has fallen in love.

Critique

Filmed in sumptuous colour by the celebrated cinematographer Kazuo Miyagawa of *Rashômon* (1950) and *Ugetsu Monogatari* (1953), *Floating Weeds* is Ozu's remake of his own silent film *A Story of Floating Weeds* (1934). In part, it is a gentle, comforting film, depicting close friendships and peaceful lives to the sound of pattering rain and humming planes. Scenes are leisurely-paced and interspersed with pensive still lives of flowers or furniture. Ozu's camera is notoriously self-effacing, sitting motionless and often at ground level so that it gazes humbly up at the action and, in dialogue scenes, it nestles invisibly between the speakers so that they gaze straight into its lens, creating a cosy and reassuring intimacy.

But just as the title has connotations of tranquility so it also has connotations of melancholy, and the film tells a tragic tale. It is Komajuro's misplaced pride that is the source of all the troubles: ashamed of his profession and determined to become a great thespian, his ambition has denied Kiyoshi a father all of his life, and Oyoshi a husband. He sees himself in fellow actors Aiko and Sumiko and, when he beats them, it is with the force of his own shame. In this scene and others, white blossom petals flutter to the ground in the foreground of the shot as though we are seeing the action through a veil of tears. In their beauty and impermanence, blossoms are a cultural symbol of *mono no aware* or 'the pathos of things', or as one troupe-member says, 'the sky is so blue, it's sad'. The depiction of the earnest, awkward Kiyoshi is bathed in pathos, not least in the heartbreaking scene in which he peers dubiously at his reflection, unable to fathom why the beautiful Aiko has shown an interest in him. The film's title evokes the hopelessly-drifting actors – but in Japanese 'floating' also has connotations of being in love, and Kiyoshi's union with Aiko is the one happy outcome of his father's visit.

Alanna Donaldson

The Funeral

Oshoshiki

Studio:
Toho

Director:
Juzo Itami

Producer:
Seigo Hosogoe

Screenwriter:
Juzo Itami

Cinematographer:
Yonezo Maeda

Art Director:
Hiroshi Tokuda

Composer:
Joji Yuasa

Editor:
Akira Suzuki

Duration:
124 mins

Cast:
Tsutomu Yamazaki
Nobuko Miyamoto
Kin Sugai

Year:
1985

Synopsis

A seemingly-disagreeable 69-year-old man dies suddenly in his comfortable rural home. His eldest daughter, a successful actress, and her equally successful actor-husband are informed of his passing while filming on set. Even before leaving contemporary Tokyo, with their manager and two young sons in tow, immediate decisions must be made. They must choose a coffin, sight unseen, with price being their only frame of reference. In the pouring rain they rush to the country-side home of her parents to attend to matters mundane and monu-mental. We follow them through the next three days that are broken down as: the preparation, the wake and the funeral.

Critique

Early in *The Funeral*, one character says, completely without irony, that it is 'my first funeral, I hope all goes right.' In this situation, not knowing what to do is the natural, universal feeling but it becomes compounded and complicated in the Japanese world. Keeping 'face', doing what is expected within the context of family, neighbours and, most importantly, society, is the most obvious action. The situation is so foreign to the characters that they must learn protocol thorough a 'how to' VHS cas-sette, as they are guided by a funeral director who adopts the manner and attire of a film director. It would be easy to imagine this universal passage as backdrop for a Woody Allen film, either funny or serious, or a Robert Altman ensemble piece, although the primary concerns of both those film-makers would have been character interaction and the conflict and enlightenment that results during a period of highlighted stress. While this is also a concern of Itami's film, *The Funeral* is more a comedy of manners, an almost sociological look at the mores, the chaos and the struggle to do the right thing within an unfamiliar situation.

This film has invited comparisons to the social satire of Luis Bunel's *The Discreet Charm of the Bourgeoisie* (1972) and the work of Jaques Tati as regards its style. *The Funeral*, as with many examples of Itami's work, comes close to sentimentality at times and also has comedic moments that verge on slapstick. His style is solid and energetic, although the use of the point of view of a corpse is gimmicky and irrational, and nearly every scene and every character is both surprising and interesting. Comparisons to the work of Yasujiro Ozu are expected with regard to any Japanese film that examines family life, though it is likely Ozu would have ended the film where this one begins, with the death of the father, and would almost certainly not have shown, the actual death on the screen. The dissolution of the family unit is located in the near-future Japan of 1988, where the family unit is already frac-tured by the very nature of the ways lives are led: fast-paced with less communication, less time together, and more technology. *The Funeral* was the first film directed by Juzo Itami. Fifty-years-old at the time, he had already enjoyed a lengthy and successful career as an actor. The two principal actors in this film, Tsutomo Yamazaki and Nobuko Miya-moto, were to become the reliable leads in most of his other films.

Fred Shimizu

The Harp of Burma

Biruma no tategoto

Studio:
Nikkatsu

Director:
Kon Ichikawa

Producer:
Masayuki Takaki

Screenwriter:
Natto Wada

Cinematographer:
Minoru Yokoyama

Art Director:
So Matsuyama

Composer:
Akira Ifukube

Editor:
Masanori Tsujii

Duration:
116 minutes

Cast:
Rentaro Mikuni
Shoji Yasui
Tanie Kitabayashi

Year:
1956

Synopsis

Captain Inouye is the leader of a platoon of Japanese soldiers fighting in the jungles of Burma. As a former music school graduate, Inouye has trained his troops to sing and has also discovered that one of the men, Mizushima, has a natural talent for playing the harp. When the platoon realizes that the war has been declared over, they readily surrender to British troops. But whilst most are moved to a holding camp in Mudon, Mizushima volunteers to persuade rebel Japanese soldiers to give up their mountain hideaway. When his entreaties are rejected, Mizukawa is presumed dead in the resulting bomb blast. It transpires, however, that Mizushima has been rescued by a local Buddhist monk and, after stealing his rescuer's clothes, he attempts to reach Mudon on foot.

Critique

Remade by Kon Ichikawa as a colour film in 1985, *The Harp of Burma* is regarded as a post-war classic and also received an international release after becoming a prize-winner at the Venice Film Festival. The film is based on the children's novel by Michio Takeyama that was serialized in the *Akatonbo* magazine, 1947–1948. Takeyama wanted the novel to introduce readers to aspects of Buddhism and, as a critic and academic, it is notable that he also attempted to tread a middle path within the partisanship of post-war Japanese politics. Previously, Buddhism and Japanese Shinto freely intermingled but the Meiji government later turned Shinto into a state religion and used it to support both Japanese nationalism and the teachings of its colonial regimes. In this way, Takeyama made a break with long-standing religious discourses in Japan.

Mizushima's transformation into a real priest is, however, also linked to his integration with Burma itself. The film continuously emphasizes the grandeur of the Burmese landscape, and the film, of course, ends with Mizushima heading into the desert accompanied by the repetition of a poem about the Burmese land. The Burmese people are also very hospitable to the Japanese, not simply to Mizushima but also in their appreciation of the singing of the troops. Even the old Burmese woman who trades with the platoon becomes more interested in friendship than in economic exchange. When Mizushima finally heads into the distance, however, he clearly still has the parrot that he exchanged with Inouye and presumably the bird is destined to keep repeating Inouye's request for him to return to Japan. As with his declaration to bury the Japanese war dead, Mizushima will always have a connection with his homeland despite his self-imposed exile. Even if the rousing singing of the troops appears to promise transcendence, in this context the singing of 'Hanyu no nado' (the Japanese version of 'Home Sweet Home' introduced at the end of the nineteenth century) cannot promise any easy resolution.

Whilst Buddhist temples are sometimes presented in dazzling brightness, the film, even in its conclusion, typically mixes pools of light and darkness without either value gaining the upper hand. Aside from the irresolution of light, the film also uses painterly compositions of figures in depth, particularly in the presentation of groups. Whilst as a 'chorus' most soldiers receive little individuation, this contrasts with the abrupt shift at the end of the film, in which the sporadic voice-over is revealed as not emanating from Inouye but from one of the anonymous soldiers. This is coupled by the film's occasional use of close-ups, where the characters are strangely expressionless rather than emotive and, rather than a melodramatic representation of the horrors of war, the film's strength is perhaps the way image and music can thus so effectively carry vacillating memories and feelings.

Christopher Howard

High and Low

Tengoku to jigoku

Studio:
Toho Company, Ltd.

Director:
Akira Kurosawa

Producers:
Ryuzo Kikushima
Tomoyuki Tanaka

Screenwriters:
Hideo Oguni
Eijiro Hisaita
Ryuzo Kikushima
Akira Kurosawa

Cinematographers:
Asakazu Nakai
Takao Saito

Art Director:
Yoshiro Muraki

Composer:
Masaru Sato

Editor:
Reiko Kaneko

Duration:
143 minutes

Synopsis

A wealthy shoe executive, Gondo (Toshiro Mifune), attempts to stealthily take over the company from greedy shareholders in an effort to save the company he cares about so strongly, and has worked at for years. But when his son is kidnapped outside his mountaintop mansion while playing with the chauffeur's son, his attentions are understandably diverted. Gondo agrees to the kidnapper's demands and to pay the ransom, until it is discovered that it was not Gondo's son snatched but the chauffeur's. Gondo initially refuses to pay the money, justifying that if he were to allocate the takeover money to the kidnapper he would be ruined financially, as he has borrowed against his home and property. Gondo's honour and decency wins out, however, and he agrees to pay the ransom, but the hand-over does not go as planned.

Critique

Building on the moral and socio-economic thematic concerns that are dealt with to varying degrees in his earlier crime films – *Stray Dog* (1949), examining how everyday people were forced into criminal acts to survive and *The Bad Sleep Well* (1960), with its corporate violence – *High and Low* finds Kurosawa and his screenwriters clearly delineating how capitalism divides and conquers in the post-war Japan of big business, leaving a few to reap the rewards and the majority to sweat it out in poverty. While the film is not overtly political, as it is first and foremost a masterpiece of police detection, *not* psychology or politics, Kurosawa does seem troubled by the capitalist reimagining of Japan after the US occupation and of a forced democracy that aimed to extinguish the equally problematic economic structure that led to World War II in the first place. Yokohama, teeming with drunken US servicemen, Japanese drug addicts wasting away in filth and squalor, and a wealth of material goods gleaming in storefront windows ready to be purchased by the emerging middle class consumer, is a city stratified to extremes.

Cast:
Toshiro Mifune
Tatsuya Nakadai
Kyoko Kagawa

Year:
1962

Gondo, a decent man who has worked his way up through the company from the bottom, is seemingly oblivious to the economic realities literally festering below his big house on the hill, and becomes an easy target for the kidnapper, who can see Gondo's residence from his claustrophobic, stiflingly-hot, shack. But despite expertly showing how an environment can breed criminal behaviour in some individuals, Kurosawa makes no excuses for the crime. Although the kidnapper's actions are given no justification other than envy for Gondo's wealth, the crime nevertheless seems rooted in something more intangible and inexcusable. By the end of the film, when the shrewd yet earnest Gondo agrees to meet with the man responsible for bringing so much destruction to so many lives, the businessman is forced to confront the harsh reality that there is nothing to be learned from this kidnapper and murderer.

Kurosawa is working at the height of his craft here, as are his long-time cinematographers Nakai and Saito, who utilize the telephoto lens to magnificent and meaningful effect throughout. The film's lurid subject matter would seem to impose an overwrought, sensationalistic approach to the material. But by focusing on the minutiae and drudgery of police work and by framing his actors in rigorously-composed telephoto shots for most of it, sentimentality thankfully has no room to fester. It is a frequently astonishing work, and one that confirmed that Kurosawa did not have to visit the past with samurai warriors in furious tow in order to achieve great meaning.

Derek Hill

High And Low, 1963. Produced by Toho

The Idiot

Hakuchi

Studio:
Shochiku Kinema Kenkyû-jo

Director:
Akira Kurosawa

Producer:
Takashi Koide

Screenwriters:
Eijiro Hisaita
Akira Kurosawa, from the novel
by Fyodor Dostoyevsky

Cinematographer:
Toshio Ubukata

Art Director:
Takashi Matsuyama

Composer:
Fumio Hayasaka

Editor:
Akira Kurosawa

Duration:
166 minutes

Cast:
Setsuko Hara
Masayuki Mori
Toshiro Mifune

Year:
1951

Synopsis

In post-World War II Hokkaido, Kameda has been left in a fragile mental state from his traumatic experiences as a wrongly-convicted prisoner of war. Travelling on a passenger ship back to the home of his sole relative, Mr. Ono, he befriends Denkichi Akama, a man who has recently inherited his father's fortune. Upon his arrival at the Ono residence, Kameda is thrown into a tense situation surrounding Taeko Nasu, a woman of ill repute whose lover is virtually selling her off for marriage with a dowry of ¥600,000. Kayama, a weak-willed suitor, accepts the offer, though he is stricken with hesitation mainly caused by his lingering feelings for Ayako, Mr. Ono's daughter. Further complicating matters is the reappearance of Denkichi, who also pursues Taeko, and Kameda's own strong, painfully-sincere love for both Taeko and Ayako. Manipulated, fought over, and regarded as an outsider, Kameda tries his best to maintain moral purity in a world riddled with greed, pettiness and danger.

Critique

After completing *Rashômon* (1950), Akira Kurosawa seized the chance to pay tribute to Dostoyevsky, one of his favorite writers, by translating his literary classic *The Idiot* to the screen. He delivered a passionate four-and-a-half-hour epic which was shown only once at the Japanese premiere, then subsequently re-cut by Shochiku, with the studio shedding 100 minutes of footage. With Kurosawa's cut considered lost forever, the project represents one of the most frustrating periods of the director's long career and, in this altered form, *The Idiot* remains an interesting yet flawed work.

At times, the film struggles with the weight of its storyline, relying upon a number of expository devices such as onscreen text and voice-over narration. Also, as an inevitable result of the studio's cuts, there is often the sense of unfulfilled potential about it, with great ambition always falling short of complete fulfilment. However, the film is undeniably graced with a good share of noteworthy qualities, among them an impressive cast consisting of some of Japan's finest actors. Masayuki Mori gives an unforgettable performance as the childlike Kameda, a man who embraces goodness after having witnessed the tragedies of human cruelty. Toshiro Mifune plays Denkichi with compelling emotional intensity, deftly wielding charisma, menace and broiling madness. In the crucial role of Taeko, Setsuko Hara is absolutely mesmerizing, her sultry temptress serving as a nice counterpoint to the characters she often played in her films with Yasujiro Ozu.

In using the wintry landscape of northern Japan, Kurosawa was able to retain the European flavor of the source material while filling it with many beautiful images. The splendid art direction and cinematography immerse the characters in an icy, inhospitable realm of wind, snow and shadows. In one particularly effective scene, Kameda pays a visit to Denkichi's house, a gloomy labyrinth of frozen corridors and darkened chambers. Afterwards, his walk home is depicted as a nightmarish odyssey, through which he is hauntingly pursued. In another dreamlike sequence, all of the principal characters are unexpectedly reunited at a winter festival: a surreal gathering of ice-skating, torch-bearing masked figures. Such powerful moments provide an idea of what Kurosawa's complete vision might have offered in full had it not been interfered with. Regardless of studio tampering, the work that remains still has much to reward curious viewers, including a unique blend of Eastern and Western styles, a wide selection of excellent performances and the lingering fragments of true cinematic greatness.

Marc Saint-Cyr

I Live in Fear

Ikirumono no kiroku

Studio:
Shochiku

Director:
Akira Kurosawa

Producer:
Shojiro Motoki

Screenwriters:
Shinobu Hashimoto
Hideo Oguni
Akira Kurosawa

Cinematographer:
Asakazu Nakai

Art Director:
Yosiro Muraki

Composer:
Masaru Sato

Editor:
Akira Kurosawa

Duration:
99 minutes

Cast:
Toshiro Mifune
Takashi Shimura
Minoru Chiaki

Year:
1955

Synopsis

Ten years after Hiroshima and Nagasaki and shortly after the events at Bikini Atoll, Kiichi Nakajima is gripped by a fear of nuclear weapons. He decides to sell his business, uproot three generations of his family and emigrate to Brazil, which he is convinced is the only place safe from hydrogen bombs and their effects. His family, as well as his extended family of two mistresses and children, are appalled by this plan and take him to court to be declared incompetent. Faced with the possibility that he might lose the case and be forced to stay in Japan, Nakajima takes increasingly desperate measures to convince his family to take him seriously and make the move that he believes will save their lives.

Critique

In 1954, American nuclear testing sent a radioactive cloud over the ocean that enveloped a fishing boat and took 23 lives. The Cold War had only just begun, and Hiroshima and Nagasaki were events in recent memory. *I Live in Fear* is most successful at portraying not only the fear of the time, channelled through Toshito Mifune's performance as a man twice his age (he was then 35), but also the apathy. Nakajima's family are not only unresponsive to his concerns, they are unsympathetic, shrugging their shoulders and pointing out that everybody dies eventually. There is also a lot of anger in the film, amplified by a summer so hot it becomes claustrophobic. Everyone involved is trapped, sweating and uncomfortable, but Nakajima and his second son, Jiro, are stubborn and furious. Each is determined to get his own way but both are shown to be bullies, and it is difficult to sympathize with either one. Dr. Harada, the most sympathetic character, is torn between the two viewpoints and, ultimately, the debate is put to one side in favour of focusing on the hope that the next generation will be crippled by neither fear nor apathy.

Despite being a Kurosawa film, *I Live in Fear* was not popular or even well-regarded until relatively recently, due in part to an unwillingness to face the controversial subject matter. However, it offers very little in the way of comments on the morality or righteousness of nuclear weapons or testing, instead focusing on the merits of action versus inaction about an issue too overwhelming and unpredictable to clearly comprehend. This basic question remains relevant today when applied to different issues, but part of the film's value is in giving contemporary viewers a glimpse of life for people who had witnessed the power of atomic bombs and had no idea if or when the next one might fall.

Amelia Cook

I Was Born, But ...

Otona no miru ehon: Umarete wa mita keredo

Studio:
Shochiku

Director:
Yasujiro Ozu

Screenwriter:
Akira Fushimi
Geibei Ibushiya

Cinematographer:
Hideo Shigehara

Art Director:
Yoshiro Kimura

Composer:
Donald Sosin

Editor:
Hideo Shigehara
Takejiro Tsunoda

Duration:
100 minutes

Cast:
Hideo Sugawara
Seiichi Kato
Tatsuo Saito

Year:
1932

Synopsis

The Yoshii boys are having the typical troubles associated with adjusting to a new home in the suburbs. The son of their father's boss, Taro, is the bully Kamekichi, and his motley gang of rascals taunt the new kids and a brawl ensues. The next day, the Yoshiis skip school for fear of reprisals, with the older one forging a grade 'A+' on his calligraphy assignment. When they see their father walking home with the teacher, however, they know they are in trouble and Mr Yoshii explains that excelling in school is the only way 'to become somebody'. Taro sells admission to a screening of his father's home movies but, after a couple of reels of street traffic, zoo animals and geishas, a sequence of shots of Mr Yoshii clowning for his boss' camera appears, causing the boys to become disillusioned with their father and his insistence on hard work.

Critique

By 1932 Yasujiro Ozu had made almost two dozen films and most of the stylistic strategies that define his subsequent three decades of work – flat compositions with prominent foreground objects; low camera height; frequent 180-degree camera repositionings, and near direct-to-camera eyelines – were all in place. But what made *I Was Born, But ...* a popular success and a perennial component of the critical canon were its comic genius and its meticulous illustration of what David Bordwell refers to as 'the social use of power'. Throughout his career Ozu's casting and direction of children was impeccable. Here, the Yoshii boys form a classic comic pair: the older only slightly taller but considerably leaner than his younger brother. The elder's quiet, thin-lipped, piercing, sceptical stare complements his brother's exceptionally wide mouth and brash, volatile nature. The two flaunt exaggerated walks and stylized poses and they often act in perfect unison, with the younger mirroring the elder's more serious deportment. Ozu does not eschew low humour either, with the younger Yoshii regularly scratching his rear and picking at his crotch.

Stern-faced Kamekichi, a head taller than the rest of the gang, controls the boys via his patented 'fingers of death': a kind of evil-eye plus pointing gesture in response to which the weaker boys must fall backwards to the ground and lie supine until a kind of reverse sign of the cross, possibly intended as a parody of Christian magic, calls them back to life. Still more outrageous is Taro, as he is introduced wearing a black bowler hat that draws attention to his protruding ears whilst wearing an absurdly anomalous plaid shirt, with its top button fastened to constrict the neck in its collar. Ozu has smartly cast a relatively shrimpy boy in this role, highlighting the importance of Taro's family's wealth in his schoolmates' treatment of him.

The Yoshii boys get a taste of politics to come when the teenage sake delivery boy, who helped them usurp Kamekichi's role as gang leader, refuses to terrorize Taro, whose parents are his employer's best patrons. In the fields in which the boys play brute force and bluster go a long way. It is significant, and hilarious that the first boy that the elder Yoshii pushes aside in his initial skirmish with the Kamekichi-Taro gang is a helpless four-year-old with a stomach ache. But it is made clear that, in the world of adults, the world of increasingly Western-style capitalism, wealth – not strength, or brains, or character – trumps all.

Bob Davis

Late Spring

Banshun

Studio:
Shochiku Kinema Kenkyû-jo

Director:
Yasujiro Ozu

Producer:
Yasujiro Ozu

Writer:
Kogo Noda
Yasujiro Ozu
Kazuo Hirotsu (original novel)

Cinematographer:
Yuuharu Atsuta

Art Director:
Tatsuo Hamada

Composer:
Senji Ito

Editor:
Yoshiyasu Hamamura

Duration:
108 minutes

Synopsis

Late Spring focuses on Noriko, a young woman in her late twenties who lives alone with her widowed father, Shukichi. At an age traditionally appropriate for Japanese women to be married, Noriko seems reluctant to commit to any sort of relationship, instead preferring the happy routine of life caring for her father. Feeling that it is in her best interest to wed, Noriko's father conspires with her aunt to set her up with an interested and upstanding bachelor. So she will not worry about how he will manage without her, Shukichi has to lie to Noriko about his own plans to remarry.

Critique

Late Spring is the first part of the Noriko Trilogy. The three films were all directed by Ozu, and made with much of the same cast and production crew, revolving around three separate individual characters named Noriko, played each time by Setsuko Hara. The films are conceptually linked by themes that run through much of Ozu's work and concentrate on domestic family dilemmas and generational divide in post-war Japan. Late Spring focuses on the father-daughter relationship between Shukichi and Noriko, and their reliance on each other. The narrative is quite simple and explores a small number of characters and the story feels intimate, with small moments that have an emotional impact. In a famous scene, Noriko is attending a kabuki play with her father and notices a glance between him and a woman she suspects he is involved with. Worried that her father may have found someone else to look after him, she is deeply saddened. Without using any dialogue, Noriko's feelings in this scene are told through her facial expressions and, although very simple in its construction, the scene carries a heavy emotional weight.

Main Cast:
Chishu Ryu
Setsuko Hara
Haruko Sugimura

Year:
1949

Ozu's films are recognized for being slow-placed and having a contemplative atmosphere. This is evident in *Late Spring* where shots often linger for a moment or two after the action has ceased, and even when all the characters have left the frame, and also in the director's use of 'pillow shots', which are shots that have no particular narrative relevance, like telephone cables or the view from a window, allowing the viewer time to contemplate the preceding scene. Ozu also achieves a sense of realism by using a minimalist approach to editing and production. As in many of his films, the action in *Late Spring* is slow and the scenes are often quite lengthy, with the camera being placed in one position, and nearly all the shots are static. Natural lighting is used where possible, shot transitions are often straight cuts, and there is very limited use of cinematic techniques, with the same locations often appearing repeatedly, and natural framing, such as doorframes or hallways, being used. This helps to create a fly-on-the-wall sensation that makes it seem that, rather than simply watching drama, the action is taking place around you.

Late Spring, along with many of Ozu's films, is considered to be distinctly Japanese but, while aspects of the narrative, such as arranging a marriage, are more applicable to traditional Japanese society, the basic theme of a father giving up his daughter has universal relevance. Ozu's formal film-making approach makes the drama in *Late Spring* both realistic and intimate, as well as allowing lead actress Hara to shine in an unusually raw and emotional performance. The film is very bittersweet and emotionally affecting, and remains a beautiful and interesting study of human behaviour in the familial environment.

Matthew Holland

Late Spring / Banshun, 1949. Produced by Shochiku

The Life of Oharu

Saikau ichi-dai onna

Studio:
Shintoho

Director:
Kenji Mizoguchi

Producer:
Hideo Koi

Screenwriters:
Yoshikata Yoda
Kenji Mizoguchi (from novel by
Saikaku)

Cinematographer:
Yoshimi Hirano

Art Diector:
Hiroshi Mizutani

Composer:
Ichiro Saito

Editor:
Toshio Goto

Duration:
148 minutes

Cast:
Kinuyo Tanaka
Tsukue Matsura
Toshiro Mifune

Year:
1952

Synopsis

Oharu is a beautiful young woman of high social rank on course for
a good marriage and a good life. Inappropriately, she falls in love
with a lowly page so beneath her social standing that their affair is
considered criminal. When they are discovered, she and her family
are banished in ruined exile, and her lover is executed. They now live
a much bleaker life. When the city is scoured for a concubine needed
immediately to produce a great lord's heir, Oharu fits the exacting criteria. Upon encouragement by her father, anxious for wealth and prestige, she journeys to the court. Oharu is successful in bearing the lord
an heir but, soon, jealousy and fear lead to her dismissal. Upon her
return home, her dismayed father insists that she be sold as a high-
end courtesan. She has a marriage proposal from a wealthy itinerant,
seemingly happy to throw his money around. Her ill-fortune leads her
to living with a wealthy merchant and working as a hairdresser for his
wife; married to a fan-maker; and beginning the process of becoming
a nun.

Critique

Made towards the end of his career, *The Life of Oharu* is the first
film in what is regarded as director Kenji Mizoguchi's great jidaigeki
(period story) trilogy. *Ugetsu* (1953) and *Sansho the Bailiff* (1954)
were to follow, and these are the films that largely and rightfully
define Mizoguchi's masterful reputation. While perhaps not quite an
epic in the later installments, this is the most ambitious exploration
of societal structure – in this case feudal Japan – as detrimental to
a woman's happiness and survival. As we follow Oharu through her
steady decline, we are also taken through a tour of sorts through the
descending social rank: samurai to upper merchant to lower merchant
to a religious enclave. None provide refuge from the oppression of
feudal Japanese society and, as usual, men are the offenders and
beneficiaries, with patriarchal figures being the most prominently
insidious.
   There are many of the signature Mizoguchi 'one shot scenes', with
fluid, choreographed tracking shots, more often than not playing
out as 'sequences' as there is usually a shifting in character- and
plot-point. The court messenger conducts his Cinderella-like search
though the town's main street in a scene that is as striking in humour
and story delineation as it is in its masterful craftsmanship. In another
sequence, the camera diagonally tracks a haughty Oharu down a
flight of stairs as she disregards the words of her employer. At the foot
of the stairs, she becomes contrite after being threatened. She quickly
follows her employer as they move left as the camera dollies along. In
a final reversal, the news that a rich merchant requests Oharu exclusively, she turns away as her boss turns to her and bows emphatically.
A true genius of Japanese cinema, Kazuo Miygawa was Mizoguchi's
regular director of photography but, for whatever reason, he did not
work on this film. It speaks to the director's strong visual sense and
style that those elements remain just as elegant and sturdy.

In one of his few borderline romantic roles, the appearance of Toshiro Mifune is as startling as the higher timbre of the voice he employs for the role. Oharu is played by Kinuyo Tanaka, the great lady of Japanese film, who worked with every major director – her greatest association being with Mizoguchi during this period. Oharu is generally thought of as her most transcendental work and, around this time, she also became the first female director in the history of the Japanese film industry.

Fred Shimizu

The Lower Depths

Donzoko

Studio:
Toho

Director:
Akira Kurosawa

Producers:
Shojiro Motocki
Akira Kurosawa

Screenwriters:
Akira Kurosawa
Hideo Oguni
Maxim Gorky

Cinematographer:
Kazuo Yamasaki

Art Director:
Yoshiro Muraki

Composer:
Masaru Sato

Editor:
Akira Kurosawa

Duration:
125 minutes

Cast:
Toshiro Mifune
Isuzu Yamada
Kyoko Kagawa

Year:
1957

Synopsis

Set during the Edo period, *The Lower Depths* focuses on the lives of a group of run-down tenement inhabitants. The main storyline follows the thief Sutekuchi as he carries on an affair with the landlord's wife, Osugi, only to fall in love with the wife's sister, Okayo. Surrounding this intrigue are the lives of the other penniless and destitute characters, and the situation alternates between comedy and despair. Into this mix comes Kahei, a wizened old man who takes on the role of mediator and grandfatherly figure.

Critique

Akira Kurosawa's film is a faithful adaptation of Maxim Gorky's play, with much of the dialogue taken directly from the source material. Kurosawa even limits the film to the few sets used by Gorky and all of the action takes place either in the tenement, the landlord's house, or the bleak courtyard that contains them both. This allows the viewer to become further involved with the few characters and examine the interplay between the lies they tell themselves and the bare truth of their reality, while Kurosawa would later use this technique in the more surreal *Dodes'uka-den* (1970).

No single character in *The Lower Depths* can be called the focus of the film. Certainly, Sutekuchi's affair might propel much of the action but every character has their chance to shine, depicting the hopes and dreams of the other hovel inhabitants: an alcoholic actor, a former samurai, a deluded courtesan, and an indigent craftsman. On the sidelines are the cynical gambler Yoshisaburo, who believes in nothing, and the itinerant priest Kahei, who does his best to support the other characters despite being aware of the lies they tell themselves. Some of the characters continuously live in denial of their situation, while others embrace the 'nothing-matters' ethos and spend their time drinking and gambling. Kurosawa is able to tap into the core of the play's dilemma by finding both the tragedy and hilarity within these lives. The despair implicit in the play is almost overshadowed by the comedic antics and while the *The Lower Depths* may end on a dark note, the last words are given to Yoshisaburo, who pokes fun at the final tragedy.

Justin Howe

One Wonderful Sunday

Subarashiki nichiyobi

Studio:
Toho Company

Director:
Akira Kurosawa

Producer:
Sojiro Motoki

Screenwriter:
Keinosuke Uekusa

Cinematographer:
Asakazu Nakai

Art Director:
Kazuo Kubo

Composer:
Tadashi Hattori

Editor:
Kenju Imaizumi

Duration:
109 min.

Genre:
Drama

Cast:
Isao Numazaki, Chieko
Nakakita, Atsushi Watanabe

Year:
1947

Synopsis

On a busy Sunday morning in downtown Tokyo, young World War II veteran Yuzo and his girlfriend Masako meet for their weekly date. Both unemployed and living separately with friends and family, they pool together their money only to find they have 35 yen to spend between them for the entire day. Regardless of their poverty and Yuzo's glum spirits, they set out into the city with Masako determined to make the best of things for both of them.

Critique

One Wonderful Sunday was made by Akira Kurosawa at an early point in his career and, like *Stray Dog* (1949), it uses a simple plot to freely explore and examine post-war Tokyo. In the spirit of Italian neorealist films such as Vittorio De Sica's *Bicycle Thieves* (1948), he and cinematographer Asakazu Nakai take their camera to the streets and provide an unflinching portrait of everyday life in the still-recovering capital of their nation. Episodically structured, the film works best when freely venturing with its two main characters into various corners of the city, discovering its inhabitants. Throughout their day, Yuzo and Masako encounter a cross-section of interesting people, including desk clerks, war orphans, bar hostesses, food vendors and ticket scalpers, with each one illustrating a different facet of life on the lower rungs of society. As the film begins, its two heroes are, at once, fully-fleshed-out individuals and emblematic representatives for a generation of disillusioned youth who maintain opposing attitudes towards their impoverished predicament, Yuzo's often-depressed mood is contrasted by Masako's persistent efforts to cheer him up and keep faith in the power of dreams and imagination. Indeed, their emotional highs and lows are communicated strongly and with many bold strokes, at one point resulting in a complete standstill in Yuzo's apartment in a lengthy sequence of crushing despair. This film tugs on the heartstrings more blatantly than other films by Kurosawa and some may find such strategies too deliberate or heavy-handed, although they come from a genuine place and, as a result, succeed despite their evident weaknesses.

When placed alongside his other achievements, *One Wonderful Sunday* stands out as one of Kurosawa's more headstrong efforts to address one of the recurring themes within his films: the inability of people to be happy, or more specifically, their inability to be happy together. In *One Wonderful Sunday*, he shows the less attractive side of human nature and puts forth hope as a source of strength and redemption. Along the way, he adopts the lens of an astute documentarian to focus on Japanese society, using a visibly dilapidated Tokyo as both a lively backdrop and an active participant in this socially affectionate work.

Marc Saint-Cyr

Osaka Elegy

Naniwa Erejii

Studio:
Daiichi Eiga

Director:
Kenji Mizoguchi

Producer:
Masaichi Nagata

Screenwriter:
Yoshikata Yoda, from the serial 'Mieko' by Saburo Okada

Cinematographer:
Minoru Miki

Composer:
Koichi Takagi

Duration/ Format:
66 mins./ B/W

Cast:
Isuzu Yamada
Seichi Takegawa
Benkei Shiganoya

Year:
1936

Synopsis

Ayako is a young woman working in a menial, subservient job at a successful pharmaceutical company in Osaka. Her much older, married, boss pressures her to become his mistress and she seeks the advice of her boyfriend, Nishimura, a young co-worker who feels powerless as he is unable to help. With her brother away at college, Ayako lives with a younger sister and a father who has incurred a substantial and pressing amount of debt. After an argument with her father, she leaves her home and stops going to work. Giving in to her boss, she moves into a western-style hotel that he has arranged as a 'love nest.' This gives her a better lifestyle while saving her family from financial ruin but it also creates a dilemma as Nishimura proposes to her. Shortly afterwards, she is caught by the wife of her boss and their affair comes to an abrupt end. Now a free woman, Ayako encounters her sister who tells her that their brother's future is dependent upon him finishing school and he is therefore badly in need of tuition. Once again she must choose between sacrificing herself and her dreams for the good of her family.

Critique

With *Osaka Elegy*, and later with the companion piece *Sisters of the Gion* (1936), Kenji Mizoguchi made the shift from Meji mono (Meji Era-based stories) to gendaigeki (modern story). Already a highly-regarded veteran of nearly 60 films, it was not until this point that Mizoguchi found the themes and the style that would eventually characterize his reputation both in Japan and abroad. *Osaka Elegy* was Mizoguchi's first collaboration with screenwriter Yoshikata Yoda, who he would work with on nearly all other films. Together they established the themes most associated with the director's work: human suffering (particularly from a woman's point of view), the injustice of society, and the exploitative nature of inequitable traditions. In *Osaka Elegy* these social issues include urban economic hardship and the limited, demeaning options available to young women, such as the heroine Ayako. The backdrop is Osaka in a time of industrialization and modernization, which in pre-war Japan is aligned with, if not wholly synonymous with, Westernization. What is entirely Western-based is the Japanese 'moda', or modern, girl: flighty, self-gratifying and materialistic, derived from the American flapper in style and attitude. As a 'moda' girl, Ayako is also a symbol of the pull between the traditional and the modern. The traditional is even less kind than the exploitative economic landscape, as the Confucian orders of family and patriarchy are destructive to her. The conflict between obligation and self-interest is magnified to become a matter of survival and self-preservation.

There are several references to going to the theatre and, in fact, a scene does take place there. It is not a coincidence that the play is about betrayal and manipulated love and that the performance is by *bunraku* puppets that are indigenous to Osaka. This is significant because, besides Ayako, who is played with wonderful nuance by a nineteen year old Isuzu Yamada, the most important character in the film is the city of Osaka itself. The centre and symbol of the merchant class and merchant mentality, Osaka is often thought of as being a bit crass and different compared to the refined traditions of Kyoto and the dominant vastness of Tokyo. The distinct dialect of Osaka is used here in film for the first time and *Osaka Elegy* begins and ends with the neon-lit night skyline, a modern hotel, a department store restaurant, and a brand new subway system, which are all intentionally integrated backdrops to the story. As with his trilogy of masterworks, *Life of Oharu* (1952), *Ugestu* (1953) and *Sansho the Ballif* (1954), *Osaka Elegy* suggests that life is about enduring hardship and suffering.

Fred Shimizu

Passing Fancy

Dekigokoro

Studio:
Shochiku Kinema Kenkyû-jo

Director:
Yasujiro Ozu

Screenwriter:
Tadao Ikeda, James Maki
(original story)

Cinematographer:
Shojiro Sugimoto

Art Director:
Yonekazu Wakita

Editor:
Kazuo Ishikawa

Duration:
100 minutes

Cast:
Takeshi Sakamoto
Nobuko Fushimi
Den Obinata

Year:
1933

Synopsis

Kihachi is a single father living with his son, Tomio, in 1930's Tokyo. Uneducated and employed at a brewery, he works alongside his friend and neighbour, Jiro, and spends most of his spare time at the restaurant near his home. A born rascal, Tomio unapologetically causes much mischief but makes up for it with an affectionate loyalty towards the two men. After a night of drinking, Kihachi meets Harue, a young woman new to the neighbourhood and looking for work. Immediately attracted to her, he helps her to get a job at the restaurant. Along with his amorous predicament, Kihachi must also tend to other responsibilities regarding both his financial situation and, most importantly, Tomio's upbringing.

Critique

Passing Fancy comes from Yasujiro Ozu's fruitful silent period, which he prolonged until 1936, beyond the emergence of sound in the Japanese film industry. Continuing his insightful study of lower-class family life, it feels more relaxed and lively than his later, eloquently-composed masterpieces. This can most likely be attributed to his talent for comedy, which he demonstrates through clever editing and charming performances from his actors. Though it has moments of seriousness, the film mostly maintains a light tone, channelling subtle humour and a warm humanity. What makes *Passing Fancy* one of Ozu's most memorable films is its central duo. Kihachi is played by Takeshi Sakamoto, who would revisit the character with Ozu in *A Story of Floating Weeds* (1934), *An Innocent Maid* (1935) and *An Inn at Tokyo* (1935). Joining him as his onscreen son is the young Tomio Aoki, who earlier made a strong impression as one of the two rascally brothers in Ozu's *I Was Born, But...* (1932). Together, they strike up a priceless chemistry, portraying beneath their frequent squabbling and scolding a strong, mutual love for each other. Kihachi, though preoccupied with his age, often ironically comes across as the more childish of the two, his sometimes careless nature kept in check by Tomio on a number of humorous occasions, including one amusing scene in which the boy acts as a makeshift alarm clock for Kihachi and Jiro by giving their shins a good whack.

Ozu devotes much of his film to character and setting. The silent format ideally suits this purpose, allowing him to smoothly establish his desired ambience through small visual details: Tomio working on a sketch of a clock; torn leaves lying on the floor as the result of a temper tantrum; laundry fluttering in the breeze; a tall silo standing imposingly in the background. They are not unlike the famous 'pillow shots' he would later use in films such as *Tokyo Story* (1953), piecing together snippets of ordinary life to great poetic effect. Eventually, the small area where Kihachi, Tomio and Jiro live becomes an equally familiar locale for the viewer – the restaurant, apartments and neighbors all forming a friendly, close-knit community. Amid its inviting atmosphere, *Passing Fancy* tells a story of mixed interests and duties. Upon her arrival, Harue becomes the object of much conflict and jealousy, disrupting not only Kihachi and Jiro's friendship, but also the relationship between Kihachi and Tomio. Consequently, Kihachi undergoes a great reassessment of his role as a father while managing his troubles with both love and money, struggling to decide how he can best provide for his son. With his regular theme of family dynamics explored through the new perspective of single parenting, Ozu offers in *Passing Fancy* a film as entertaining as it is touching.

Marc Saint-Cyr

Rashômon

Studio:
Daiei Motion Picture Company,
Daiei Studios

Director:
Akira Kurosawa

Producer:
Minoru Jingo

Screenwriters:
Akira Kurosawa
Shinobu Hashimoto

Cinematographer:
Kazuo Miyagawa

Art Director:
So Matsuyama

Composer:
Fumio Hayasaka

Synopsis

At the Rashômon Gate in Kyoto, a woodcutter and a priest are discussing an event so horrific that the priest is in danger of 'losing my faith in the human soul'. A peasant seeking shelter from the rain joins them and asks to hear their story. They describe how a man has been murdered in the woodlands and his wife raped by a notorious bandit named Tajômaru. What has filled the pair with horror is that, at the trial, each witness gave an entirely different account of what happened after the woman was raped. Just as the priest is despairing of man's untrustworthiness, they hear an abandoned baby crying; the woodcutter offers to take care of it and this act of altruism restores the priest's faith in humanity.

Critique

Arguably the film that first bought Akira Kurosawa and Japanese cinema to a Western audience, *Rashômon* is beautifully filmed in the sun-dappled woodland, in a minimalist style reminiscent of the silent cinema that Kurosawa so admired. The film is remarkable for its unreliable narration, now so common in cinema but almost unheard of at the time, as each character gives their version of events. Those events are depicted in flashback, despite their erroneousness. It is one

Rashomon, 1951. Produced by Daiei

Editor:
Akira Kurosawa

Duration:
88 minutes

Cast:
Toshiro Mifune
Machiko Kyo
Masayuki Mori

Year:
1950

thing for the characters to lie but it is quite another for the images to collude in that lie and, in deceiving his audience in this way, Kurosawa removes the barrier between art and life until, just like the priest, we learn to distrust everything we are told. The Rashômon Gate surrounds the men like a stage, and is steadily dismantled by the peasant, tearing off pieces of wood to burn, mimicking the way in which Kurosawa here dismantles the very structure of cinema.

Aside from the final burst of optimism, the film is unremittingly bleak. As if the core story of murder and rape was not dark enough, each character embellishes their account to cast the others in a worse light than themselves: the man presents his wife as a whore, she presents him as a tyrant, and the woodcutter presents all three as cowardly and base. 'Is there anyone who's really good?' asks the peasant, 'Maybe goodness is just make-believe.' It seems that, for Kurosawa, who spoke of 'the *essential evil* in human nature', man's goodness can only be glimpsed fleetingly – as is the sun behind the trees in woodland. Weather is used for symbolic effect throughout Kurosawa's films: the torrential rain that obscures the landscape (dyed with black ink so as to be visible on camera) suggests the priest's confusion, while the sun that breaks through in the final scene suggests his newfound hope. The ending is more optimistic than intended by Kurosawa, however, who had pessimistically hoped to film an ominous black rain cloud hovering over the sunlit scene – but none appeared.

Alanna Donaldson

Rhapsody in August

Hachigatsu no Rhapsody

Studio:
Shochiku

Director:
Akira Kurosawa

Screenwriters:
Akira Kurosawa
Ishiro Honda

Producers:
Toru Okuyama
Hisao Kurosawa
Seikichi Iizumi
Mike Y. Inoue

Cinematographer:
Takao Saito
Masaharu Ueda

Art Director:
Yoshiro Muraki

Composer:
Shinichiro Ikebe

Editor:
Akira Kurosawa

Duration:
98 minutes

Cast:
Sachiko Murase
Mitsunori Isaki
Richard Gere

Year:
1991

Synopsis

Four children spending an idyllic summer with their grandmother become interested in her stories about the atomic bombing of Nagaski, in which she lost her husband. They visit the Peace Park in Nagasaki and return to their grandmother angry at the Americans who dropped the bomb. She tells them that war itself, not the Americans, is to blame. The children have a chance to meet a real American when Clark, the son of the grandmother's long-lost older brother, pays a visit. The brother, who went to Hawaii as a young man and made a fortune in pineapples, is now dying and wishes to see his sister one last time. Clark has come to escort her to Hawaii.

Critique

'It was a very strange summer.' So begins Akira Kurosawa's thirtieth feature film, *Rhapsody in August*. The initial foreign reaction to this tale of an old woman's search for her past during a summer holiday with her four grandchildren was strange or perhaps I should say, sharply-divided. The audience at the Cannes Film Festival applauded *Rhapsody* and its director loud and long, but foreign reporters at a pre-Cannes press conference in Tokyo bombarded him with questions about the film's historical one-sidedness. Why did the *Rhapsody in August* make so much of the Nagasaki bombing, and yet so little of Japanese deeds during World War II?

'It isn't that kind of film,' Kurosawa replied. He was right: Rhapsody is about family relationships and remembrance, not the war as such. But after four decades, the bombing still shapes those relationships. *Rhapsody* is a didactically-political film, with a message familiar to anyone who has sampled the many Japanese TV programmes and movies about the events of August 1945: remember the victims and end the wars that produce them. Kurosawa states this message simply and poignantly, with signature touches. When the children are looking at the memorials to the bombing victims erected by foreign countries in the Peace Park, the younger boy asks why there is no American memorial. 'Of course there's no American memorial,' his older sister replies, as though stating the obvious. 'They're the ones who dropped the bomb.'

Was Kurosawa trying to cast America as the villain and Japan as the victim, they asked? The answer, I think, is no. Experiencing the reality of the bombing for the first time, the children are understandably shocked and angry at what they consider to be the perpetrator: America. But the grandmother, who lost her husband in the bombing, tells them that war itself, not America, is to blame. She has gone beyond anger at the bombers, if not sorrow at the tragedy they brought. Playing the grandmother's nephew, Richard Gere tries hard to blend in with the Japanese cast, but he comes across as a Hollywood star visiting the set. With his big smile and easygoing ways, he is an American all right, but not a credible Nisei relation. His All-Americaness, however, is perfect for his key scene: a heart-to-heart talk with the grandmother. Clark, who has just heard that her husband was killed in the Nagasaki bombing, expresses his apologies. The grandmother tells him that he has nothing to apologize for.

This US-Japan reconciliation scene rubbed some members of the American press the wrong way. 'Why should only the American have to apologize?' they asked. But it was Clark's uncle, not an anonymous victim, who died; his words of sympathy and regret sound natural and right. Kurosawa doubtless knew that his latest cinematic statement about the atomic bombings would be a gamble. His earlier film on the same theme, *Record of a Living Being* (1955), was a critical and box office failure. That he went ahead and made another anyway is admirable. *Rhapsody in August* is minor-key Kurosawa; it lectures too much, engages too little. But it is still Kurosawa. Who else could have filmed the children's sobering encounter with a jungle gym twisted by the nuclear blast? Or the grandmother's final, tragic run in a driving rainstorm? In these scenes, and others, Kurosawa showed that, even at the end of his career, he could still make moments of what he called 'real cinema.'

Mark Schilling

Scandal

Shubun

Studio:
Shochiku Company

Director:
Akira Kurosawa

Producer:
Takashi Koide

Screenwriters:
Ryuzo Kikushima
Akira Kurosawa

Cinematographer:
Toshio Ubukata

Art Director:
Tatsuo Hamada

Composer:
Fumio Hayasaka

Editor:
Yoshi Sugihara

Duration:
105 minutes

Synopsis

Ichiro Aoe is a painter of moderate renown. While working on a new picture in the mountains, he meets the famous singer Miyako Saigo by chance and offers her a lift on his motorcycle. They both stay at the same inn, where they are spied upon and photographed together by two paparazzi. After the picture is published in the tabloid *Amour*, images of Aoe and Saigo are plastered across Tokyo and their reputations are put at risk by false allegations of an affair. Infuriated, Aoe seeks retribution and takes it upon himself to sue the gossip magazine. He is approached by Otokichi Hiruta, a down-and-out attorney who offers the artist his services. Upon further investigation, Aoe meets Masako, Hiruta's angelic, tuberculosis-stricken daughter, and is immediately overcome with sympathy for her and promptly hires him. Their respective careers disrupted by unwanted public attention as a result of the scandal, Aoe and Saigo do what they can to prepare their case. However, even as he tries to help them, Hiruta succumbs to temptation and accepts bribes from *Amour*'s editor. Tortured by his conscience, he struggles to make the right decision but redeems himself as the trial looms closer.

Critique

Of all the films Akira Kurosawa made between the end of World War II and the internationally successful *Rashômon* (1950), *Scandal* is possibly the most solidly assembled. Taking a critical stance towards the tabloid press and the way it abuses its freedom of expression, it is both sharply insightful and constantly engaging. Kurosawa propels the viewer through the first act with a flurry of energetic montage

Cast:

Toshiro Mifune
Yoshiko Yamaguchi
Takashi Shimura

Year:

1950

sequences and skilfully-executed scenes. Later on, the film adopts a calmer pace, delving into more emotional territory while still maintaining a high degree of effectiveness and tact.

A film of considerable substance, *Scandal* owes much of it to its impressive cast. Toshiro Mifune certainly fulfills his leading-man status as Aoe, epitomizing cool, gentlemanly charm. Holding her own opposite him is the beautiful, doe-eyed Yoshiko Yamaguchi, who would later appear in Samuel Fuller's *House of Bamboo* (1955). Also deserving recognition are the numerous, talented supporting players who populate a conflicted world of both purity and corruption. However, the true star of the film is Takashi Shimura as Hiruta, deftly portraying one of the most complex and fascinating characters in Kurosawa's oeuvre. Truly the beating heart of the film, Hiruta appeared to Kurosawa quite unexpectedly during the writing process, taking on a life of his own and eventually commandeering the screenplay. Later, Kurosawa would recall that his pathetic lawyer was, in fact, inspired by a man he had met years earlier who, as Hiruta does in the film, would repeatedly spend his nights drinking and lamenting to the world his inferiority and worthlessness to his ailing daughter. Stemming from this reality-based figure, Shimura gives one of his most striking performances, bringing Hiruta to life with a soul-baring blend of desperation, self-loathing and an enduring desire to do good.

Long overshadowed by the director's other early films, such as *Drunken Angel* (1948), *Stray Dog* (1949) and, of course, the towering *Rashômon*, *Scandal* is just as demonstrative of his then-blooming artistic abilities. Highly rewarding, it marks the director's successful venture into legal drama while continuing his cinematic exploration of morality within Japan's post-war cultural climate.

Marc Saint-Cyr

Snow Country

Yukiguni

Studio:

Toho

Director:

Shiro Toyoda

Producer:

Ichiro Sato

Screenwriter:

Toshio Yatsumi, Based on novel by Yasunai Kawabata

Synopsis

Shimamura, a young amateur artist of leisure and means, travels from Tokyo to the spas of the snow country. On the train he is engrossed by a young woman who aids her sickly male companion and he is taken by her attentiveness and kind manner. They all get off at the same station. Returning to an inn where he had stayed the previous year, he arranges to meet a young woman, Komako, then on verge of becoming a geisha, with whom he had a brief affair. Komako has now become a full-time geisha and the feelings that the two have for each other become deeper and more complicated. He has a family and life back in Tokyo and his natural inclination is indecisive. She has constricting financial obligations. After more than a year, Shimamura again returns to the snow country. He and Komako sort through the frailty of their relationship and the disappointing nature of their present and future.

Cinematographer:
Jun Yasumoto

Art Directors:
Kisaku Ito and Makoto Sono

Composer:
Ikuma Dan

Editor:
Hiroichi Iwashita

Duration:
120 minutes

Cast:
Keiko Kishi
Ryo Ikebe
Kaoru Yachigusa

Year:
1957

Critique

Snow Country is a finely-crafted movie, adapted from an even more finely-crafted novel by Yasunari Kawabata, the only Japanese author to win the Nobel Peace Prize. Aside from a few details (Mizoguchi is not an artist in the book, but a European ballet connoisseur and therefore even more of an idler than in the film version), Shiro Toyoda's film remains doggedly faithful to its source material. This is the greatest strength of *Snow Country*, but also its greatest weakness. Wherever possible, long passages of dialogue are lifted verbatim, with internal thoughts being attempted visually, again verbatim. This is effective, particularly so in the opening train sequence, where images can be read ambiguously for mood rather than for the minimal plot machinations.

The novel itself is sparse in activity with oblique motivations and feelings that are only hinted at. This is the uniquely-Japanese concept that unspoken feelings are the truest, most pertinent ones. Also, the characters feel the even-more common Japanese concept – the pull between responsibility and personal desire. In the internalized form of Kawabata's prose, this often works well, beautifully even, and makes the reading experience quite satisfying. For years, Toyoda had longed to make this film and spent additional years in preparation, but his steadfast loyalty to the novel does not fully service the work as a feature film and, as the narrative advances, the dialogue becomes repetitive, character actions and motivations rendered vague. However, there is much to admire about the film, including the fine, restrained performances of the leads and the assuredly precise compositions and editing. The isolated locale of the snow country is perhaps the film's greatest character as the silence of the snow provides beauty and clarity but can also be viewed as limiting and oppressive. Similarly, the comings and goings of the train frame most of the action. The sound of the train almost always draws a reaction, as it is the lifeline of the snow country to the rest of the world, and these sights and sounds of the novel become beautifully specific during the film's finest moments.

Fred Shimizu

Stray Dog

Nora inu

Studio:
Toho Company, Ltd.

Director:
Akira Kurosawa

Producer:
Sojiro Motoki

Screenwriters:
Ryuzo Kikushima
Akira Kurosawa

Cinematographer:
Asakazu Nakai

Art Director:
Shu Matsuyama

Composer:
Fumio Hayasaka

Editors:
Toshio Goto
Yoshi Sugihara

Duration:
122 minutes

Cast:
Toshiro Mifune
Takashi Shimura
Keiko Awaji

Year:
1949

Synopsis

Post-World War II Tokyo; a sweltering, humid day in the city. A young police detective has his loaded gun stolen on a Tokyo bus and becomes obsessed about trying to retrieve it before it can be used in a crime. But the detective's honour is blackened when the pistol is used in a robbery and a murder. Feeling immense guilt, the neophyte detective teams up with a more experienced older detective to hit the mean streets of the city and hunt down the murderer before he can kill again.

Critique

Kurosawa's ninth feature may have a deceptively simple storyline but the film is stylistically revelatory and features a complex dissection of criminality, superceded only by the director's later police procedural, *High and Low* (1963). Influenced by French crime writer Georges Simenon and inspired by a real-life incident involving a cop and his stolen gun, Kurosawa attempted to write this as a novel, until he realized that it would work better as a film. The film's journey into the dark heart of the Tokyo post-war years – where normally law-abiding citizens mixed with junkies, prostitutes, thieves and murderers in order to survive during the American occupation – is gritty, unromantic, and startling in its straightforward neorealist style. While the script is multi-layered and the performances are strong, the film's major achievement is in its chronicling of everyday criminality with a stunning nine-minute sequence in which the young detective, played by Toshiro Mifune in one of his most controlled performances, disguises himself as a soldier and journeys into the black market to track his prey and to reclaim his gun.

Filming with a hidden camera in many scenes, Kurosawa never flinches from the suffering and squalor that defined this period of Japanese history, visually explicating the idea that the greatest sin of war is how it corrupts everyone, as crushing unemployment, food rationing, and petty crime taint everyone's lives. Kurosawa's characteristic humanity is also on display, exemplified yet again in the performance of one of the director's favourite performers, Takeshi Shimura. Although Kurosawa would build on this film's visual and thematic richness with *The Bad Sleep Well* (1960) and the masterful *High and Low*, both subsequently taking very different approaches to the crime genre, *Stray Dog*'s overheated, exquisitely-suspenseful plot is nevertheless a brilliant examination of how blurred a sense of justice can be in a society struggling in the aftermath of a far greater violence.

Derek Hill

Streets of Shame

Akasen chitai

Studio:
Daiei

Director:
Kenji Mizoguchi

Producer:
Masaichi Nagata

Screenwriter:
Masahige Narusawa

Cinematographer:
Kazuo Miyagawa

Art Director:
Hiroshi Mizutani

Composer:
Toshiro Mayuzumi

Editor:
Keniichi Sakane

Duration/Format:
94 mins/ b&w

Cast:
Machiko Kyo
Aiko Mimasu
Ayako Wakao

Year:
1956

Synopsis

As the impending ban on prostitution looms over the Dreamland Café and other establishments of the three-century-old Yoshiwara pleasure quarter, the employees have yet another addition to their woes. They are told by the mercenary husband and wife owners that they must work even harder as they are fortunate to have the opportunity to sell their bodies. They live day-to-day, barely getting by, and there is no escape and no future, only an acceptance of hardship. Hanae supports her infant son and unemployed sickly husband, often doing so without milk or medicine. Yumeko must confront her grown son who has moved to Tokyo from the countryside, where he was raised without her. The least-suited for the profession is an aging Yorie, who dreams of domestic tranquility. Yasumi is by far the best earner and the best saver. With a natural knack for monetary dealings, she accumulates even more wealth by lending to the other women, who are always in need, at substantial interest rates. Spirited newcomer, the Western-dressed Mickey (for Michiko) lives and spends so recklessly that severe debt and an indentured life is inevitable.

Critique

This was the last film made by the great director Kenji Mizoguchi. While it is not a summing-up of his career in any way, and he was actually preparing another film at the time of his death, it is very much consistent with the style, themes and issues of his other work. Women at the lower rung of society spiral downwards as they are forced to struggle in a world not of their making. As in most of his other films, the women's lives are subject to the bad behaviour of the men in their lives. Tokyo, as depicted here, is in the transitional period between the hardships of the post-war period and the start of the economic boon. Prostitution and the Yoshiwara pleasure district, which has thrived since the Edo Period, were threatened by this progress, and the great success of Mizoguchi's final film is said to have been instrumental in making prostitution illegal.

There are no outlets for the characters in this film, nor is there anyone to rely on, certainly not family or spouses. Children and parents are either severe disappointments or hindrances. The younger two women fare a bit better. The manipulating Yasumi has learned to count on no one and, at film's end, may have made herself a better life. The thoughtless, irrepressible Mickey manages by virtue of her youth and looks, but will likely fall into irretrievable debt and a fate as desperate as the others. As always with Mizoguchi, it is society in part but ultimately the men in particular who are at fault. The customers are either 'suckers' or necessary evils, either way unlikable. Hanae's husband is needy and weak, while Yumeko's son Shuichi is ungrateful and unsympathetic, unwilling to understand his mother's plight. As always in Mizoguchi's world, the patriarchs (the club owner and Mickey's father) are the most hypocritical and the most damaging.

While *Streets of Shame* does not exhibit the flow and stately beauty of the roving camera-work found in the director's best work, there are many striking frame-within-a-frame compositions by his long time cinematographer, Kazuo Miyaguchi and the dissonant soundtrack is at first a bit distracting but then highly effective. The ending is heart-breaking, as a young apprentice, yet another lost soul, continues the vicious cycle. Fittingly for Mizoguchi, it is shown in a single shot, a coda as strong and as memorable as any ending in any film: a worthy final image from a true master.

Fred Shimizu

Tales of Moonlight and Rain

Ugetsu Monogatari

Studio:
Daiei Studios

Director:
Kenji Mizoguchi

Producer:
Masaichi Nagata

Screenwriters:
Matsutaro Kawaguchi
Kyûchi Tsuji
Akinari Ueda
Yoshikata Yoda

Cinematographer:
Kazuo Miyagawa

Art Director:
Kisaku Ito (Production Design)

Composers:
Funio Hayasaka
Tamekichi Mochizuki
Ichiro Saito

Editor:
Mitsuzo Miyata

Duration:
94 minutes

Cast:
Masayuki Mori
Machiko Kyo
Kinuyo Tanaka

Year:
1953

Synopsis

Set during the civil wars of the sixteenth century, *Ugetsu Monogatari* tells the story of an ambitious potter named Genjuro who, discovering that 'war is good for business', sets off for the city with his friend Tobei to seek his fortune, leaving his wife and child at home. Meanwhile, Tobei has a lofty ambition of his own – to become a famous samurai – and at the first opportunity he abandons his own wife in pursuit of his reckless dream. But for Genjuro and for Tobei, it is only when they are reunited with their wives that they discover the tragic cost of their ambitious natures.

Critique

Like his contemporaries Yasujiro Ozu and Akira Kurosawa, Kenji Mizoguchi was a master within Japanese cinema, tirelessly innovative and hugely influential. He has been called a feminist film director and certainly *Ugetsu Monogatari* is concerned with the plight of women, and yet it does not judge Genjuro and Tobei: 'War drove us mad with ambition,' confesses Genjuro, and it is war that the film condemns. Mizoguchi does not preach to his audience, however; his camera is famously impartial and unobtrusive, patiently documenting events from a distance in long unbroken takes. Close-ups are avoided and the central character in a scene will often have his back to the camera, so adamantly does the director refuse to manipulate his audience.

The film moves effortlessly from these scenes of grim realism to the ethereal fantasy sequences in Lady Wasaka's castle, in which Genjuro's dream of wealth and luxury takes shape around him and, in a delightfully dreamlike touch, his crude rough-hewn pottery now appears delicate and ornate. Machiki Kyo's performance as Lady Wasaka is most subtle – and all the more unsettling for it, as we are never quite sure what we are seeing: she seems to move in slow motion, gliding across the ground, and the fleeting, dark expressions that pass across her face are supremely sinister. The heady love scenes between the couple are amongst the most celebrated in the film, in particular the dazzling sequence in which they frolic beside a blissfully-glistening lake. But the heart of the film lies in an earlier magical scene in which Genjuro, flushed with his success in the marketplace, imagines his wife excitedly trying on expensive kiminos. This moment is entirely sympathetic with Genjuro, revealing that he pursues wealth for his wife's sake but in doing so, tragically misunderstands her. As she said when he last gave her such a gift: 'It is not the kimino but your kindness that makes me happy.'

Alanna Donaldson

Those Who Make Tomorrow

Asu wo tsukuru hitobito

Studio:
Toho

Directors:
Akira Kurosawa
Hideo Sekigawa
Kajiro Yamamoto

Producers:
Keiji Matsuzaki
Sojiro Motoki
Ryo Takei
Tomoyuki Tanaka

Screenwriters:
Yûsaku Yamagata
Kajiro Yamamoto

Cinematographers:
Takeo Ito
Taiichi Kankura
Mitsuo Miura

Art Directors:
Takeo Kita
Keiji Kitagawa

Composer:
Noboru Ito

Duration:
82 minutes

Cast:
Kenji Susukida
Chieko Takehisa
Chieko Nakakita

Year:
1946

Synopsis

A family consisting of a salaryman father, the housewife mother, and daughters Yoshiko, a script girl, and the younger Aiko, a revue dancer, barely make a living. They rent the top floor of their apartment to a railroad engineer, who is involved in unionization activities. Despite the father's strict opposition to this kind of 'disloyalty' to employers, the daughters also become involved with the labour movement. Dissatisfaction is spreading amongst the technicians and actors at Yoshiko's movie company, just as unrest brews among Aiko's colleagues when a dancer is fired for being sick. When the father is unfairly laid off, along with employees that had been active in the union, his belief in the management is crushed. When he sees the engineer continuing the unionization struggle despite the tragic death of his child, he considers joining.

Critique

Co-director Akira Kurosawa famously struck *Those Who Make Tomorrow* from his filmography, apparently finding its lack of directorial signature and its heavy-handed didactics to be a personal embarrassment. The film was produced at the major studio Toho, but mainly made by the Toho labour union, while its production was encouraged by the American occupation government to promote unionization – a policy of the early post-war years that would soon be reversed. The employment of the main characters clearly mirrors Toho's film, theatre, and railroad business, providing the film with a peculiarly self-reflexive thrust that was possibly rooted in the National Congress of Industrial Unions' decision to single out the high-profile film industry as a priority for union activity. Only a few months after the film's release, Toho was shaken by a major strike that led to the establishment of another major studio, Shin-Toho. Two years later, another intense strike rocked Toho but, with the cold war escalating, the occupation forces now sided with the studio and helped crush the upheaval with a display of military muscle. The occupation-initiated 'red purge' subsequently exiled many leftist film-makers from the studios, leading to a general disillusionment with occupation policy.

Made in only one week, *Those Who Make Tomorrow* is full of pro-union slogans, songs, and somewhat stiff dialogue explaining the merits of labour unions. Despite a fairly simplistic portrayal, and a lacklustre dramatic arc, it is nonetheless a fascinating document of politics in Japan directly after the war and the mix of a spirit of hope with the contradictory stance held within the post-war leftist movement. For all the expounding on the merits of unionization, the final arguments that convince both the father and the larger crowd are purely emotional: the engineer's perseverance despite his child's death or Yoshiko's tearful appeal to group consciousness. The gender roles are similarly conflicted: on the one hand, star actress Hideo Takamine makes a self-confident appearance as herself, arguing the merits of labour organization, but Yoshiko's final appeal to the crowd is strictly sentimental and, once the workers are won over by her tears, the male union leader takes over to provide the actual arguments and leadership. Regrettably, this intriguing piece of post-war film history is currently not available on VHS or DVD, and has only been screened very occasionally at the National Film Centre in Tokyo.

Alexander Zahlten

Throne of Blood

Kumonosu jô

Studio:
Toho Company

Director:
Akira Kurosawa

Producers:
Akira Kurosawa
Sojiro Motoki

Screenwriters:
Shinobu Hashimoto
Ryuzo Kikushima
Akira Kurosawa
Hideo Oguni

Cinematographer:
Asakazu Nakai

Art Director:
Kohei Ezaki

Composer:
Masaru Sato

Editor:
Akira Kurosawa

Duration:
109 min

Cast:
Toshiro Mifune
Isuzu Yamada
Akira Kubo

Year:
1957

Synopsis

Throne of Blood transports Shakespeare's *Macbeth* to feudal Japan, but follows the core narrative of the play. Two samurai named Washizu and Miki triumph in battle and, returning to Cobweb Castle through Cobweb Forest, encounter a witch. She predicts that the men will be promoted when they reach the castle, and that Washizu will one day be Lord of the castle, succeeded by Miki's son. The two friends laugh off her words, but when they are indeed promoted they begin to suspect the truth of her other prophecies.

Critique

Filmed high up on mist-enshrouded Mount Fuji, *Throne of Blood* is a visually-spectacular film and one of Akira Kurosawa's most critically-acclaimed works. The director strays from Shakespeare's story and dispenses with his dialogue, but adaptations should be judged on their coherence as opposed to their fidelity and *Throne of Blood* is a taut and thrilling masterpiece. The play is distilled into a bleak and spartan narrative; peripheral characters are dispensed with and instead of three witches there is only one, white-faced and terrifying, kneeling at a spinning-wheel in a bamboo cage. In a further condensation, the guilt-ridden Asaji will later come to resemble this witch when she kneels, pale-faced, and scrubs her pristine hands. Literary critics have discussed the witchiness of Lady Macbeth and, in Kurosawa's interpretation, Asaji foretells her husband's death with the line: 'Arrows will seek your life from the rear too.'

From the cage of arrows, that pins Washizu to the spot, to the birds that get caught in the castle eaves, the film's dominant motif is that of entrapment. Cobweb Castle is the literal translation of the film's Japanese title and, if the ghost at her spinning-wheel is the spider in Cobweb Forest, Washizu and Miki, filmed through the criss-crossing branches, are flies caught in her web. As they flee the forest they become lost in the fog, riding towards and away from the camera for what seems an eternity: metaphorically they have lost their way and lost sight of each other, the witch's words having sown seeds of distrust between them. Compared to the blustering, gurning Washizu, Miki remains almost expressionless throughout the film, his unnerving impenetrability encapsulated in the scene in which Washizu addresses him through the great, locked, castle door and receives no answer. But Washizu's greatest mistake is to distrust his best friend and the extraordinary scene in which Miki's impassive ghost appears at the feast is as tragic as it is chilling.

Alanna Donaldson

Tokyo Monagatori / Tokyo Story, 1953. Produced by Shochiku

Tokyo Story

Tokyo Monogatari

Director:
Yasujiro Ozu

Studio:
Shochiku

Producer:
Takeshi Yamamoto

Synopsis

Shukichi and Tomi Hirayama, an elderly retired couple living with their youngest daughter in the small port town of Onomichi, leave for Tokyo to visit their other children. They first stay with the oldest son, Koichi, a pediatrician with a wife and two sons, too busy with his work to show his parents around. Their other daughter , Shige, runs a hairdresser's salon at the house where she lives with her husband and is also too preoccupied with her own schedule and asks Noriko, her widowed sister-in-law, to act as their guide. On their way home, Tomi becomes ill on the train and, she although appears better after a night spent in Osaka with their youngest son, Keizo, her condition gets critical and everyone hurries to Onomichi to pay farewelli.

Screenwriters:
Kogo Noda
Yasujiro Ozu

Cinematographer:
Yuuharu Atsuta

Production Design:
Tatsuo Hamada
Itsuo Takahashi

Editor:
Yoshiyasu Hamamura

Composer:
Kojun Saito

Duration:
136 minutes

Cast:
Chishu Ryu
Chieko Hagashiyama
Haruko Sugimura

Year:
1953

Critique

The familial drama *Tokyo Story* is considered to be Ozu's signature film as it is a richly-profound experience, both visually and dramatically. Set in post-war Japan, it reflects on the ongoing changes to the simple and modest life of the past by juxtaposing meditative pace and everyday dialogue with scenes of urbanization and the accelerating speed of modernity. Ozu highlights the fragility and transience of life by placing the focus on an aging couple and revealing their perspective on the rapidly changing and ever-more distant world that they are soon to depart. Although Shukichi and Tomi are obviously neglected by their children, left to themselves even after making such a long and demanding journey, they always exhibit a childlike joy and appreciation of life, and it is only Noriko herself, left alone after the passing of her husband, who is appreciative of their company. Her final resolution is to make better use of the time she has and this is made clear through her holding on to Tomi's watch, which has been given to her as a memento by Shukichi.

With the gap between the generations, the differences between the rural Omichi and the growing Tokyo, and the constant presence of modernity in the repeated shots of trains and telephones, *Tokyo Story* is as much about time as it is about family relations. Deliberately choosing to show only the most private scenes, Ozu opts for intimacy and an insider's look into the family dynamics rather than from a stance of a detached observer that could have been achieved if the director had shown the couple actually travelling on the train or walking amongst the Tokyo crowds. Ozu, instead, offers multiple points of view from the positions of different characters, with the narrative developing through the communication between them, although it is through the eyes of Shukichi and Tomi that the audience is looking at everybody else. A classic *shomin geki*, *Tokyo Story* offers an overview of the director's now classical style.

Jelena Stojvokic

Under the Flag of the Rising Sun

Gunki hatameku motoni

Company:
Toho

Director:
Kinji Fukasaku

Synopsis

It is 26 years since the surrender of the Japanese in World War II. A war widow, Sakie Togashi, is unable to receive benefits because the government has listed her husband Katsuo, who had been a sergeant in the Japanese Army, as a deserter. Sakie refuses to accept the ruling, or that her husband was a traitor, and mounts a seemingly-quixotic quest to uncover the truth surrounding his mysterious death. Sakie gains a list of names of men who served with her husband and she interviews each one, trying to piece together what happened on the days leading up to his death, in an effort to restore honour to Katsuo's blackened reputation. The truth is out there, but it is not pretty.

Producers:
Seishi Matsumaru
Eigasha Shinsei
Shohei Tokizane

Screenwriters:
Kinji Fukasaku
Norio Osada
Kaneto Shindo

Cinematographer:
Hiroshi Segawa

Art Director:
Tatsuya Irino

Composer:
Hikaru Hayashi

Editor:
Keiichi Uraoka

Duration:

96 minutes

Cast:
Tetsuro Tamba
Sachiko Hidari
Yumiko Fujita

Year:
1972

Critique

Although *Under the Flag of the Rising Sun* works as a frenetic but equally powerful and haunting companion piece to Kon Ichikawa's anti-war film *Fires on the Plain* (1959), Kinji Fukasaku's scathing political mystery can also be viewed as the Japanese equivalent to Costa Gavras' political thrillers *Z* (1969) and *State of Siege* (1972), as well as anticipating the American films of paranoia and dread, such as *All the President's Men* (1976), that were released during and after the Nixon era. Fukasaku's *Râshomon*-like puzzle is a film of bitterness, regret and pure rage. It is also a brave film, refusing to deviate from the unpleasant truths Sakie confronts and not absolving the citizens of Japan, who would rather not think of such taboo subjects. Fukasaku offers up no comfort at the end of Sakie's quest, and Sachiko Hidari's quiet performance is heartbreaking to watch as we also seek some consolation, but are offered only pain.

Although director Fukasaku is understandably better-known in the West for his explosively violent *jitsuroku* yakuza films, this personal project is one of his finest films. It is also arguably one of the greatest post-war Japanese films and would be better-known if perhaps Fukasaku had become a critical darling in the West a long time before he eventually did at the turn of the millennium with his brilliant dystopian action film *Battle Royale* (2000). Retrospectives of the director's work were held, especially in the United States, and many cinemagoers encountered for the first time this occasionally challenging, idiosyncratic and always entertaining film-maker. Perhaps if Fukasaku had not built his career on making yakuza pictures and, instead, focused more on making dramatic non-genre work such as *Under the Flag of the Rising Sun*, he would have been talked about in the same breath as Kurosawa, Ozu, Mizoguchi, et al. But, as it stands, we are lucky to have this film at all. Plenty of film-makers who have made war films claim them to be anti-war testaments, although they are anything but. While perhaps being cynical about conflict, these film-makers still delight in the grandiose adolescent fantasies of war adventure. Fukasaku, who witnessed the horrors of war at first hand, refuses to deal in good and bad dichotomies to ease our discomfort. It is a remarkable work, savage and ultimately haunting.

Derek Hill

When a Woman Ascends the Stairs

Onna ga kaidan wo agaru toki

Studio:
Toho Company

Director:
Mikio Naruse

Producer:
Ryuzo Kikushima

Screenwriter:
Ryuzo Kikushima

Cinematographer:
Masao Tamai

Art Director:
Satoshi Chuko

Composer:
Toshiro Mayuzumi

Editor:
Eiji Ooi

Duration:
111 minutes

Cast:
Hideko Takamine
Masayuki Mori
Reiko Dan

Year:
1960

Synopsis

Keiko is a middle-aged bar hostess who works in the classy Ginza district of Tokyo. Night after night, she drinks her fill and entertains a revolving array of businessmen, making a living but going nowhere. Known amongst her co-workers and customers as Mama, she is well-liked and respected, firmly maintaining a dignified, proper demeanour in matters of business and possible romance. Approaching the point where her age could become ill-suited for her occupation, Keiko decides to embark on a different course in her life. In doing so, she must consider two options: starting up a bar of her own or marriage.

Critique

When a Woman Ascends the Stairs peels back the glossy surface of Japan's hospitality industry to reveal the everyday challenges faced by its hostesses. Their jobs require them to uphold a costly lifestyle, as expensive clothes, perfumes and apartments all contribute to the impression of luxury that attracts their customers. This is familiar territory for director Mikio Naruse, who, throughout his career, specialized in making women's films. Even though he was not discovered by Western audiences until years after his death in 1969, today he is recognized as one of the greatest Japanese film-makers. He regularly chose to depict strong, working-class female characters, and devoted a great deal of attention to the all-important, ever-present spectre of money. Bills, debts, credit, receipts, stamps – these are the governing forces that so often dominate his films, forming barriers of ink and paper that can only be overcome one payment at a time.

The performances in Naruse's films are not so much controlled by his sensibilities as a film-maker but are, instead, complemented by them. Without the incomparable Hideko Takamine in the lead role, When a Woman Ascends the Stairs would be a much lesser film. A regular collaborator with Naruse, she brings a fine balance of courage and weariness to Keiko, whose deep-rooted feelings of sadness and longing can only be kept beneath her façade of refinement for so long. Naruse's cinematic style is simple, clear and intelligent, informed by a sharp sense of logic. He occasionally allows himself small, poetic touches, such as the brief segments featuring the streets, traffic and bright, flickering signs of Tokyo over which Keiko narrates her story, but even they are presented in moderation.

However, the wisdom behind his tact occasionally reveals itself in moments of astonishing emotional impact, made all the more impressive by how slight their execution is. One particular shot of a defeated Keiko facing another woman with a series of tall smokestacks looming behind her is, at once, a mini-masterpiece of composition and a poignant encapsulation of Naruse's melancholic vision. *When a Woman Ascends the Stairs* is a moving, assuredly-told tale of making ends meet. Through an unbiased lens, it follows a memorable heroine who, despite her flaws, one cannot help but admire as she bravely meets each challenge that arises before her. Tracking her odyssey of daily errands and nightly responsibilities, the film portrays a realistic, resolute breed of femininity.

Marc Saint-Cyr

J-HORROR/
JAPANESE HORROR

Ju-On: The Grudge, 2003. Produced by Oz Company Ltd

Ever since the release of Hideo Nakata's *Ring* in 1998,
Japanese horror has enjoyed an unprecedented level of
attention. Now considered to be one of the most important and influential genre traditions, prior to 1998 western
knowledge of this aspect of Japanese cinema was effectively
limited to a handful of notable period-set ghost stories –
Masaki Kobayashi's *Kwaidan* (1964), for example, which was
Oscar-nominated in 1964 (Best Foreign Film, the only time
Japan has submitted a horror film to the Academy) and which
won the Special Jury Prize at the Cannes Film Festival the
following year. This circumstance has lead to an unfortunate
belief that Japanese horror was dormant between the 1960s
and the release of *Ring* but, despite sinking to its lowest ebb
in the 1970s, Japan's genre tradition has been active since the
earliest days of the nation's film industry.

Many of the earliest Japanese horror films were based on
ancient tales written during the Edo period (1603–1865),
often as *kabuki* plays. A heavily-stylized form of theatre,
kabuki was the most popular form of entertainment during
the Edo period, and the most well-known stories remained
popular well into the twentieth century, providing an obvious source of material for the earliest Japanese film-makers.
Among the most famous of these is the *Yotsuya kaidan*, the
story of a penniless samurai who drives his wife to suicide in
order to marry a rich woman only to find the disfigured ghost
of his dead wife pursuing him. The story features many of the
most common characteristics of the Japanese ghost story or
kaidan: murder, betrayal and vengeance from beyond the
grave, usually at the hands of an *onryō*, or vengeful spirit. The
Yotsuya kaidan was first filmed in 1912, and has since been
filmed more than 20 times; one of the most recent versions
was directed by Kinji Fukasaku, best-known as director of

Battle Royale (2000). Other stories were less moralistic in tone, like the popular *Botandoro*, which tells of a man who enters into a sexual relationship with a woman he later discovers to be a ghost. Like the *Yotsuya kaidan*, *Botandoro* has been adapted for the screen many times, and was actually the first of the traditional tales to be filmed, in 1910. It was given a contemporary update in Nobuhiko Obayashi's excellent *Ijintachi tono natsu* (1988) and continues to be a very popular tale.

The onset of war and Japan's eventual defeat had a major impact on the national cinema, but the years of the Allied occupation saw the beginnings of a recovery. However, the occupying forces frowned upon subjects that recalled Japan's feudal, and hence military, past, a definition which included the many period-set ghost stories that had been popular in the pre-war years. In response, Japanese film-makers began to explore other genres, most of them informed by recent Hollywood hits, like Shinsei Adachi's *The Invisible Man Appears* (1949) and *Claws of Iron* (1951). The first is a relatively straightforward rehash of Universal's *Invisible Man* series, while *Claws of Iron* mixes elements of *Dr Jekyll and Mr Hyde*, *King Kong* (1933) and *The Wolf Man* (1940) into a bizarre but entertaining mélange. Even after the end of the occupation, western films were a common source of inspiration; the Italian gothic of Mario Bava and his contemporaries was recreated in Hajime Sato's *The Ghost of the Hunchback* (1965) and Michio Yamamoto paid tribute to Hammer's *Dracula* series in three films: *Legacy of Dracula* (1970), *Lake of Dracula* (1971) and *Evil of Dracula* (1974).

The success of Ishiro Honda's *Godzilla* (1954) – itself inspired by Eugène Lourié's *The Beast from 20,000 Fathoms* (1953) – ensured that Japanese pulp cinema in the 1950s and '60s had a strongly science-fiction bent. In between creating a slew of giant monsters for Toho, Honda also directed several offbeat sci-fi/horror films, most notably *The Human Vapor* (1960) and the excellent *Attack of the Mushroom People* (1963). Despite the typically overstated US title, *Attack of the Mushroom People* is a disturbing, surreal film that prefigures the body-horror nightmares of Shinya Tsukamoto's *Tetsuo* films and Higuchinsky's *Uzumaki* (2000). A group of sea-going socialites find themselves stranded on an island with only one source of food: enormous multicoloured mushrooms. Unfortunately those who eat the mushrooms find their bodies undergoing a transformation into something less than human. Similar themes cropped up in Hajime Sato's *Goke – Body Snatcher from Hell* (1968), a psychedelic riff on Robert Heinlein's *The Puppet Masters*, featuring a glob of pink slime that crawls into the heads of the survivors of a plane crash. Filled with strong, oddball characters (grieving Vietnam War widow, yakuza thug, government hit man), political and social commentary, and cheap but grotesque special effects, *Goke* is one of the best Japanese horror films of the period and a firm cult classic.

The end of the Allied Occupation allowed Japanese film-makers to return to the traditional tales that had been the mainstay of pre-war horror cinema, ushering in something of a golden age. Many of the classic films date from this period, including Kenji Mizoguchi's *Ugetsu monogatari* (1953), a haunting and beautiful tale of ambition and greed, now considered to be one of best Japanese films ever produced. The key figure of the period was Nobuo Nakagawa, a veteran director who produced a string of popular horror stories for Shintoho in the 1950s and '60s. Although best-known for directing the definitive version of the *Yotsuya kaidan*, 1959's *Tokaido Yotsuya kaidan*, his other works are no less interesting. Another Edo-period tale was the inspiration for *Kaidan Kasane-ga-fuchi*, one of the darkest and most terrifying Japanese ghost stories, later reworked by Hideo Nakata himself (*Kaidan*, 2007). Set across two generations, it is the story of a samurai who murders a blind masseuse and falls prey to his victim's post-mortem fury. Twenty years later, the samurai's son becomes involved with a schoolteacher, eventually betraying her to marry a younger girl; unbeknown to him, the teacher is the daughter of the masseuse murdered years before and his fate comes to echo his father's. Although his period-set ghost stories are generally excellent, Nakagawa's best film was the little-seen *Jigoku* ('hell'), a contemporary morality fable released in 1960 but subsequently lost in the collapse of its parent studio Shintoho. Unlike the atmospheric chills of *Tokaido Yotsuya kaidan* and *Kaidan Kasane-ga-fuchi*, *Jigoku* presents a man's blood-drenched journey through hell, complete with graphic torture and mutilation – and three years before H.G. Lewis's pioneering splatter film, *Blood Feast* (1963).

As the 1960s progressed, Japanese film-makers were beginning to spice up their period horror stories with a dash of sex and violence. Kaneto Shindo's *Onibaba* reduced the supernatural elements in favour of political commentary and erotica, resulting in a powerful film that works on a number of levels. The rise of the *pinku eiga* – Japanese soft-core pornography – also affected the horror film, with tales like the *Botandoro* being ideally suited to sexually-explicit adaptations, notably Chusei Sone's *Hellish Love* (1972). Long unavailable in Japan and only recently released on DVD in the US, Teruo Ishii's *Horrors of Malformed Men* (1969) mixed the supernatural trappings of the kaidan with a parade of grotesquery possibly inspired by Tod Browning's *Freaks* (1932), and an appearance from author Edogawa Rampo's celebrated master detective Akechi. Like *Jigoku* and *Attack of the Mushroom People*, *Horrors of Malformed Men* is obsessed with transformation of the human body, a frequent theme of post-war domestic horror.

The decline of Japanese cinema in the early 1970s had a serious impact on the domestic horror scene, which reached an all-time low by the middle of the decade. The form did not disappear entirely, however, and a few worthwhile efforts managed to secure a release. Some of these, like Tatsumi Kumashiro's respectable remake of *Jiguko* (Teruo Ishii would direct a third version in 1999, with the US title *A Japanese Hell*) looked to the past for inspiration, while others sought different paths. Despite the period setting, Nobuhiko Obayashi's *House* (*Ie*, 1977) is a thoroughly-modern haunted-house tale that utilizes the many camera techniques the director picked up during his work in TV commercials. For all the flashy visual tricks on display, *House* is also genuinely creepy and sharply insightful, with the psychology of sexual maturity and adolescence playing a key part in the story. For his next horror film, 1988's *Ijintachi tono natsu*, Obayashi transplanted the *Botandoro* into contemporary Tokyo. Harada, a bored, middle-aged and divorced scriptwriter, begins a relationship with one of his neighbours. He also encounters a couple who claim to be his long-dead mother and father; despite his initial misgivings, he comes to believe they really are his parents. Although he is overjoyed to spend time with them again, Harada does not see that his nightly meetings with his deceased mother and father are causing him to prematurely age and are robbing him of his vitality. Equal parts horror and nostalgic drama, *Ijintachi tono natsu* won several awards in its native country but, aside from a single screening on UK television, is still largely unknown elsewhere. Even more suitable for international audiences is Kiyoshi Kurosawa's *Sweet Home* (1989), a haunted-house movie featuring excellent special effects from Dick Smith and a number of first-rate shocks.

Away from the mainstream other directors were exploring different avenues, and the 1980s also saw a low-key wave of violent and graphic Japanese horror films. The best of these is undoubtedly Toshiharu Ikeda's *Evil Dead Trap* (1988), a stylish and terrifying slasher movie about a TV crew who find themselves lost in an abandoned military base. Ikeda, a well-known director of pink and V-cinema (direct-to-video) films, lines up a series of gory and surprising deaths, each of which cranks the tension up a notch or two. A classic of 1980s' splatter, *Evil Dead Trap* was followed by two in-name-only sequels: Izo Hashimoto's nonsensical but bloody *Evil Dead Trap 2: Hideko* (1991) and Ikeda's own *Evil Dead Trap 3: Broken Love Killer* (1993), a slick but predictable psycho-thriller. The slasher movie was also a notable influence on Kazuo Komizu's pair of low-budget V-cinema monstrosities, *Entrails of a Virgin* (1986) and *Entrails of a Beauty* (1986). As the titles suggest, neither of these films are characterized by restraint or good taste but even their graphic blend of sex and splatter was superseded by the notorious *Guinea Pig* series, one instalment of which attempted to pass itself off as a genuine snuff movie.

By the early '90s, Japanese horror cinema was showing undeniable signs of life. The sprawling *Haunted School* franchise, based on a series of bestselling books about Japanese urban legends, exploited the growing interest in horror among children and teenagers. The franchise would eventually include four theatrical movies, countless made-for-TV and direct-to-video specials and an animated series, some of which featured future luminaries of Japanese horror, including Hideo Nakata, Hiroshi Takahashi, Kiyoshi Kurosawa and Takashi Shimizu. Inspired by the success of the *Haunted School* films, director Norio Tsuruta put together a series of direct-to-video anthologies called *Scary True Stories* (*Honto ni atta kowai hanashi*), while popular schoolyard ghost Hanako-san appeared in several feature films. This steady increase in genre activity finally exploded in 1998 with the release of Hideo Nakata's *Ring*, a film that transformed Japan's domestic horror scene into a lucrative and influential movement.

The combination of traditional and contemporary elements proved to be immensely popular and *Ring* was followed almost immediately by a wave of sequels, follow-ups and knock-offs. The best of these – Takashi Shimizu's *Ju-on* series, for example – built on the foundations laid by Nakata's film and achieved their own well-deserved success. Despite the presence of a large number of uninspired copies, this period was also marked by some truly innovative films, such as the Junji Ito adaptations *Uzumaki* (2000) and *Love Ghost* (2000), or Kiyoshi Kurosawa's bleakly-terrifying *Pulse* (2001) – the best of the post-*Ring* techno-horrors. Nakata himself returned to the genre in 2002 with the excellent *Dark Water*, a subtle but powerful ghost story set in a miserable, damp-infested block of flats. At the same time, Japanese horror was attracting international attention, leading to a slew of Hollywood-produced remakes, including Gore Verbinski's *The Ring* (2002) and the Takashi Shimizu-directed *The Grudge* (2004), both of which performed well enough to warrant sequels of their own.

In recent years there has been something of a shift away from the territory carved out by the *Ring* and *Ju-on* franchises. While Hideo Nakata and Takashi Shimizu have struggled to repeat their early successes, epic manga adaptations like *Death Note* and *20th Century Boys* have scored at the box office, with notable critical and commercial returns also going to Yukihiko Tsutsumi's *Forbidden Siren* (2006), a computer game adaptation, and Shinya Tsukamoto's *Nightmare Detective* (2006). A surprisingly-mainstream effort from one of

Japan's most respected independent film-makers, *Nightmare Detective* is also one of the best Japanese horror films since *Ring*. Although the main story appears to be a simple reworking of *A Nightmare on Elm Street* (1984), it is actually an ambitious, original film about a man who possesses the ability to enter other people's dreams. When a series of mysterious – and bloody – suicides occurs, the police turn to this 'nightmare detective' for help, bringing the hero into conflict with a psychopath who has the same ability. At a time when Japanese horror is being derided for churning out nothing more than a string of *Ring* and *Ju-on* clones, *Nightmare Detective* proves that there is still plenty of life left in the genre, and plenty of reasons to be optimistic about the future.

Jim Harper

Audition

Ôdishon

Studio:
AFDF, Creators Company
Connection, Omega Project

Director:
Takashi Miike

Producers:
Satoshi Fukushima
Akemi Suyama

Screenwriters:
Daisuke Tengan, from the novel
by Ryû Murakami

Cinematographer:
Hideo Yamamoto

Art Director:
Tatsuo Ozeki

Composer:
Koji Endo

Editor:
Yasushi Shimamura

Duration:
115 minutes

Synopsis

Audition begins with a man named Aoyama watching helplessly as his wife passes away in her hospital bed, leaving him alone to raise Shigehiko, their young son. Years later, Shigehiko suggests to his father that he begin seeing other women again. The widower discusses the idea with Yoshikawa, a friend and fellow film producer who comes up with a plan to hold an audition for a fake film project, allowing Aoyama to preview several women at once. While looking over the many applications, he is intrigued by one from Asami, a young woman whose dreams of becoming a dancer were halted by a hip injury. After meeting her at the audition, Aoyama is positively smitten and begins dating her. Yet a circumstance arises which finally prompts Aoyama to investigate her himself, producing strange new suspicions concerning his would-be beloved.

Critique

Of the many films in Takashi Miike's vast and varied body of work, *Audition* is also one of his best. A macabre classic, it occupies a unique place alongside its J-horror counterparts and has inspired comparisons with the work of the Italian *giallo* masters such as Dario Argento, while there are also similarities with the techniques of Alfred Hitchcock. Like the master of suspense, Miike plays with his viewers' expectations, carefully presenting the audience with what is, at first, a romantic melodrama before it veers into entirely different territory. The tone that Miike adopts throughout *Audition* is quiet and observational, his characters frequently framed in long shots as they occupy various public spaces with anonymous strangers. Amongst the topics that arise in their dialogue is the scarcity of truly happy people in Japan, subtly dovetailing with Aoyama's own search for happiness. Musician and actor Ryo Ishibashi portrays him as a decent and well-meaning man who bears enough of a conscience to turn the picture of his wife away before looking over the applications of

Cast:
Ryo Ishibashi
Eihi Shiina
Tetsu Sawaki

Year:
1999

various actresses, and voices his feelings of guilt before beginning the semi-exploitative audition. Through slight touches, such as Shigehiko's own experiences with love, and a coworker of Aoyama's whose behaviour hints towards feelings for him, Miike invites a consideration of male-female relationships, morality and responsibility in contemporary Japanese society alongside the more genre-based elements of the film.

Asami, played by Eihi Shiina in one of her first roles, is the great riddle of *Audition*. In her first meetings with Aoyama, she appears to be the ideal woman for him: shy, sweet and a kindred lonely spirit. However, as Yoshikawa, then Aoyama, try to learn more about her on their own, they only emerge with more questions than answers and, by the time the final act unfolds, one of the few real certainties left about her is a strong determination driven by her still-enigmatic code of beliefs. The legendary final reel is a shocking, remarkably-executed departure from the rest of the film, confronting the viewer with a disorienting sequence of hallucinatory images before landing back in the trappings of stark, definite reality. *Audition* takes advantage of the cinematic capabilities of horror. It shows a deeper consideration for its audience members than most other films within the genre, smartly guiding them through an elegantly-constructed maze right up to a disturbing conclusion. With its deliciously-manipulative traits, confident direction and enduring mysteries, its cult reputation is rightfully deserved.

Marc Saint-Cyr

Blind Beast

Môjû

Company:
Daiei

Director:
Yasuzo Masumura

Producers:
Masaichi Nagata
Kazumasa Nakano

Screenwriter:
Yoshiro Shirasaka

Cinematographer:
Setsuo Kobayashi

Art Director:
Shigeo Mano

Synopsis

A blind sculptor named Michio obsesses over a beautiful model, Aki, and kidnaps her. Trapping her in his gigantic warehouse, where he lives with his accomplice and mother and where he also stores massive sculptures of female bodies and abstract anatomical parts, the sculptor systematically rapes her and subjugates her to extreme mental torture. Eventually, though, the young woman goes blind and succumbs to Michio's sadomasochistic wishes, entering into a relationship that transgresses all morality.

Critique

Based on a serialized short story by the legendary Japanese writer Edogawa Rampo (the Japanese pronunciation of Edgar Allan Poe and the pseudonym for Taro Hirai), *Blind Beast* was for years a much-sought-after film for Western horror film aficionados, largely due to its obscurity. Its semi-legendary reputation among connoisseurs was heightened by its lack of critical appraisal, except for a notable entry in Phil Hardy's Aurum Film Encyclopedia. Not surprisingly, Yasuzo Masumura's film could never live up to the expectations gleaned from the short yet luridly-enticing entry once the film eventually surfaced

Composer:

Hikaru Hayashi

Editor:

Tatsuji Nakashiju

Duration:

86 minutes

Cast:

Eiji Funakoshi

Mako Midori

Noriko Sengoku

Year:

1969

from obscurity. But while the reality is not as graphically violent as its entry led many to believe, Masumura's film is an extraordinary depiction of aberrant sexual power games, while still maintaining its strict thriller-genre dramatic beats.

Although not technically a *Pinku eiga*, Masumura's story constantly straddles the line of reactionary erotica which defines the genre as a whole by never giving Aki the ability to define herself away from how Michio defines her; or Masumura for that matter. The underlying meaning to Michio's and Aki's not-so-subversive relationship may be disturbing and even repulsive to many viewers, but there is a sort of twisted purity of inevitability to their union, shockingly realized by the end when Michio severs Aki's limbs. In his own strange and sordid way, Masumura displays remarkable fidelity to his material. In that respect, he should be commended for his integrity in plunging us far down the rabbit hole of twisted love and keeping us there.

Derek Hill

Dark Water

Honogurai Mizu no Soko Kara

Studio:

Kadokawa Shoten

Director:

Hideo Nakata

Producer:

Takashige Ichise

Screenwriters:

Yoshihiro Nakamura

Ken'ichi Suzuki

Cinematographer:

Junichiro Hayashi

Art Director:

Katsumi Nakazawa

Composers:

Kenji Kawai

Shikao Suga

Editor:

Nobuyuki Takahashi

Duration:

97 minutes

Synopsis

Fighting to keep her child in an acrimonious custody battle, Yoshimi and her young daughter Ikuko hurry to move into the best apartment Yoshimi can afford to make a fresh start. While Yoshimi searches for a job for the first time since giving birth, their cheap apartment starts to show signs of damp which are consistently ignored by the apartment manager and estate agent who sold her the home. To make matters worse, Ikuko has made an imaginary friend and started behaving strangely at school, a fact that Yoshimi's ex-husband is trying to use to gain custody of his daughter. The damp in the apartment spreads unnaturally quickly, and Yoshimi herself begins to hear noises in the empty apartment upstairs, catching glimpses of a little girl in a yellow raincoat and seeing memories of a lonely childhood that are all-too familiar, but not her own. As these incidents grow more violent, and Ikuko's life appears to be in danger, Yoshimi becomes desperate to learn the story behind the memories and protect her child at all costs.

Critique

Dark Water comes from the short-lived 'J-horror' wave that was sparked by Nakata's previous film, *The Ring* (1998). One reason given for the popularity of J-horror films in their original incarnations is their combination of traditional Japanese culture and Hollywood film-making techniques. This mixture is certainly evident in *Dark Water*, which combines the Japanese *onryō*, the 'vengeful spirit' archetype, with the atmosphere and imagery of such films as *Don't Look Now* (1973) and *The Shining* (1980), with the storyline updated to provide a social commentary on present-day Japan. A traditional *onryō* is usually a woman brought back as a spirit to exact revenge on the man who has wronged her and anyone else who gets in the way, but does not

Cast:

Hitomi Kuroki
Rio Kann
Mirei Oguchi

Year:

2002

completely apply to *Dark Water*. The unworthy men in this story are very minor characters, used mostly to provide the context for the actions and emotions of the female character, rather than the motivation. Mitsuko is a child, wronged by her neglectful, abusive parents and seeking comfort rather than revenge, while Yoshimi, who was similarly neglected and abused as a child, responds to Mitsuko with sympathy and compassion even when feeling threatened.

The characters and their interaction reflect the changing demographics of Japanese society, in which divorce is on the rise and many women have had to quickly learn how to balance the care of their children with a return to the workplace that they may well have been pressured to leave when they married. Fatherhood is not considered in depth in *Dark Water*, but the shifting expectations of motherhood and the relatively recent willingness to examine dysfunctional families in Japanese society are highlighted through Yoshimi, Mitsuko and Ikuko's relationships with their parents and, in this respect, *Dark Water* is a story in which characters face unfair consequences for doing what they believe to be for the best. The lack of moral compass of Hollywood horror cinema will be refreshing for some and unnerving for others, but the real appeal of *Dark Water* is in its slow, measured build-up, focused far more on fear within human relationships than on external terrors. The pace can be challenging for viewers used to Hollywood shock machines, and the pay-off is more heartbreaking than horrifying, but the best J-horror films are engaging because they are distinctly different from the Western counterparts, and *Dark Water* is no exception.

Amelia Cook

Dark Water, 2002. Produced by Kadokawa Shoten

Demon Woman

Onibaba

Studio:
Kindai Eiga Kyokai

Director:
Kaneto Shindo

Producer:
Hisao Itoya

Screenwriter:
Kaneto Shindo

Cinematographer:
Kiyomi Kuroda

Art Director:
Kaneto Shindo

Composer:
Hikaru Hayashi

Editors:
Toshio Enoki
Kazuo Enomoto

Duration:
103 minutes

Cast:
Nobuko Otowa
Jitsuko Yoshimura
Kei Sato

Year:
1966

Synopsis

In rural, war-torn fourteenth-century Japan, an old peasant woman awaits her son's return from battle. A summer frost has killed the crops and she and her daughter-in-law are struggling to survive. In the tall susuki grass that surrounds their hut, they lie in wait for lost samurai, killing them for their valuable armour and concealing the bodies in a well. When their neighbor Haichi returns from battle alone and announces that the man that binds them is dead, animosity begins to grow between the two women. The girl is soon seduced by Haichi and, upon discovering their affair, the older woman is overcome with envy and despair at her own loveless existence and determines to come between them.

Critique

Demon Woman is a highly stylized and heavily symbolic film which draws on the classical Noh theatre of the era that it evokes. The well is the film's central symbol, evoking at once the old woman's murderousness and the young girl's lust (like her wantonly open mouth as she runs to meet her lover each night). When the old woman descends into the well and stands amongst her victims' bones, the shadows lend her face a skull-like aspect. If she is a symbol of death, then the young couple is a symbol of life and the film's imagery celebrates their union: two raindrops roll and dance around each other on a water lily before merging into one, and the softly swaying susuki grass, filmed in slow motion, seems to move with the lovers' sensuality. Filmed on location in high-contrast black and white, the film is justly celebrated for its imagery, while the eerie day-for-night lighting and a soundtrack of drums and cries adds to its charged atmosphere. Shindo is a powerful silent film-maker whose 1960 feature *The Naked Island* was entirely dialogue-free, and the lengthy dialogue sequences in *Demon Woman* are regrettable, diluting tension and rendering it overlong.

Shindo has been preoccupied with Hiroshima throughout his career and *Demon Woman* is no exception. The old woman's make-up in the unmasking scene was based on photographs of the radiation victims, and when Haichi returns from battle and tells how 'strange things are happening in Kyoto: the sun rose black in the sky and a horse gave birth to a calf", he evokes the radioactive 'black rain' that fell in the aftermath of the bomb and its devastating effects. Throughout the film the characters debate the existence of monsters and in the opening scene we are made to share their uncertainty: a monstrous-looking creature appears on the horizon, staggering and swaying through the grass, its two heads lolling and gasping. Slowly it begins to take shape, and we see two injured samurai, leaning together – they have been fighting one another and are close to death. Shindo's point, here and throughout the film, seems to be that it is only the self-destructive man who is truly monstrous.

Alanna Donaldson

Evil Dead Trap

Shiryo No Wana

Studio:
Phaedra Cinema

Director:
Toshiharu Ikeda

Screenwriter:
Takashi Ishii

Cinematographer:
Norimichi Kasamatsu

Art Director:
Yuji Hayashida

Composer:
Masa Kitamura

Duration:
100 minutes

Cast:
Miyuki Ono
Aya Katsuragi
Hitomi Kobayashi

Year:
1988

Synopsis

Nami, the hostess of a late-night clip show, receives a videotape from one of her viewers. It appears to show a woman being tortured and murdered, and provides directions to a disused military base where the killing apparently took place. Sensing a story that might provide her with a way to break into mainstream journalism, Nami and her production crew follow the directions on the tape and begin to explore the abandoned military base. Although it appears to be deserted, someone has constructed a series of elaborate and deadly traps. As the friends split up to look around, they quickly find themselves falling prey to these brutal constructions.

Critique

Toshiharu Ikeda's *Evil Dead Trap* is arguably the most well-known Japanese horror film of the 1980s, and one of the best Japanese splatter movies ever made. Like Kiyoshi Kurosawa's *Sweet Home* (1989) and *The Guard from the Underground* (1992), *Evil Dead Trap* is obviously influenced by a number of international horror films. The plot is heavily reminiscent of US slasher movies, relying on the same stalk-and-slash procedure as *Friday the 13th* (1980). There are also several references to the films of Italian director Dario Argento, in particular *Suspiria* (1977); although Ikeda himself was not aware of Argento's films, scriptwriter Takashi Ishii and composer Tomohiko Kira were both admirers of the Italian director. In keeping with his status as an important director of *pinku eiga*, Ikeda casts a handful of pink and AV (adult video) veterans in the film and includes a couple of sex scenes.

In horror terms, *Evil Dead Trap* is more than successful. Ikeda and scriptwriter Ishii (later director of 1995's *Gonin*) are certainly inventive in their brutality, employing a range of devices – including spikes, swinging blades, crossbows, nooses and many more – to impressive effect and provoking a few genuine jolts. Equally impressive are the elaborate tracking shots, atmospheric lighting and unusual shot compositions created by cinematographer Norimichi Kasamatsu, a frequent Sogo Ishii collaborator, which help to lift *Evil Dead Trap* above the majority of low-budget splatter movies. Unfortunately, after a tense and surprising first hour, the film loses pace and could comfortably stand to lose fifteen minutes. The controversial final act takes a sharp turn into the body-horror territory of David Cronenberg, culminating in a bloodily-surreal scene that has been heavily criticized but that few viewers are likely to forget. Despite its flaws, *Evil Dead Trap* is a well-made, powerful horror film that suggests Ikeda could have distinguished himself in the genre should he have wanted to do.

Jim Harper

The Face of Another, 1966.

Face of Another

Tanin no kao

Studio/Distributor:
Teshigarhara Productions

Director:
Hiroshi Teshigahara

Producers:
Nobuyo Horiba
Kiichi Ichikawa
Tadashi Oono

Screenwriter:
Kobo Abe

Cinematographer:
Hiroshi Segawa

Synopsis

Facially-disfigured from an industrial accident, Okuyama seeks the help of an unorthodox psychiatrist, who offers to build him a new face modelled upon 'the face of another': the face of a young man that they met in a restaurant in the working class area of Tokyo. Drawing on the Frankenstein myth, the construction of Okuyama's new face is a deranged experiment by his psychiatrist. The narrative maps out the philosophical and psychological ramifications of this experiment, utilizing surrealistic and impressionist techniques against a coldly-aesthetic background of black and white, and meditating on what happens when the 'face' as ultimate signifier of identity becomes a commodity like any other. The mask gradually takes over, altering Okuyama's personality, affecting not only his outside – his clothes – but his inner self.

Critique

Face of Another is one of four films that Teshigahara made in collaboration with the existential writer Kobo Abe and musician Toru Takemitsu, the others being *Pitfall* (1962), *Woman of the Dunes* (1964)

Art Directors:
Arata Isozaki
Masao Yamazaki

Composer:
Toru Takemitsu

Editor:
Yoshi Sugihara

Duration:
124 minutes

Cast:
Tatsuya Nakadai
Machiko Kyo
Mikijiro Hira

Year:
1966

and *A Ruined Map* (1968). While *Woman of the Dunes* was a critical success, both nationally and internationally, *Face of Another* – as with Teshigahara's other Abe films – received little of the critical attention or acclaim of the former. This is surprising as *Face of Another* has a stronger narrative drive and more familiar plot in its reinterpretation of the Frankenstein myth. The topic of surgically-switching faces was not new, having already been the subject of Georges Franju's 1959 film *Eyes without a Face* and Jess Franco's *The Awful Dr Orloff* (1962). However, in both these films, the surgery fails and the 'patients' – in both cases the daughter of the mad scientist – remain faceless and ultimately monstrous. Okuyama, however, becomes one with the mask, the face of another allowing the creation of a new identity unencumbered by the historical past. Scenes of Okuyama at home and at work imply that, at both a literal and metaphorical level, having no face, means having no identity. And it is the philosophical and psychological implications of this 'loss of face', and its impact on tradi-tional constructions of masculinity, that *Face of Another* explores.

Strangely beautiful, *Face of Another* fully realizes the potential of black-and-white cinematography with the expressionistic scenes in the psychiatrist's office and its continually shifting *mise-en-scène* providing a counterpoint to the more documentary-style aesthetics of the everyday world. The need to create a new identity unfettered by the past is without doubt an allusion to Japan's traumatic histori-cal past and the continuing scars of Hiroshima and Nagasaki on the national psyche during the 1960s. This is no surprise given that Teshigahara had not only worked with Gumio Kamei on the documen-tary *It Was Good to Live* in 1956 about Hiroshima A-bomb victims but had directed his own documentary about atomic bomb testing in 1957, called *The World Is Terrified* (1957). Together with the visually-arresting images, Takemitsu's score with its juxtaposition of traditional Japanese music – and play of sound and silence – with the Western waltz explores the impact of Westernization in the wake of the Allied Occupation on questions of national and cultural identity. The answer is an existentialist one, as signified by collapse of distinctions between 'self' and 'mask' at the film's conclusion, in which the subject is born anew through his/her own actions.

Colette Balmain

Ju-on: The Grudge

Studio:
Oz Productions

Director:
Takashi Shimizu

Producers:
Takashige Ichise

Screenwriter:
Takashi Shimizu

Cinematographer:
Tokusho Kikumura

Art Director:
Toshiharu Tokiwa

Composer:
Shiro Sato

Editor:
Nobuyuki Takahashi

Duration:
92 minutes

Cast:
Megumi Okina
Misaki Ito
Misa Uehara

Year:
2002

Synopsis

After the appointed care worker fails to show up for work, volunteer Rika is sent to take care of an old woman who lives in Tokyo's Nerima ward with her son and daughter-in-law. When she arrives, Rika finds her patient alone and the house in disarray. As she sets about her work she is alarmed to discover a small boy sealed into an upstairs wardrobe, along with his cat. Worse still, Rika sees a shadowy black shape leaning over the old woman, apparently sucking the life from her. Unknown to the latest victim, the house in Nerima was previously the scene of a series of brutal murders in which a jealous husband killed his wife and son before apparently committing suicide. The angry spirits of the mother and son are still haunting the house, taking their anger out on anyone foolish enough to enter the house.

Ju-on: The Grudge II

Studio:
Oz Productions

Director:
Takashi Shimizu

Producers:
Takashige Ichise

Synopsis

Pregnant actress Kyoko, best known for starring in horror films, appears in an episode of a TV series about curses, ghosts and super-natural events. The episode is being filmed in the house in Nerima ward, which now has a reputation as a 'haunted house'. Once the shooting is finished, the cast and crew are plagued by a wave of accidents, disappearances and mysterious deaths, including a car wreck that leaves Kyoko's fiancé wheelchair-bound and kills their unborn child. As the director and the actress try to trace the cause of these incidents, Kyoko comes to realzse that she is pregnant once again – but who or what is growing inside her?

Screenwriter:
Takashi Shimizu

Cinematographer:
Tokusho Kikumura

Art Director:
Toshiharu Tokiwa

Composer:
Shiro Sato

Editor:
Nobuyuki Takahashi

Duration:
92 minutes

Cast:
Noriko Sakai
Chiharu Niyama
Kei Horie

Year:
2003

Critique

After the *Ring* films, the most successful contemporary Japanese horror franchise has been the *Ju-on* series. Created by Takashi Shimizu, a former pupil of J-Horror luminary Kiyoshi Kurosawa, the series currently consists of two V-cinema instalments (*Ju-on* and *Ju-on 2*), two theatrically-released feature films (*Ju-on: The Grudge* and *Ju-on: The Grudge 2*), and three lucrative English-language remakes (*The Grudge*, *The Grudge 2* and *The Grudge 3*), with only the direct-to-video *The Grudge 3* not directed by Shimizu himself. The roots of the franchise can be found in two three-minute shorts the director prepared as part of a made-for-TV horror anthology (*Gakko no Kaidan G*, 1998). These shorts introduced Kayako and Toshio, the mother-and-son ghosts that appear in each of the subsequent films. The first full-length instalments, the low-budget, video-released *Ju-on* and *Ju-on 2* (aka *Ju-on: The Curse*), appeared two years later. Produced by *Ring* (1998) producer Takashige Ichise and distributed by Toei Video, with *Ring* scriptwriter Hiroshi Takahashi on board as a creative consultant, the early *Ju-on* films set the template for all the future incarnations of the story. The success of these two prompted the release of the bigger-budgeted, theatrically-released *Ju-on: The Grudge*, eventually leading to the lucrative Sam Raimi-produced Hollywood remakes.

Like many of the American films that influenced Shimizu – *A Nightmare on Elm Street* (1984) and *Friday the 13th* (1980) – the *Ju-on* movies are essentially formulaic. All the key elements – the haunted suburban house in Tokyo; the croaking, creeping ghosts; the viral nature of the curse; the fractured chronology – were present in the very first direct-to-video installment and have altered little over the years. Taking their cues from Freddy Krueger and Jason Voorhees, the 'heroes' of the *Ju-on* franchise are not the succession of attractive if slightly-unmemorable victims (Megumi Okina and Noriko Sakai, for example) that parade through the house, but Kayako and Toshio, the only characters to appear in every film (the murderous husband, played by Takashi Matsuyama, is missing from *Ju-on: The Grudge 2*). There are also a few nods to other famous horror franchises, such as a montage of empty rooms inspired by John Carpenter's *Halloween* (1978) in *Ju-on*, or the maternity ward massacre in *Ju-on: The Grudge 2* in the style of Larry Cohen's *It's Alive* (1974).

While inspired by classic American horror cinema of the 1970s and 1980s, the *Ju-on* films also owe much to contemporary Japanese horror, most obviously Hideo Nakata's *Ring* (1998). Kayako's sinister, jerky movements are a variation on Sadako's shambling gait, while Shiro Sato's score for *Ju-on: The Grudge* and *Ju-on: The Grudge 2* is occasionally reminiscent of Kenji Kawai's atonal soundscapes. Like *Ring*, the *Ju-on* films draw upon Japanese legends and folktales, most obviously in the character of Kayako, a wife brutally murdered by her jealous husband and transformed into an *onry* or Vengeful Spirit, a motif that appears in a great many of Japan's traditional tales. However, Shimizu avoids simply recycling key moments from *Ring*; significantly, he foregoes Nakata's lengthy build-up and carefully unfolding plot in favour of short, high-tension segments. If this approach does not quite add up to *Ring*'s cumulative, devastating impact, it still works, thanks to Shimizu's well-constructed, imaginative scares and his talent for turning prosaic, everyday locations (suburban houses, Japanese-style rooms, apartment buildings, offices) into claustrophobic, terrifying places. Wisely, Shimizu retained the Japanese locations for the first English-language remake, *The Grudge* (2004); the same settings that were commonplace and ordinary to domestic audiences became alien and unfamiliar to Western viewers, enhancing the sense of isolation felt by the expatriate characters. Although it is never allowed to overwhelm the horror, there is a streak of black humour running through the *Ju-on* films, including a mock-*Godfather* scene showing the desolate streets of Nerima, completely deserted but strewn with 'missing person' flyers. With the *Ju-on* series Shimizu achieved a lasting position within the world of contemporary horror. It quickly became one of the most heavily-copied Japanese horror films, resulting in a slew of inferior knock-offs, including the long-running *Ju-rei* series and the lifeless US-Japanese co-production *Apartment 1303* (2007).

Jim Harper

Kwaidan

Kaidan

Studio:
Toho

Director:
Masaki Kobayashi

Producer:
Shigeru Wakatsuki

Screenwriter:
Yoko Mizuki, from Fairy tales retold tales by Lafcadio Hearn

Cinematgrapher:
Yoshio Miyajima

Art Director:
Shigemasa Toda

Composer:
Toru Takemitsu

Duration:
164 minutes

Synopsis

Kwaidan is composed of four short stories of the uncanny spirit world. In the first, a poor samurai leaves his hard-working, loving wife to marry the daughter of a high official and live a more opulent life style. His second wife turns out to be selfish and loveless. Almost immediately he realizes his mistake and, though he longs to return to Kyoto, he finishes his tenure. When he finally returns, he is greeted with love and understanding and at first everything seems well. In the second, an apprentice woodsman is spared from a deadly blizzard by a mysterious and beautiful woman in the snow, who instructs him never to mention what has happened. In the third, a skilled blind musician, living in a temple, is called upon by a mysterious samurai figure to perform a ballad which recounts the ancient battle that ended with the heroic extinction of the Heike Clan. This becomes a nightly ritual until, one night, he is followed by temple servants to his destination – a graveyard. Finally, a story-within-a story is told by a writer who cannot finish his tale of a samurai who sees and then drinks the soul of another samurai in a teacup.

Critique

Somehow the reputation of this beautiful film has withered through near-neglect. This might be because it is generally categorized, not unreasonably, as a horror film. Today, the most highly-manufactured and influential import commodity of a struggling Japanese film industry has become the redundant J-Horror and, after more than four decades of repetitive story lines loosening constraints on violence and advanced special-effects technology, the visual punch-lines of

Cast:
Rentaro Mikuni
Keko Kishi
Tatsuya Nakadai

Year:
1964

Kwaidan, so necessary within the genre, now seem tame, predictable and unconvincing. What is still to be appreciated, however, is the beauty and colour of the stylized images, the startling innovative use of sound, the kabuki and Noh-influenced staging and movements, and the mood and atmosphere of Heian and Tokugawa Japan. The horror genre lends itself to episodic structure, with one of the earliest examples, the British production *Dead of Night* (1945), perhaps still being the best of the bunch. Within the genre format, it is the axiom that becomes a plot device: bad behaviour begets retribution, and this is particularly true in Japanese context. The stories are based on traditional moralistic fairy tales re-told by American and Greek expatriate Lafcadio and, in the first episode, the obvious lapse in judgment is greed. Less obvious is heedlessness in the second story and the taking of a life or soul in the last episode.

Kwaidan is the first film that Kobayashi made in colour and, filmed almost entirely on a soundstage, the colour is often spectacular, with swirls in the backdrops creating not only a sense of other worldliness but forming grand emotional sweeps. The unseen narrator sets the stage and provides background while many long passages without dialogue, often accompanied by only by the effects of Toru Takemitsu, are quite effective. Unfortunately, there are periods that follow which are overly talkative, covering narrative aspects that we have already seen. Another reason that *Kwaidan* might be overlooked is that it lacks the weight of social commentary that is the foundation of the director's best work. Kobayashi has said that *Kwaidan* was not primarily a horror film but a film about the spiritual importance of life. He wanted to make a film that would show the beauty of traditional Japan while extending the limits of stylized film-making. By those self-imposed standards, he has more than succeeded.

Fred Shimizu

The Machine Girl

Kataude mashin gâru

Studio:
Fever Dreams, Nikkatsu

Director:
Noboru Iguchi

Producers:
Yoshinori Chiba
Yoko Hayama
Satoshi Nakamura

Synopsis

The brother and the friend of school girl Ami Hyuga are bullied to death by the son of a yakuza boss. Wanting to understand what transpired and why, Ami confronts the son's gang, killing a number of them before being captured by the yakuza. She escapes whilst clutching the bloody stump of her amputated left arm. Later, fitted with a gatling gun where her left forearm once was, Ami confront the yakuza boss and his underlings.

Critique

The Machine Girl engages with the ramifications of bullying and revenge in a completely extravagant and absurd fashion. Yet it is the element of absurdity which transforms *The Machine Girl* from pure kitsch to a film which actually engages with the outcomes of violence. The film explores the very real practices of bullying which take place

Screenwriter:
Noboru Iguchi

Cinematographer:
Yasutaka Nagano

Composer:
Takashi Nakagawa

Editor:
Kenji Tanabe

Duration:
96 minutes

Cast:
Minase Yashiro
Asami
Ryosuke Kawamura

Year:
2008

not only in Japanese high schools but in many institutions worldwide. Ami's brother and his young friend are constantly tormented by a young yakuza and his gang, ranging from name-calling, beating to ultimately being thrown off a building. While the film is glossed with B-movie effects, laughably-over-the-top violence, and ridiculous dialogue, it uses these techniques in order to demonstrate the preposterousness of the quest for vengeance.

The film's social viewpoint on revenge is demonstrated in one key scene. Following the deaths of some of the members of the gang, Ami and Miki are attacked by ninjas who are literally ripped apart by bullets once Ami has attached a gatling gun to where her forearm once was. While this is a scene of exorbitant violence, the triumphant dynamic changes once Ami and Miki attempt to confront the yakuza boss. Having gone on a killing spree, eliminating the members of the young yakuza's gang, Ami and Miki encounter the 'Super Mourner Gang', which consists of the grieving relatives of the young men that Ami has killed. The cyclical dynamic of revenge killings is readily apparent in this scene when one quest for vengeance encounters another, as both groups have equal cause to engage the other. While the film concludes with the protagonist triumphant, it nevertheless effectively demonstrates the ludicrous barbarism that is associated with a relentless pursuit of vengeance.

Angus McBlane

Marebito

Studio:
Eurospace

Director:
Takashi Shimizu

Producer:
Kenzo Horikoshi

Screenwriter:
Chiaki J.Konaka

Cinematographer:
Tsuakasa Tanabe

Art Director:
Atsuo Hirai

Composer:
Toshiyuki Takine

Editor:
Masahiro Ugajin

Synopsis

Solitary Masuoka has an obsessive interest in filming. Even when not working as a freelance cameraman, he spends his days recording the world around him and views the footage on his computer monitors. One day, he becomes fascinated by a news film in which Furoki appears so afraid of something that he takes his own life, by stabbing himself through the eye. Wanting to encounter this fear, Masuoka retraces Furoki's steps, discovering a labyrinthine underground world beneath Shinjuku station. Here, he talks with the ghost of Furoki before stumbling upon a naked and not-quite-human young woman. After freeing her from her chains, Masuoka takes the mute, feral creature to his apartment, where he christens her 'F'. After receiving eerie phone calls saying F needs to return to the underworld, Masuoka discovers he can only care for the creature by feeding her blood.

Critique

Starring fellow horror-director Shinya Tsukamoto, Shimizu's digital video production is a more challenging and disturbing work than his celebrated *Ju-On* series. Much of this quality is no doubt down to the input of Chiaki J.Konaka, a talented anime scriptwriter who laces the film with echoes of H.P.Lovecraft. In Shimizu's hands, the film builds a tense, disquieting atmosphere, dominated by a growing sense of

Duration:
92 minutes

Cast:
Shinya Tsukamoto
Kazuhiro Nakahara
Tomomi Miyashita

Year:
2004

primordial horror. What distinguishes the film, however, is the unique way in which *Marebito*'s hidden world appears to become accessible to Masuoka through digital technology. Whilst it would be a challenge to reduce the film to a single, coherent philosophy, the fact that *Marebito* is a meta-commentary on digital technology quickly becomes apparent. Here, the digital, rather than analogue, nature of the production is emphasized by constant changes in image quality, as the film incorporates various diegetic camera and video sources. This is motivated by Masuoka's approach to filming, which borders on an obsessive pleasure in surveillance. But if digital recording allows him to review a greater quantity of footage (often simultaneously on several monitors), it also leads to a paranoiac suspicion of what remains unknown or undecipherable, often filled by Masuoka's disturbing fantasies.

The dreamlike atmosphere of the film is particularly evident in underdetermined 'interruptions' into the story world, such as the flashes of the monstrous Deros or mysterious telephone calls. Ultimately it appears as though it is Masuoka's compulsion to go beyond the everyday world that unleashes repressed primal fantasies. The bland normality of Masuoka's encounters with superficial bosses or shop assistants is thus contrasted with his murderous hatred for his wife and his incestuous desire for F/Fumiko, which is finally consummated after Masuoka cuts open his own mouth for a bloody kiss. However, if 'digital paranoia' leads to a desire to go beyond the everyday, the fulfilment of this desire through unmediated access to primal fantasy ultimately destroys Masuoka through unbearable fear. The themes and visual construction of the film work together in a sophisticated manner. The camera often puts the audience in a position of surveillance over Masuoka and, towards the end of the film, the supposedly detached position of the spectator is further put into question by feedback effects interfering with the image track. This makes *Marebito* a complex but rewarding film that transcends the disposable thrills of many J-Horror works.

Christopher Howard

Nightmare Detective

Akumu Tantei

Studio:
Movie-Eye Entertainment,
Kaijyu Theatre

Director:
Shinya Tsukamoto

Synopsis

Having made a name for herself dealing with fraud and white collar crime, detective Keiko Kirishima has transferred to the murder squad in the hope of tackling more serious crime. Her first case involves a young woman who committed suicide, soon followed by more suicides, all of them dying in violent, bloody fashion, apparently in their sleep. After receiving little support from her superior, Keiko tracks down an individual known as the 'Nightmare Detective', who is said to be able to enter a person's dreams. When a junior officer agrees to dial the number and go to sleep, the detective enters his dreams, where he meets Zero, a psychopath using similar powers to murder his victims while they sleep.

Akumu Tantei, 2006. Produced by Kaijyu Theater/Movie-Eye Ent

Producers:

Shinya Tsukamoto
Shinichi Kawahara
Yumiko Takebe

Screenwriter:

Shinya Tsukamoto

Cinematographer:

Shinya Tsukamoto

Art Director:

Shinya Tsukamoto

Composers:

Chu Ishikawa
Tadashi Ishikawa

Editor:

Shinya Tsukamoto

Duration:

106 minutes

Cast:

Ryuhei Matsuda
Hitomi
Masanobu Ando

Year:

2007

Critique

The synopsis reads like another update of Wes Craven's classic *A Nightmare on Elm Street* (1984) but, despite the similarities, *Nightmare Detective* is not simply a copy. One of Japan's most respected and influential directors, Shinya Tsukamoto has made his name with a series of original, challenging and intelligent features – including *Tetsuo: The Iron Man* (1989), *Gemini* (1999) and *A Snake of June* (2002) – but *Nightmare Detective* is his first attempt at 'straight' horror since 1991's entertaining work-for-commission *Hiruko the Goblin* (1990), although genre elements frequently appear in his work. It is also arguably the closest to a mainstream effort that Tsukamoto has come in his entire career, featuring a pop star in her debut appearance and playing to the same crowds who turned out for blandly-commercial fodder like Takashi Miike's *One Missed Call* (2004). The comparison is an apt one since Tsukamoto's film succeeds in many of the areas in which Miike's film fails. Whereas *One Missed Call* looks like the standard post-*Ring* (1998) technophobic horror movie (albeit a slickly made one) and bears few of the hallmarks of its maverick director, *Nightmare Detective* is both mainstream and most definitely a Shinya Tsukamoto film: as well as writing and directing, he also receives production, cinematography, editing and art direction credits, and also stars as Zero, the villain of the piece.

Equally importantly, *Nightmare Detective* is noticeably more effective in horror terms than many of its contemporaries. Tsukamoto stages his violent death scenes in deserted urban locations that seem to reflect the victims' psychological state. His hand-held cameras whirl around the victim as they are hacked apart by Zero's frenzied assaults. At first it is not clear precisely what is attacking them, although Tsukamoto reveals a little more each time. Zero's 'dream monster' becomes more and more deformed and mutilated with each killing, apparently bearing the cuts he inflicts on his earthly body in order to enter his victims' dreams. These sequences are tense and scary as Zero stalks his prey around familiar but eerily-deserted locations, including an underground parking area and a maze of empty concrete roads.

Despite her relative inexperience, pop star Hitomi acquits herself well as the ambitious young detective trying to adjust to the murder squad. Her supercilious chief, well played by Ren Osugi, delights in mocking her squeamishness around corpses and her high-powered dress sense, referring to her as a 'princess'. Full acting honours go to Ryuhei Matsuda, whose excellent performance as the fragile, tormented Kagenuma makes a welcome change from the withdrawn, blank-faced and frequently psychopathic characters he has played in films like *Blue Spring* (2002) and *Love Ghost* (2000). A welcome change from the multitude of ghost stories produced in the wake of *Ring* (1998) and the *Ju-on* series, *Nightmare Detective* is smart, scary and original film.

Jim Harper

Pitfall

Otoshiana

Studio:
Teshigahara Productions, Toho

Director:
Hiroshi Teshigahara

Producer:
Tadashi Oono

Screenwriter:
Kobo Abe

Cinematographer:
Hiroshi Segawa

Art Director:
Masao Yamazaki

Composers:
Toru Takemitsu
Yuji Takahashi
Tadashi Ishikawa

Synopsis

A young man and his son drift from mining job to mining job, doing whatever they can to survive and eking out a meager existence, while a mysterious man in a white suit follows them and takes pictures. They eventually reach what appears to be a deserted ghost town and the only resident that they can find is a woman who runs a candy store and is waiting for word from her lover. The other residents are the ghosts.

Critique

From this initial premise, and using a range of stylistic genre conventions, director Hiroshi Teshigahara builds a film that is, at once, a murder mystery, a tragic tale of human desperation, a harsh criticism of political power and a creepy story about the spirits of the dead. *Pitfall* was Teshigahara's first feature-length film after several documentary shorts, and also the first in a series of four projects on which he collaborated with writer Kobo Abe and composer Toru Takemitsu. His debut feature juggles several themes via its various storylines, with references to the similarity between the survival struggles of humanity and the rest of nature being sprinkled throughout. The comparison between the harsh life of man and that of the creatures found in these desolate landscapes is just one of the many instances of 'doubling' in the film, and actions taken by one character are repeated in some way

Editor:
Fusako Shuzui

Duration:
97 minutes

Cast:
Hisashi Igawa
Sumie Sasaki
Sen Yano

Year:
1962

later on, through another character or animal. Added to this theme is the notion of voyeurism, as the characters watch, and are watched by, others. Teshigahara returned to some of these themes in even greater fashion in his later film *The Face Of Another* (1966), but they still receive fascinating treatment here. Combined with the superb black-and-white cinematography, it is a treat to see how these ideas are visually represented throughout the film.

There are aural wonders present as well. Takemitsu creates a soundtrack filled with sudden and discordant clanging, percussion thumps and tuneless music that sounds like free-form jazz being played on harpsichords and gamelan gongs. The overall sound design of the film also incorporates every small grunt, sigh and shuffle of the characters, making the audience aware of their every move. Since a basic human response to the unknown is fear, the soundtrack creates the perfect atmosphere for the ghost town and the many souls that are travelling through it. *Pitfall*, though not strictly a horror film, must have been an influence on the sound design of more recent works such as Kiyoshi Kurosawa's *Pulse* (2001) and *Cure* (1997), and Takashi Shimizu's *Ju-On: The Grudge* (2003) and *Reincarnation* (2005). The outlook of *Pitfall* might be bleak, but the film satisfies the senses like few other works of the time.

Bob Turnbull

Pulse

Kairo

Studio:
Daiei Eiga

Director:
Kiyoshi Kurosawa

Producer:
Kiyoshi Kurosawa

Screenwriter:
Kiyoshi Kurosawa

Cinematographer:
Junichiro Hayashi

Art Director:
Tomoyuki Maruo

Composer:
Takefumi Haketa

Editor:
Junichi Kikuchi

Synopsis

Two groups of friends both discover that evils spirits are using the internet to enter our world. Michi works at a plant sales company. When one of her co-workers fails to show up for his shift, she goes to his apartment, finding him alive but somewhat despondent. The moment she turns her back, he matter-of-factly grabs a rope and hangs himself. As Michi and the rest of her co-workers struggle to deal with the loss of their friend and the reasons for his suicide, they begin to encounter a ghostly woman who sends each of them into the same state of despair and solitude that the deceased Taguchi was experiencing. It is only a matter of time before Michi discovers the true meaning behind the lurking sprits that are invading our world, infecting it with sadness and solitude.

Critique

Pulse could have been played off like any other *Ring* (1998) inspired J-horror film but, instead, director Kiyoshi Kurosawa does the complete opposite. While some of the crew from *Ring* was involved in *Pulse*, most notably cinematographer Junichiro Hayashi, and it still creates that same feeling of dread that seeps through every frame of film, it does so in very different way. Kurosawa uses incredibly-subtle methods to incite a feeling of terror and isolation. Each location has

Duration:

118 minutes

Cast:

Haruhiko Kato
Kumiko Aso
Koyuki

Year:

2001

its own lighting cue, creating a sense of solitude between each of the characters and their homes, as none of them visually seem the same. It all seems so artificial. Even the natural light seems oddly false and ominous. The only time you get a sense that the lighting is natural is during the opening and the closing of the film, when Michi is aboard the ship of survivors. Because the film deals with the effect technology has on society and how it creates a deep sense of isolation, Kurosawa chooses to shoot the entire film in mostly wide shots, very rarely using close-ups of any kind. It is the environment that is affecting these people, and that is what we see. All these cinematic subtleties are very effective in creating the pervasive atmosphere of doom. It also helps that the sound track is sparse and incredibly creepy, and Kurosawa's use of the decrepit reclamation buildings helps to drive forward the impending sense of doom.

Everything in the film, every decision Kurosawa makes, is driven by the narrative and the theme of isolation. Nothing is superfluous. It all serves a purpose. It also leaves a lot open for interpretation. Unlike most Western horror films, it does not waste time trying to explain everything that is happening. There is no great piece of exposition that nicely sums up the film, no light bulb that goes off inside one of the characters heads as they figure out what exactly is going on. Rather, Kurosawa allows it to be ambiguous, to both the audience and the characters, and it is the sense of not knowing that helps create the dark, creepy atmosphere, and it is this level of interpretation that raises this J-Horror entry to the level of art.

Matthew Hardstaff

Pulse, 2001. Produced by Toho/Magnolia

Ring

Ringu

Studio:
Omega Project

Director:
Hideo Nakata

Producers:
Takashige Ichise
Shinya Kawase
Takenori Sento

Screenwriter:
Hiroshi Takahashi

Cinematographer:
Junichiro Hayashi

Art Director:
Iwao Saito

Composer:
Kenji Kawai

Editor:
Nobuyuki Takahashi

Duration:
91 minutes

Cast:
Nanako Matsushima
Hiroyuki Sanada
Miki Nakatani

Year:
1998

Synopsis

While investigating her teenage niece's mysterious death, journalist Reiko Asakawa discovers that three of her friends died at exactly the same time, and in the same unusual fashion. Following their trail to a holiday cabin where the four of them stayed a week before their deaths, Reiko finds a video tape, apparently watched by her niece and her friends. Although the images on it are apparently meaningless, she connects her discovery to a currently popular urban legend about a tape that kills you seven days after you watch it – unless you can find some way to avoid the curse. Recruiting her intellectual ex-husband, Reiko begins to investigate the tape, convinced it holds the key to her niece's death. Her quest takes on a greater urgency when she wakes up one night to find her six-year-old son sat in front of the television watching the cursed tape, giving her less than seven days to save the life of her son, her ex-husband and herself.

Ring 2

Ringu 2

Studio:
Oz Productions

Director:
Hideo Nakata

Producer:
Takashige Ichise

Screenwriter:
Hiroshi Takahashi

Cinematographer:
Junichiro Hayashi

Art Director:
Iwao Saito

Composer:
Kenji Kawai

Editor:
Nobuyuki Takahashi

Duration:
95 minutes

Cast:
Nanako Matsushima
Hiroyuki Sanada
Miki Nakatani

Year:
1999

Synopsis

Having discovered the body of her lecturer, Mai Takano attempts to uncover the circumstances of his mysterious death. Her first task is to track down his ex-wife Reiko, who called at his apartment on the day he died and has since disappeared, along with their six-year-old son Yoichi. Enlisting the help of another journalist, Mai manages to find the pair, but Reiko is killed soon afterwards. Even more disturbing is the realization that Yoichi has begun to show signs of possessing powerful and destructive psychic abilities, probably as a result of his exposure to the cursed video tape. When a psychiatrist claims that he might be able to help the boy, Mai agrees to cooperate in the hope of removing Yoichi's increasing powers before more fatalities ensue.

Ring 0: Birthday

Ringu 0: Bâsudei

Studio:
Oz Productions

Director:
Norio Tsuruta

Synopsis

Returning to the incidents before her murder, we see Sadako as a young adult, joining a theatre group. When the lead actress in the group's forthcoming performance dies suddenly, the director gives Sadako her role, despite her lack of experience. This obvious favouritism does not endear her to the other performers, who already disliked the strange young woman; ever since she joined the group, a long-haired apparition has been seen by a number of people. Meanwhile a journalist is investigating Sadako's life: her husband died in the ill-fated demonstration of her mother's psychic powers, and she is eager for revenge.

Producers:
Takashige Ichise

Screenwriter:
Hiroshi Takahashi

Cinematographer:
Takahide Shibanushi

Composer:
Shinichiro Ogata

Duration:
99 minutes

Cast:
Yukie Nakama
Seiichi Tanabe
Kumiko Aso

Year:
2000

Critique

Hideo Nakata's *Ring* has often been described as the Japanese *Halloween* (1978), and there is definitely some truth to the assertion. Both are straightforward, low-key horror movies that rely heavily upon atmosphere rather than flashy special effects, over-the-top violence or star power for their effect. They are also exceptionally well-written, hanging a simple and memorable plot upon a set of strong, like-able characters (despite its Japanese origins, *Ring*, like *Halloween* is largely culturally universal, requiring little amendment to fit into other cinematic settings). They were made for budgets that would have Hollywood accountants weeping for joy and became amongst the most profitable films of their day, giving rise to a multitude of official sequels, spin-offs and knock-offs. Like John Carpenter's film, *Ring* has had a profound impact upon its genre, and it is safe to say that with-out it the landscape of contemporary horror would look very different indeed.

Sadako's curse started its life as the smallpox virus, and *Ring*'s original form was Koji Suzuki's 1991 bestseller of the same name. A combination of technophobic horror and medical thriller, the novel was not an immediate success, but its mounting popularity resulted in a made-for-TV adaptation broadcast in 1995. Directed by Chisui Taki-gawa, *Ringu: Kanzenban* stuck fairly closely to Suzuki's story, despite the addition of high levels of gratuitous nudity and a noticeable lack of the chilling atmosphere that characterized Nakata's film. How-ever, *Ringu: Kanzenban* proved to be a hit with Japanese audiences, confirming the commercial potential of the property. A theatrical adaptation was commissioned, with Hideo Nakata appointed director and Hiroshi Takahashi handling the script. Nakata and Takahashi had already collaborated on several projects, most importantly *Ghost Actress* (1996), a 75-minute horror film that featured many of the con-cepts that would be honed to perfection in *Ring*.

In adapting Suzuki's original novel, Nakata and Takahashi removed most of the medical and scientific elements in favour of supernatural occurrences, effectively turning the tale into a contemporary ghost story. The most significant alteration was the depiction of Ryuji's death and Sadako's emergence from the television (in the novel the victims are only found, and their final moments not described). It is a key scene, the culmination of Nakata's steadily building tension, and a moment frequently described as one of the scariest moments in the history of cinematic horror. Essential to *Ring*'s impact is Kenji Kawai's excellent score: a heavily-processed, discordant mix of metallic clang-ing and scraping that adds greatly to the atmosphere of tension and unease. As well as nods to Western horror classics like *The Haunting* (1963), *Poltergeist* (1982) and *Videodrome* (1983), *Ring* also takes inspiration from traditional Japanese folktales: Sadako's appear-ance – long dark hair covering one side of her face, long white gown, a single grotesque eyeball – is informed by depictions of Oiwa, a vengeful spirit (*onryō*) found in one of Japan's most famous legends, the Yotsuya Kaidan.

In an unusual move, *Ring* was released alongside *Spiral* (1998), an adaptation of the second novel in Suzuki's trilogy, directed by

Joji Iida, one of the co-writers of *Ringu: Kanzenban*. Unlike Nakata's film, *Spiral* remained largely faithful to its source material, reinstating many of the elements discarded from Suzuki's novel. The result was a less-than-satisfactory sequel, although that did not stop Fuji Television from broadcasting two spin-off TV series: the first based on *Ring*, the second on *Spiral*. In response to the lukewarm performance of Iida's pseudo-sequel, producer Takashige Ichise hired Nakata and Takahashi to create an 'official' follow-up, while *Spiral* was quietly forgotten. Picking up where the first film finished, *Ring 2* (1999) focused mainly on Yoichi while expanding on a handful of lesser characters. Like many sequels – for example, *Exorcist II: The Heretic* (1977), an acknowledged influence on the film – *Ring 2* was faced with the difficult challenge of continuing an essentially self-contained, simplistic story and, predictably, the results do not match the achievements of *Ring*, despite some interesting ideas and solid performances.

After the difficulties of *Ring 2*, Nakata withdrew from the series, although Takahashi stayed on to script a third film, the prequel *Ring 0: Birthday* (2000), with Norio Tsuruta in the director's chair. Based on one of Koji Suzuki's short stories, *Ring 0* explores the events leading up to Sadako's murder. As with the previous instalment, the film sacrifices the simplicity of the original in favour of a more detailed look at the central character. Unfortunately the need to portray Sadako as both a tragic heroine and a truly evil creature resulted in some unlikely plot contortions that stop *Ring 0* from achieving the same impact as either of its predecessors. Wisely, producer Takashige Ichise brought the series to a close with *Ring 0*, paving the way for the release of Gore Verbinski's English-language remake *The Ring* (2002).

Jim Harper

Suicide Club

Studio:
Omega Project

Director:
Sion Sono

Producers:
Masaya Kawamata
Junichi Tanaka

Screenwriter:
Sion Sono

Cinematographer:
Kazuto Sato

Synopsis

Dozens of schoolgirls throw themselves in front of a high-speed train as it hurtles through the station, drenching the waiting passengers in blood. Soon afterwards, a wave of suicides strikes Japan: schoolchildren jumping off the roofs of their schools, nurses climbing out of open windows, theatre groups killing themselves on stage. At the scene of many of the mass suicides police find hold-alls containing neatly stitched rolls of human skin, apparently removed when the victims were alive. A website seems to be keeping score of the number of deaths but the updates appear *before* the suicides take place. Believing that there is a great conspiracy at work, the police attempt to track down the individual behind the suicides but find themselves inexorably drawn into a web of murder and mutilation.

Art Director:
Yoshihiro Nishimura

Composer:
Tomoki Hasegawa

Editor:
Masahiro Onaga

Duration:
99 minutes

Cast:
Ryo Ishibashi
Masatoshi Nagase
Akaji Maro

Year:
2002

Critique

Even if the rest of it were complete rubbish, Sion Sono's *Suicide Club* would probably be afforded the status of cult classic on the strength of the first ten minutes alone. Although Sono clearly (and understandably) found it difficult to come up with a conclusion worthy of his jaw-dropping, memorable opening, *Suicide Club* is not without interest. Building on the same themes as Kiyoshi Kurosawa's *Cure* (1996) – ordinary people suddenly becoming violent, in this case self-destructive and suicidal – Sono turns the spotlight on the trends and fashions that he suggests sometimes dominate Japanese society, in particular the young. While there is apparently a malign influence at work, probably broadcast through the songs of winsome pre-teen pop group Dessert (although how is never precisely explained), there are plenty of others committing suicide because it is the trendy thing to do at the time.

Although the focus is on policeman Ryo Ishibashi and Masatoshi Nagase, it quickly becomes apparent that, for all their capabilities as detectives, they are out of their depth on this case. Their investigation struggles from the start – they cannot even agree whether a crime has actually been committed, and their attempts to determine a conventional motive are less than successful. The majority of the victims are young people and children but the detectives are hampered by their 'adult' sensibilities and their failure to understand the attitudes and emotions of the victims. The mature Ishibashi has two teenage children who provide him with access to the main conspiracy, through the pop group they watch on TV and the websites they browse, but the knowledge does him little good. He fails to comprehend the nature of the threat that faces him; when he arrives home one day to find his entire family dead, the detective shoots himself. His younger partner begins wearing hoodies and sitting in darkened rooms surfing the Net, but comes no closer to unravelling the mystery.

After a gripping first half, *Suicide Club* begins to lose focus and direction. A lengthy, irritating scene shows a ludicrous glam-rock singer performing in front of kidnap victims in a deserted bowling alley, but it has almost nothing to do with the rest of the film. In the rushed final act, a minor character succeeds where the police could not and traces the suicides back to the kiddie-pop group, but Sono still does not manage to tie all his disparate threads together. This lack of resolution is not *Suicide Club*'s biggest flaw, however; it is Sono's failure to find a single thread to follow throughout the film that does the most damage. Having created a powerful opening and an intriguing set-up, Sono simply does not know where to go next. Nonetheless, *Suicide Club* is a unique film, that is – for the first half at least – truly memorable.

Jim Harper

Versus

Studio:
KSS

Director:
Ryuhei Kitamura

Producers:
Hideo Nishimura

Screenwriter:
Ryuhei Kitamura
Yudai Yamaguchi

Cinematographer:
Takumi Furuya

Composer:
Nobuhiko Morino

Editor:
Shuichi Kakesu

Duration:
120 minutes

Cast:
Tak Sakaguchi
Hideo Sakaki
Chieka Misaka

Year:
2000

Synopsis

After escaping from custody, Prisoner KSC2–303 finds himself on the run from both police and rival yakuza, with another escapee, the Girl, in tow. Unfortunately the forest they take refuge in is actually the 444th portal between the world of the living and the world of the dead, also known as the Forest of Resurrection. As the casualties start to pile up they also start to come back to life, causing problems for both the Prisoner and his enemies. The situation is further complicated by the arrival of the Man, a mysterious individual who seems to be heading for an apocalyptic showdown with Prisoner KSC2–303.

Critique

Despite its low-budget origins, the high-octane zombies-and-martial-arts splatter flick *Versus* has drawn appreciative audiences around the globe and pushed director Ryuhei Kitamura into the front line of Japanese directors. Largely thanks to *Versus*, Kitamura has since taken over Japan's most famous movie franchise with *Godzilla: Final Wars* (2004) and travelled to Hollywood to make his English-language debut with the Clive Barker adaptation *The Midnight Meat Train* (2008). The roots of *Versus* can be found in *Down To Hell*, a 45-minute Super-8 short put together in 1997 by Kitamura and a handful of friends, most of whom acted as both cast and crew, including the director's regular composer Nobuhiko Morino.

As the synopsis suggests, *Versus* is comparatively light on plot, and what there is serves mainly to provide an excuse for the various characters to fight – a lot. This does mean that the film is unlikely to hold much attraction for those with no love for graphic violence and lengthy fight scenes, and even those who do respond favourably might well feel that the two-hour running time is simply too much.

However, Kitamura's technical bravado does go some way to compensating for these flaws and, at its best, *Versus* is a jaw-dropping feast of hyperkinetic delights, equally inspired by the old-school splatter of the *Evil Dead* films, the choreographed combat acrobatics pioneered by John Woo and the bloody-handed martial arts antics of 1970's action star Sonny Chiba. It helps that Kitamura is endlessly inventive when it comes to devising new ways to inflict grievous bodily harm on his combatants, whether it is severed limbs, exploding heads or flying eyeballs. All this mayhem is achieved with a relentless energy that carries the viewer through the occasional slow scenes and glosses over the periodic repetition.

Jim Harper

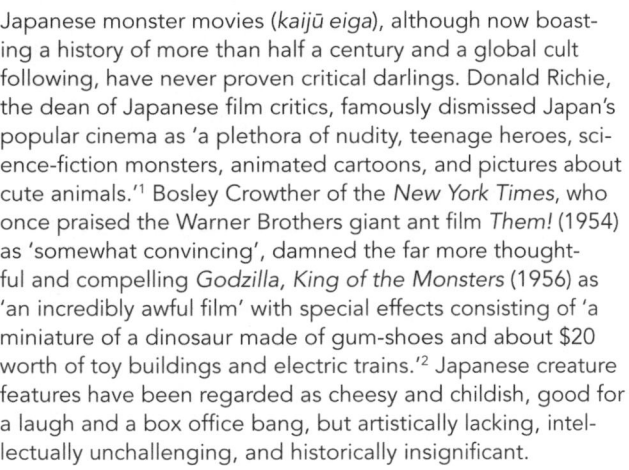

Japanese monster movies (*kaijū eiga*), although now boasting a history of more than half a century and a global cult following, have never proven critical darlings. Donald Richie, the dean of Japanese film critics, famously dismissed Japan's popular cinema as 'a plethora of nudity, teenage heroes, science-fiction monsters, animated cartoons, and pictures about cute animals.'[1] Bosley Crowther of the *New York Times*, who once praised the Warner Brothers giant ant film *Them!* (1954) as 'somewhat convincing', damned the far more thoughtful and compelling *Godzilla, King of the Monsters* (1956) as 'an incredibly awful film' with special effects consisting of 'a miniature of a dinosaur made of gum-shoes and about $20 worth of toy buildings and electric trains.'[2] Japanese creature features have been regarded as cheesy and childish, good for a laugh and a box office bang, but artistically lacking, intellectually unchallenging, and historically insignificant.

Despite such highbrow derision, Japan's cinematic monsters have been an enduring part of Japanese film-making, not to mention the global imaginary, since the 1950s. Toho studios' Godzilla franchise, which featured the irradiated giant saurian in some 28 films from 1954 to 2004, is arguably the longest series in world cinema history. Many of the ingenious creations of the Japanese monster movie genre, like Godzilla, Mothra (a gigantic, colourful lepidopteron), and Gamera (a tusked flying turtle), have become international pop icons. And Japanese monster-on-the-loose films have spawned imitations worldwide: from Britain (*Gorgo*, 1960) and Denmark (*Reptilicus*, 1962) to Korea, both south (*Yongary*, 1967) and north (*Pulgasari*, 1985).

The reputation of Japanese monster movies as playful, lightweight entertainment products designed for youth audiences is, in many respects, deserved. The special effects of

classic Japanese creature features, dubbed 'suitmation' at Toho and based on actors in latex monster costumes moving through miniature model landscapes, contributed to their comic, juvenile appeal. The 'man in a rubber suit' convention, which has persisted in Japanese monster movie-making even in an age of sophisticated CGI, has long been scorned by American studios as primitive, cheap, and unconvincing. Yet the cinematic spectacle of rubbery humanoid monsters, wrestling exuberantly in tiny-scale cities, has proven enduringly and globally popular for its joyous physicality, its resolute difference from Hollywood standards of special effects verisimilitude, and the campy delights of its cheesy production standards.

Such monstrous slapstick notwithstanding, Japanese creature features, especially the Godzilla series, have consistently engaged with issues of contemporary social, political, and moral significance. The original *Gojira* (1954), for example, was a sober and thoughtful reflection on H-bomb tests, atomic age anxiety and Japanese vulnerability in the Cold War world. Made less than a decade after the bombings of Hiroshima and Nagasaki, *Gojira* had a clear agenda: 'Believe it or not', the film's idealistic (and pacifist) director once remarked, 'we naively hoped that the end of Godzilla was going to coincide with the end of nuclear testing.'[3] Even in later decades, as the series targeted a much younger and less politically aware demographic, the Godzilla films continued to address some of the weighty issues confronting Japanese society: corporate corruption, pollution, school bullying, remilitarization, and rising Japanese nationalism, just to name a few. Indeed, the evolution of Japanese creature features has closely reflected changes in Japan's political life, economic fortunes, and culture over the post-war period, tracking the nation's recovery from the ruins of war, to the heady days of the 'miracle economy' growth and optimism, to the more recent experience of bust in the 1970s oil shocks, followed by boom in the overheated 'Bubble Economy' of the 1980s, and the hard landing of the 'Lost Decade' of economic recession, political drift, and social malaise from the 1990s into the new millennium. The Japanese monster movie has remained a vital genre for over fifty years not just because it provides distracting and dependable family entertainment, with the reassuring look of suitmation and the tried-and-true monster-on-the-loose formula, but also because the genre has proven adaptable over time and monster movies have remained closely engaged with developments in Japanese society and the changing fashions of post-war popular culture.

Japanese monster films were initially derivative of Hollywood, appearing in the wake of the 1952 re-release of the classic *King Kong* (1933) and *The Beast from 20,000 Fathoms* (1953), both of which were hits in Japanese theatres. *Gojira*, which launched the creature-feature genre in Japan, boasted a big budget (by local standards of the day), a talented cast and production crew (including director Ishiro Honda and special effects master Tsuburaya Eiji), and a message which hit home with post-war Japanese audiences. The story of a Jurassic survivor, mutated by US H-bomb testing and intent on destroying Tokyo, *Gojira* evoked memories of the war just lost and stirred fears of a nuclear holocaust yet to come. The movie also contained thinly-veiled anti-American sentiments and, in its climax, a therapeutic re-writing of the end of World War II (with Japan coming out on top this time around) that clearly left American distributors uneasy. When the film was edited for release in the United States as *Godzilla, King of the Monsters*, 40 minutes of the most politically-charged footage was left on the cutting-room floor, censored out for sensitive American consumers.

The monster films that followed immediately in the wake of *Gojira* in the 1950s and early 1960s – *Gojira no gyakush* (*Godzilla Raids Again*, aka *Gigantis* the Fire Monster, 1955), Radon (Rodan, 1956), Mothra (1961) – continued to be relatively sombre in tone, reflecting Japan's postwar vulnerability, Cold War tensions, and ongoing nuclear fears. During the 1960s, however, when Godzilla emerged as the leading man of Toho's growing stable of cinematic monsters, Japan's national mood was beginning to change as atomic anxieties faded, economic growth accelerated, and Japanese confidence swelled. Under such circumstances, Godzilla was transformed from a vengeful and implacable threat to Japan into a defender and champion of Japan against legions of other monsters, credulity-stretching aliens, and even residents of a reclusive undersea civilization. In the lighthearted Kingu Kongu tai Gojira ('King Kong vs. Godzilla', 1962), for example, the giant ape (representing America) and Godzilla (representing Japan) battle to a draw at the base of Mount Fuji; in Kaij daisens ('Godzilla vs. Monster Zero', 1965), Godzilla saves Japan from invasion by the scheming Planet X and its resident monster, the three-headed dragon King Ghidorah; and in Godzilla tai Hedora ('Godzilla vs. the Smog Monster', 1971), Godzilla averts environmental catastrophe by besting a giant creature born from the toxic effluvia of Japanese industry. Although Godzilla maintained some of the trappings of its atomic origins – most notably the nuclear ray that shot from its mouth – in the films of the 1960s and beyond, Godzilla's irradiation became more of a gimmick than a chilling warning as the monster was tamed and recast as Japan's hometown superhero.

Hard times in the Japanese film industry during the 1960s also had an impact on monster movies. Suburbanization (that left many potential moviegoers far from downtown cinemas), the proliferation of other leisure options (such as golf) and, above all, the rise of television, combined to drain audiences from Japan's movie theatres. In 1960, Japan boasted 7,500 movie screens nationally; by 1970, this had withered to just 3,000 and movie attendance declined by more than 50 percent. In this new economic reality, movie budgets were slashed, creative and artistic aspirations were sacrificed, and creature features were churned out as cheap and predictable fare for undiscriminating youth audiences. Toho catered to the short attention spans of its audience with bright, colourful and action-packed pictures, with plenty of monster-on-monster combat, humorously-stylized violence, and storylines and characters that appealed to school-aged children. Godzilla was even physically altered to meet the supposed demands of a younger audience: by the 1970s, the king of the monsters had taken on a friendlier, more cartoonish look, with a larger head, bigger eyes, a cute pug nose, and a long, comically-snakelike tail. And when the Gamera franchise was launched in 1965 by Toho's rival Daiei studios as a Godzilla knock-off, the giant turtle protagonist was styled from the start as a 'friend of all children'.

By the twentieth anniversary of the Godzilla series in 1974, the Japanese monster-movie genre appeared to have run its course. Suffering from creative fatigue and dwindling box office receipts – Kingu Kongu tai Gojira had sold 12.6 million tickets in 1962 while Gojira tai Megaro ('Godzilla vs. Megalon', 1973) could not even manage a million a decade later – Toho pulled the plug on creature features after the 1975 release of Mekagojira no gyakushū ('Terror of Mechagodzilla'). After a hiatus of less than a decade, however, the Godzilla series was revived as Toho recognized the significant demand from nostalgic fans, both in Japan and globally, who had grown up watching the king of the monsters. Seven new films were made between 1984 and 1995, all of which featured improved special effects (while still retaining the tradition of suitmation) and a darker, more serious tone, aimed at an adult audience. In 1995's Gojira vs. Desutoroia ('Godzilla vs. Destoroyah'), Toho killed off its leading man, allowing Godzilla to succumb to a spectacularly-fatal internal meltdown, in order to move the series to a new – and potentially much more lucrative – venue. The 1998 *Godzilla*, directed by Roland Emmerich, was an attempt to re-establish the franchise in Hollywood. But the Tristar film, which featured an hysterical and fecund raptor based loosely on Godzilla and slick special effects (but no actor in a latex suit), was a disappointment critically and financially, closing the door on any American-made sequels.

Despite Godzilla's failure in Hollywood, the resurgence in Japanese monster movies was apparent from the mid-1990s. A new trilogy of Gamera films, beginning with *Gamera: Daikaijū kuchu kessen* ('Gamera: Guardian of the Universe', 1995) drew inspiration from Japanese animation and set new standards for special effects, suspense, and innovation in the genre. Toho brought back Godzilla with *Gojira nisen: Mireniamu* ('Godzilla 2000: Millennium', 1999), subsequently releasing a new feature annually in the busy New Year's season. A blockbuster fiftieth-anniversary film, *Gojira: Fainaru uōsu* ('Godzilla: Final Wars'), heavily marketed as featuring, yet again, the death of Godzilla, premiered in Los Angeles in 2004, to mixed reviews and disappointing box office numbers. In the wake of this letdown, the king of the monsters was once more given a pink slip, as Toho decided to place all its Godzilla projects on indefinite hold.

Despite Godzilla's furlough, imaginative and innovative Japanese monster movies continue to be produced, suggesting the continued dynamism and relevance of the genre even in a new millennium. Recent features have been surprisingly diverse in their tone, subject matter, and target markets, running from polished action films aimed at family audiences, like *Chisaki yūsha tachi, Gamera* ('Gamera the Brave', 2006), to more comic, tongue-in-cheek offerings like *Girara no gyakushū: Tōyako samitto kiki ippatsu* ('The Monster X Strikes Back', 2008). A new departure for Japanese creature features is comedian Matsumoto Hitoshi's *Dai-Nipponjin* ('Big Man Japan', 2007), a parodic mockumentary that combines a heartfelt nostalgia for the golden age of Toho science-fiction films with a scathing critique of Japan's cynical and troubled twenty-first-century society. Beyond Japan as well, giant monster films creatively reinterpreting and paying homage to Japanese *kaijū eiga* have seen a renaissance. From South Korea have come *D-War* ('Dragon Wars', 2007), a big-budget (and critically panned) blockbuster, as well as Bong Joon-ho's *Gwoemul* ('The Host', 2006), a subtle, imaginative, and politically-charged film that broke all Korean box office records. With *Cloverfield* (2008), J.J. Abrams' edgy tribute to classic monster movies from Hollywood and Japan, Godzilla has been ingeniously and chillingly recontextualized for a post-9/11 world. And so, as new generations of outsized cinematic creatures follow in Godzilla's capacious footsteps, the Japanese monster movie continues to be redefined, revitalized, and reaffirmed as a touchstone of global popular culture.

Notes

1. Donald Richie, (1990) *Japanese Cinema: An Introduction*, New York: Oxford University Press, p.80.
2. *New York Times*, April 28, 1956.
3. Honda Ishirō quoted in Stuart Galbraith IV, (1998), *Monsters are Attacking Tokyo*, Venice, California: Feral House, p.49.

William M. Tsutsui

Dai-Nipponjin, 2007. Produced by Realproduct/Yoshimoto Kogyo Company

Big Man Japan

Dai-Nipponjin

Studio:
Yoshimoto Kogyo Company

Director:
Hitoshi Matsumoto

Producers:
Akihiro Okamoto
Hiroshi Osaki
Isao Yoshino

Screenwriter:
Hitoshi Matsumoto
Cinematographer:
Hideo Yamamoto

Art Director:
Etsuko Aikou and Yuji Hayashida

Composer:
Towa Tei

Synopsis

A 'documentary' film crew follows Masaru Daisato, a third generation superhero who protects Japan from what he calls 'baddies'. However, Daisato is not the national hero that his ancestors were. Instead, his battles are broadcast live, via the various national news stations, and Daisato's very unflattering figure is instantly seen by millions of people and the often awkward, always destructive, battles are analysed and criticized almost immediately. In an effort to boost his popularity ratings, his manager sells his various oversized body parts to advertisers so that their various brands can be seen during the televized battles, but only a winning streak will really boost his ratings. But can Daisato – a depressed, out-of-shape, anachronistic man – pull himself out of his slump?

Critique

Hitoshi Matsumoto is a comedic giant in Japan. He rose to prominence in the late-1980s as the funny man to Masatoshi Hamada's straight man, with their Manzai comedy act *Downtown*. Manzai is a two-person comedy act which has more of an emphasis on timing and delivery than the actual content of the joke. Hitoshi's identity has become filtered throughout Japanese culture; his love of Tetris and billiards has led to televised competitions. He has been on television

Editor:

Hisaya Shirawa

Duration:

113 minutes

Cast:

Hitoshi Matsumoto
Ua
Ryunosuke Kamiki

Year:

2007

so much, and people have become so used to his comedic style, that it was hard to predict how audiences would react if he changed his act. Before *Dainipponjin* was released, no one was allowed to see it until it opened nationally. It was kept under tight control, and for good reason. Hitoshi Matsumoto had a lot riding on the film, but it opened at number one at the box office, beating Takeshi Kitano's *Glory to the Filmmaker* (2007).

Dainipponjin is Hitoshi Matsumoto channelling Christopher Guest. While the material lends itself to some truly outrageous Kaiju battles, this is really not what the film is about. Daisato spends most of his time alone, depressed, in his small, miserable home with his stray cat, and this is what Hitoshi decides to capture: a mockumentary about a man who hates his job, and who is looked down upon by citizens of the city, and even his own family. The film is quiet and subtle. Daisato has been beaten so much psychologically, that he is struggling to be a man. We follow Daisato through his miserable, isolated existence, which is occasionally broken up with an insanely-outlandish battle with a giant creature. *Dainipponjin* is not a laugh-out-loud comedy, but it is smart, touching and subtly incredible.

Matthew Hardstaff

Gamera the Invincible

Daikaijû Gamera

Studio:

Daiei

Director:

Noraiki Yuasa

Producers:

Hidemasa Nagata
Yonejiro Saito
Masaichi Nagata

Screenwriters:

Nisan Takahashi, Yonejiro Saito

Cinematographer:

Nobuo Munekawa

Composer:

Artie Butler

Editor:

Tatsuji Nakashizu

Synopsis

A Soviet bomber carrying atomic weapons is shot down by the American military, and crashes down in the barren ice plains or the Arctic Circle. The atomic explosion which results from the crash serves to revive the prehistoric turtle Gamera. Understandably annoyed about being so rudely awakened after a long rest of 7,000 years, Gamera proceeds to travel to Japan and to destroy major landmarks, while the Japanese government brings together a team of scientists and enlists the assistance of international military power to stop Gamera from bringing an abrupt end to civilization as we know it. The scientists believe they have succeeded in their mission when they use an explosion to knock Gamera on his back, but when the monster reveals that it can fly, a new plan must be devised.

Critique

Daiei intended *Gamera* to compete with the massively-successful *Godzilla* series, which was produced by rival studio Toho, but had much lower technical and artistic aspirations for their own creature franchise. Ishiro Honda's *Godzilla* (1954) had served as a precautionary message about the dangers of nuclear power, but *Gamera* largely ignores such issues. Instead, this occasionally amusing cash-in offers a simple race-against-time scenario, and an overall tone more suited to young audiences, as exemplified by the sub-plot involving Toshio, a young boy who is sympathetic to Gamera, and a theme tune which is actually quite catchy, although this may be because the lyrics consist

Duration:

80 minutes

Cast:

Eiji Funakoshi
Harumi Kiritachi
Junichiro Yamashiko

Year:

1965

of the repetition of the monster's name. *Godzilla* was an ambitious production which sought to ground the monster mayhem within a recognizable social-political reality by creating credible sets and impressive visual effects, and offering a convincingly-jaded scientist in the character of Dr. Serizawa-hakase, but the producers of *Gamera* were content to deliver a briskly-paced B-movie in which some unremarkable set pieces are glued together by a hole-ridden plot and dramatically stilted exposition. The scenes set in the arctic – and some of the military footage – seems to come from stock and, unfortunately, the same can also be said of the characters: a forgettable mix of commanders, scientists, innocent bystanders, and a lonely boy who believes that Gamera has been 'misunderstood'. After devouring his way through fuel reserves and oil refineries, Gamera is baited into a rocket bound for Mars and banished to outer space, receiving the surprisingly sentimental send off, 'Sayonora, Gamera!'

Although *Gamera* would be the first film in a long-running series, comprised of official sequels and re-boots, it also represented the end of an era in that it was the last monster movie to be filmed in black and white – a technical decision that was necessitated by the use of stock footage. While the series has gained a cult following outside Japan, the first film was the only instalment to be released theatrically in the United States, with other entries being screened on television. This review of *Gamera* refers to the international version released by World Entertainment Corporation and Harris Associates, which added new footage of American actors, and featured a wide shot of Gamera attacking the nuclear reactor which was not seen in the original Japanese version.

John Berra

Godzilla

Gojira

Studio:

Toho Company

Director:

Ishiro Honda

Producer:

Tomoyuki Tanaka

Screenwriters:

Ishiro Honda
Takeo Murata
Shigeru Kayama (story)

Synopsis

After receiving several distress calls from sinking ships around Japan, a group of scientists are dispatched to an island close to the area where the incidents took place. It is here they learn about Gojira, a monster god, feared by the island's fisherman. When the fishing grows scarce, they blame the angry Gojira, and sacrifice a female to appease his fury. One fateful night, a storm slams the island, the thunder vibrating the very ground, houses collapse and the scientist's helicopter is destroyed. The next morning they discover a giant footprint and that the ground is highly radioactive. Then, beyond the cliffs of the island, a large creature appears, sending out a primitive roar before diving back into the ocean. Upon their return to the mainland, the scientists try to convince the sceptical public of what they saw. It is not until this creature, now known by all as Gojira, tramples the shores of Japan that people heed their warning.

Cinematographer:
Masao Tamai

Art Directors:
Satoshi Chuko
Takeo Kita

Composer:
Akira Ifukube

Editor:
Kazuji Taira (as Yasunobu Taira)

Duration:
98 minutes

Cast:
Akira Takarada
Momoko Kochi
Takashi Shimura

Year:
1954

Critique

The *Godzilla* of today is not the *Gojira* that Ishiro Honda had envisioned. The *Godzilla* of today is nothing more than a pop icon, used to make flashy, entertaining fare to put smiles on our faces. Not that there is anything wrong with that, but Honda's *Godzilla* was a monster god in every respect. He was meant to inspire fear. Honda was a close acquaintance with Kurosawa, even assisting him on such films as *Ran* (1985) and *Dreams* (1990), and he was also a man who wanted to make films with meaning and conscience. While the bastardized American version of *Godzilla*, featuring Raymond Burr, had all evidence of a social conscience removed, *Godzilla /Gojira* was a film of protest.

It is fairly evident that Gojira himself is a metaphor for the atomic bomb. He is highly radioactive, and his devastation of Tokyo is representative of the nuclear attacks on Hiroshima and Nagasaki but slow and more drawn out. The attack is spectacular, and inventive in every aspect of its construction. It is also brutal and horrific. Families are killed, with mothers covering their children's eyes as Gojira sends them into the next life. It is shocking and heart-wrenching, and the aftermath is even worse. The survivors develop radiation sickness and, as with the aftermaths of Hiroshima and Nagasaki, they are permanently disfigured. Beyond the political and anti-nuclear message of *Godzilla* is also an expertly-crafted film. *Godzilla* is poetic and lyrical in its construction, dwelling on the destruction and aftermath of Gojira's attack. It is classic Japanese film-making and it is a shame that the creature *Godzilla* developed into is not at all a reflection of what Honda set out to create.

Matthew Hardstaff

Godzilla: Final Wars

Gojira: Fainaru uôzu

Studio:
Toho

Director:
Ryuhei Kitamura

Screenwriters:
Ryuhei Kitamura
Isao Kiriyama

Synopsis

Godzilla is buried in the Antarctic ice by blasts delivered from the *Goten*, a submarine helmed by a mustachioed side of beef named Captain Gordon. To guard against this sort of monster eruption, we learn, the United Nations has formed the Earth Defence Force, which has developed special monster-fighting technology. In the EDF vanguard is the M-Organization, an elite unit of mutants with superhuman fighting skills. Among the best of the unit's best are Shinichi Ozaki and arch-rival Kazama. Monsters start springing up in Shanghai, Sydney, Paris, New York and other corners of the globe. Godzilla reappears as an unlikely ally in humanity's battle with the aliens.

Critique

Godzilla: Final Wars, was Ryuhei Kitamura's send-off to Godzilla, who went into retirement in 2004 after a 50-year run. The film is like one of those adulatory documentaries dedicated to blues or rock or R&B

Producer:
Shogo Tomiyama

Cinematographer:
Takumi Furuya

Art Director:
Deborah Riley

Special Effects:
Eiichi Asada

Composers:
Keith Emerson
Nobuhiko Morino
Daisuke Yano

Duration:
110 minsutes

Cast:
Don Frye
Masahiro Matsuoka
Kane Kosugi

Year:
2004

greats. The old guys can still play the notes and rock the house, we see, but now they are really in the nostalgia business. A once-time wunderkind with a gift for action, Kitamura is the master of the cool move and the eye-popping fight sequence – as seen in his *Versus* (2000) and *Azumi* (2003) – and he uses his skills to the full in *Final Wars*. He is also a pastiche artist whose assembly of the best bits from the 27 past Godzilla movies gives fans the shocks of recognition that they are paying for, with more style and flair than they are used to. With an ancient 'TohoScope' banner, he even references the Shaw Brothers' tribute that Quentin Tarantino slipped into the opening credits of *Kill Bill Vol. 1.* (2003).

Kitamura also tries to rope in non-fans (or former fans who grew tired of the corny effects and absurd stories soon after their tenth birthdays) with self-referential humour, formerly verboten in the Godzilla oeuvre. (One of the funnier bits is a TV-panel discussion with a well-known UFO crank and sceptic. with the crank winning the argument.) Mostly, though, he plays down the middle, while providing meticulous 'fan service', including cameos from such series veterans as Kumi Mizuno, Kenji Sahara and Akira Takarada (the last two being cast members of the original 1954 film). This is no doubt what series producer Shogo Tomiyama wanted, but those expecting a fresh, hip, post-millennial Godzilla movie will be disappointed.

As with so much of Kitamura's work, *Final Wars* is less an integrated film than a series of gonzo action-sequences that, after the initial rush, feel very much the same. Kitamura does not filter this material through his own sensibility, as Tarantino did with Asian B-movies in *Kill Bill*, instead assembling it like a club mix of Motown tunes, all with the same hammering beat. Some fans will dance, while others will reject *Final Wars* as a last desecration. But given that, throughout its existence, the series has latched onto new trends, if not quite technologies (Big G always being played by a man in a rubber suit), this latest – and perhaps last entry – is business as usual.

Mark Schilling

Gunhed

Studio:
Toho, Sunrise, Bandai, Kadokawa Shoten and Imagica

Director:
Masato Harada

Screenwriters:
Masato Harada
Jim Bannon

Synopsis

The setting: an artificial island – a dimly lit jungle of pipes, beams, and industrial junk – where a mad supercomputer reigns. The island's evil genius is the Biodroid: a powerful 'living robot' programmed to do the computer's dirty work, including the killing of unwanted intruders. The intruders come anyway and meet sudden, horrible ends. Two, however, survive: an ex-pilot named Brooklyn who has landed on the island with a gang of cut-throat treasure hunters (the treasure in this case being computer chips), and a female security officer named Nim, who has arrived with her elite unit – the Texas Air Rangers – in pursuit of the renegade Biodroid.

Producers:
Tomoyuki Tanaka
Eiji Yamaura
Yoshishige Shimatani
Tetsuhisa Yamada

Cinematographer:
Junichi Fujisawa

Art Director:
Fumio Ogawa

Composer:
Toshiyuki Honda

Editor:
Yoshitami Kuroiwa

Duration:
100 minutes

Cast:
Masahiro Takashima
Brenda Bakke
James Brewster Thompson

Year:
1989

Critique

In *Gunhed*, writer-director Masato Harada has exploited a Hollywood trend without understanding its roots. The trend in question began with *Star Wars* (1977), George Lucas's paean to the sci-fi of his youth. The film spawned a host of successors in a variety of modes and moods, from the jack-in-the-box horror of *Alien* (1979) to the twenty-first-century angst of *Blade Runner* (1982), but they retained the *Star Wars* look of grubby realism and its assumption – expressed most vividly in the character of Han Solo – that our distant descendants will still be recognizably, even degenerately, human. Shiny, futuristic cities on the hill are conspicuously absent in these films. In some, such as *Robocop* (1987), the outlook is frankly pessimistic, with Hobbes' war of all against all become a grim reality.

The parallels between *Gunhed* and *Alien* are especially obvious. Harada tries to create the same feeling of edgy camaraderie and the same atmosphere of gut-wrenching suspense, but falls short of his model. His failure is both technical and cultural and, given the poorly structured story line, probably inevitable. Brooklyn needs only about fifteen minutes of screen time to discover the true nature of the treasure hunters and to kill most of them. These action scenes, presented in a choppily-edited blur, make it hard to tell who is doing what to whom. This confusion is compounded by the dialogue. The American actors speak English in hard-boiled clichés, and the Japanese actors speak in standard Japanese. As a consequence, the characters often appear to be talking at, but not with, each other – an impression strengthened when they mispronounce phrases in each other's languages.

In not only its English but its look, such as the treasure hunters' B-17 and their leader's World War II-vintage flight cap, *Gunhed* tries to evoke a *Star-Wars*-like nostalgia for the movie past, but it is an alien past, imperfectly understood. Lucas made his take-off of old serials work because he had grown up with the material, had real affection for it and understood its limitations. Harada either uses his American influences trivially – as a design motif – or in oddball earnest. Before the penultimate battle the hero's robot delivers a rousing speech on the glories of the old Brooklyn Dodgers. The effect is jarring and sad, like spotting an old Armed-Forces-edition paperback, alone and out of place, in a Jimbocho used-book bin. Even sadder, however, is the acting of Brenda Bakke, yet another minimally talented gaijin carrying too-large a dramatic load in a Japanese film. Cast as a superwoman, she comes across as a supremely-bored waitress. Her partner in adventure, Masahiro Takashima, is an easygoing hunk who has neither the intensity nor charisma that the part requires. The real star of the movie is Gunhed – the fighter robot that Takashima's Brooklyn uses to defeat the forces of evil. When he appears in his clanking splendour, the movie's real inspiration becomes apparent – the good-robot-versus-bad-robot TV shows that Japanese boys teethe on. If I were ten years old, I might daydream through the dull parts, sit enthralled through the climactic scenes and then rush out to buy my very own Gunhed (sold, thoughtfully, by Bandai). Not being ten, I simply suffered – until the noise stopped.

Mark Schilling

Mothra, 1962. Produced by Toho

Mothra

Mosura

Studio:
Toho

Director:
Ishiro Honda

Producer:
Tomoyuki Tanaka

Synopsis

When a ship sinks in the Ocean, the survivors find themselves stranded on the island of Beru, a site that is being used for atomic bomb testing. After they are rescued, tests reveal that they have not been affected by radiation poisoning, probably because of a special 'juice' they were given by the natives of the island. The government sends an expedition team to explore Beru, with one scientist almost being killed by hostile plant-life only to be saved by two little fairies. When an unscrupulous member of the team captures the two girls and takes them back to civilization, with the intention of putting them in a show for his own financial gain, Mothra, a giant moth, awakens and travels to the city to rescue the fairies and return them to their natural environment of Beru.

Critique

As he was responsible for the original *Godzilla* (1954), director Ishiro Honda could orchestrate this kind of monster mayhem in his sleep and although *Mothra* contains plenty of destruction, as the giant moth lays waste to a miniature metropolis, it is not his most inspired addition to the genre. The film suffers from a comparatively-lengthy preamble as the survivors explore the island and meet the natives, while Mothra is not the most imposing beast to tread on plastic vehicles and building as she only attacks when provoked, and is generally lacking in killer instinct. This can be seen as the basis for an ecological, as opposed to nuclear, subtext, with Honda pointing his finger of blame at 'Rolithica', a fictitious nation which is obviously intended to represent the United States.

As with Honda's more enjoyable *Rodan* (1956), the characters are derived from the American science-fiction films of the period, with the principals including a journalist with a nose for a good story, his plucky female photographer assistant, and a nervous linguist who, implausibly, also doubles as a scientist whenever events require some exposition or explanation. However, the real star of the show is Mothra herself, and she is perhaps the most sympathetic monster in the Toho canon as her intention is to preserve her island and rescue to the abducted fairies, with her destruction of the city being an unfortunate side-effect of her well-intentioned mission. In this sense, *Mothra* is less a monster movie than an eco-fable, with the bright cinematography and child-friendly tone suggesting that it may have been more effective as an animated feature. At the risk of ruining the film for first-time viewers, it is interesting to note that *Mothra* was the first *kaiju eiga* film in which the monster does not get killed at the end and, despite its technical shortcomings, the titular monster went on to feature in a number of *Godzilla* movies, their enduring association beginning with *Godzilla vs. Mothra* (1964).

John Berra

Rodan

Sora no daikaijû Radon

Studio:
Toho

Director:
Ishiro Honda

Special Effects:
Eiji Tsuburaya

Synopsis

On the island of Kitamatsu, a mining town at the base of Mt. Aso becomes the epicentre of a series of bizarre events – a mining tunnel starts to take in water and a miner goes missing. The miner is found dead, floating at the bottom of the flooded tunnel. The death is investigated as murder but eventually more miners go missing, including the murder suspect. A giant caterpillar-like creature, dubbed a meganulon, attacks the village and is revealed to be the true killer. The engineer and fellow miners track the gargantuan insect back through the mines and into a massive cave within the mountain: the nest of a prehistoric pteranodon called Rodan. Sightings of Rodan are reported all over the world, and soon the great beast terrorizes the Japanese

Producer:
Tomoyuki Tanaka

Screenwriters:
Takeshi Kimura
Takeo Murata, based on a story
by Takashi Kuronuma

Cinematographer:
Isamu Ashida

Art Director:
Akira Watanabe

Composer:
Akira Ifukube

Editor:
Koichi Iwashita

Duration:
82 minutes

Cast:
Kenji Sahara
Yumi Shirakawa
Akihiko Hirata

Year:
1956

city of Saseabo, with his supersonic shock waves and destructive wing blasts, and things become worse when a second bird joins the apocalyptic jubilee.

Critique

When Toho Studios decided to keep their more infamous monster creation, Godzilla, in the retirement closet after the rushed, lacklustre sequel *Godzilla Raids Again* (1955) failed to generate much box office excitement, *Rodan* was given the green light to become Japan's first colour *kaiju eiga*. But unlike *Godzilla*'s dour mood and earnest plea for nuclear disarmament, director Ishiro Honda's take on *Rodan* adheres more to overt horror elements and then-popular Hollywood science-fiction films like *Them!* (1954), as exemplified by the opening scenes with the missing miners and the attack of the meganulon on the village. The scenes concerning the search for the missing miners are effectively suspenseful and even generate a sinister, albeit brief, surrealistic power when mining engineer Shigeru Kawamura (Kenji Sahara) becomes trapped in the mammoth cave to behold the hatching of Rodan, while the creepy-crawly caterpillars scurry away from their imminent devouring.

However, the film's true strength, and its value as an important *kaiju eiga*, is predicated on its marvellous scenes of the massive havoc waged by the tremendous birds, commandeered by the legendary special effects director Eiji Tsuburaya, and these moments of mayhem are some of the finest in Tsuburaya's long career, as well as Honda's. But while the requisite spectacular destruction is impressive, it is Honda's shift toward the melancholic in the film's final moments that leaves us with an unexpected moment of strangeness when one of the pteranodons nosedives into the crater of the erupting volcano to sacrifice itself while its mate perishes in the lava. Only moments in the historical *kaiju eiga Daimajin* (1966) and the ending of *Yokai Monsters:*

Rodan The Flying Monster, 1956. Produced by Toho

Spook Warfare (1968), both produced by the rival Daiei Studios, equal or surpass *Rodan* in that regard. Like his more infamous and profitable partner in chaos, Godzilla, Rodan would be resurrected in the 1960s to battle it out with a gaggle of other Toho monsters, with each encounter more and more resembling a pro-wrestling match instead of an apocalyptic parable. None of these punch-ups would feature Rodan as the star attraction, though, and his brief appearances would be relegated to the supporting slot in films such as *Ghidorah, the Three-Headed Monster* (1964) and *Destroy All Monsters* (1968).

Derek Hill

Tetsuo: The Iron Man

Tetsuo

Studio:
Sen, Kaijyu Theater, K2 Spirit, JHV

Director:
Shinya Tsukamoto

Producer:
Shinya Tsukamoto

Screenwriter:
Shinya Tsukamoto

Cinematographers:
Kei Fujiwara
Shinya Tsukamoto

Art Director:
Shinya Tsukamoto

Composer:
Chu Ishikawa

Editor:
Shinya Tsukamoto

Duration:
67 minutes

Cast:
Tomorowo Taguchi
Kei Fujiwara
Shinya Tsukamoto

Year:
1989

Synopsis

A Japanese salaryman accidently strikes another man with his car. Unfortunately, the bystander is a 'metal fetishist', and the salaryman is 'infected' by metal and mechanic growths soon begin to develop all over his body. As the salaryman struggles to cope with the process of becoming a cyborg, he decides to track down his tormentor and confront him.

Tetsuo 2: Body Hammer

Tetsuo II

Studio:
Kaijyu Theater

Director:
Shinya Tsukamoto

Producer:
Shinya Tsukamoto

Screenwriter:
Shinya Tsukamoto

Cinematographers:
Fumikazu Oda
Shinya Tsukamoto
Katsunori Yokoyama

Art Director:
Shinya Tsukamoto

Composer:
Chu Ishikawa

Editor:
Shinya Tsukamoto

Duration:
83 minutes

Cast:
Tomorowo Taguchi
Shinya Tsukamoto

Year:
1992

Synopsis

A Japanese salaryman is attacked and injected with something as his son is kidnapped whilst on an outing with the family. As the salaryman chases after the kidnappers he beings to sprout mechanical growths, which eventually turn into weaponry. The salaryman is unable to save his child as he loses control of himself and beings to fire the weaponry, which has grown from his chest and arms when confronting the kidnappers. Later, the salaryman is captured by the group that originally attacked him. It becomes apparent that the salaryman and the leader of the group are brothers and were raised to be human-mechanical weapons by their father. Eventually, the two brothers face each other in an ultimate confrontation to see who has the greater 'will-to-kill.'

Critique

By opening both films with scenes of urban decay and degradation, writer-director Shinya Tsukamoto enacts a meditation on the technological encroachment into the everyday and the inevitability of the symbiosis of the organic and the technological. Decay, trash, industry and rust all feature prominently in both films and serve as an all-encompassing backdrop which heralds the ultimate symbiotic relationship between humanity and technology as one which sits between the poles of the technophilic and the technophobic. Tsukamoto presents themes and imagery that simultaneously valorize and deny each pole, never making it clear which side these films fall on. However, this enables Tsukamoto to create a far more nuanced take on technology than many contemporary Western films, such as *The Terminator* franchise, which discuss similar issues.

Utilizing a heavy dose of cyberpunk imagery, *Tetsuo 2* contains the requisite mirror-shaded villains, the technological encroachment into the everyday being presented far more appropriately in the first film. As the salaryman's body becomes covered in 'junked' technology, his daily routine becomes difficult to maintain; he is unable to shave as technological growths begin to appear on his face and, in perhaps the most disturbing scene, he is unable to have sex with his girlfriend as his penis has turned into a pneumatic drill, which ultimately kills her. This cyborg is not the comparatively clean-cut cyborg that is found in *Ghost in the Shell* (1995) as the salaryman is comprised of machine junk, the leftover waste of daily technology.

Technology in these films does not purely mediate on the interactions between individual human actors but rather becomes the site of interaction. If the cyborg transformation in *Tetsuo* is one of embracing machine 'junk', then it must be asked what remains of human 'junk'. *Tetsuo 2* tackles this issue to a much greater degree, whilst enacting a far more conventional plotline and obviously taking advantage of a bigger production budget. The second film closely explores the direct role that humanity has in relation to technology and technology is here utilized in relation to human will, specifically the will to kill. The machine growths are less viral in the central characters, and are imbued with the direct will of a human actor as Homo faber, with technology becoming value-neutral, standing by in reserve until it is held by a human agent. The full cyborgification of the salaryman in *Tetsuo 2* is directly tied to his losing control of his emotions, and becoming a being of pure rage. Technology does not encroach into the everyday of human interactions to the extent that it does in the first film; rather, it is the human factor which encroaches into the technological.

While possessing a setting of decay and rust can be viewed as leaning distinctly towards the pole of the technophobic, the *Tetsuo* films undercut this presentation by uniting the two lead characters, both cyborgs, in their finales. The process of uniting flesh and metal is one of deep psychological and bodily trauma for the salarymen and the finished product, when united with his antagonist, is one which becomes the harbinger of a new epoch; his new entity is able to more fully grasp and engage with the world as it is, revelling in the industrial degradation of the urban sprawl, and ultimately becoming one with it. This distinctly phallic entity enacts a representation of the posthuman, in which no matter what the classification, machine, human or otherwise, all entities are marked by technology.

Angus McBlane

Tokyo Gore Police

Tôkyô zankoku keisatsu

Studio:
Fever Dreams, Nikkatsu

Director:
Yoshihiro Nishimura

Producers:
Yoshinori Chiba
Yoko Hayama
Satoshi Nakamura

Screenwriters:
Kengo Kaji
Sayako Nakoshi
Yoshihiro Nishimura

Cinematographer:
Shu G. Momose

Art Director:
Nori Fukuda

Synopsis

It is sometime in the near future, and Japan's police force has been transformed into a corporation. Ruka is a cop who specializes in hunting down and killing 'engineers': mutants who grow biological weaponry out of any wound or injury. The only way to kill them is to remove a key-like tumour that is found somewhere in their body. Ruka is tortured by the suicide of her mother and the murder of her father, who was a just and righteous police officer opposed to the corporatization of the police force, and she pursues his killer with relentless focus, epitomizing the alienation of the Japanese citizen, whose only connection to others is through violence.

Critique

Over the last few years, there has been a growing trend in Japanese cinema, as well as other Asian film industries, to create films with a certain international audience in mind. While the trend for overseas consumption has existed since the success of Akira Kurosawa, it has always been one with an emphasis on artistic integrity, creating films that would be popular with high-brow audiences. The new trend, however, is to create genre films that will attract the obsessive cult fans. Takashi Miike was one of the forerunners of this new movement, after the success of films like *Audition* (1999) and *Dead or Alive* (1999). Tokyo Shock and Fever Dreams recently began producing Japanese films aimed specifically at Western audiences, despite the fact that they have little impact in their native country. The first of

Composer:

Koh Nakagawa

Editor:

Yoshihiro Nishimura

Duration:

110 minutes

Cast:

Eihi Shiina
Itsuji Itao
Yukihide Benny

Year:

2008

these was the bloody, tongue-in-cheek revenge tale *The Machine Girl* (2008) and the follow-up, *Tokyo Gore Police*, takes the splatter from the earlier films and blends it with social commentary, producing a surreal, subversive, blood bath.Although the plot could be played for laughs, director and co-screenwriter Yoshihiro Nishimura, the special effects mastermind behind *The Machine Girl* as well as most of Sion Sono's films, plays it dead serious. He adapts his short film *Anatomnia Extinction* (1995) into a Japanese hybrid of *Robocop* (1987), *Blade Runner* (1982), and *Videodrome* (1983). But to say it is merely an amalgamation of other films would not do it justice. With help from co-screenwriter Kengo Kaji, they drive much of their social commentary and satire with Verhoeven-inspired commercials, some directed by none other than *The Machine Girl* maestro Noboru Iguchi. There is no wink or nod to the audience in this film.

While the film has obvious Western influences and is primarily aimed at a Western audience, it remains uniquely Japanese. Nishimura injects an Edogawa Rampo-esqe subversive spirit into the film, from the bizarre, urinating, living chair to the strange, sadomasochistic perversions of the head engineer, known simply as the Key Man. Even though there are enough film references to make even the most jaded genre fans smile, great action choreography by Tak Sakaguchi transforms what could have been a psychedelic splatterfest into a brilliant, anarchistic tale of the corporatization of the modern urban landscape, whilst also pushing the very limits of what is deemed acceptable for celluloid. Penis guns, acid-squirting breasts, living chainsaw arms and real-life maggot consumption are just a few of the delights awaiting the viewer. Verhoeven may have pushed the limits of American cinema when *Robocop* received the X-rating, but Nishimura pushes that envelope through the roof. It may be hard for most to see past the vast amounts of gore that, on first viewing, will seem pointless and excessive but, if you can, you will experience a rewarding and original film filled with blood-soaked mayhem that, at the centre of it all, still has a heart and a soul.

Matthew Hardstaff

Virus

Fukkatsu no Hi

Studio:
Haruki Kadokawa Office

Director:
Kinji Fukasaku

Producer:
Haruki Kadokawa

Screenwriters:
KojiTakada
Kinji Fukasaku
Gregory Knapp

Cinematographer:
Daisaku Kimura

Art Director:
Yoshinaga Yokoo

Composers:
Kentaro Haneda
Teo Macero

Editors:
Akira Suzuki
Pieter Hubbard (international version)

Duration:
156 minutes (US: 108 minutes)

Cast:
Masao Kusakari
George Kennedy
Olivia Hussey

Year:
1980

Synopsis

A submarine emerges in the Tokyo bay and sends out a drone that broadcasts pictures of a city covered with rotting corpses. A flashback reveals what led to the catastrophe: a deadly virus stolen from an East German lab, accidentally released, begins to eradicate the population all over the globe. The President of the United States learns that the virus was originally developed by the American military and, with no antidote available, humanity is doomed. Eventually, only 800 international scientists stationed in Antarctica are spared as the virus is not active in sub-zero temperatures. The Japanese seismologist Yoshizumi is amongst them, and he joins this new community of scientists in grappling with uneasy questions, such as how to organize social life with only eight women remaining, and how to develop a vaccine. Yoshizumi, who falls in love with the Norwegian scientist Marit, finds that an earthquake is imminent in the Washington area and that this could trigger an automatic missile attack against the Soviet Union, whose response missiles are also aimed at the Antarctic station. A submarine departs with the goal of bringing the uneasy pairing of Major Carter and Yoshizumi to Washington to dismantle the missile system in a desperate race against time.

Critique

Virus was the highest-budgeted Japanese film of its era, and its international ambitions would inadvertently change the business strategy of its legendary producer Haruki Kadokawa for many years to come. In the late-1970s the flamboyant Kadokawa, heir to a publishing company, shook up the industry by introducing multimedia marketing techniques and deftly using the remains of the disintegrating studio system for his blockbuster productions. At a time when Japanese audiences saw domestic films as being divided into old-fashioned entertainment and sexploitation, the populist Kadokawa marketed films as being cool and contemporary, although his critics insisted that they were simply shallow. Kadokawa had already used his flair for foreign locations with *Proof of the Man* (1977), the first Japanese film to be partially shot in New York, and had minor overseas success with *G.I. Samurai* (1979). With budgets for his films skyrocketing, *Virus* was an attempt to tap into foreign markets and it utilized a global theme, predominantly foreign actors, and a genre that seemed to be internationally successful but had actually overstayed its welcome. Like most Kadokawa films, it was based on a book that the producer had previously published: a 1964 novel by Sakyo Komatsu, who also authored the Japanese disaster epic, *Japan Sinks*. An American scriptwriter was hired, although his version was eventually discarded, and an American editor assembled the 'international version'.

Nonetheless, *Virus* failed miserably in the US market. With its raving generals and conciliatory but doomed American president, the film heavily evoked the arms race pessimism of its time, and the national stereotypes put forth on the Antarctic station are almost nostalgically

charming. However, *Virus*'s theme of the necessity of global coop-
eration is as relevant today as in 1980, and the multinational cast's
interaction is still curiously appealing. The epic scale of the story is
captured very competently by director Kinji Fukasaku, at least in the
longer version, and Yoshimizu is a genuinely-intriguing figure, both
in his world-destroying failure and his final triumph. Although the film
was not quite the financial disaster it is often claimed to have been, its
performance was disappointing enough to change Kadokawa's business model. Until the renewed blockbuster attempt of *Heaven and
Earth* (1993), also the most expensive film to be produced in Japan at
that time, Kadokawa would switch to smaller productions with market-
able teenage stars, allowing for up to eight or nine films annually,
spreading the risk of financial failure and increasing revenues from the
burgeoning home-video market.

Alexander Zahlten

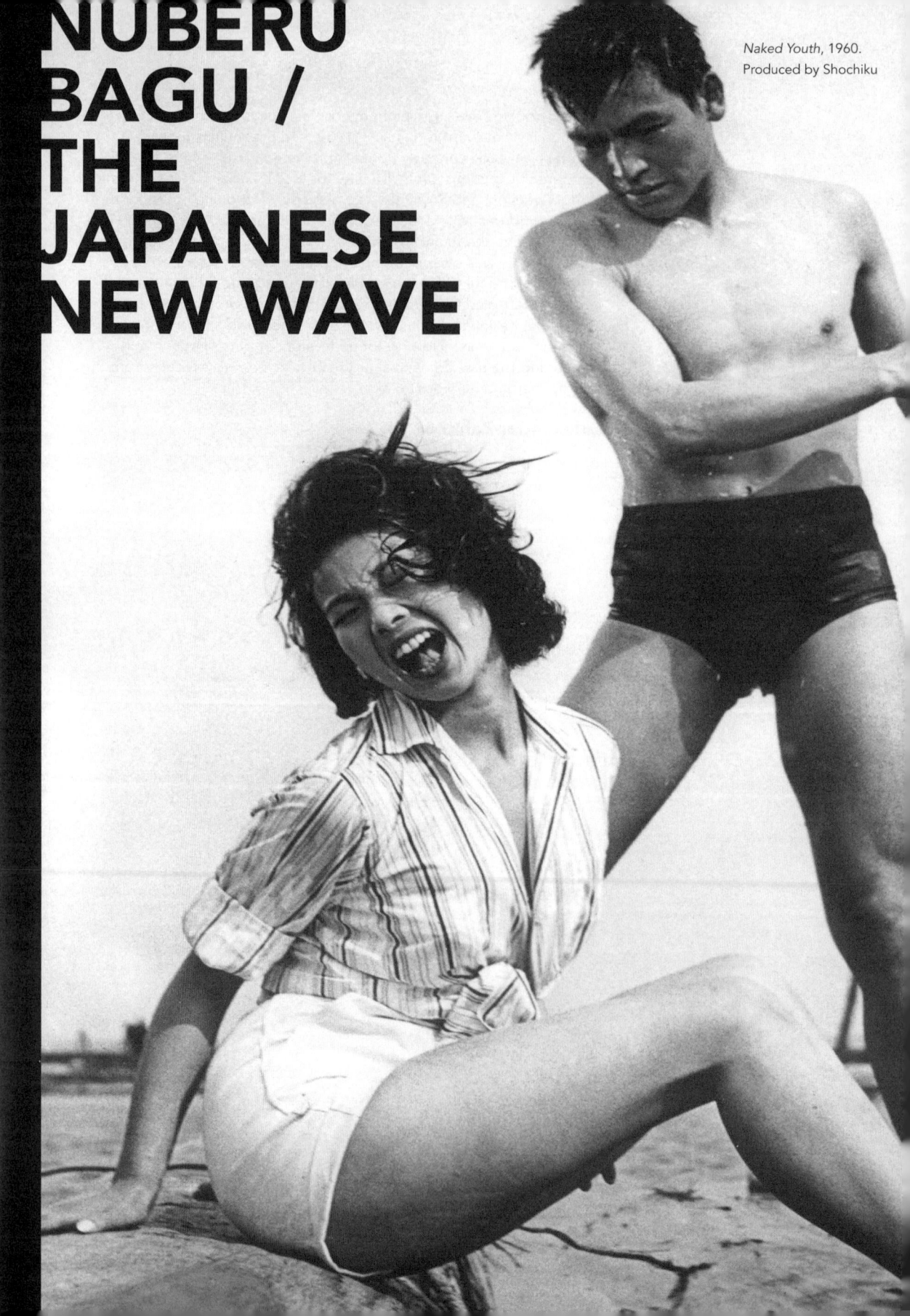

NUBERU BAGU / THE JAPANESE NEW WAVE

Naked Youth, 1960.
Produced by Shochiku

The Japanese New Wave, or *Nuberu Bagu*, refers to a fearless group of Japanese film-makers who emerged in the 1950s, and the term is applicable to examples of Japanese cinema from the 1960s and the early 1970s. As with many 'waves' that have occurred within the medium of cinema, an exact definition of this movement has frequently been debated by both scholars and enthusiasts. In addition, even those who agree on certain criteria for what constitutes a *Nuberu Bagu* film will frequently disagree about the inclusion of certain directors and films within the social-political or industrial framework that they perceive to be an appropriate means of discussing the movement. This is perhaps because, unlike the French New Wave, or *Nouvelle Vague*, which occurred at the tail-end of the 1950s, or the growth of the American Independent sector in the 1960s, the Japanese New Wave occurred within the supposedly-restrictive confines of the studio system.

As with the new cinema that emerged from France and the United States, the films were made by young, largely inexperienced, but mostly cine-literate directors, yet these Japanese directors were working with studio resources, effectively being sponsored to subvert the system from within, rather than burrowing their way into the popular conscience from the industrial margins. However, what began as a fascinating case of studio experimentation did rapidly evolve into a genuine sector of independent production, and independent thought, especially when the movement gained credibility through the films of Nagisa Oshima, who was known as a serious film critic and leftist activist before embarking on a career as a film-maker.

As Phillips and Stringer (2006) have noted, the rise of the Japanese New Wave coincided with the arrival of television and with the growth of cine-literate audiences seeking novelty beyond the boundaries of more conventional studio entertainment, with this audience being predominantly based in major metropolitan cities. Although the Japanese New Wave was initially sponsored by the studio system, with Shochiku Studios funding Oshima's initial entries: *A Town of Love and Hope* (1959) and *Cruel Story of Youth* (1960), the distribution network that was provided by the Art Theatre Guild, which had previously specialized in foreign imports, would provide exposure to such fascinating films as Matsumoto Toshio's *Funeral Parade of Roses* (1969) and Shinoda Masahiro's *Double Suicide* (1969). These two titles exemplify the aesthetic extremes of the New Wave movement, with *Funeral Parade of Roses* being an unflinching excursion into the gay sub-culture, with the story being abruptly intercut with interviews with real-life members of the scene, while *Double Suicide* is a more formally-detached experience, using the techniques of Brecht to study the racial discrimination which existed in Japan regarding Korean minorities. While the initial studio investment in the New Wave can be seen as a cynical corporate ploy to exploit the emerging youth, or student, market, it afforded opportunity to film-makers such as Oshima and Shohei Imamura, who were allowed the artistic freedom necessary to create works which felt authentically 'independent' in that they dealt with a shifting social and cultural landscape in a manner which was raw, immediate, confrontational and uncompromising, frequently encountering censorship issues.

As Oshima already had a public persona due to his work as a film critic and his outspoken political views, he made an ideal figurehead for the movement, just as Godard and Truffaut were popularly associated with the term French New Wave by audiences outside of the cinephile set. For this reason, and also because of the remarkable films that he delivered in quick succession due to studio production resources, Oshima serves as an ideal entry-point for those uninitiated in the provocative wonders of the Japanese New Wave, as he swiftly explored his political disillusionment with two films that were both released in 1960, *The Sun's Burial* and *Night and Fog in Japan*. His second feature, *Cruel Story of Youth*, is often cited as being the first film in the Japanese New Wave, and concerns and follows the sexually-charged relationship between a delinquent university student and a high-school girl who feel alienated from adult, consumerist society, and yet have not been swept up by the fervour of the activist movement, with their confused feelings about society and each other ultimately leading to their tragic deaths.

While his frequent use of hand-held camera, long takes, quick-pans and his interest in the urban sub-culture lead to comparisons with the French New Wave, *Cruel Story of Youth* is more politicized, with newspaper headlines employed as graphic backgrounds to establish the mood of the time, which saw students demonstrating against the Japanese Prime Minister, Kishi Nobusuke, launching a political movement which would rapidly lapse into disillusionment. Oshima films of this period, most notably *The Sun's Burial* and *Pleasure of the Flesh* (1963), were examinations of the lower social class, and dealt with teenage gangs, prostitutes, violence, and rape, but *Night and Fog in Japan* focuses on former student activists who meet at a wedding and argue over their subsequent political compromises. It was clear that Oshima was as frustrated with the failings of the leftist movement as he was with the Japanese government.

Other directors associated with the Japanese New Wave include Susumu Hanu, Hiroshi Teshigahara, Yasuzo Masamura, and Imamura. Although these directors would work separately, rather than as part of a collective film-making community, their works shared similar protagonists in that they often focused on criminals or delinquents, and explored sexuality in a frank manner that was shocking at the time and added to the debate about the changing role of women within society.

Imamura also started working within the studio system, making films for both Sho-chiku and Nikkatsu, but formed his own production company, Imamura Productions, in 1965 to concentrate on more adventurous projects, such as *The Pornographers* (1966). However, he struggled financially when the costly 1968 production *The Profound Desire of the Gods* proved to be a box-office failure, and his status as a New Wave director is best exemplified by *Pigs and Battleships* (1961), which concerns small time yakuza mixing with American soldiers stationed at a local military base and taking them to brothels, and *The Insect Woman* (1963), which is an examination of incestuous brothel life. Both of these projects were financed by Nikkatsu, which had to deal with political repercussions from releasing *Pigs and Battleships* as the film was widely seen as exhibiting anti-American sentiment.

Imamura often declared that he liked to make 'messy' films that were reflective of shifting social structures, and he would later fully embrace this aspect of his unique style by embarking on documentary projects such as *A Man Vanishes* (1967) and *History of Postwar Japan as Told by a Bar Hostess* (1970). By contrast, Susumu Hanu actually started as a documentary film-maker, and it could be argued that he effectively brought *cinema-verité* to Japan, later encouraging his actors to improvise when working on such features as *Bad Boys* (1961) which was based on the actual experiences of Japanese youth in a reformatory. However, he would work less frequently than his contemporaries, and subsequently return to his documentary roots.

Directors who had already established themselves within the industry prior to the phenomenon of the Japanese New Wave were occasionally linked the movement, either due to some of the social concerns in their work or their aesthetic sensibility, although such allegiances were temporary or actually non-existent. For instance, Seijun Suzuki is a film-maker who is often connected to the Japanese New Wave, largely due to his vibrant, unconventional aesthetic sensibility and a refusal to succumb to the demands of studio executives, which ultimately led to his dismissal from Nikkatsu following an infamous screening of his surreal yakuza thriller *Branded to Kill* (1967). However, in his acceptance of genre trappings and popular iconography in such films as *Youth of the Beast* (1963) and *Tokyo Drifter* (1966), not to mention his freewheeling excursions into surreal humour and filmic satire, Suzuki is less overtly political than more widely-accepted members of the New Wave, although his deconstructionist approach to genre, particularly when working within the framework of melodrama, was definitely an influence on film-makers with more pressing social concerns.

If the French New Wave is perhaps more widely celebrated and culturally acknowledged, largely due to the enduring appeal of Goddard's *Breathless* (1960), the Japanese New Wave provided a more substantial selection of films and perhaps, ultimately, had a greater influence on cinema as a whole in terms of its social critique rather than because of its, admittedly impressive, aesthetic attributes. Imamura would become one of only four directors to win the Palme d'Or at Cannes for multiple films with *The Ballad of Narayama* (1983) and *The Eel* (1991), finding his greatest acclaim on the world stage after the movement he is so intensely associated with had come and gone. While contemporary Japanese cinema is often seen to be embracing the spirit of the New Wave, largely due to auteur status of some of its leading directors and the freedom they have been afforded through their own production companies and their success on the international festival circuit, these recent films are not as socially challenging or technically invigorating, perhaps a reflection of the fact that the Japanese New Wave is an unflinching encapsulation of a nation experiencing political turmoil and social unrest.

John Berra

Blackmail is my Life

Kyokatsu Koso Waga
Jinsei

Company:
Shochiku

Director:
Kinji Fukasaku

Producer:
Akira Oda

Screenwriter:
Shinji Fujiwara

Cinematographer:
Keiji Maruyama

Art Director:
Kiminobu Sato

Composer:
Hajime Kaburagi

Editor:
Kinji Fukasaku

Duration:
90 minutes

Cast:
Hiroki Matsukata
Tomomi Sato
Tetsuro Tamba

Year:
1968

Synopsis

Shun Muraki is a small-time blackmailer taking advantage of the moral lapses of wealthy Tokyo businessmen. His crew consists of former yakuza member Seki, a failed boxer named Zero and the alluring Otoki, who is on the payroll simply because she is so attractive. They make easy money by running simple scams but matters become more complicated when Zero's father is murdered by drug traffickers and Sun's gang seeks vengeance. Then, becoming disenchanted with his lifestyle choices and the world around him, Shun's emerging political conscience involves his gang in a scheme to expose a corrupt politician, but their street-level methods are no match for the overarching influence of the establishment.

Critique

Much like Seijun Suzuki, the prolific Kinji Fukasaku takes his directorial inspiration from the French New Wave but, unlike his contemporary, he integrates his stylistic sensibility within a recognizable social-economic milieu and comments on the corrupt underbelly of the economic boom. The first half of *Blackmail is my Life* is bright, colourful, amoral fun, as Shun introduces the audience to his gang through a series of easily-accomplished scams, with some striking black-and-white flashbacks to his previous life as a lower-class worker, toiling away in menial jobs before embracing the 'get rich quick' ethos of the period. The political blackmail which features in the third act was reportedly inspired by real-life real-estate swindles that involved Kakuei Tanaka, who was then the Finance Minister of Japan, and would later become the nation's Prime Minister, and the episodic structure of the film serves to illustrate how greedy even small-time operators were becoming in an era of economic growth. Shun's targets are initially anonymous adulterers but he and his gang become more ambitious, gradually targeting wealthier individuals as they develop ideas above their station as low-rent scam artists, eventually believing that they can bring down representatives of government power.

Fukasaku references Suzuki's significance to the crime genre by having its characters whistle the theme tune to Suzuki's cult classic *Tokyo Drifter* (1966), and he invigorates the fairly routine plot with jump-cuts and freeze-frame, which causes some confusion with regards to the chronology of events. However, the freewheeling spirit of the first half leads to a subtle shift in tone as Fukasaku's opportunistic hustlers become more politically engaged. The director is also keen to underline the fact that these characters will remain at the bottom of the social ladder, no matter how much money they steal or extort; Shun blackmails a famous television actress into a sexual relationship, but he is ultimately used by the actress, who has actually enjoyed the illicit novelty of having an affair with a 'bad man' and is now ready to marry a more socially-acceptable partner. As with Michel Poiccard, the central protagonist of Jean-Luc Godard's legendary *Breathless* (1960) portrayed so energetically by Jean-Paul Belmondo, the over-ambitious Shun dies an anonymous death, collapsing on the street after suffering a fatal knife wound (one of Fukasaku's signature acts of onscreen violence) and being largely ignored by his fellow urbanites as he curses his fate. A dynamic yet thoughtful New Wave thriller that is ripe for rediscovery.

John Berra

Black Rose Mansion

Kuro bara no yakata

Studio:
Shochiku

Director:
Kinji Fukasaku

Producer:
Akira Oda

Screenwriters:
Kinji Fukasaku
Hiro Matsuda (based on the play by Yukio Mashima)

Cinematographer:
Takashi Kawamata

Art Director:
Kumagai Masao

Composer:
Hajime Kaburagi

Editor:
Kinji Fukasaku

Duration:
90 minutes

Cast:
Akihiro Miwa
Eitaro Ozawa
Masakazu Tamura

Year:
1969

Synopsis

The beautiful Ryuko turns the head of every male she meets and all the men who come to see her sing at the private club where she works become completely infatuated. It is not only the patrons of the club that are ensnared, since her ex-lovers begin to show up as well and trouble ensues from their appearance. Kyohei, the owner of the club, decides to take Ryuko as his lover while his son Wataru also falls under her spell and becomes dangerously obsessed. The story unfolds in typically-melodramatic style, as we learn of the past histories of some of the characters and their previous and current affairs. The little that is known of Ryuko is that she carries a black rose at all times in the hope that it will turn bright red one day in order to indicate that she has found her own true love.

Critique

The first thing we learn in Kinji Fukasaku's *Black Rose Mansion* is that a beautiful sunset is always followed by a terrible storm, suggesting a stylized and slightly surreal treat; the opening scenes are filmed through a red-orange filter to simulate a sunset, while the private club where Ryuko sings is a gorgeous set filled with gothic touches and the object of male desire is actually played by a man – the legendary female impersonator Akihiro Miwa. That last detail is never utilized as a plot point, with Ryuko being treated as a woman throughout the film despite the very manly crooning voice 'she' uses during all of her torch song performances. However, the trick works in that Miwa's performance, the makeup and the stunning gowns, all come together to create a believable character that might actually inspire feelings of obsessive love. But even as she accepts their flirtations, she tells them, 'I like to play make-believe'.

Fukasaku piles on the mirroring story elements: the club owner's bed-ridden wife and her previous dalliance that directly led to tragic events, while Wataru's old love that he suddenly left has married his brother. Along with the style of the film, this makes for a fun first hour but once we focus on the relationship between Wataru and Ryuko, it progresses to the foreshadowed conclusion. The later scenes are not without directorial merit but *Black Rose Mansion* ends up being awkwardly located somewhere between a dark fantasy and a character study of obsession. *Manji* (1964), *In the Realm of the Senses* (1976) and even *Blind Beast* (1969) are other Japanese films that cover similar ground but tackle the subject more thoroughly, although Fukasaku's film is never boring and his framing of his actors alone is worth witnessing to see how he plays them off each other. Miwa's performance is quite extraordinary here, re-teaming with Fukasaku after *Black Lizard* (1968), in which he portrayed a female jewel thief.

Bob Turnbull

Boy / Shonen, 1969. Produced by Sozosha

Boy

Shonen

Production Company:
Art Theater Guild

Director:
Nagisa Oshima

Producers:
Masayuki Nakajima
Takuji Yamaguchi

Screenwriters:
Takeshi Tamura
Nagisa Oshima
Masato Hara
Mamoru Sasaki

Cinematographer:
Yasuhiro Yoshioka

Art Director:
Jusho Toda

Synopsis

An expressionless ten-year-old boy plays hide-and-seek alone at a dilapidated roadside shrine. He reminds himself that he is supposed to cry when he gets caught. His father, a veteran who claims an invisible disability that prevents him from finding a job, enlists his wife, the boy's stepmother, in an extortion scheme. She throws herself into oncoming traffic, threatening to involve the police unless the driver pays her medical bills and two weeks' worth of recovery compensation. When a legitimate injury prevents her from working such scams, the father forces the boy into 'service'. At first, injections simulate bruises, but soon, real wounds begin to appear.

Critique

Oshima set to work on *Boy* ten days after the September 1966 events that inspired the film shocked Japan when a couple forced their ten-year-old son to walk into a slow-moving automobile in order to claim compensation. Production, however, did not begin until two years later, after Oshima had completed four more features and his casting team had scoured dozens of Tokyo children's homes. They finally discovered Tetsuo Abe, an orphan who had briefly lived with a stepmother and whose stiff-backed stoicism in the face of potentially traumatic circumstances lends the film much of its affective power. *Boy* was shot on location in seventeen cities with a crew of only fifteen for a miniscule 20 million yen.

Composer:

Hikaru Hayashi

Editor:

Keiichi Uraoka

Duration:

97 minutes

Cast:

Tetsuo Abe

Akiko Koyama

Fumio Watanabe

Year:

1969

For Oshima, perhaps the most stylistically eclectic director of the Japanese New Wave, *Boy* represented an opportunity to 'return to the psychological state of a novice'. Indeed, though the director and his crew often used *Boy*'s widescreen format to create strikingly decentered images and occasionally drained scenes of their colours, they employed none of the radically-Brechtian bare sets, extreme performances, and mechanical compositions and cutting technique of *Death by Hanging* (1967). *Boy*, then, is Oshima's most classical 1960s' film. Critics such as Turim and Desser have seen *Boy* as a study in psycho-sexual subjectivity (Turim) and as an indictment of post-war militarism but *Boy*'s double ending points more overtly to broader concerns about identity and, by extension, national identity. Abe perfectly embodies the role of the guarded, emotionally-detached boy. When he cries at his pretend grandmothers, he cries mechanically, on cue. And when he winces in pain for the physicians who examine him, he winces according to a well-rehearsed script. He cultivates a robotic impassivity. 'I don't know anything about anything', he claims, and he identifies not with humans but with space aliens.

Boy's visual design suggests that, for Oshima and his collaborators, the boy's specific identity problem is tied to a greater, national problem. Japanese flags are ubiquitous in the film. Art director Jusho Toda has placed the distinctive red-on-white emblem in every exterior location: the father twiddles, unmotivated, a Japanese flag throughout a long bus ride; the opening credits consist of red lettering in a circle on a white background; a giant Japanese flag is, somehow, hanging in the Hokkaido inn where the father delivers a ranting lecture on what it means to live, and then strangles his wife. These two threads – the boy's identity crisis and the national symbol – come together in the penultimate chapter as the boy builds a snowman, white on a snowy white background, and decorates it with the red snow-boot he has rescued from the scene of an accident. At first he identifies with the flag-echoing snowman: 'This snowman is not an ordinary snowman, but one from outer space', he tells his brother, 'he's not afraid of monsters or trains or cars. He never gets hurt. He never cries. He doesn't even have tears. He has no parents. He's all alone. I'm going to become someone just like him.' But then, unexpectedly, the boy rises, scolds the pile of snow and then demolishes it. The camera emphasizes this rare burst of emotion by gradually increasing the frame rate, slowing the motion.

The boy's potential for transformation from being a representative of the future of a nation that has lost its way to a real human being is hinted at in Oshima's final shots. Earlier, he had insisted that he had nothing to do with his father's scam and when shown a photo of himself at an accident scene, he had claimed: 'That's a man from outer space'. But when a kindly police escort treats him like the boy he is, inviting him to brag about having flown in a plane, the boy – after Oshima has cut to pregnant shots of the snowman, an accident victim, and a close-up of the red boot in a field of snow – admits, 'Yes, I went to Hokkaido.' Only then, as the boy begins to accept a degree of responsibility for his past, does a real, spontaneous tear roll down his cheek.

Bob Davis

Double Suicide

Shinju ten no Amijima

Studio:
Hyogensha | Art Theatre Guild

Director:
Masahiro Shinoda

Producer:
Masahiro Shinoda
Masayuki Nakajima

Screenwriters:
Taeko Tomioka
Masahiro Shinoda
Toru Takemitsu

Cinematographer:
Toichiro Narushima

Art Director:
Kiyoshi Awazu

Composer:
Toru Takemitsu

Editors:
Kiyoshi Awazu
Yoshizaku Hayashi

Duration:
104 minutes

Cast:
Kichiemon Nakamura
Shima Iwashita
Hosei Kamatsu

Year:
1969

Synposis

Double Suicide begins with traditional *bunraku* puppeteers preparing for a performance, as an off-screen conversation discusses the outcome of the story which is about to unfold: in eighteenth-century Osaka, a couple are found dead under a bridge. Jihei, a paper merchant, and Koharu, a beautiful courtesan, are obsessively in love. Jihei's unstable financial situation and marriage to Osan prevents him from buying out her contract to fulfil their dream of being together. Merchant Tahei expresses candid interest in purchasing ownership of Koharu, whilst Osan's family criticize Jihei's *amour fou* affair and demand a divorce. Since their desires conflict with the realities of their lives, they discuss the enactment of a 'love suicide' to consummate their spiritual unity. Blinded by love and convinced of their passions, the couple charge towards their fate.

Critique

Double Suicide structurally destabilizes the boundaries between Western modernism and local traditions in search of a creative affinity between two ostensibly-separate arenas of creative thought. Although a faithful adaptation of the 1720 doll-drama written by Chakamatsu Monzaemon, the text is resuscitated by Shinoda with formal vitality, reflecting the urge for cultural experimentation that permeated Japanese art in the late-1960s. Eradicating the illusion of reality, *Double Suicide* consciously foregrounds its artificiality, flattens the depth of field, and exposes the fragility and versatility of its set. Though evidently influenced by Brecht's notion of distanciation, the film is very much attached to its origins and locality. Indeed, Brecht and other theorists, including Eisenstein, drew on eastern traditions in art and linguistics to expand on their preoccupations with audience awakening; *bunraku* theatre and Buddhist Noh theatre consciously expose their own models and devices to initiate audience enlightenment. It is this complicated negotiation of Western and Eastern thought that is central to the unique vision of Shinoda's film. In a meta-textual interplay between temporal dimensions, Shinoda further disavows filmic escapism by allowing the *kurogo* figures, hooded puppeteers of *bunraku* theatre, to interrupt the diegesis as they determine their characters' destinies. Through subtle close-ups that linger on their veiled expressions and their return of our gaze, Shinoda suggests the *kurogo* figures share our sympathy for the characters and are our surrogate observers within the filmic vision. Deemed voiceless, they reluctantly lure the human puppets towards their fate – they, too, controlled by a greater force of spiritual destiny.

   Against the rigidly-patriarchal backdrop of eighteenth-century Japan, Shinoda radically deconstructs traditional gender politics through his portrayal of Osan and Koharu as familial and societal obligations conflict with passionate sensuality. Jihei is torn between duty and desire, whereas his female counterparts perform with self-assurance, showing mutual respect for each other within this tempestuous situation. Shinoda's real-life partner Shima Iwashita plays both lover

Double Suicide, 1969. Produced by Art Theatre Guild / HYOGENSHA

and wife, symbolically representing the limitations of female roles yet revealing the emotional complexity that transcends these social structures that impinge on their existence. Ironically, it is through death that the couple achieve their desired freedom; the beautifully composed shot of blood splattered kimonos and hair scattered in a delirious mess remains in our mind as their silent outcry.

Julian Ross

Funeral Parade of Roses

Bara no soretsu

Production Company:
Art Theater Guild

Director:
Toshio Matsumoto

Producers:
Mitsuru Kudo
Keiko Machida

Screenwriter:
Toshio Matsumoto

Cinematographer:
Tatsuo Suzuki

Art Director:
Setsu Asakura

Composer:
Joji Yuasa

Editor:
Toshie Iwasa

Duration:
107 minutes

Cast:
Osamu Ogasawara
Yoshio Tsuchiya
Emiko Azuma

Year:
1969

Synopsis

Transvestite Leda runs the Bar Genet, a celebrity hang-out where Eddie is one of her most popular 'girls'. Both are having affairs with Gonda, a drug runner and the bar's financial manager. After Leda sees Eddie with Gonda, she plots to have her star employee disfigured. But when Gonda figures out her plan and leaves her for good, the heartbroken Leda poisons herself, leaving her lifeless body dressed in drag on a bed covered with roses.

Critique

An introductory quotation from Baudelaire's *Flowers of Evil* – 'I am the wound and the blade, the torturer and the flayed' – points to the dissolving of boundaries that epitomizes Toshio Matsumoto's *Funeral Parade of Roses*. Part documentary, part fiction, and part avant-garde experiment, Matsumoto's first feature feels punch-drunk with the late Sixties revolutions of art, politics, sexuality, life. The director sets a re-sexed Oedipus myth – Eddie kills his mother and sleeps with his father – in a world of fluid gender identity. In one sequence three transvestites shop for mod bargains in the women's department, piss in the men's restroom's urinals, and then tussle with a butch leather-clad proto-*Sukeban* girl gang. In another, a dozen or so youths pass around a joint, then play a strip version of 'walk-the-line'. Soon, they are all dancing under strobe lights in their underwear, a polymorphous mass of undulating flesh.

Formally, too, *Funeral Parade of Roses* rejects strict dichotomies. Fictional episodes are intercut with interviews with 'gay-boys', some apparently unarranged, others planned if not carefully scripted. Actors, fashion photographers, and film directors (including Masahiro Shinoda) patronize Bar Genet using their real names. And popular film critic Choji Yodogawa appears as 'a film critic' in a short clip that disrupts the narrative flow at its dramatic climax. His 'review' of the scene that the audience is watching is 'Frightening! What a mix of cruelty and laughter. Let's look forward to the next show.' Scenes in which a strange procession of men in funeral attire and gas masks carry extralarge white boxes through the Tokyo streets mix performance art (the members of the mini-parade are in fact the Zero Dimension Group) and documentary (the bystanders who react to the procession have no idea what is going on) and fiction (Eddie is part of the crowd). And later, when Matsumoto cuts from close-ups of Eddie moaning in the throes of passion to a wider shot in which we see a film crew shooting the scene, layers of filmic partial 'truths' are juxtaposed.

Matsumoto blends pornography and documentary, catfight comedy and Greek tragedy, *verité* and experiment – the cine-club even screens a lengthy segment of Matsumoto's own 1969 avant-garde short, *Ecstasis* – not so much to call into question these categories as to advocate the necessity of all of them, and the variety of human experience, in any tenable worldview. When, towards the end of the film, gay-boy Eddie dresses the wounds of a very serious young man who has been wounded in the student demonstrations, Matsumoto's film deftly illustrates his world's wide range of identity options and perhaps, for him, the ultimate détente.

Bob Davis

The Naked Island

Hadaka no Shima

Studio:
Kindai Eiga Kyokai

Director:
Kaneto Shindo

Producers:
Kaneto Shindo
Matsumura Eisaku

Screenwriter:
Kaneto Shindo

Cinematographer:
Kiyoshi Kuroda

Composer:
Hikaru Hayashi

Editor:
Toshio Enoki

Duration:
92 minutes

Cast:

Nobuko Otawa
Taiji Tonoyama
Masanori Horimoto

Year:
1960

Synposis

The Naked Island follows the quotidian lives of a peasant family of farmers who are the only inhabitants of a small, remote, island. From dusk till dawn, the mother, Toyo, and father, Senta, must row back and forth to the mainland to procure precious water, which they pour into large buckets and carry on their shoulders. The water is used for feeding the crops and must be collected from the mainland as the salt water that surrounds their isle is useless. When Taro falls seriously ill, his father must row back to the mainland to find a doctor to save his child.

Critique

The Naked Island is a hypnotic example of how the economical use of images can evoke the most vivid emotional responses. The patience of the images, the persistence of repetition and the meticulous introspection of the details of everyday struggles synthesize to form this profoundly-minimalist cine-poem. Shindo allows his images to get caught up in their own rhythms, both within and between the frames, to summon a spiritual transcendence that is deeply humanist, echoing his western counterpart, Robert Bresson. The omnipotent rhythms and oscillating tempos pulsate throughout the story and compensate for the lack of narrative. The seemingly-flawless fluctuation between objective and subjective perspectives conjures up a filmic language very much of its own. The protagonists' cyclical daily rituals seem alien as we watch in awe, yet we gradually realize their lives underline our everyday realities which permeate humanity's existence on earth. We are invited to observe the futility of their quotidian exertions against the overwhelming indifference of their landscape. Yet simultaneously we are asked to respect and celebrate their humble perseverance and share their embrace of the simple moments of happiness that transcend their hardships, and instances of tragedy that overrule their travails. In a world where actions speak louder than words, the film is entirely absent of dialogue. Shindo himself cited an old Japanese proverb in reference to the film: 'the eye can express as much as the mouth can'. Composer Hikaru Hayashi meditates on a single melody for the majority of the film, extracting and interposing when it suits, reflecting on the patient approach of the camerawork.

As one of the most prominent independent film-makers in post-war Japan, Shindo and his small crew of thirteen inhabited the desolate island and performed many similar farming tasks, enabling them to experience the minutiae of peasant life. Recalling Shinsuke Ogawa's documentaries, the collective approach to film-making and the distillation of boundaries between subject and object proved appropriate for Shindo's intentions and informed his future oeuvre. As Alex Cox has suggested, the making of the film itself was a political act, where they risked the limited financial reserves of Kindai Eiga Kyokai to invest in the creation of art that left no concessions to commercialism. Fortunately, the film was showered with international awards, including the Grand Prix at the Moscow International Film Festival, and saved the company from financial ruin.

Julian Ross

Naked Youth

Seishun Zangoku
Monogatari

Studio:
Shochiku

Director:
Nagisa Oshima

Producer:
Tomio Ikeda

Screenwriter:
Nagisa Oshima

Cinematographer:
Ko Kawamata

Art Director:
Koji Uno

Composer:
Riichiro Manabe

Editor:
Keichi Uraoka

Duration:
97 minutes

Cast:

Yusuke Kawasu
Miyuki Kuwano
Kei Sato

Year:
1960

Synopsis

A story of juvenile delinquency amongst the post-war generation, *Naked Youth* follows a teenage couple, Makoto and Kiyoshi, who roam the Tokyo backstreets, leading an aimless existence. Dissatisfied with high school life, Makoto pursues an unintelligible thrill by wandering the neon-lit city by night and hitching lifts from businessmen. Inevitably, she encounters trouble when a perverse middle-aged man attempts to rape her, a situation that is brought to a halt by Kiyoshi, who is walking by. The courageous act sparks a vehement relationship, as Kiyoshi reveals that he is far from a hero.

Critique

'In the rip of a woman's skirt and the buzz of a motorboat, sensitive people heard the heralding of a new generation of Japanese film.' Those were the words that Nagisa Oshima used to voice his admiration for the *taiyo-zoku* (sun tribe) genre that ruptured the Japanese cinema scene in the mid-1950s. A profound influence on *Naked Youth*, the *taiyo-zoku* films captured an essence of the Japanese post-war generation, resonating with youthful energy and offering a refreshingly honest outlook on contemporary society. Although Oshima's second feature with Shochiku echoes their thematic concerns and imagery, it is an altogether more sombre, darker experience. In a desperate attempt to redeem their audience numbers, Shochiku reinstated Oshima after a six-month 'suspension' due to the commercial failure of his first feature, *A Town of Love and Hope* (1959). Fortunately, *Naked Youth* was a box-office success, and the film launched a movement within Shochiku that was given the title 'Ofuna Nouvelle Vague'. These film-makers, with Oshima at the eye of the storm, would lead Japanese cinema into its most exciting period amidst the pervading chaos of the new decade.

Naked Youth immediately paints the socio-political backdrop of the teenage lovers in its introductory sequences. The audience is confronted with forceful images of newspaper clippings, footage of student demonstrations in South Korea, and Zengakuren protests against the renewal of the Anpo US-Japan Security Treaty on the streets of Tokyo. Although his characters are ultimately detached from these experiences, as Oshima was a student revolutionary in his own youth these political upheavals occupy a significant space in his heart, and the discontented masses generate a pessimistic milieu that permeates the screens of *Naked Youth*. Oshima provides no space for sentimentality and assigned himself the task of abolishing the colour green, as he felt it was too calming. He avoids glorifying the young couple, whose everyday life is saturated with self-absorbed nihilism, allowing his audience to relate to their disenchantment but never asking for admiration. The downbeat moments in the aftermath of Makoto's abortion are clearly symbolic of a future stifled before it could begin, and the apple Kiyoshi munches on had connotations with Adam and Eve and the demise of humanity from there on. The vivid colours and widescreen set-ups capture nothing but the melancholy of these hopeless youths.

Interactions with elders reveal the conflict between generations that would fracture Japan's sense of a national identity. The amoral scams that the couple embark on confront the older generations, fiercely demonstrating their inability to adjust the nation's moral compass. Kiyoshi's parents are never mentioned and Makoto's father is hopelessly impotent. Makoto's sister Yuki, along with her ex-boyfriend and now-abortionist Akimoto, were once student activists in the 1950s, but are now just left-over crumbs of the movement. Released only a few months after the renewal of the Anpo treaty that signified another failed uprising, all generations in *Naked Youth* are united in their dismay of a nation in crisis.

Julian Ross

Night and Fog in Japan

Nihon no Yoru to Kiri

Studio:
Shochiku

Director:
Nagisa Oshima

Producer:
Tomio Ikeda

Screenwriters:
Toshiro Ishido
Nagisa Oshima

Cinematographer:
Takashi Kawamata

Art Director:
Koji Uno

Composer:
Naozumi Yamamoto

Editor:
Keiichi Uraoka

Duration:
107 minutes

Cast:
Kenzo Kawarazaki
Miyuki Kuwano
Takao Yoshizawa

Year:
1960

Synopsis

The setting is the wedding of two members of the *zengakuren*, a national left-wing student activist group. Nozawa (Kawarazaki) was an active member in his student days in the early 1950s but had become disillusioned with the ideals of the group until he met Reiko (Kuwano), a current student who is full of the enthusiasm that he once shared with his classmates, now guests at his wedding. However, what should be a happy occasion is tainted as an unexpected guest, a radical protester currently on the run from police, arrives to accuse the bride, groom and their guests of hypocrisy and posturing.

Critique

While indisputably a film of great significance, *Night and Fog in Japan* is a difficult film to watch. Oshima intended to provoke a discussion about politics, a bold move in 1960 when such subject matter was at the heart of intense debate and protests, and the film was shelved by its studio only a few days after its release. In the 1950s, students were united as members of the *zengakuren* group, a national union with ties to the Japan Communist Party. However, there was considerable discontent at the restrictions in place by this affiliation and in 1959 the *zengakuren* detached itself from the Communist Party, just in time for the Anpo protests. The US-Japan Security treaty (abbreviated to 'Anpo' in Japanese), originally signed at the end of the US Occupation of Japan, was up for renewal in 1960 – a decision many left-wing groups were against. Students led the protests, which became more and more agitated until a student was trampled to death. It is at this point that Reiko is introduced, lying injured in the hospital where she meets Nozawa, who is covering the events in his capacity as a journalist.

The film is based around heated accusations, defensive responses and flashbacks that provide some context for these characters' backgrounds. The cast is large, their discussion mostly political, and any emotional interaction tied firmly to the political framework. The wedding scenes are not cut, with, instead, the camera pulling in and out and panning from face to face, giving a theatrical feel to the film that is reinforced by flashbacks filmed on a black stage with spotlights. Viewers are kept at a Brechtian distance throughout, allowing us to observe the events without being swayed by sympathy for any one character. *Night and Fog in Japan* showcases the dissent within and between these two generations of student activists, exposing the intense yet fragmented nature of the student movement and questioning the nature of activism and the requirements of a commitment to political change. It is ultimately one of those films that viewers are more likely to appreciate than enjoy – exactly as Oshima intended it to be.

Amelia Cook

Story of a Prostitute

Shunpu den

Studio:
Nikkatsu

Director:
Seijun Suzuki

Producer:
Kaneo Iwai

Screenwriter:
Hajime Takaiwa, from a novel by Taijiro Tamura

Cinematographer:
Kazue Nagatsuka

Art Director:
Takeo Kimura

Composer:
Naozumi Yamamoto

Editor:
Akira Suzuki

Duration:
96 minutes

Synopsis

Set in 1937 during the Japanese conflict with China, *Story of a Prostitute* focuses on title character Harumi after she is betrayed by her lover. She is transported with a group of other prostitutes to the Manchurian front, where they intend to offer their services to the hundreds of troops stationed there. However, immediately upon her arrival, Harumi is singled out by the hateful, abusive Lieutenant Narita. Simultaneously used and regarded with contempt by him, she is inspired to take a stand of rebellion, and she does so by becoming involved with Mikami, Narita's gentle-natured subordinate. The lovers find themselves increasingly at odds with the demands of Japan's military system. Soon enough, their situation becomes more complicated after they are taken prisoner by the Chinese side, forcing them to reconsider where their loyalties truly lie and what they must do to uphold them.

Critique

Story of a Prostitute begins with a quick, dizzying series of events. Following the opening title sequence, which introduces her emerging from a desolate landscape, Harumi is given a brief back-story surrounding her love affair in the Chinese city of Tianjin, which ends with her angrily cutting the man who dared to jilt her. Soon after, she is shown sitting with the other prostitutes being taken them to the front, in a truck that is suddenly attacked by enemy forces. The rest of the film is similarly paced, giving way to moments of abruptness and unexpected action. In this way, it remains constantly engaging, playing with, and often thwarting viewer expectations.

The most interesting aspect of *Story of a Prostitute* is its three main characters. Harumi is a complex, intriguing heroine, possessing a fierce, confrontational nature as she at once recognizes her lowly stature in the eyes of the men she services and tries to defend it and her self-esteem. She becomes locked in a battle of wills with Narita, who

Cast:
Yumiko Nogawa
Tamio Kawachi
Isao Tamagawa

Year:
1965

makes her an object of his venomous loathing. A significant portion of the film's conflict is based around their relationship, which pits her defiant femininity against his authoritative masculinity. Mikami forms the third, most passive part of their destructive triangle, a reader of Diderot's philosophy who is ill-suited to the strict regimen of service to the Japanese military.

Suzuki's portrayal of womanhood caught in the sidelines of a male-dominated world is reflected not just by Harumi but also the other prostitutes who inhabit the military outpost, who occasionally act as a Greek chorus as they discuss the developments between Harumi, Narita and Mikami. They also must cope with the suppression of their desires, which is most painfully reiterated when one woman's hopes for a proper marriage fall apart, and her broken dreams are represented in a shot of her bowls, glasses and utensils lying scattered across the ground. Along with the restriction of individuality, the film's main theme is honour, be it Harumi's despite her profession, or Mikami's as he is pressured to uphold his duties as a soldier. Brimming with ideas and innovation, *Story of a Prostitute* is a revealing critique of Japan's patriotic mentality.

Marc Saint-Cyr

The Sun's Burial

Taiyo no Hakaba

Studio:
Shochiku

Director:
Nagisa Oshima

Producer:
Tomio Ikeda

Screenwriters:
Toshiro Ishido
Nagisa Oshima

Cinematographer:
Ko Kawamata

Art Director:
Koji Uno

Composer:
Riichiro Manabe

Editor:
Keichi Uraoko

Synposis

Set in the ghetto slums of 1960s' Osaka, *The Sun's Burial* follows a group of juvenile delinquents who find themselves amongst poverty-ridden streets infested with criminals and addicts who indulge in a life segregated from civil existence. Takeshi and Tatsu join Shin's street gang of pimps who pursue a living through prostitution. They meet Hanako, a young malefactor who has set up a clinic to sell blood to cosmetic companies in collaboration with an older generation of petty criminals led by Yosehei. Takeshi experiences the reality of their marginalized existence, where his everyday encounters involve acts of rape and violence as part of the nature of being. As acts of deception accumulate, the criminal community begins to decay, dissolving into a miscellaneous mass as each individual is urged towards their destiny of total destruction and irredeemable annihilation.

Critique

Fuelled by nihilistic energy, Oshima made three films in quick succession during the year 1960, with what has been described as 'journalistic speed'. The second of the three, *The Sun's Burial*, was already in the making when the preceding *Naked Youth* (1960) was released. The film was part of Shochiku's new canon that was given the title 'Ofuna Nouvelle Vague', a studio-led movement that diminished the hierarchical system of in-house ascendance to allow assistant directors a chance to direct. Shochiku gave the go-ahead for these projects in

Duration:

87 minutes

Cast:

Kayoko Honoo
Isao Sasaki
Masahiko Tsugawa

Year:

1960

reaction to the tidal wave of television that was eroding their audience share, desperately attempting to resuscitate their box office statistics. The attention that Nikkatsu's *taiyo-zoku* (sun tribe) films received in the mid-1950s, along with the French Nouvelle Vague's international success, encouraged the studio to explore new territory in order to engage with the post-war generation. However, Oshima's career gave birth to an altogether different kind of monster, with *The Sun's Burial* being no exception.

Oshima here slices open the masquerade of the newly-affluent Japan to reveal the reality behind the statistics. As suggested by its title, perhaps more accurately translated as *Graveyard for the Sun*, Oshima orchestrates a requiem for Japan and its future. The vultures of the underground constitute a microcosm of contemporary society, where a crowd of heterogeneous voices aimlessly stray the back-streets of Osaka. Shot on location with hand-held cameras, Oshima pursues a rigorous realism that rejects all forms of sentimentalism. A carnal physicality radiates from the individuals, whose emotions are veiled by sweat and dirt, shown in intense close-ups that swallow up the screen. The fierce red of the sun engulfs the characters, metaphorically blaming the entire nation for the anti-social state of these lost souls. The widescreen images squash the characters and emphasize the distance and alienation of their existence, while Oshima allows no space for audience identification, as subjectivity is abandoned and replaced by a corporeal sense of reality, which snarls at the viewer rather than inducing any sympathy. The irredeemable sense of hopelessness, the unpalatable portrayal of lowlife criminals, and the rampant physicality of the action recalls the films of foreign contemporaries Pier Paolo Pasolini and Luis Bunuel, specifically *Accatone* (1961) and *Los Olvidados* (1950), and Oshima cited the latter as an influence.

In a world where every man stands for himself, Hanako seems to be the only individual with some sense of narrative agency amidst the chaos. A refreshing refusal of the misogyny that pervades films from the period, Hanako is cast as the puppet master of the crowd, an unassailable presence that mediates between the gangs and orchestrates their destiny as the society around her crumbles. As Oshima's surrogate, she is the one that initiates the climactic destruction of everything, an existential annihilation and a hygienic removal for the future; yet she also leads the waltz towards another cycle of criminality.

Julian Ross

A Town of Love and Hope

Ai to kibo no machi

Studio:
Shochiku

Director:
Nagisa Oshima

Producer:
Tomio Ikeda

Screenwriter:
Nagisa Oshima

Cinematographer:
Hiroyuki Kusuda

Art Director:
Koji Uno

Composer:
Riichiro Manabe

Editor:
Yoshi Sugihara

Duration:
62 minutes

Cast:
Hiroshi Fujikawa
Yuki Tominaga
Yuko Mochizuki

Year:
1959

Synopsis

Fatherless Masao lives in a derelict area of Kawasaki, Greater Tokyo, and whilst his sick mother Kuniko wants him to stay in school, Masao is determined to support financially his mother and younger sister Yasue. Masao forms a friendship with Kyoko, the daughter of a wealthy electricity company president, after selling her his pet pigeons, and both Kyoko and Masao's schoolteacher, Miss Akiyama, attempt to persuade the company hierarchy to employ Masao if he passes his school exams. In the meantime, Miss Akiyama also becomes romantically involved with Kyoko's older brother Yuji, a manager at the company. However, despite his success, Masao is rejected by Koyo Electric when Yuji discovers that Masao is swindling people by selling pigeons that always return to him and are subsequently sold again. Whilst Masao's scheming initially enrages both Kyoko and Miss Akiyama, they eventually take very different views on his actions.

Critique

A Town of Love and Hope was Oshima's first feature film as writer-director. Made at Shochiku Studios, it was conceived as a programmer and screened on a double-bill. Whilst it has some hallmarks of a Masaru Ofuna melodrama, the film does contain themes that set the scene for his future work, particularly with regards to the sympathy that is afforded towards the 'delinquent' protagonist, Masao (Hiroshi Fujikawa). Rather than being scathing of his petty crimes, the target of the Oshima's critique is instead the bourgeois world of Kyoko and Yuji. Whereas gas tanks and factory chimneys surround Masao's decrepit home, Kyoko's light and spacious house offers a commanding view over the city.

What is particularly interesting about the film, however, is the implicit criticism of the 'liberal' response of both Kyoko and Miss Akiyama to Masao's plight, and this is notable in relation to their condemnation of Masao's swindling after the two had both been so charitable to his family. Indeed, in concentrating on the responses of Kyoko and Miss Akiyama, it is interesting that Masao is largely absent from the final minutes of the film. Miss Akiyama often appears to be somewhat superficial in her kindness as she is a keen participant in the new consumerist riches of Japan, spending her time in the cafes and expensive restaurants from which Masao and his family are obviously excluded. Although her sudden realization of the inseparable gap between Masao's family and Kyoko's family may be psychologically underdetermined, it is visually marked by a striking use of light and shade in her final meeting with Yuji. This is counterbalanced by the subsequent ferocity of Kyoko in her decision to kill Masao's pigeon to sabotage his future 'crimes'.

Whilst Oshima's subsequent films for Shochiku were bigger-budget productions, produced in colour and photographed in widescreen format, A Town of Love and Hope's monochrome photography allows Oshima to capture the grim poverty of families such as Masao's who were struggling to be part of Japan's rapidly-improving economy.

Whilst it is difficult to ignore the class conflict in this particular film, subsequent works such as *Cruel Story of Youth* (1960) demonstrate that Oshima was moving on to thinking about crime and delinquency as part of a wider rejection of organizational structures, rather than indicating sympathy towards leftist reform, making *A Town of Love and Hope* an intriguing debut by a director who was still developing his own social-economic stance.

Christopher Howard

Vengeance is mine

Fukushû suru wa ware ni ari

Studio/Distributor:
Imamura Productions, Eureka Entertainment

Director:
Shohei Imamura

Producer:
Kazuo Inoue

Screenwriter:
Masaru Baba

Cinematographer:
Shinsaku Himeda

Art Director:
Shinsaku Himeda

Composer:
Shinichiro Ikebe

Editor:
Keiichi Uraoka

Duration:
140 minutes

Cast:
Ken Ogata
Mayumi Ogawa
Rentaro Mikuni

Year:
1979

Synopsis

A loose account of the real-life exploits of serial killer and conman, Akira Nishiguchi, renamed Iwao Enokizu, the narrative details the events leading up to his capture following a 78-day killing spree in 1963. Beginning with Enokizu's capture, the story is related in a stream-of-consciousness manner in which past and present events become diffused. Enokizu is a chameleon, changing identities as he evades capture – at one point taking on the persona of a university professor. Women fall in love with Enokizu even when they know the truth about his murderous impulses: for example, Haru (whose mother is an ex-convict) enters into a passionate affair with Enokizu.

Critique

Shohei Imamura is one of the key directors of the Japanese New Wave. Starting out within the studio system, first at Shochiku (where he was assistant director to Yasujiro Ozu) and then Nikkatsu, he established his own independent production company, Imamura Productions, in 1965. In the 1970s, as the film industry slumped, Imamura turned his hand to television documentaries, many of which explored the lasting scars of World War II. It is clear to see the influence of the documentary mode in *Vengeance is Mine*, – use of hand-held camera, inter titles to add factual evidence to Enokizu's crimes, and location shooting – even though the film continually blurs the boundaries between fact and fiction, as did his first independent feature, *A Man Vanishes* (1967). At the same time, the relationship between Enokizu (Ken Ogata) and his father, Shizuo (Rentaro Mikuni), foregrounds Imamura's continuing obsession with the consequences of war on the national psyche.

A short flashback details Shizuo's humiliation at the hands of a naval officer when forced to give over his fishing boats to the military effort. This is juxtaposed with a later scene of Enokizu harassing a young Japanese woman who is out with a group of American soldiers. This cinematic shortcut creates an analogy between authority, subservience and terror which is carried into the present through Enokizu, who seems at times like an unstoppable force of nature, wreaking destruction everywhere he goes: a metaphor for the persistence of historical trauma in the construction of Japanese nationhood. Immoral and fundamentally flawed, Enokizu submits to his fate when captured, repeating his father's earlier submission to the authorities. In his disdain for authority and societal rules, and with his handsome exterior hiding the sociopath beneath, Enokizu's character captures the zeitgeist of Japan in the 1960s.

Ken Ogata provides a powerful turn as Enokizu, imbuing the character with charm even while his diffidence to others shines through. Although Ogata had played a similar part in Yoshitaro Nomura's *The Demon* (1978), it was the role of Enokizu that propelled Ogata to national and international stardom. While Japanese critics at the time were perplexed by Imamura's refusal to posit a definite motivation for Enokizu's actions, after all he was not a working class anti-hero but a member of the privileged middle classes, the film won six awards, including best film and best director, from the Japanese Academy.

Colette Balmain

Woman in the Dunes

Suna No Onna

Studio:
Toho Film (Eiga) Co. Ltd,
Teshigahara Productions

Director:
Hiroshi Teshigahara

Producers:
Kiichi Ichikawa
Tadashi Oono

Screenwriter:
Kobo Abe

Cinematographer:
Hiroshi Segawa

Art Directors:
Totetsu Hirakawa
Masao Yamazaki

Composer:
Toru Takemitsu

Editor:
Fusako Shuzui

Synopsis

Weary of life in the hectic city, an entomologist decides to spend a few peaceful days in the desert collecting rare insects. Exploring the dunes, he dozes off in the sun and is awoken by a villager who tells him that the last bus has gone. Unperturbed, and tickled by the novelty of the experience, the man agrees to spend the night in a hut that stands on solid sand at the bottom of a pit. He descends a rope ladder and is greeted by a demure young woman who cooks him dinner and makes a bed for him. When he awakes in the morning, however, the rope ladder has disappeared. He soon learns that the villagers have trapped him there so that he can assist the woman in her work: the endless and seemingly senseless task of clearing the pit of sand.

Critique

Woman in the Dunes is based on a novel of the same name by absurdist novelist Kobo Abe and is essentially a retelling of the Sisyphus myth, as hinted at in the opening shot in which a grain of sand, filmed in extreme close-up, appears like a giant boulder. The unrelenting sandiness of the film is extraordinary: sand underfoot, sand through fingers, sand cascading like water, sand blown by the wind, sand in eyes and hair, sand on skin and in between toes, sand in food and water, sand swallowed and spat out – to the point where the mirage of a cool sun-dappled pool that appears to the parched man seems genuinely wondrous. The film's emphasis on the physical discomfort of its characters serves to acutely attune us to their sensations, which in turn heightens the film's simmering eroticism for which it is renowned.

Woman Of The Dunes / Suna No Onna, 1964. Produced by Teshigahara

Duration:

123 minutes

Cast:

Eiji Okada
Kyoko Kishida

Year:

1964

Seen through Teshiguhara's camera, the entomologist and his insects appear of equal size – in one shot an insect's head fills the frame; in another, the man, filmed from a distance, wriggles through the sand like a bug – with the implication that, insect-like, he now toils unthinkingly for his survival and that of his species; the reason that they must clear the pit is that, if the house is buried, the neighbouring house will be next. What we are meant to make of his eventual acceptance of this existence is a moot point but, at the very least, the implication is that, in its simple purposefulness, it has become preferable to his 'unfathomable' life in the city. Like the Sisyphus of Albert Camus' essay, so in vogue in the 1960s, we are asked to imagine him happy. The film won the Special Jury prize at the 1964 Cannes Film Festival and was nominated for two Oscars the following year. Its unearthly score is by avant-garde composer Toru Takemitsu and is justly celebrated.

Alanna Donaldson

PINKU EIGA / PINK FILMS

Kimyo Na Sakasu, 2005.
Produced by Sedil

Japanese pink cinema, or *pinku eiga*, is the name given to a type of independent 'sexploitation' cinema which was distinguishable from the typical independent films of the time in terms of its direct approach to sexuality and frequent number of sex scenes. These films were originally termed 'eroductions', until the phrase *pink eiga* ('pink cinema') was coined in 1962 as a description of a new type of low-budget stag film that was becoming increasingly popular in response to falling cinema audiences.[1] While Hunter argues, as do other critics, that Tetsuji Takechi's *Daydream* (1964) was the first pink film,[2] Sharp dates the genre earlier, back to *Flesh Market* by Satoru Kobayashi in 1962.[3] There are roughly three waves of pink cinema: The first between 1962 and 1972 (if we take *Flesh Market* rather than *Daydream* as the first pink film) comprised mainly independent films. The second wave (1971–1982) saw the mainstreaming of pink cinema when one of the largest Japanese studios at the time, Nikkatsu, abandoned its usual action films for erotic films, known as romantic pornography (*roman porno*), the most [in]famous of which are the Angel Gut Series of films. Quick to realize the profitably of mainstream erotic cinema, Toei produced its own type of pink cinema known as 'pinky violence', which focused more on violence than sex as the term suggests. The third distinct wave dates from 1992 onwards and is marked by the re-emergence of the independent pink film with directors such as Hisayasu Sato and Takahisa Zeze .[4]

While it would be easy to argue that because the pink film never showed actual intercourse it should be categorized as 'softcore' pornography as opposed to 'hardcore', this division is far too simplistic and does not take into consideration the particular specifics of production at the time in Japan. In fact, in some sex scenes in pink films, intercourse did take place and sex was not regulated against (neither was sexual violence). As long as certain things were not shown (those deemed obscene), film-makers had much more creative freedom than in the West. At the time, Japanese cinema was regulated by Eirin (Administration Commission of Motion Picture Code of Ethics), which was set up in 1949. In terms of obscenity, Eirin defined three specific areas as not suitable for public consumption: (1) genitalia; (2) pubic hair and (3) penetration shots. Any films which transgressed these prohibitions were charged under Article 175 of the Penal Code, although, as in the case of *Daydream* and Oshima's *In the Realm of the Senses* (1976), such prosecutions were rarely successful. Pink film-makers self-regulated their films by using either digital mosaics, fogging or blocking (the careful positioning of objects) to cover up the offending areas and thereby avoid prosecution. This meant that as long as the film-makers abided by Eirin's guidelines anything was permissible. This was particularly problematic in terms of the representation of sexual violence; as Allison points out: 'imagining a woman tied up, held down, or forcibly penetrated is acceptable ... whereas revealing the reality of her pubic hair is not.'[5] This helps to explain the number of Japanese pink films, and later studio productions, that detail violence towards women and particular scenes of rape, the most lurid of which are the Rapeman (*Reipuman*) series of films in the 1990s.

With the advent of *roman porno*, and other studio variations of the pink film, pink cinema became less political and more explicit. Any genre was fair game for the pink treatment including the traditional ghost film (*kaidan eiga*) – *Immortal Love* (1972). At a time when the studios were suffering from dwindling audiences in response to the competition from television, films with large numbers of sex scenes in them guaranteed box-office success. Hunter writes: 'Roman porno saved Nikkatsu, and some critics have suggested it even saved the entire Japanese film industry from imminent disaster.'[6] Sexual violence became a convention of the genre, so much so that a sub-genre, the torture film, emerged. Mainly associated with Toei studio and the director, Teruo Ishii, the first film was *Criminal Woman* (1968). Ishii directed eight films in the series between 1968 and 1973, collectively known as the *Joys of Torture* series. In 1974, Nikkatsu introduced its own type of sexually-violent pink offshoot, S&M, and then later the Violent Pink genre in 1976. It needs to be pointed out that, although much of the violence was directed towards women, men were not immune from being the victims of torture in these films.

Hunter points out that the *Joy of Torture* films belong to 'the genre of Japanese exploitation cinema known as *ero-guro* – short for "erotic-grotesque."'[7] A key early film of the *ero-guro* genre was Yasuzo Masumura's *Blind Beast* (1969), based upon a short story by the Edogawa Rampo. Another important *ero-guro* film, also owing its genesis to the works of Rampo, was Ishii's *Horror of the Malformed Men* (1969). However, like mainstream pink cinema, the *ero-guro* film got more and more explicit as time went on. In the first two films of the notorious direct-to-video Guinea Pig films (1985–1989):*Guinea Pig: Devil's Experiment* (1985) and *Flower of Flesh and Blood* (1985) – loosely based upon the manga of Hideshi Hino – narrative is dispensed with. Instead both films focus solely on the torture and mutilation of a woman, with the second film trying to pass itself off as found-footage of a real assault on a woman. Rumours suggest that Charlie Sheen saw the film and was convinced that it was real, with his insistence leading to an FBI investigation. However, not only can such a rumour not be substantiated but it is difficult to understand how anyone could think that cold entrails being thrown at a woman constituted real-life torture, or that any of the kicks or hits were actually hitting the actress at the film's beginning. While such films are problematic in terms of portraying violence towards women, the cinematic pretensions of the Guinea Pig films deconstruct the concept of an unproblematic identification between the characters on screen and those in the auditorium. Here the pornography collapses into the horrific and, as Sharp notes, 'Japanese cinema became notorious for its excesses.'[8] The media furore surrounding the case of Tsutomu Miyazaki in 1989, known as the Otaku killer who abducted and murdered four young girls and was found to have a large quantity of pornographic films in his possession including, purportedly, the Guinea Pig films, resulted in Japanese cinema moving away from the excesses of the early 1980s and, by the late 1990s, sexually violent and S/M fantasies had all but disappeared from Japanese cinema.

However, while some pink films played out misogynistic fantasies of male dominance, such as the torture, S&M, and *ero-guro* genres, Toei's 'pinky violence' series offered powerful woman in central roles who, rather than being repeatedly tortured and subject to sexual violence, were positioned as the perpetrators of violence whose very presence and activity subverted traditional Japanese patriarchal concepts of appropriate femininity. Particularly of note are the Female Prisoner Scorpion series, which began with *Female Prisoner #701: Scorpion* in 1972. Though ostensively Women in Prison films, much of the action of the first three films in the series directed by Ito takes place outside the prison. Together with *Sex and Fury* (1973), the Scorpion films have been credited as a direct influence on Tarantino's *Kill Bill* films (2004/2005).

The emergence of the home-video market, and hardcore pornography (Adult Video), resulted in the 1980s led to Eirin laying down more restrictive guidelines for sexually-explicit and violent films. With these new easily-accessible forms of pornographic films, it would have seemed that the market for pink cinema would no longer exist. This was not the case, and it continued with its main directors, Genji Nakamura, Banmei Takahashi and Mamoru Watanabe, known collectively as 'The Three Pillars of Pink'.[9] It was in the 1990s, however, that pink cinema saw a renaissance with a new generation of directors known as the Four Devils (shitennô). The Four Devils are Kazuhiro Sano, Hisayasu Sato, Toshiki Sato and Takahisa Zeze.[10] Key films include the acid hallucinatory *The Bedroom* (1992), with its cameo from the real-life Japanese cannibal Issei Sagawa, and Zeze's *The Woman in Black Underwear* (1997). The newest group of pink directors are known as the *Seven Lucky Gods* (*shichifukujin*) and are Toshiya Ueno, Yuji Tajiri, Shinji Imaoka, Yoshitaka Kamata, Toshirô Enomoto, Mitsuru Meike, and Rei Sakamoto.[11] Like the first wave of pink cinema, these films are focused less on sex and more on politics. Toshiyo Ueno's *Ambiguous*, which was voted the pink film of the year in 2004, is not interested in sex for sex's sake but instead provides a social commentary on recent outbreaks in Japan of group suicides. The pink film continues to be a significant part of Japanese film-making practice and, despite the arrival of Adult Video, will continuously flourish if the last ten years are anything to go by.

Notes

1. Jack Hunter (1998) *Eros in Hell: Sex, Blood and Madness in Japanese Cinema*, London: Creation Books, p. 26
2. Hunter, p. 7
3. Jasper Sharp (2008) *Behind the Pink Curtain: The Complete History of Japanese Sex Cinema*, Godalming, Surrey: FAB Press, p. 46
4. Yuko Mihara Weisser and Thomas Weisser (1998) *Japanese Cinema: Encyclopaedia – The Sex Films*, Vital Books, p. 20
5. Anne Allison, 'Cutting the Fringes: Pubic Hair at the Margins of Japanese Censorship Laws', in *Hair: Its Power and Meaning in Asian Cultures*, A. Hiltebeitel and B. D. Miller (eds), State of New York University Press, New York, 1998, p. 185
6. Hunter, p. 23
7. Hunter, p. 69
8. Sharp, p. 247
9. Weisser, p. 231
10. Sharp, p. 249
11. Sharp, p. 311

Colette Balmain

Ambiguous

Aimai

Studio/Distributor:
Kokuei

Director:
Toshiya Ueno

Producers:
Nakato Kinukawa
Kazuto Morita
Kyoichi Masuko

Screenwriter:
Hidekazu Takahara

Cinematographer:
Yasumasa Konishi

Duration:
63 minutes

Cast:
Hidehisa Ebata
Noriko Murayama
Nikki Sasaki

Year:
2003

Synopsis

Five strangers: a battered wife; an AV actress; a schoolgirl; a lowly restaurant worker and a maker of *hanko* (a signatory stamp) – brought together by loneliness and despair – make a pact through the Internet to commit suicide together. Purportedly based loosely on real events, *Ambiguous* introduces us to each character, focusing in on their despair; while the restaurant employee, Innocent, finds difficulty in adopting a deferential attitude towards his customers, the battered wife is shown being brutally beaten by her husband; the AV actress being ignored by her boyfriend (a pornographic film director) who tries to convince her to work in S&M films; the schoolgirl being bullied by her classmates as they help themselves to her expensive make-up; and finally the *hanko* maker taking part in an aborted marriage interview and being roughly rejected after having sex with his prospective bride. These disparate characters come together one evening to fulfill their suicide pact.

Critique

Ambiguous was named pink film of the year at the sixteenth Annual Pink Taishô awards which took place in April 2004 at the refurbished Shingungei-zei. One of the latest generations of directors of pink cinema, or the Seven Lucky Gods (*shichifukujin*) as they are known, Toshiya Ueno shows great promise in this his second pink film. While *Ambiguous* has the requisite number of sex scenes, these scenes are perfunctory, often highlighting the character's despair and loneliness. Sex here, like food, is seen as a basic instinctual need which, while it can be a signifier of one person's power over another (as in the case of the abused wife and AV actress), allows the reaffirmation of one's humanity through intimacy with another. Like Sion Sono's *Suicide Circle* (J2000) and *The Suicide Manual* (2003), *Ambiguous* comments on the relatively high rates of suicide amongst the young and the aged in Japan compared to elsewhere. Statistics show that, in 2000, 33,000 people committed suicide in Japan, directly leading to the development of a special programme by the Ministry of Health to tackle the issue, and this followed the success of Wataru Tsurumui's instruction book *The Complete Manual of Suicide* in the early-1990s. Emphasizing the individual's right to commit suicide, the book has sold over 1.2 million copies in Japan and has been found at the site of a number of group suicides, with one particular location identified in the book providing the place for 74 suicides in 1998.

Using the form of the pink film, Ueno is commenting on what is a critical socio-political concern in contemporary Japan. At the same time, *Ambiguous* is decidedly more hopeful than other films on the topic in that it ultimately affirms the potentiality inherent in living over the negation of death. This is demonstrated through the transformation of Innocent, from socially inept otaku, to a fully-functioning individual in one of the last scenes of the film. 'Are You Alive?' – the final words of the film spoken by the schoolgirl as she stands on the roof of her school – are a direct address and/or challenge to the audience. *Ambiguous* clearly demonstrates that pink cinema cannot be dismissed as simply pornography or erotica but that the genre can allow contemporary Japanese film-makers the freedom to interrogate crucial philosophical and political issues in a similar manner to the first wave of independent pink cinema directors, such as Koji Wakamatsu, in the 1960s.

Colette Balmain

Entrails of a Virgin

Shojo No Harawata

Studio:
Rokugatsu Gekijo

Director:
Kazuo Komizu [Gaira]

Producers:
Matsuo Sato, Hiroshi Hanzawa

Screenwriter:
Kazuo Komizu [Gaira]

Cinematographer:
Akihiro Ito

Art Director:
Yuji Hayashida

Composer:
Hideki Furusawa

Editor:
Kan Suzuki

Duration:
72 minutes

Cast:
Saeko Kizuki
Naomi Hagio

Year:
1986

Synopsis

A group of fashion photographers and their models wrap up a day's shooting and retreat to a cabin in the middle of nowhere. As they settle down to a night of non-stop sex, they're interrupted by a misshapen, humanoid monster determined to impregnate a human female.

Critique

As the succinct synopsis suggests, *Entrails of a Virgin* is not exactly challenging stuff. As a blend of graphic sex and over-the-top splatter it is on a level with the *Guinea Pig* series, and only likely to appeal to people who enjoyed those films. A former scriptwriter for *pinku* legends like Koji Wakamatsu and Masaru Konuma, director Komizu (aka Gaira) pushes the boundaries as far as he can without breaking Japanese censorship laws. Without the obligatory optical 'fogging', *Entrails of a Virgin* would count as hardcore pornography.

In genre terms, *Entrails of a Virgin* resembles *Friday the 13th* (1980) and its slasher brethren, with the victims picked off one by one as they separate from the group or wander off into the woods. Komizu throws in a few moments that might just about qualify as gory comedy were they not so completely tasteless. It also does not work particularly well as pornography, since the sex and nudity is frequently interrupted by graphic blood and gore. Anyone who does enjoy *Entrails of a Virgin* should try the pseudo-sequel *Entrails of a Beautiful Woman*, (1986) which features even more sex and violence, this time inspired by rape-revenge 'classics' like *I Spit on your Grave* (1978). The Gaira-directed *Female Inquisitor* (1987) is often considered to be a third film in the series but the similarities are minimal; here Gaira is more interested in sex, and the film boasts a noticeably higher budget.

Jim Harper

Female Prisoner #701: Scorpion

Joshuu 701-gô: Sasori

Studio/Distributor:
Toei

Director:
Shunya Ito

Screenwriters:
Fumio Konami
Hiro Matsuda

Cinematographer:
Hanjiro Nakazawa

Art Director:
Tadayuki Kuwana

Composer:
Shunsuke Kikuchi

Editor:
Osamu Tanaka

Duration:
87 minutes

Cast:
Meiko Kaji
Isao Natsuyagi
Fumio Watanabe

Year:
1972

Synopsis

Nami is a police informant who is passionately involved with the police detective, Sugimi, who is acting as her mentor and case worker. However, he simply uses her as a means to developing links with the yakuza and advancing his position within the department. After attacking the corrupt detective, Nami is sentenced to hard labour in a women's prison where the inmates are routinely victimized by the violent and sadistic guards, and often fight amongst themselves. Nami develops ties with several inmates who help her survive in the dangerous environment and, when a riot breaks out, she takes advantage of the situation and escapes, leading to a final confrontation with Sugimi.

Critique

Based on the cult comic book by Tooru Shinohara, the legendary exploitation item *Female Prisoner #701: Scorpion* blends the revenge thriller with the women in prison genre. It also mixes elements of the pink film to deliver an exciting experience which owes as much to arthouse as it does to grindhouse. Ito's adaptation is certainly violent, with Nami taking beatings from her guards and fellow inmates and being tortured with boiling hot soup, yet it is also beautifully staged and shot with innovative sets-within-sets production design and virtuoso camera work during the action sequences. The soundtrack features appropriately cool 1970s' tunes, all of which perfectly complement the visual cues and scene transitions, and obviously served as stylistic reference point for Quentin Tarantino's *Kill Bill* films (2003/2004). The cine-literate American independent director also 'borrowed' the central revenge plot of Ito's film, with Nami seeking vengeance after being betrayed by her professional mentor and lover, although it is a shame that Tarantino's double-bill was not nearly as lean and mean as his structural model. Shunya Ito, making his directorial debut, wastes little time on exposition, and concentrates on serving up consistently-exciting and inventive scenes, and an erotic encounter in solitary confinement when an undercover police officer is so seduced by Nami that she fails to report anything of significance to her superior and then begs to be returned to the cell so that she can spend more time with the prisoner known as Scorpion

Female Prisoner #701: Scorpion is often referred to as a Women in Prison film, although not all of the narrative takes place behind bars, and its heroine is more empowered than her equivilants in the American quickies that were served up by the Roger Corman school of low-budget exploitation film-making, best exemplified by Jonathon Demme's *Caged Heat* (1974). While *Female Prisoner #701: Scorpion* does offer some of the key ingredients of the WIP film, such as torture, sex, shower scenes, and corrupt prison guards, the core of the narrative is the aforementioned relationship between Nami and Sugimi the police detective who abused her willingness to act as his informant so that he could climb up the department ladder and simultaneously carve out a lucrative sideline as an associate of the yakuza. Meiko Kaji is a strong, if largely silent, presence as Nami, demonstrating her physical prowess in fast, effective moves and exhibiting a steely resolve when threatened with torture, or being forced to dig holes and then fill them in again as punishment for rebelling against the order of the institution, while Isao Natsuyagi's Sugimi makes for a suitable adversary, a swaggering villain who revels in his amorality, with the palpable tension between the two leading to an intense conclusion.

John Berra

Go, Go Second Time Virgin

Yuke yuke nidome no shojo

Studio:
Wakamatsu Production

Director:
Koji Wakamatsu

Producer:
Koji Wakamatsu

Screenwriter:
Izuru Deguchi

Cinematographer:
Hideo Ito

Composer:
Meikyu Sekai

Duration:
65 minutes

Cast:
Mimi Kozakura
Michio Akiyama

Year:
1969

Synopsis

On the roof of an apartment house in Tokyo, a young girl is gang-raped by a group of hippy-ish vagabonds as a young man looks on. When she awakes the next day, the young man is still watching her, and she greets him with a cheery 'good morning!' As they watch the traffic below and ruminate about the time interval between jump and impact, she tells the young man, who already sports slashed wrists, of her tragic family history and her wish to die. The girl recites a poem for him, naming herself the 'Second Time Virgin'. As the two individuals build a tentative relationship, and slowly reveal their respective traumas, their conversations increasingly revolve around death, killing, suicide and love.

Critique

KojiWakamatsu is often heralded as the king of pink film. While this acclaim serves to ignore many much more successful and very talented directors, he certainly is the best-known brand name in the genre. However, his films always skirted the borders of a genre that, in the 1960s, was already notoriously hard to pin down. Caught between sexploitation and experimentation, and between political activism and grindhouse conventions, Wakamatsu eventually broke out of the pink film mould but even in the late-1960s his films were wiggling their way out of any limiting definitions. After his *Affairs Within Walls* (1965) was shown at the Berlin Film Festival and caused a national scandal in 1965, Wakamatsu founded his own production outfit and recruited some experimentally-inclined and politically-minded young talents, who often jointly wrote scripts under the pseudonym Izuru Deguchi. Production circumstances were rough, and *Go, Go Second Time Virgin* was shot on location on the roof of the apartment building where Wakamatsu lived, in the now highly fashionable district of Harajuku. The male lead was played by one of his assistant directors.

The film was first screened at a Wakamatsu film event at the Sasori-Za, an event space under a theatre run by independent film distributor/producer ATG, then one of the centres of Tokyo underground culture. This alone shows how little he was confined by the then developing circuit of pink film theatres, and his influence was thus more widely felt. Critic Masao Matsuda commented on the development from the claustrophobic *The Embryo Hunts in Secret* (1966) to the isolated but open rooftop of *Go, Go...* with an article titled 'From Closed Rooms to Landscape', triggering an influential body of film theory in Japan that would become known as 'landscape theory'.

The memorable title is taken from a poem by Yoshinori Nakamura, as are the lyrics of the song that the boy somewhat bizarrely sings on the rooftop, with musical arrangement by film-maker and later Japanese Red Army member Masao Adachi. The abstract handling of the grim subject matter of disillusioned youth, with no course of action left but more or less focusing violence against both oneself and others, was visible in many Wakamatsu productions at the time. Adhering to decidedly non-PC pink film conventions, the violence most often manifested itself against the female body, transforming it into a symbol of both national and generational despair. This carried a diffuse but recognizable leftist message, endearing Wakamatsu to a young audience caught up in the student movement. Three years after *Go, Go Second Time Virgin*'s first screening in Tokyo, it was shown at the Pesaro Film Festival, and the recent resurgence of interest in Wakamatsu has since repositioned it in numerous retrospectives on the international film festival circuit.

Alexander Zahlten

In the Realm of the Senses

Ai no corrida

Studio/Distributor:
Argos Films, Nouveau Pictures

Director:
Nagisa Oshima

Producer(s):
Anatole Dauman,
KojiWakamatsu

Screenwriter(s):
Nagisa Oshima

Cinematographer:
Hideo Ito

Composer:
Minoru Miki

Editor:
Patrick Sauvion, Keiichi Uraoka

Synopsis

In the Realm of the Senses is based upon a real-life event. In 1936 a geisha called Abe Sada was found wandering the stress of Kyoto with her lover Kichi's severed penis in her hands. In *In the Realm of the Senses*, Sada is an ex-prostitute who works as a maid in Kichizo Ishida's (Tatsuya Fuji) house. Sada becomes sexually obsessed with Kichizo and they begin an affair, which becomes increasingly more extreme as time passes. On only one occasion do we see Kichizo and Sada passing time together as lovers outside the confines of the rooms in which they conduct their increasingly sadomasochistic affair, often having sex while watched by other women who sometimes participate.

Critique

Nagisa Oshima is one of the noted directors of the Japanese New Wave. His 1968 film *Death by Hanging* is typical of the youth-centred dramas of New Wave Directors. It is perhaps, though, his 1983 *Merry Christmas Mr Lawrence* for which Oshima was best known in the West, before *In the Realm of the Senses* eventually made it onto video in a heavily-cut form. The film still divides audiences and critics alike as to whether it is pornography masquerading as art cinema or a masterpiece of Japanese cinema. There can be little doubt that *In the Realm of the Senses* was politically motivated and that the explicit nature of the sex was used as a direct challenge to the Japanese censorship

Duration:

98 minutes

Genre:

Erotic Cinema

Cast:

Tatsuya Fuji, Eiko Matsuda, Aoi Nakajima,

Year:

1976

system at the time, which allowed any configuration of sexual perversion and sexual violence as long as the film abided by strict guidelines. Female genital hair was one of the three things deemed obscene by Eirin, the statutory body in charge of Japanese cinematic censorship. So it is significant that the first time we meet Sada she lifts her kimono to show an old man – perhaps a figuration of the censor – her pubic hair. This challenge did not go unheard, and Oshima was arrested and charged with obscenity, although found not guilty at his trial.

The set design and costumes, which evoke Japan in the 1920s before modernization and Westernization transformed Japan and are signifiers of Oshima's aesthetic sensibility, provide a beautiful background (some scenes are almost straight out of Sunga *ukiyo-e* woodprints) to the highly-charged sex scenes between Sada and Kichizo. However, the sex scenes, although inventive, become repetitive, and the addition of a rape scene – which was par for the course in pink cinema at the time – is nothing if not problematic. *In the Realm of the Senses* attempts to subvert the codings of pink cinema by showing what was at the time unrepresentable and, in doing so, exposing the hypocrisy of Japanese censorship regulations. However, in its representation of the sexually-voracious woman who signifies death, it is no less misogynistic than other examples of pink cinema. The only explanation we are offered for Abe's behaviour is that she suffers from hypersensitivity.

The insatiable woman is of course another common trope of pink cinema and much mainstream pornography in the 1970s – for example *Sex Psycho* (1970) or *Deep Throat* (1972). As such, Abe is the epitome of the femme fatale who fascinates her male prey, seducing him before finally killing and castrating him. Here, female sexuality as castrating is literal rather than metaphorical. Oshima's next film, *Empire of Passion*, sometimes seen as a sequel to *In the Realm of the Senses*, while considerably less explicit, manages to more authentically chart the destructive relationship between two star-crossed lovers. Having said this, there can be no doubt that *In the Realm of the Senses* is an important film in the history of Japanese cinema, but perhaps its posterity lies within the debates that surround it rather than with the attributes of the film itself.

Colette Balmain

Snake Of June, A / Rokugatsu No Hebi, 2002. Produced by Kaijyu Theater

A Snake of June

Rokugatsu no hebi

Studio:
Kaijyu Theater

Director:
Shinya Tsukamoto

Producer:
Shinya Tsukamoto

Screenwriter:
Shinya Tsukamoto

Cinematographer:
Shinya Tsukamoto

Art Director:
Shinya Tsukamoto (Production Design)

Composer:
Chu Ishikawa

Synopsis

Rinko is a beautiful young woman who loves her balding businessman husband Shigehiko very deeply, but feels the need to be more of a caretaker to him in order to support his career and, therefore, does not want to bother him with her own needs. So she represses her desires, which begin to eat away at her. Meanwhile, as she works at her job on a mental-health hotline, a former caller gets in touch to tell her that, since she helped him, he now wants to return the favour. He turns her own advice back on her – 'You've got to do what you really want' – and expresses his belief that the sexual fantasies she has been having in private should be acted out in public. He begins to force the issue with pictures he has taken of her during her private moments, and slowly intertwines himself into her and her husband's lives.

Critique

Shinya Tsukamoto's *A Snake of June* is a gorgeously-filmed tale of repressed desires coming to the surface. The beautiful blue-and-white photography not only looks fabulous and quite unique, but also emphasizes the constant presence of water throughout the film. Water is indeed found everywhere, casting fluid shadows, glistening as beads of sweat, and pouring from drainpipes, serving to represent the rebirth of these characters from the rather tame and bland lives they are initially seen to be leading.

Editor:

Shinya Tsukamoto

Duration:

77 minutes

Cast:

Asuka Kurosawa

Yuji Kohtari

Shinya Tsukamoto

Year:

2002

The role of the photographer/blackmailer is played by Tsukamoto himself, and it is certainly a tricky character for the director to tackle in that he must show himself to care for Rinko, and to truly want to help her, but also carry out some cruel behaviour. He essentially acts as her, and eventually her husband's, guide through Hell so that they may be reborn on the other side and bring closure to the disconnection between them. Shigehiko, for his part, sees his wife as someone to cherish and protect and, because of this, he sinks himself into his work and sleeps in another room to avoid temptation, but this also makes him quite jealous. Tsukamoto's photographer is the catalyst for bringing all of these repressed feelings out into the open, as exemplified by a scene in the rain in which Shigehiko spies on his wife stripping down while the photographer snaps away.

The film runs a scant 77 minutes and Tsukamoto keeps it moving at a good clip. With Rinko's story taking up the first half, the rest of the movie pulls in Shigehiko's tale, further machinations by the photographer and a number of surreal scenes that help bring out Shigehiko's own feeling. One memorable scene shows the husband being forced to be a voyeur whilst wearing a funnelled mask as he witnesses two women engage in sexual activity. It is not meant to be taken completely literally, but such scenes are very effective in conveying the emotions of Shigehiko. Even though Tsukamoto's visuals are centre stage, Asuka Kurosawa's performance as Rinko is the dominating factor of the film and she is quite stunning, putting everything into her bravura performance. Ultimately, *A Snake of June* is probably the best example of Tsukamoto's skewed vision of humankind's difficulty in relating to each other in a personal and sexual manner.

Bob Turnbull

Strange Circus

Kimyo no Circus

Studio:

Sedic

Director:

Sion Sono

Producers:

Koji Hoshino

Toshihiro Sato

Screenwriter:

Sion Sono

Cinematographer:

Yuichiro Otsuka

Synopsis

Wheelchair-bound erotic novelist Taeko is writing a book about the relationship between a husband and wife and their young daughter, involving incest, child abuse, violence and suicide. It might be based on the novelist's own childhood, and her assistant Yuji is determined to uncover the truth about his employer, but his investigations uncover a world where it becomes difficult to separate fantasy from reality.

Critique

After achieving acclaim for the memorable but flawed *Suicide Club* (2001), Sion Sono returned with the even more bizarre *Strange Circus*. Dropping the over-the-top splatter of the earlier film, Sono weaves a tale of twisted sexuality that might be equal parts fantasy, reality and hallucination. From the opening scene – an overweight drag queen introduces us to the 'strange circus' – nothing is entirely what it seems and following the permutations of the plot becomes very tricky indeed. The fusion of sex, horror and mystery in *Strange Circus* is

Art Director:
Hayato Oba

Composer:
Sion Sono

Editor:
Junichi Ito

Duration:
108 minutes

Cast:
Masumi Miyazaki
Issei Ishida
Rie Kuwana

Year:
2005

characteristic of the *ero-gro* or 'erotic-grotesque' tradition, a concept most often associated with the works of acclaimed Japanese writer Edogawa Rampo (1894–1965). Although primarily a writer of detective fiction influenced by Arthur Conan Doyle (among others), Rampo also produced a number of works that are closer in tone and content to the horror genre, exploring the dark side of the human psyche, from lust and depravity to violence and murder.

These stories have been the basis for many films over the years and their influence can be clearly seen in several recent works, including Takashi Miike's English-language debut, the made-for-TV *Imprint* (2006), the four-part anthology *Rampo Noir* (2005) and John Williams' *Starfish Hotel* (2006). *Strange Circus* also carries a few direct references to the author's work, such as the cello case in which a person can hide: a variation on the hollowed-out furniture used by one of Rampo's characters for a similar purpose. Literature as a whole plays a key part in the film, whether it is the influence of Edogawa Rampo, Taeko's torrid erotic novels or the opening quote from *À Rebours*, J Huysman's fictional account of thrill-seeking Satanic cultists in nineteenth-century Paris. With its scenes of cruelty and abuse, *Strange Circus* is not an easy film to like although, like *Suicide Club,* it is almost impossible to forget. It is also an engrossing mystery that serves up enough bizarre twists (including one which rivals anything in *Suicide Club*) to make it genuinely difficult to switch off. Not a film for all tastes, but certainly a rewarding one for those who are brave enough to try.

Jim Harper

Tokyo Decadence

Topazu

Studio/Distributor:
Ryu Murakami Office, Japan Video Distribution

Director:
Ryu Murakami

Producers:
Chosei Funahara
Tadanobu Hirao
Yousake Nagata
Akiuh Suzuki
Hank Blumental

Screenwriter:
Ryu Murakami

Synopsis

Ali works for a specialist sadomasochist sex agency and is repeatedly degraded and humiliated in a number of encounters with clients, who include a member of the yakuza, a rich businessman, and a crack addict. The opening encounter sets the tone for the ensuing narrative: Ali is repeatedly forced to strip for the pleasure of her male client as she stands in the glass window of a luxurious hotel room overlooking the glittering night city of Tokyo. While she strips, her male client snorts copious amounts of cocaine and, with some pride, proclaims to be perverted. Ali's virginal exterior (signified through her prim dress outside of sexual encounters) like that of Tokyo, hides the seeming perversions that exist just beneath the surface. But in a city like Tokyo, romance and love has no place and the film disintegrates into hallucination as Ali, high on drugs, goes to her ex-lover's house, where she is made fun of and turned away.

Critique

Tokyo Decadence is not an example of Japanese pink cinema, although it is often marketed as such. It is too long for one thing – the complete version is reputedly 135 minutes long. However it shares

Cinematographer:
Tadash Aoki

Composer:
Ryuichi Sakamoto

Editor:
Kazuki Katashima

Duration:
112 minutes

Cast:
Miho Nikaido
Sayoko Amano
Tenmei Kano

Year:
1991

with pink cinema an obsession and fetishization of female sexuality and of sadomasochism as a mechanism for subverting the repressive nature of Japanese society. Constrained by censorship regulations at the time, *Tokyo Decadence's* sexual imagery is not particularly explicit, although the scenarios that it visualizes, including one in which a client wants Ali to pretend she is dead so that he can rape her, explore the very margins of human sexuality. Miho Nikaido's performance is outstanding, capturing the very vulnerability of Ali and her isolation even while she caters to her clients' most perverse demands. The glittering surfaces of Tokyo, which hide the corruption beneath, comprise a *mise-en-scène* of desire that is devoid of human emotion.

As such, *Tokyo Decadence* is reminiscent of the earlier cycle of *roman porno* associated with Nikkatsu studios. Ali is not far removed from the archetypical Nami – the central female protagonist of all their official and unofficial *Angel Guts* (1979–1988) films – who is unable to enter into a satisfactory relationship with her male counterpart, Muraki. While some have criticized the film for its hallucinatory sequences in which Ali seeks her lost love, which are far removed from the more realistic sequences of sex that comprise the first two-thirds of the film, these sequences are central to its themes of alienation, loneliness and isolation that form the underside of Japan at the height of the economic boom. While *Tokyo Decadence* is not a particularly enjoyable film to watch, it is an interesting and relevant document of the contradictory nature of Japanese society.

Colette Balmain

Violated Angels

Okasareta hakui

Studio/Distributor:
Wakamatsu Productions

Director:
KojiWakamatsu

Producer:
Takashige Ichise

Screenwriters:
Masao Adachi
Juro Kara
KojiWakamatsu
Haruno Yamashita

Cinematographer:
Hideo Ito

Synopsis

Violated Angels is loosely based upon the real-life exploits of Richard Speck who, on 14 July 1966, murdered eight young nursing students, one by one. Two of his victims were Phillippino exchange students who had only arrived in Chicago two months previously. A third Phillippino, Corazon Amurao, who hid under a bed, was the only one to survive the attacks. *Violated Angels* follows the true story relatively faithfully, although the man is invited into the White Lily Nurse Dormitory and asked by the nurses to watch a lesbian encounter that is taking place in one of the bedrooms. Voyeurism soon turns to aggression and the attacker rapes and murders the women one by one as the others watch helplessly. As in the real-life story, one nurse survives, but the ending differs significantly.

Critique

Shot predominantly in black and white, *Violated Angels* is an example of the type of political exploitation cinema that fuelled the first cycle of pink cinema in the 1960s. KojiWakamatsu, a pioneer of pink cinema, is one of the most important directors of the Japanese New Wave, yet his films remain either banned or not widely available in the

Composer:

Koji Takamura

Editor:

Fumio Tomita

Duration:

56 minutes

Cast:

Juro Kara

Keiko Koyanagi

Miki Hayashi

Year:

1967

West. Wakamatsu began his career working as a director for Nikkatsu. His 1963 film *Secrets Behind the Wall* was selected for the Berlin Film Festival in 1965 and the scandal it caused in Japan, where the film had not been passed for exhibition by Eirin, together with the general critical success in the West paved the way for Wakamatsu to set up his own independent film company, Wakamatsu Productions.

A prolific and political director, Wakamatsu shot *Violated Angels* in just three days. Due to financial constraints – the budget for Wakamatsu's early films rarely exceeded 1,000,000 yen ($5,000) – *Violated Angels* was shot in black and white, with the more expensive colour film limited to the tableau of death where the bodies of the dead nurses are laid out in a mockery of the Japanese flag. The use of black and white, punctured with colour and freeze frames, removes the film from purely exploitation and adds to the political dimension of the

Violated Angels, 1967. Produced by Wakamatsu/Shibata

narrative. Wakamatsu's films have been described as owing as much to the works of Karl Marx and those of Marquis de Sade. Wakatmasyu was the first director of pink cinema to bring avant-garde techniques to the genre. In addition, the repeated use of deep focus and internal framing adds to the feeling of claustrophobia and entrapment that mirrors the isolation and alienation of the young generation in Japan in the 1960s. This, of course, was the time of the Red Army and militant student riots: a militancy that would end up being an exercise in futility. For Wakamatsu, sexuality and death are inextricably linked and, while the inherent misogyny of the genre of pink cinema is problematic here as elsewhere, there is no denying the political intention or impact of the film. As a study in voyeurism and male aggression, *Violated Angels* should be considered the Japanese counterpart to Michael Powell's *Peeping Tom* (1960) and Alfred Hitchcock's *Psycho* (1960).

Colette Balmain

The Woman with Red Hair

Akai Kami no Onna

Studio:
Nikkatsu

Director:
Tatsumi Kumashiro

Producer:
Ro Miura

Screenwriter:
Haruhiko Arai

Cinematographer:
Yonezo Maeda

Art Director:
Kazuo Yagyû

Composer:
Yuukadan

Editor:
Akira Suzuki

Duration:
73 minutes

Synopsis

Kôzo and the somewhat hapless Takao work on a large construction site in the countryside. Kôzo lures Kazuko, the boss's daughter, to a remote place, and he and Takao gang-rape her. On another day they pick up a hitchhiking woman with their cement truck, and she ends up at Kôzo's bleak apartment. As the rain pounds down without end, the two embark on an emotionally-rocky but physically-passionate affair. The woman discloses only fragments of her past: she has left behind two young boys and an abusive, amphetamine-addicted husband. Kôzo is torn between his fascination for the woman, her suffering and impulsiveness, and conflicted feelings he cannot articulate. Meanwhile, Kazuko claims she has become pregnant and pushes Takao to marry her. Takao, shaken, asks Kôzo to allow him to sleep with the woman in his apartment. Reluctantly, Kôzo agrees and one day arranges for Takao to burst in during sex and rape the woman. Afterwards, he strays through the bars, unable to face himself for what he has done, and unsure if she will ever return to the shabby little apartment.

Critique

The Woman with Red Hair was one of the most critically-acclaimed of the *Roman Porno* line of films produced by the major studio Nikkatsu. *Roman Porno* were softcore sex films, shot on fairly large budgets with trained studio staff and often quite ambitious directors, that were initially meant to appeal to a youthful demographic. Tatsumi Kumashiro was the most prominent, and one of the most stylistically-deft, of the directors who contributed to the genre. Nikkatsu had switched its formerly action-film and blockbuster-oriented production to sex films in 1971 in a desperate and successful bid to save the oldest film studio

Cast:
Junko Miyashita
Renji Ishibashi
Ako

Year:
1979

in Japan from bankruptcy, but the decision garnered much criticism and eventually led to a very public obscenity trial. By 1979, however, the films were regarded as a regular part of the film industry by most critics; *The Woman with Red Hair* was heaped with prestigious awards for best director and screenplay and made number four on the annual best-of list by leading film magazine Kinema Junpo.

The film is based on a story by author Kenji Nakagami, one of the central figures of 1970s' Japanese literature. A vocal and very public intellectual, Nakagami himself had a background based in the much-discriminated minority of the so-called Burakumin. Star scriptwriter and outspoken left-winger Haruhiko Arai retains much of the social ambiance and ambivalent thrust of Nakagami's books: Kôzo is a working-class figure weighed down by a harsh social climate, the impossibility of engaging with his situation through reflection, and a resultant penchant for tragic, verbal, and often physical, violence. The elliptic story and the very sketchy character histories, combined with precise performances from Ishibashi and Miyashita, almost paradoxically provide the characters with a degree of immediacy that quietly works against the obviously male-centred perspective.

Kumashiro, with his reduced colour palette and skilful switches between long takes and shaky telephoto shots, crafts a kind of social-realist counterpiece to Nagisa Oshima's *In the Realm of the Senses* (1976). Reminiscent of the sexual solipsism of Oshima's characters, Kôzo's dreary apartment becomes a refuge filled with desperate sexual and emotional clutching, but a refuge nonetheless in a world where the endless rain conjures up an atmosphere of clammy unease. In this context, the small degree of comfort that the two main characters afford each other becomes almost touching. True to the logic of genre film production, Kumashiro later shot a similarly-titled film on location in West Germany, *The Woman with a Red Hat* (1984).

Alexander Zahlten

YAKUZA/GANGSTER

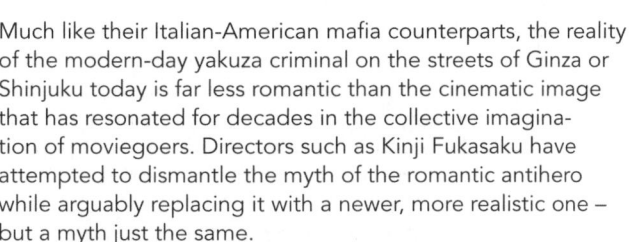

Much like their Italian-American mafia counterparts, the reality of the modern-day yakuza criminal on the streets of Ginza or Shinjuku today is far less romantic than the cinematic image that has resonated for decades in the collective imagination of moviegoers. Directors such as Kinji Fukasaku have attempted to dismantle the myth of the romantic antihero while arguably replacing it with a newer, more realistic one – but a myth just the same.

As with the iconic samurai hero, the figure of the gambling-obsessed, violence-prone gangster has been a mainstay in Japanese cinema since the earliest days of the industry. But it was not until the post-World War II years that the genre exploded in new, fascinating, and profitable ways. Yet yakuza films failed to find a critical legitimization in the West comparable to that of the samurai film. The samurai genre had the charisma of actor Toshiro Mifune, who became a worldwide star through his many samurai performances in Akira Kurosawa's films, such as *Seven Samurai* (1954), *Yojimbo* (1961), and *Ran* (1985). Yakuza films have never made as deep a cultural mark outside of Japan. That is not to suggest that the hard-boiled yakuza films of the 1960s (the heyday of the genre) and early 1970s have not belatedly found critical and audience appeal; they certainly have, due to film festival screenings and availability on DVD by various specialty companies, but the genre has never resonated in the collective imagination as its more mythic cinematic brethren – the samurai.

Although both genres trade in similar subject matter – the struggle of a lone anti-hero to maintain his sense of personal honour while having to serve a larger cause that he may disagree with, and the fight for traditional warrior values in an ever-changing world – the neon-lit underworld of the yakuza is decidedly more sleazy, violent, and nihilistic, making the stories

Left: *Sonatine*, 1993. Produced by Right Vision/Bandai   Yakuza / Gangster   267

of these two-fisted, tattooed thugs with missing fingers a little difficult for many viewers to warm to. The samurai genre is populated with similar characters: killers and gamblers with sword skills, but perhaps the historical distance (most *chambara* are set in the idealized distant past, while the yakuza films are in the all-too-real modern-day) has enabled audiences to fall under their spell without feeling much guilt or queasiness regarding the onscreen carnage. Nevertheless, audiences all over the world love celluloid crime tales and some of the finest have come from the relatively peaceful country (in terms of violent crime) of Japan.

In the post-war years, the two most successful major studios cranking out these lurid yet captivating tales of sin and violence were Toei and Nikkatsu. Known as *ninkyo eiga* (chivalry films), these tightly-plotted yet routine action pictures usually focused on a lone hero – generally played by stars such as Ken Takakura, Akira Kobayashi, Kei'ichiro Akagi, or Jo Shishido – having to take a stand against a dec-adent Westernized villain who personified the new booming yet soulless Japanese economy of the 1960s. Many of the films are forgettable and are simply the same story told over and over again. But the finest films from this time period, specifi-cally some of the films from the iconoclastic director Seijin Suzuki, are exemplary crime melodramas with style to burn and a cheeky attitude to match.

Suzuki, who worked for Nikkatsu, was initially viewed by many as an efficient though undistinguished film-maker. But a striking, outlandish, and increasingly surreal visual sense started to creep into his crime films, at first only during the violent climaxes, as in *Kanto Wanderer* (1963) and *Tattooed Life* (1965), then peppered throughout, as in *Youth of the Beast* (1963), and eventually overshad-owing everything else, as in *Tokyo Drifter* (1966) and *Branded to Kill* (1967). The last film, starring the oddly charismatic, puffy-cheeked Jo Shishido, is an absurd-ist classic and one that quickly derailed Suzuki's studio career. After the head of Nikkatsu, Kyusaku Hori, watched Suzuki's giddily-crazed overthrow and decon-struction of the yakuza action film, he immediately fired him, effectively derailing the director's career for years to come. Viewed now, Suzuki's wild career and body of work (yakuza films being the most widely-known, though hardly the most interesting) are remarkable testaments of an idiosyncratic genius – a mix of Sam Fuller, Jean-Luc Godard, and David Lynch.

For many cinemagoers Suzuki is the most wonderfully potent (and best) gate-way director into the yakuza genre. But for others, the finest director to contrib-ute to the genre is Kinji Fukasaku. While Suzuki chose to overthrow the clichés and conventions of the genre by showing us how silly and ridiculous his hard-headed antiheroes truly were, Fukasaku opts for a double-barrelled shotgun to blow holes into the myth of the honourable gangster. Fukasaku, like Suzuki, had tried his hand with various genres over his long career: from science fiction, with *The Green Slime* (1968) and the notorious *Battle Royale* (2000), to war drama with *Tora! Tora! Tora!* (1970) and *Under the Flag of the Rising Sun* (1972), taking in youth rebellion with *If You Were Young: Rage* (1970), historical epics such as *Shogun's Samurai* (1978), and the just plain indefinable *Black Lizard* (1968), How-ever, it is in his gritty, brutal yakuza films that his reputation earns its keep.

By the time that Fukasaku unleashed his 1972 film *Street Mobster*, starring Bunta Sugawarwa, the yakuza genre had grown flabby and self-satisfied. It needed a creative transfusion if it wanted to make it through the next few years, as audiences (primarily young males) had grown tired of the old-fashioned morality tales of stoic criminals fighting for the weak against the corrupt strong. The *ninkyo* films no longer reflected the turbulent times of the late-1960s/early-1970s. But *Street Mobster*, and more importantly the five-film series *Battles without Honour and Humanity*, did reflect the chaos and uncertainty of the times. Gone were the clean-cut and morally-certain assassins that had drawn in audiences a generation before. Now the culturally-subversive sensations of violence, rape, and nihilism lured audiences into the cinema, and Fukasaku was the reigning lord of cinematic misrule. Like his Western counterpart Sam Peckinpah – whose finest work is ferociously brave and political in the way that he exposes and dissects the disease at the heart of the so-called American Dream, and the manner in which audiences romanticize violence and turn cinematic killers into idols of the silver screen – Fukasaku is a fearless dissector of his own country's hero-worship of the outlaw and of the intricate political and cultural systems that keep such killers in power.

Frequently compared to Francis Ford Coppola's *Godfather* films, the *Battle without Honour and Humanity* series is just as complex as the more famous Italian-American mafia saga, but thankfully lacking Coppola's sentimentality and romantic excesses. Fukasaku's tightly-coiled epic is lean, sinuous, and volatile film-making at its best. Ruthlessly realistic and filmed in a crazed documentary-styled fashion, Fukasaku's films (known as *jitsuroku rosen* or 'line of realism') are perhaps too dishevelled and emotionally detached (despite a swaggering charismatic lead performance by Bunta Sugawarwa) to ever generate the kind of adoration that Coppola's films understandably have. But for accuracy and an almost fetishistic attention to criminal backroom dealing and politics, nothing surpasses these films. After the immense success of Fukasaku's series, the new grittiness ruled the cinema screens and a number of directors (including Fukasaku) delivered more of them to audiences ready for new criminal exploits stripped of glamour and heroic deeds. By the middle of the decade, the *jitsuroku* films were on their way to extinction and pretty much dead and buried by the end of the 1970s, much like the genre of the Western film in the United States. Through the 1980s and 1990s, the vast majority of yakuza films were made for the burgeoning direct-to-video market and catered to an increasingly-small audience. But while the genre stayed out of fashion with mainstream audiences, two significant and major auteurs of the genre did rise up and carve out their international reputations with their own particular and vastly different takes on the yakuza film.

The emergence of television personality and character actor 'Beat' Takeshi Kitano onto the world stage in 1993 with the film *Sonatine* was a surprise to many in Japan, where the film did not perform particularly well financially. But throughout the decade, Kitano's icy, deadpan, yet explosively brutal (and funny) yakuza films – the antithesis of Fukasaku's tempestuous, boozy film-making style – did earn him a fervent cult audience in America and the UK. His 1997 film *Hana-Bi* would eventually go on to win the top prize at that year's Venice Film Festival. The film, which is arguably Kitano at his best, turns the genre on its topsy-turvy head yet again to such an extent that it was difficult to see how any director after him could ever approach similar material.

But former straight-to-video hack Takashi Miike, who has been known to crank out up to four films a year, has been a worthy successor to the other auteurs of the genre. Known for his giddy, abrasively cartoonish style – with enough sex, drugs, sadomasochism, rape, murder, and gore for numerous exploitation films – and rabid energy, Miike's films are wildly uneven but infectiously entertaining. Some of his most infamous and successful films (at least in the West) occupy the yakuza genre and are also his most outrageous, particularly *Dead or Alive* (1999) and *Ichi the Killer* (2001). Miike is insidiously inventive in his depravity toward his characters, but his work is also paralysing because of it. It is definitely not for timid tastes.

While the yakuza genre may never capture the imagination of Western filmgoers in the same way that the samurai films have, there is still plenty of exemplary work to be savoured. And while those discussed here are merely the four prominent auteurs of the genre, and a great place to start for the beginner, the intrepid watcher will quickly discover his or her own favourites.

Derek Hill

Boiling Point

3-4 x jûgatsu

Studio:
Shochiku

Director:
Takeshi Kitano

Producer:
Kazuyoshi Okuyama

Screenwriter:
Takeshi Kitano

Cinematographer:
Katsumi Kanagishima

Editor:
Toshio Taniguchi

Duration:
96 minutes

Cast:
Yurei Yunaga
Gadarukanaru Taka
Takeshi Kitano

Year:
1990

Synopsis

After causing the defeat of his team in a junior baseball game, slow-witted Masaki returns to his job in a local garage. Assigned to valet the car of a yakuza, the gangster's abuse finally causes the otherwise-passive Masaki to snap and launch a sudden, if rather feeble, attack. Whilst Masaki's act of revolt seems to give him the courage to finally find a girlfriend, his action also draws the wrath of local yakuza boss Otomo. Masaki's baseball coach, and former Otomo gang-member, Iguchi, tries to settle the matter but, in his new 'civilian' role, Iguchi's actions ultimately land him with a severe beating. Seeking revenge, Iguchi vows to travel to Okinawa to acquire some illegal guns. However, Masaki and his friend Akira decide to travel to the island in place of their injured coach and, upon arrival, team-up with the delinquent Uehara, himself aiming to take retribution on his own local gang.

Critique

Boiling Point was Takeshi Kitano's follow up to *Violent Cop* (1989) and further develops some of the thematic and aesthetic trends evident in more well known works such as *Sonatine* (1993) and *Hana-Bi* (1997). By focusing on everyday people as well as yakuza, however, *Boiling Point* also adds an extra dimension missing in these subsequent works. In particular, we can see how the appeal of the yakuza is something that shapes male self-perceptions even amongst ordinary Japanese men. The film, however, also seems to suggest that Japanese masculinity is universally plagued by repression. Whilst the yakuza world may initially appear as detached from the pressures of everyday life, in the cynical 1990s this lifestyle is evidently also structured by bitter internal politics, ultimately only escapable in the form of self-destruction. The film's mixture of violence and comedy is as shocking as in any of Kitano's later works. This is perhaps most evident when a drunken party quickly degenerates into an uncomfortable display of Uehara's sadistic perversions before, once again, returning to outright farce as Uehara tries to sever Tamagi's finger. There is also an emphasis on repetition, which functions both as a source of comedy, as in Uehara's bar fight, or audience discomfort, exemplified in his later abuse of 'girlfriend' Fumiko.

With repetition also a feature of everyday life, any resistance in breaking these cycles only leads to a short-lived catharsis. Just as any attempts to stand up to Uehara's violence simply leads to further retaliation, so Uehara himself later receives a predictable, and indeed non-dramatic, execution for trying to stand-up to his gang. Even games and parties seem to quickly regress to hierarchies of power, suggesting that there is ultimately no escape from authority. Indeed, even though Iguchi's return to civilian life sees him achieve some degree of independence, his work as bar-owner still positions him as servile to insulting customers. The end of the film appears to pose the question of whether the whole story should be treated as a dream. Perhaps it is less important to analyse whether this is the case, or to

Boiling Point, 1990. Produced by Yamada Right Vision

ask whether the film has a coherent story world, and, instead, simply see the work as itself part of the circulation of images and fantasies interweaving with real-world self-perceptions. With some of his most astutely-judged comic characters and an intriguing narrative structure, *Boiling Point* should be situated right towards the top of Kitano's oeuvre.

Christopher Howard

Branded To Kill

Koroshi no rakuin

Studio:
Nikkatsu

Director:
Seijun Suzuki

Producers:
Kaneo Iwai
Takiko Mizunoe

Screenwriters:
Hachiro Guryu
Takeo Kimura
Chusei Sone
Atsushi Yamatoya

Cinematographer:
Kazue Nagatsuka

Art Director:
Sukezo Kawahara

Composer:
Naozumi Yamamoto

Editor:
Matsuo Tanji

Duration:
98 minutes

Cast:
Jo Shishido
Mariko Ogawa
Anne Mari

Year:
1967

Synopsis

An organized crime killer, Hanada, fails an assassination assignment when a butterfly lands on the end of his gun, and becomes a target of his peers. He had been looking to reach the pinnacle of his profession (he is currently the No. 3 Killer in the organization), but now that others are trying to kill him, including the never-before-seen No. 1 Killer, achieving that status has been made that much harder. Further complications are the women in his life: his wife despises him, but is crazed for sex, and the mysterious woman who brought him the job that he bungled has become his new infatuation. He just cannot shake off thoughts of her, and he becomes almost as obsessive about her as he is about the smell of boiled rice.

Critique

What Seijun Suzuki does in *Branded to Kill*, his last film with the Nikkatsu studio before they fired him and he became a director without a home for a decade, is to play with the form and structure of typical narrative film-making. The plot and storyline still come across, but the images are not exactly what you would expect along the way, and may not even make logical sense. However, they provide the information you need to keep you moving through the story without the film-maker having to always fall back on long bits of exposition or narration. After so many years in the studio system making 'B'-picture after 'B'-picture, you cannot blame Suzuki for trying different things by experimenting and tinkering with the parameters of story-telling.

Along with its style, *Branded to Kill* is also a solid piece of genre entertainment. If you give in to its images – let them tickle your brain for a while – the story just flows out of them. The 'B'- movie yakuza plot is filled to the brim with interesting character moments, as well surprising devices used to impart information. For example, Hanada does not need a shot of Scotch to calm down, he just needs to get out the rice cooker and inhale its vapours. It is odd character details like these that add so much more to the enjoyment of the story. These are not just randomly-assigned quirks as they flesh out these people and tell us more about their personalities. In addition, the actors are perfect for their roles: Jo Shishido working his way from cool to crazed as Handa, Anne Mari as the icy object of the hitman's obsession, and Mariko Ogawa as his loony wife.

Amongst many terrific sequences is one in which Hanada takes care of three separate jobs: using a huge billboard lighter as cover, shooting a victim through a sink drain from basement pipes, and escaping on top of a hot-air balloon. It all happens within a frame that is constantly shifting perspectives, angles, and timelines while also filled with interesting scenery, sets and props. By the end of the film, rooms filled with butterflies, a boxing ring and torrential rain showers have all played parts in what could pass for a swirling fever dream in the mind of Hanada. Who says that stories have to be told in a straight line?

Bob Turnbull

Brother, 2000, Recorded Picture/Office Kitano. Photographed by Suzanne Hanover

Brother

Studio:
Office Kitano

Director:
Takeshi Kitano

Producers:
Masayuki Mori
Jeremy Thomas

Screenwriter:
Takeshi Kitano

Cinematographer:
Katsumi Yanagijima

Composer:
Joe Hisaishi

Editor:
Yoshinori Ota

Synopsis

Senior yakuza Yamamoto is forced to flee to the US after his boss is killed in a Tokyo gang war and he is tipped off that the opposition want him dead. In a strange new country, where he does not speak the lingo, Yamamoto seeks out his younger brother who 'studies' in California, only to find him hanging out with petty criminals and dealing drugs for the local Mexican mafia. After killing the supplier who mistreats his brother, Yamamoto and his small-fry, makeshift, family find themselves at war with the Mexicans. Gradually growing in wealth and power, the motley crew of Japanese and African-Americans begin to learn and appreciate the yakuza spirit of honour, loyalty and brotherhood.

Critique

By no means on a par with *Hana-Bi* (1997) and *Sonatine* (1993), which won Takeshi Kitano international recognition and his overseas fan-base, *Brother* is nonetheless an entertaining feature. Its predictability washes down well with its over-emphasis on cultural stereotypes so that what emerges from the rubble of potentially damning defects is a satirical, though still sympathetic, caricature of Japanese and,

Duration:

114 minutes

Cast:

Takeshi Kitano
Omar Epps
Masaya Kato

Year:

2000

particularly yakuza, culture. Kitano may have been accused of being naïve about his own culture, due to the apparent exaggeration involved in depicting Japaneseness, but such criticism is unfounded. If the flashback sequence, which depicts the lead up to Yamamoto's escape from Tokyo, does not convince the viewer that this is all good-humoured comedy, then the scene in which one yakuza demonstrates his fake pinkie to another, amidst impressed remarks about no longer having to be turned out from Golf Clubs, certainly will.

The acting is by no means commendable, and often even cringe-worthy. On the plus-side, the violence is graphic, the humour dead-pan, and Kitano's central character has that weird inscrutability that is loveable. Without it, *Brother* would have even less to boast of. In fact, a bartender's closing remark to Yamamoto about the Japanese being so inscrutable defines the significance of this film. *Brother* is not about the yakuza opening shop in America and its foreseeable consequences. It is Kitano drawing a comparison between the Eastern and Western psyche. Beyond Yamamoto and Kato's poker-face facade and their ability to resort to violence without batting an eyelid lies a deep sensitivity. When Kato becomes frustrated over an American gang-member's inability to chop off his pinkie in recompense for his betrayal, we witness the sincerity and the dedication to honour that is intrinsic to Kitano's rendition of the yakuza, which deems hesitation incomprehensible to Kato.

In contrast to the graphic violence are sequences of men at peace with their surroundings, often framed in extreme long-shot. These scenes, such as the one in which Yamamoto and his boys are playing on the beach or the one which follows the flight of a paper airplane Kato launches from a rooftop, suggest a capacity for juvenile wonder-ment that is akin to innocence. It is not like anything the Americans have ever known or experienced, and it is also what brings about the gang's final undoing. The poignant purity of spirit and mad selfless-ness of the yakuza cannot thrive when faced with ruthless ambition and self-interest.

Elest Ali

Bullet Ballet

Studio:

Kaiju Theatre

Director:

Shinya Tsukamoto

Producer:

Igarashi Maison

Screenwriter:

Shinya Tsukamoto

Synopsis

Goda, a salaryman type, is distraught after losing his love of ten years, Kiriko, to suicide. He is also obsessed with guns – the method Kiriko used to end it all. In the course of his drunken wanderings through the back streets of Tokyo, he encounters Chisato, a sultry cutie in skintight leathers who belongs to a gang that once pounded him to a bloody pulp. When Goda begins to rave at her for the beating, the other gang members appear, and continue where they had left off. Humiliated and enraged by this fresh insult, Goda decides to blow his tormentors away. First, however, he has to find a gun – no easy task, as he discovers. He tries to make his own piece, but learns to his woe

Cinematographer:
Shinya Tsukamoto

Art Director:
Mari Ehara

Composer:
Chu Ishikawa

Editor:
Shinya Tsukamoto

Duration:
87 minutes

Cast:
Shinya Tsukamoto
Kirina Mano
Tatsuya Nakamura

Year:
1998

that he is as ineffective a gunsmith as he was a street fighter. Failing to off his tormentors, he is drawn irresistibly into their orbit. But while the gang's male members are bad boys playing naughty games, Chisato has a genuine death wish. The climax comes in a war with another gang that offers Goda – a working gun finally in hand – a chance for his long-contemplated revenge, and Chisato, for her long-desired end.

Critique

At a time when the emotional temperature of many Japanese independent films ranged from medium-low to icy-cold, Shinya Tsukamoto was boiling over with *Tetsuo: The Iron Man* (1989), *Tetsuo II: The Body Hammer* (1992) and *Tokyo Fist* (1995) – films that were the essence of urban alienation and rage. In *Bullet Ballet* Tsukamoto continues to work out his various artistic and personal obsessions, including, as he states, 'the relationship between the metropolis and human physical existence'. But in place of writhing robots, slamming fists and other images straight from the seething core of the Japanese pop-culture imagination, Tsukamoto creates an underworld more recognizably like Shibuya at three in the morning. In short, he has returned to earth, if not quite to everyday life.

The change is not all for the better. Along with the extremity, the originality of his earlier work has largely disappeared. Instead, *Bullet Ballet* is a grim, if essentially romantic, journey through a noirish urban jungle where fashionable young outlaws play violently-nihilistic games. This theme was a popular one with younger Japanese directors in the 1990s but, too often, the aim was to attitudinize rather than to truly explore or expose. Tsukamoto, by contrast, is blazingly sincere in his rage against the Japanese social machine, but in *Bullet Ballet* he also has a tendency to fall into mangaesque poses, more self-regarding than self-revealing. Once the most personal of film-makers, willing to cinematically expose his own nerve endings, Tsukamoto has since become more distanced from his material. He now focuses more on coordinating his lighting and camera moves than journeying to the heart of his hero's obsessions. Despite its visual invention and narrative intensity, the film feels uninflected, like a drummer slamming out the same beat at the same tempo for a ten-minute solo.

In telling his story of a salaryman's jouney into the Tokyo underworld, Tsukamoto uses harshly-lit black-and-white photography and jittery camera work to create the right end-of-the-tether, edge-of-the-night mood. The industrial-noise score by Chu Ishikawa adds to this mood, as does a spare, intense performance by Tsukamoto as Goda. But all the atmospherics cannot disguise yet another recycling of familiar themes and motifs. What was stunningly *sui generis* in *Tetsuo* has started to feel banal in *Bullet Ballet*. We've taken this particular death trip once too often.

Mark Schilling

The City of Lost Souls

Hyôryû-gai

Studio:
Daiei Motion Picture Company

Director:
Takashi Miike

Producers:
Kazunari Hashiguchi
Toshiki Kimura
Hiroshi Yamamoto

Screenwriters:
Ichiro Ryu
Seishu Hase (original novel)

Cinematographer:
Naosuke Imaizumi

Art Director:
Reiko Kobayashi

Composer:
Koji Endo

Editor:
Yasushi Shimamura

Duration:
103 minutes

Cast:
Teah
Michelle Reis
Mitsuhiro Oikawa

Year:
2000

Synopsis

Brazilian-Japanese criminal Mario immediately sets about the daring and violent rescue of his Chinese girlfriend, Kei, as she is being deported from Japan to her homeland. They travel together to Tokyo, where, with the aid of Mario's friends in the Brazilian-Japanese community, the couple hopes to find help to get out of the country. After their false passports are ruined in a confrontation with Chinese crime-lord Ko, a former lover pursuing Kei, they discover they will need money to leave Japan a different way. So Mario, two of his friends and Kei form a plan to rob a local cock-fighting and gambling den, hoping that the money they steal will be sufficient. On the run, and with a price on their heads, Mario and Kei fight for their future in a city where nothing is ever straightforward.

Critique

The City of Lost Souls is an archetypal Takeshi Miike film that combines wild, anarchic and often experimental methods of shooting with a narrative that explores characters from marginalized sectors of Japanese society, in a contemporary Japan at odds with a cleaner, traditional perspective. The main characters are almost entirely immigrants, as is in fact the case with most of the speaking parts, and this, combined with some location shooting in California – doubling for parts of Japan – creates a sense that the film is consciously disrupting a sense of place and nationality. The film is expressing the idea that Japan is no longer Japanese and, as such, is set mostly in the confines of the Brazilian-Japanese community of Tokyo, with the plot involving members of the community and some Chinese immigrants and gangsters. The few Japanese characters even comment at times about 'foreigners' taking over in modern Japan, although Miike does not present this situation in a negative way and, instead, simply relates it as a symptom of contemporary society.

Despite having an intelligent commentary to make on the interesting subject of multiracial contemporary society in Japan, *The City of Lost Souls* falls short of having any real depth, partly due to a rather clichéd narrative tangent about a young blind girl who becomes involved with the proceedings, also because of vacant performances from the two leads: Teah as Mario as Michelle Reis as Kei. Their performances are vapid and their emotionless portrayals do nothing to make the audience warm to their struggle. The film features the excessive violence that is typical of Miike, from the yakuza firing a grenade-launcher in the street to Mario's bloody assault on their headquarters, armed with a shotgun. There are also some stylized moments of farce like 'Love' spelled out in blood spatter from a gunfight, and a CGI cockfight. As a result, *The City of Lost Souls* is best enjoyed as the fun spectacle it remains and although there is more going on, in order to appreciate the subtext, the audience needs to look beyond a couple of glaring flaws.

Matthew Holland

A Colt is my Passport

Koruto Wa Ore No Pasupoto

Studio:
Nikkatsu Corporation

Director:
Takashi Nomura

Screenwriters:
Shuichi Nagahara
Nobuo Yamada

Cinematographer:
Shigeyoshi Mine

Composer:
Harumi Ibe

Duration:
84 minutes

Cast:
Jo Shishido
Jerry Fujio
Ryotaro Sugi

Year:
1967

Synopsis

A gangland boss hires a hitman to knock off his rival. He agrees and, along with his sidekick, performs the task with precision and efficiency. Unfortunately, they are almost immediately double-crossed by the very man who hired them but, thanks to some quick thinking, they narrowly manage to escape. They hide out at an inn in Yokohama, hidden away by one of the female staff drawn to their cool swagger. However, after a failed attempt at leaving Yokohama, the hitman manages to smuggle out only his loyal sidekick, remaining behind to confront the boss and his gang for the climactic showdown.

Critique

Nikkatsu Corporation churned out its borderless brand of 'Action Cinema' like a well-oiled machine, using the same stars, playing variations on the same role, in very similar films, re-imagining and re-inventing Western genre cinema and its motifs. Narratively, and to some degree cinematically, Takashi Nomura's film owes much to the French New Wave, and the films of Jean-Pierre Melville in particular, as A Colt is my Passport echoes his tragic, minimalist films noirs. Shishido seems to embody the quintessential 'cool' that Jean Paul Belmondo and Alain Delon captured so well on screen, and this influence precedes the slew of Hong Kong Heroic Bloodshed films, such as John Woo's The Killer (1989). Although Nomura does not take the tragic elements of the genre to the extremes of Melville or Woo, all three directors do channel the same ideals into their central protagonist: a man who follows his own strict code, regardless of whether it will bring about his own death. These characters never crack and never break, always maintaining an air of confidence and panache. The completely random musical performance by Jerry Fujio evokes images of Elvis Presley, someone who heavily influenced the first generation of Nikkatsu Action films in the late-1950s, and the score obviously has roots in Spaghetti westerns.

The fusion of these influences is epitomized wonderfully in the final shoot-out, in which Shishido takes on a small army of yakuza goons at a dusty reclamation area. The scene is reminiscent of many Sergio Leone films, both in its expansive, desert-like location and its treatment of its lone-gunman protagonist. Despite the limitations under which Nomura's film was made, as part of the conveyor belt film factory that Nikkatsu had become, it channels the French New Wave, the American gangster film, the Spaghetti Western, and even a little Elvis, into becoming a completely original and inspiring film that embodies everything that is great about cinema. It is entertaining, compelling, and visually striking, and the perfect embodiment of Nikkatsu's borderless style.

Matthew Hardstaff

The Flower and the Angry Waves

Hana to Doto

Studio:
Nikkatsu

Director:
Seijun Suzuki

Screenwriters:
Kazuo Funabashi
Keiichi Abe
Takeo Kimura

Producer:
Takeo Yanagawa

Music:
Hajime Okumura

Cinematographer:
Kazue Nagatsuka

Art Director:
Takeo Kimura

Composer:
Hajime Okumura

Editor:
Akira Suzuki

Duration:
92 minutes

Cast:
Akira Kobayashi
Tamio Kawachi
Chieko Matsubara
Hiroyuki Nagato

Year:
1964

Synopsis

The time: the Taisho Period (1912–26). The place: Asakusa, a popular Tokyo entertainment district. Ogata, a former yakuza, is working as a common labourer. Manryu, a popular geisha who has her pick of clients, becomes sweet on Ogata, even bankrolling a successful gambling spree. This favouritism stirs the wrath of Izawa, a yakuza who wants Manryu for himself. Ogata is working for the Murata-gumi, which has won a big construction job from Daito Denryoku, an electric power compay. Tamai-gumi, with which Izawa is allied, is angling to steal the job away. Ogata is drawn into this struggle when he knocks down an old man who seems to be trespassing on the work site and learns that he is Mr. Shigeyama, an industry fixer and Murata ally.

Critique

The second pairing of Seijun Suzuki and Akira Kobayashi, following *Kanto Wanderer* (1963), *The Flower and the Angry Waves* unfolds in Suzuki's beloved Taisho Era Asakusa, whose colourful demi-monde echoes both old Japan and the new cultural influences from the West. Though the story, with its conflict between the salt-of-the-earth construction workers and grasping gangsters, is standard genre material, Suzuki films it with characteristic theatrical flair: the hitman, played by Tamio Kawachi, with his cape, bolero hat and Man-of-Mystery air, is the most obvious example, although Suzuki admits that the costume was the idea of Takeo Kimura, the production designer who also co-wrote the script. Similar scenes include the escape of Oshige and Ogata from Asakusa and the final confrontation in Niigata.

Characters struggle for their lives within a setting of stark, bizarre beauty, killing and dying with a stylized grace. Suzuki films all this without an obvious wink, but the very abruptness of the shifts from the straightforward to the surreal indicates an antic, subversive spirit at work. But, compared with Suzuki's later outrages, *The Flower and the Angry Waves* is still well within the boundaries of film industry and social conventions, from its story of true love thwarted by fate to Ogata's spurning of the feisty, rule-defying geisha Manryu for the weepy, pure-hearted servant girl Oshige (though given that Ogata is married to the latter, his choice is at least honourable). Even so, certain story choices belie a more unconventional, if not yet outwardly rebellious, attitude. One is the vicious beating by the supposedly 'good' oyabun that leaves half of Ogata's face a grotesque mess. Was Suzuki having a joke at the expense of his handsome star – or simply trying to give the audience a jolt?

Mark Schilling

Rainy Dog

Gokudo kuroshakai

Studio:
Daiei

Director:
Takashi Miike

Producer:
Tetsuya Ikeda

Screenwriter:
Seigo Inoue

Composer:
Koji Endo

Editor:
Yasushi Shimamura

Duration:
95 minutes

Cast:
Sho Aikawa
Lian-mei Chen
Tomorowo Taguchi

Year:
1997

Synopsis

After gang problems have forced him into exile, former Japanese yakuza Yuji is left stranded in Taiwan. Living in a cramped, run-down Taipei apartment, Yuji holds down a meatpacking job while still undertaking occasional hits for a local Taiwanese gang, and being tracked by the beleaguered Honami, a Japanese detective indefinitely posted in Taiwan until he has been able to indict his nemesis. Yuji's solitary life is interrupted when a former lover leaves him with a seemingly-mute boy, Ah Chen, who the lover claims is his son. Yuji remains inhospitable to the new arrival until he strikes up a relationship with a Taiwanese prostitute and a fragile family bond begins to form between the three alienated characters.

Critique

Rainy Dog forms the second part of Miike's *Shinjuku Triad Society* trilogy. Whilst it draws on similar themes of alienation, its focus is more on the dislocations of exile rather than mixed ethnicity. This sense of estrangement is particularly palpable in the representation of Taipei as a gloomy conurbation of weathered concrete and corrugated iron. As suggested by the title, it is also a city in which the overcast skies consistently break out into heavy downpours. Yuji's attempts to avoid the rain echo his self-imposed isolation from the world around him but, even when viewing Japanese monster films on his computer screen, he cannot block out its monotonous sound. The sense of the low value of human life is evident in the opening sequences of Yuji travelling in a lorry-load of animal carcasses and his impassive witnessing of a back-street stabbing. After he realizes that Lily also uses the computer as an attempt to overcome isolation, it is the mutual sense of disaffection that allows him to forge a connection. Rather than continuing to treat Ah Chen as a stray dog looking for a master, this link further develops into a makeshift family bond between the three characters.

With its serious tone, rounded central characters and little in the way of Miike's characteristic eccentricity, *Rainy Dog* is one of the director's more straightforward dramatic pieces. Miike even demonstrates his skills of *mise-en-scène*, particularly in the way in which he positions and moves the three central characters in such a way as to evoke the tentativeness of these unstable family bonds. The most creative act is probably to mix the yakuza genres with some conventions of the Western, and this is signalled most obviously in the slide-guitar music, but is also evident in the final showdown. Indeed, some degree of self-consciousness returns with the clichéd use of a cigarette case to save a life. But whilst Lily at one point threatens to become one of Miike's more interesting heroines, her fading narrative importance and off-screen death suggest that, in the world of Rainy Dog, revenge is the right of men rather than women. Whilst it is encouraging to see Miike turn his hand to more straightforward film-making, many of his seemingly more haphazard or incoherent productions are actually more challenging, perhaps making *Rainy Dog* the least interesting of the *Shinjuku Triad Society* series.

Christopher Howard

Sonatine

Sonachine

Studio:
Shochiku

Director:
Takeshi Kitano

Producers:
Masayuki Mori
Hisao Nabeshima
Takio Yoshida

Screenwriter:
Takeshi Kitano

Cinematographer:
Katsumi Yanagishima

Art Director:
Osamu Sasaki

Composer:
Joe Hisaishi

Editor:
Takeshi Kitano

Duration:
94 minutes

Cast:
Beat Takeshi
Aya Kokumai
Tetsu Watanabe

Year:
1993

Synopsis

Murakawa, a pokerfaced Tokyo-based yakuza underlord, is sent to Okinawa with his henchmen to mediate a truce between two feuding clans only to discover the clans are not in fact at war. Instead, a bomb rips through his headquarters and gunmen ambush him and his gang in a local bar. What is left of Murakawa's troops – the aging, slightly fey Uechi, the middle-aged, stern Katagiri, and two fledglings, Ken and Ryoji – hole up at a seaside cottage. There, the neophyte killers play with dolls, throw Frisbees, wrestle in the sand, spurt roman candles at each other, shower in the rain, and otherwise frolic on the beach. Their boss sometimes joins in, otherwise observing their youthful enthusiasms with nostalgia. When a peculiarly robotic assassin puts an end to the gang's impromptu beach-baseball game by firing a bullet into the pitcher's temple, Murakawa is drawn back into the internecine war for one last time and violence escalates.

Critique

Actor-writer-director-editor-media-icon Takeshi Kitano's perfectly paced gangster-film-cum-Ravelian-daydream possesses the violent eruptions and quiet eroticism of an unwritten Mishima masterpiece leavened by the director's trademark detached, absurdist worldview. The film both exploits and mocks yakuza conventions – sunglasses and tattoos, on the one hand; business suits and 'hostesses', on the other – and romanticizes its yakuza hero: the stoic and nostalgic, paternal and mischievous, philosophic and impulsive Murakawa. Obviously, Kitano feels both the insignificance and the humanity of his subjects. The miracle of *Sonatine* is his integration of contrasting elements – play and gunplay, reverie and brutality, suppressed *eros* plus massacre – so that each gains from the other. The violence jolts by contrast with the relaxed pace, and the melancholy of Murakawa's nostalgia for youth as he mentors his apprentices is deepened by our fear that the bloodbath that will inevitably erupt around them may mean that this will be his last stand.

Sonatine's aesthetics, too, reflect these contrasts. Stillness dominates. Characters are planted in static compositions. Even Kitano's gunmen stand nailed to the floor, weapons extended stiff-armed in a locked down frame. This stillness is underlined by two more formal elements: small subject-image size and protracted shot-duration. A wide shot in which a dozen people remain motionless – like the utterly inert 'group portrait' of Murakawa's team in the aftermath of the bombing, a shot so distant that it is impossible to determine which of the characters is speaking – draws particular attention to its rejection of classical, 'realistic' filmic strategies. In addition, when the duration of the shot clocks in at seventeen seconds, as this one does, the rejection feels all the more insistent. *Sonatine's* soundtrack, too, is unusually quiet: the aural equivalent of stillness.

The austere aesthetic not only unifies *Sonatine* but also provides a convenient set-up, a visual and aural 'straight man', for moments of comedy and violence, for both punches and punch lines. The shootout in the Okinawa bar, again, is typical. Though static and wide, it is relatively quick-cut, with nine shots in fourteen seconds, compared to the twelve-second average shot-length, and it is noisy. Incessant deafening gunfire drowns out, contrasts with, the distant waft of muzak that precedes and, drolly, follows it. *Sonatine*'s default style and Kitano's deadpan portrayal of Murakawa led critics to dismiss the film as empty, cold, essentially meaningless. But distant does not mean absent, and blank is not the same as empty. Since the film's form and its cast's performances provide only minimal clues to the inner lives of its characters, with no 'meaningful' close-ups of quivering faces, no push-in at times of crisis, viewers are free, within narrative confines, to pour their own emotions into Kitano's characters from their own personal storehouse of sentiments. *Sonatine*, then, becomes a 94-minute Kuleshov experiment, or perhaps even a Bressonian action-comedy.

Bob Davis

Tattooed Life

Irezumi ichidai

Studio:
Nikkatsu

Director:
Seijun Suzuki

Producer:
Masayuki Takagi

Screenwriters:
Kei Hattori
Kinya Naoi

Cinematographer:
Kurataro Takamura

Art Director:
Takeo Kimura (Production Design)

Composer:
Masayoshi Ikeda

Editor:
Akira Suzuki

Duration:
87 minutes

Synopsis

In order to help put his younger sibling through art school, Tetsu has become a low-level yakuza. He knows his place and the limits of his influence so when the Owada family commands the assassination of the head of the Totsuka clan, he goes about taking care of the business in a clean and methodical manner. The Owadas like to keep things tidy, too, and in turn dispatch another gang member to kill Tetsu. That attempt fails and the would-be murderer is killed by Tetsu's younger brother, Kenji, who has witnessed everything. The brothers decide to escape to Manchuria and end up stuck in a fishing port, where they fall in love with a pair of sisters. The aggressive Midori pursues a reluctant Tetsu, while Kenji is smitten with the older Masayo, the wife of the construction boss for whom they work. Tetsu knows that no good can come from sitting still and putting down roots while their past catches up with them and he will not even let Midori see his body because of the yakuza tattoos he has – the markings that have essentially set the destiny for him and his brother.

Critique

Seijun Suzuki's *Tattooed Life*, like many of his 1960s films, has a story that is not overly complicated or original, and which uses stock themes such as destiny, loyalty and sacrifice as its foundation, while the inevitable climax looms in the distance. *Tattooed Life* is reasonably entertaining but it is the film's style and narrative method that really grab the attention. Suzuki liked to play with the rules, so he developed shorthand ways of moving the plot along and avoiding long sequences of exposition. He might edit a scene in an unexpected way, or drop in some out of context images in order to impart the information the audience needed to know – just not necessarily in the way in which the audience might expect to receive it.

Cast:
Hideki Takahashi
Akira Yamauchi
Hiroko Ito

Year:
1965

For much of *Tattooed Life* these techniques are kept to a minimum, but its final reel is an explosion of colour and violence and is such a marvel of creativity that It feels like Suzuki has been saving it all up for that final stretch. In the climactic battle sequence, we get out-door shots that make the most of a thunderstorm and indoor shots that highlight typical Japanese architecture of the depicted time period (mid-1920s – the start of the Showa era). As the pace quick-ens, the camera angles become more severe and, suddenly, rooms and characters are bathed in saturated colours – with no points for guessing what red signifies. While the floodgate's opening during the climax helps to emphasize the emotional intensity of the film, the finale would not have been as effective without the deliberately slow journey that the story takes, and the emphasis on the relationships between the brothers and the sisters. These are complex characters that Suzuki is happy to spend time with and although the ending is what most viewers will remember, it is all the more effective because of everything that precedes it.

Bob Turnbull

Tokyo Drifter

Tokyo nagaremono

Studio:
Nikkatsu

Director:
Seijun Suzuki

Producer:
Tetsuro Nakagawa

Screenwriter:
Kohan Kawauchi

Cinematographer:
Shigeyoshi Mine

Composer:
Hajime Kaburagi

Editor:
Shinya Inoue

Duration:
89 minutes

Cast:
Tetsuya Watari

Synopsis

Tetsu decides to follow his yakuza boss Kurata and abandon the life of a gangster. Kurata's old enemy, Otsuka, unsuccessfully endeavours to take Tetsu into his clan so sends one of his killers to assassinate him, but Tetsu decides to leave Tokyo and lead the life of a wanderer. Kurata, however, betrays his former protégé and conspires with his yakuza rival, Otsuka. After surviving this conspiracy, Tetsu returns to Tokyo to confront Kurata and then finally leaves Tokyo for good, after settling his accounts with old friends and enemies.

Critique

Seijun Suzuki's *Tokyo Drifter* is such an explosive mixture of different genres and heterogeneous elements that one can hardly believe it was studio-produced. Resembling more an avant-garde manifesto of the 1960s, *Tokyo Drifter* seems to be parodying the yakuza genre. It is no wonder that Suzuki's playfulness with conventions revealed him as Nikkatsu's black sheep, ultimately leading to his dismissal for produc-ing overly-alternative films that went beyond studio-enforced bound-aries. With influences that range from Pop Art to 1950s' Hollywood musicals, and from farce and absurdist comedy to Surrealism, Suzuki shows off his formalistic acrobatics in a film that is clearly meant to mock rather than celebrate the yakuza film genre. Moreover, the experimental form together with the often incomprehensible narrative create a Brechtian platform on which Suzuki can unfold his syllogisms on the conformism dominating Japanese cinema and Japanese society in general. The first images are static shots of large grey buildings from the Tokyo business district and clearly contrast with

Chieko Matsubara
Hideaki Nitani

Year:
1966

the rest of the film. The primary colours are full of life and apart from subverting the yakuza aesthetics could also be expressing the sensibility and creativity that was suppressed under the boot of industrial standardization.

At the heart of the film is the absurd and delirious saloon sequence where Suzuki digresses from the narrative only to make fun of America, the conveyor of Japanese society's new formation. This sequence, though, does not signify Suzuki's denial of everything American or Western as he exploits Hollywood for the sake of his cinematic alchemy. The protagonist's whistling reminds us of cowboy films, while the Art-Deco club seems to have been painted by Vincent Minnelli's art director. Suzuki does not omit French cinema from his hybrid oeuvre: the Michel Legrand-type singing of Tetsu's girlfriend and the ridicule with which the villains are portrayed seem to be clear references to Nouvelle Vague. In the case of *Tokyo Drifter*, the oppressiveness of the studio almost seems beneficial for a director who did not reach the same levels of creativity once he was actually granted his artistic freedom.

Nikolaos Vryzidis

Tokyo Drifter / Tokyo Nagaremono, 1966. Produced by Nikkatsu

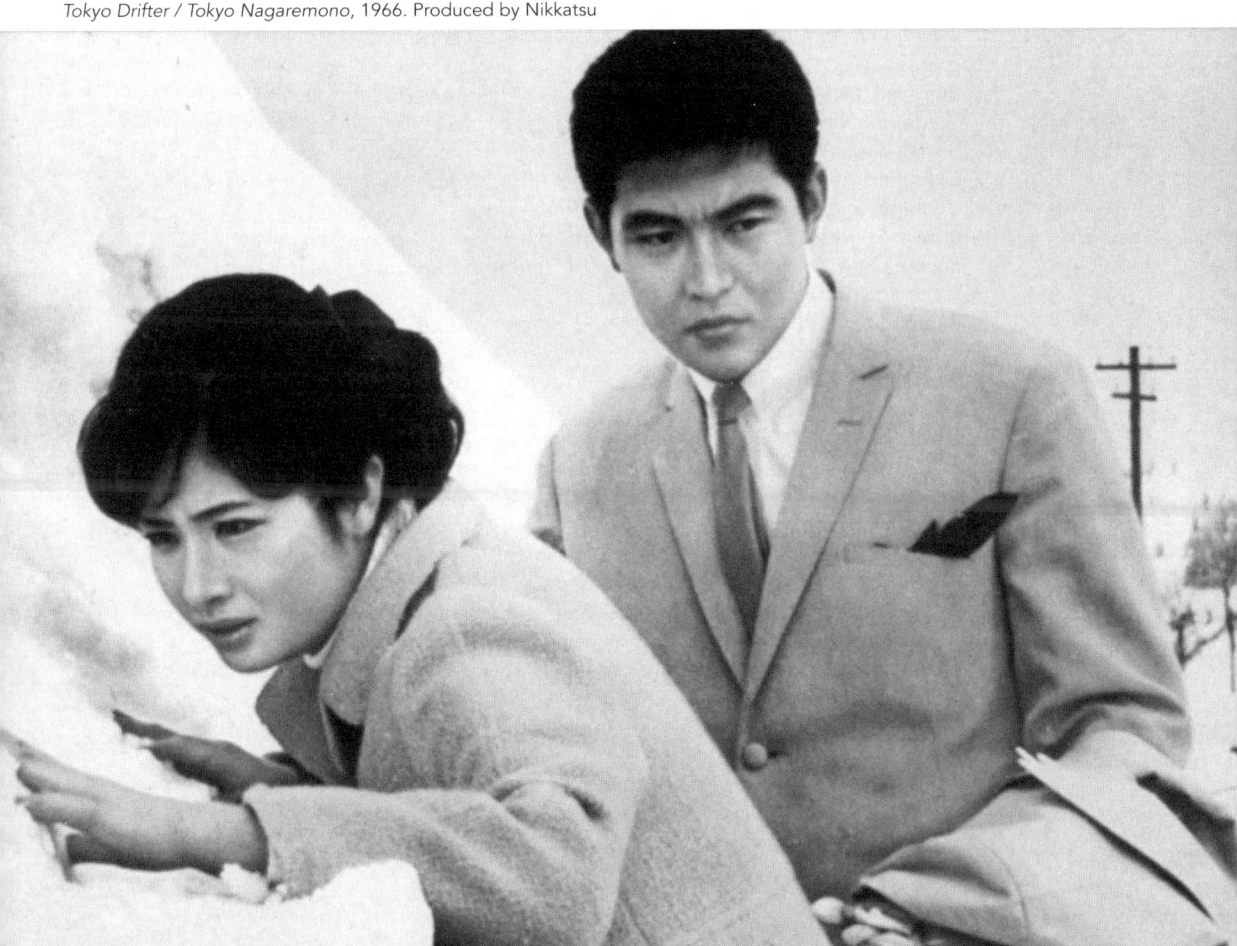

RECOMME READING

Anderson, Joseph & Ritchie, Donald (1982) *The Japanese Film: Art and Industry*, Princeton, NJ: Princeton University Press.

Balmain, Colette (2008) *Introduction to the Japanese Horror Film*, Edinburgh: Edinburgh University Press.

Barrett, Gregory (1989) *Archetypes in Japanese Film: The Sociopolitical and Religious Signifiers of the Principal Heroes and Heroines*, Selinsgrove: Susquehanna University Press.

Bolton, Christopher (2007) *Robot Ghosts and Wired Dreams: Japanese Science Fiction from Origins to Anime*, Minneapolis & London: University of Minnesota Press.

Bordwell, David & Thompson, Kristen (2006) *Film Art: An Introduction*, 8th edition, New York: McGraw-Hill.

Bower, Justin (2004) *The Cinema of Japan and Korea*, London: Wallflower Press.

Broderick, Mick (1996) *Hibakusha Cinema: Hiroshima, Nagasaki, and the Nuclear Image in Japanese Film*, New York: Routledge.

Brown, Stephen T (2008) *Cinema Anime*, New York: Palgrave Macmillan.

Buckley, S (2009) *The Encyclopaedia of Contemporary Japanese Culture*, London: Routledge.

Buruma, Ian (1984) *A Japanese Mirror: Heroes and Villains of Japanese Culture*, London: Jonathon Cape.

Cavanaugh, Carole (2000) *Word and Image in Japanese Cinema*, New York: Cambridge University Press.

Cardullo, Bert (2008) *Akira Kurosawa: Interviews (Conversations with Filmmakers)*, Jackson: University Press of Mississippi.

Cavallaro, Dani (2006) *The Anime Art of Hayao Miyazaki*, Jefferson, NC: McFarland & Co.

Cavallaro, Dani (2006) *The Cinema of Mamoru Oshii: Fantasy, Technology and Politics*, Jefferson, NC: McFarland and Co.

Cavallaro, Dani (2007) *Anime Intersections: Tradition and Innovation in Theme and Technique*, Jefferson, NC: McFarland and Co.

Cazdyn, Eric (2003) *The Flash of Capital: Film and Geopolitics in Japan*, Durham: Duke University Press.

Clements, Jonathon & McCarthy, Helen (2007) *The Anime Encyclopedia*, London: Titan.

Davis, William Darrell (1996) *Picturing Japaneseness: Monumental Style, National Identity, Japanese Film*, New York: Columbia University Press.

Desjardins, Chris (2005) *Outlaw Masters of Japanese Film*, London: I.B. Tauris.

Desser, David (1983) *The Samurai Films of Akira Kurosawa*, Ann Arbor, MI: UMI Research Press.

Desser, David (1988) *Reframing Japanese Cinema: Authorship, Genre, History*, Bloomington: Indiana University Press.

Desser, David (1997) *Ozu's Tokyo Story*, Cambridge: Cambridge University Press.

Desser, David (1998) *Eros Plus Massacre: An Introduction to the Japanese New Wave Cinema*, Bloomington: Indiana University Press.

Galloway (2005) Patrick, *Stray Dogs and Lone Wolves: The Samurai Film Handbook*, Berkeley, CA: Stone Bridge Press.

Galloway, Patrick (2006) *Asia Shock: Horror and Dark Cinema from Japan, Korea, Hong Kong and Thailand*, Berkeley, CA: Stone Bridge Press.

Gerow, Aaron (2007) *Kitano Takeshi (World Directors)*, London: BFI.

Harper, Jim (2008) *Flowers from Hell: The Modern Japanese Horror Film*, Noir Publishing.

High, Peter (2003) *The Imperial Screen: Japanese Film Culture in the Fifteen Years' War*, Madison: University of Wisconsin Press.

Hunter, Jack (1999) *Eros in Hell: Sex, Blood and Madness in Japanese Cinema*, London: Creation Books.

Jacoby, Alexander (2008) *A Critical Handbook of Japanese Film Directors: From the Silent Era to the Present Day*, Berkeley, CA: Stone Bridge Press.

Joso, Estudio (2006) *The Monster Book of Manga*, London: Collins.

Kalat, David (2007) *A Critical History and Filmography of Toho's Godzilla Series*, Jefferson, NC: McFarland & Co.

Kurosawa, Akira (1983) *Something like an Autobiography*, London: Vintage Books.

Macias, Patrick (2001) *Tokyoscope: The Japanese Cult Film Companion*, San Francisco: Cadence.

Mellen, Joan (2004) *In the Realm of the Senses*, London: BFI.

McCarthy, Helen (2003) *Hayao Miyazaki: Master of Japanese Animation: Films, Themes, Artistry*, Berkeley, CA: Stone Bridge Press.

McDonald, Keiko I (1983) *Cinema East: A Critical Study of Major Japanese Films*, Rutherford, NJ: Fairleigh Dickinson University Press.

McDonald, Keiko I (2006) *Reading a Japanese Film: Cinema in Context*, Honolulu: University of Hawaii Press.

McRoy, Jay (2005) *Japanese Horror Cinema*, Edinburgh: Edinburgh University Press.

Mes, Tom (2003) *Agitator: The Cinema of Takashi Miike*, FAB Press.

Mes, Tom (2005) *Iron Man: The Cinema of Shinya Tsukamoto*, FAB Press.

Mes, Tom & Sharp, Jasper (2004) *The Midnight Eye Guide to New Japanese Film*, Berkeley, CA: Stone Bridge Press.

Marciano, Mitsuyo Wada (2008) *Nippon Modern: Japanese Cinema of the 1920s and 1930s*, : Honolulu: University of Hawaii Press.

Napier, Susan (2006) *Anime from Akira to Howl's Moving Castle: Experiencing Contemporary Japanese Animation*, New York: Palgrave MacMillan.

Nogami, Teruyo (2006) *Waiting on the Weather: Making Movies with Akira Kurosawa*, Berkeley, CA: Stone Bridge Press.

Nolletti, Arthur Jr. & Desser, David (2005) *Reframing Japanese Cinema: Authorship, Genre, History*, Bloomington: Indiana University Press.

Osmond, Andrew (2008) *Spirited Away (BFI Film Classics)*, London: BFI.

Phillips, Alastair & Stringer, Julian (2006) *Japanese Cinema: Texts and Contexts*, London & New York: Routledge.

Prince, Stephen (1999) *The Warrior's Camera: The Cinema of Akira Kurosawa*, Princeton, NJ: Princeton University Press.

Ritchie, Donald (1972) *Japanese Cinema: Film Style and National Character*, London: Secker & Warburg.

Ritchie, Donald (1990) *Japanese Cinema: An Introduction*, Hong Kong, New York: Oxford University Press.

Ritchie, Donald (1996) *The Films of Akira Kurosawa*, Berkeley, CA: University of California Press.

Ruh, Brian (2004) *Stray Dog of Anime: The Films of Mamoru Oshii*, New York: Palgrave MacMillan.

Sato, Tado (2008) *Kenji Mizoguchi and the Art of Japanese Cinema*, Oxford: Berg.

Schilling, Mark (2000) *Contemporary Japanese Film*, New York: Weatherhill.

Schilling, Mark (2003) *Yakuza Movie Book: A Guide to Japanese Gangster Films*, Berkeley, CA: Stone Bridge Press.

Schilling, Mark (2007) *No Borders, No Limits: Nikkatsu Action Cinema*, FAB Press.

Sharp, Jasper (2008) *Behind the Pink Curtain: The Complete History of Japanese Sex Cinema*, FAB Press.

Standish, Isolde (2000) *Myth and Masculinity in the Japanese Cinema: Towards a Political Reading of the Tragic Hero*, London: Routledge.

Standish, Isolde (2006) *A New History of Japanese Cinema: A Century of Narrative Film*, New York: Continuum.

Thornton, Sybil (2007) *The Japanese Period Film: A Critical Analysis*, Jefferson, NC: McFarland & Co.

Tsutsui, William (2004) *Godzilla on My Mind: Fifty Years of the King of Monsters*, New York: Palgrave MacMillan.

Weisser, Yuko Mihara & Weisser, Thomas (1998) *Japanese Cinema: Encyclopaedia – The Sex Films*, Miami: Vital Books.

JAPANESE CINEMA ONLINE

3Yen
http://cinema.3yen.com
Network of weblogs related to everything Japanese, with contemporary cinema
being discussed alongside travel, gadgets, food, teaching in Japan, and other
aspects of popular Japanese culture.

The Association of Japanese Animation
http://www.aja.gr.jp
AJA is an industry group, consisting of Japan's leading animation production
companies, which aims to sustain the development of the Japanese animation
industry. Along with information on events organized by the Association and
its members, the site provides information relating to new developments in
Japanese animation production, training programmes and copyright issues.

Bright Lights Film Journal
http://www.brightlightsfilm.com
Bright Lights Film Journal is a popular-academic online hybrid of movie analysis,
history, and commentary, looking at classic and commercial, independent,
exploitation, and international film from a wide range of vantage points from the
aesthetic to the political.

CineMagaziNet!
http://www.cmn.hs.h.kyoto-u.ac.jp
Bilingual, online scholarly research journal, focusing on Japanese cinema.

CoFesta
http://www.cofesta.jp
The official site of the Media Contents film festival, CoFesta, gathering media
content regarding video games, anime, manga, music, broadcasting and films.

Directory of World Cinema
http://worldcinemadirectory.org/
The website for the *Directory of World Cinema* series featuring film reviews and biographies of directors. An ideal starting point for students of World Cinema.

EigaGoGo!
http://eigagogo.free.fr
Informative website devoted to Japanese cinema, with articles on key films, directors and genres, which also examines Japanese cultural life.

Hoga Central
http://www.hogacentral.com
This website features reviews of new Japanese movies and interviews with leading directors. The aim of the site is to introduce international audiences to the films which Japanese viewers enjoy on a regular basis, rather than just focusing on the titles that are released internationally or find exposure at film festivals.

Internet Movie Database
http://www.imdb.com
Leading source of information for international cinema and industry news, with pages devoted to individual films, directors, actors, crew members, and regularly updated links to breaking news and interesting articles.

Japan Arts Council
http://www.ntj.jac.go.jp
Japanese-only site which provides information on Japanese film production and supporting programmes offered by the Japan Arts Council, which collectively involves Japanese national cultural-art institutions such as the Japanese National Theatre, National Engei Hall, National Noh Theatre, National Bunraku Theatre, National Theatre of Okinawa, New National Theatre of Tokyo.

Japan Community Cinema Centre
http://www.jc3.jp
The official site of the Japan Community Cinema Centre, a non-profit organization which supports industry presence in local areas of Japan. Aside from information on its activities, the site provides information related to national and international cinema, a directory of Japanese film festivals and reports on the state of the Japanese film industry, gained from its own research studies.

Japanese Filmmakers Association
http://www2.odn.ne.jp
The official site of the Japanese Film Makers Association, formed in 1995 by Japanese film and video production industry members.

Japan Foundation
http://www.jpf.go.jp
The official website of the Japan Foundation. This organization aims to promote cultural and people-to-people exchanges in the fields of art, Japanese language education and intellectual property. It also provides information on its projects relating to film festivals and Japanese film production.

Japanese Movie Database
http://www.jmdb.ne.jp
Similar to the Internet Movie Database, but entirely focused on Japanese
cinema. The database was started in 1997 and contains information about films,
directors, actors and crew members.

Japan Media Arts Plaza
http://plaza.bunka.go.jp
This site provides media art-related information alongside the information on the
Media Art Film Festival organized by the Agency of Cultural Affairs.

Japan Times
http://www.usajapan.org/
Daily news and features on Japan, from the most widely-read newspaper in the
country. Film critic Mark Schilling is a regular writer.

J-Preview
www.jpreview.com
Comprehensive Japanese cinema review site, featuring news, images, DVD
releases, essays and a forum.

Kawakita Memorial Film Institute
http://www.kawakita-film.or.jp
The official site of the Film Institute formed by Kawakita. With information on
Japanese film screenings, the site provides access to the institute's reference
database, which includes both Japanese and foreign film-related books,
magazines, pamphlets, and event catalogues.

Kinema Club
http://pears.lib.ohio-state.edu
Kinema Club is devoted to the study of Japanese moving-image media, and is
produced through the collaboration of many scholars around the world. It keeps
everyone connected as a storehouse of information and serves as the host to the
newsgroup KineJapan.

Kinotayo
http://www.kinotayo.fr
The official site of the Japanese film festival, Kinotayo, held in Paris, France,
every year in November.

Mark Schilling's Tokyo Ramen
http://www.japanesemovies.homestead.com
Reviews and articles about Japanese films and pop culture by Mark Schilling,
reviewer for *The Japan Times* and reporter for *Screen International*.

Motion Picture Producers Association of Japan, Inc.
http://www.eiren.org
This site introduces the activities of the four leading film production companies
in Japan: Shochiku, Toho, Toei and Kadokawa Films, known as 'Eiren'. It provides
considerable statistic data on the Japanese film industry alongside 'Eiren DB',
which covers most of the works produced and distributed by above-mentioned
film production companies.

National Film Centre, the National Museum of Modern Art, Tokyo (NFC)
http://www.momat.go.jp
This site provides information on the activities that the National Film Centre
organizes within the National Museum of Modern Arts which include regular
Japanese film screenings and exhibitions, Japanese film industry-related
symposiums and lectures and activities related to the maintenance and
preservation of Japanese film archive.

Nippon Connection
http://www.nipponconnection.de
Official website of Nippon Connection, the largest festival of Japanese cinema
held in Europe. The website features information about the annual event, with
press links, timetables and achieves.

Pia Film Festival
http://www.pff.jp
The official site of the Pia Film Festival, established at Tokyo in 1977 with an aim
to discover and support new film-making talent. Besides the information related
to the festival, the site also provides information on Pia's scholarship scheme,
original library and film releases.

Senses of Cinema
http://www.sensesofcinema.com
Senses of Cinema is an online journal devoted to the serious and eclectic
discussion of cinema. *Senses of Cinema* is primarily concerned with ideas
about particular films or bodies of work, but also with the regimes (ideological,
economic and so forth) under which films are produced and viewed, and with
the more abstract theoretical and philosophical issues raised by film study.

Third Window Films
http://www.thirdwindowfilms.com
Official website for UK distributor Third Window Films; their carefully chosen
catalogue includes a number of recent Japanese films.

Tokyo FilmEx
http://www.filmex.net
The official site of Tokyo FilmEx, a festival which follows new trends in the
Japanese film industry and which aims to establish sustainable networks among
film producers.

Tokyo International Anime Fair
http://www.tokyoanime.jp
The official site of the Tokyo International Anime Fair, the world largest anime
fair organized every year in spring at Tokyo Big site.

Tokyo International Film Festival
http://www.tiff-jp.net
The official site of Tokyo International Film Festival, Japan's only officially-
approved international film festival, initiated in the year 1985 and presently
managed by Japan Association for International Promotion of Moving Images.

The Toronto Japanese Film Appreciation Pow-Wow
http://www.jfilmpowwow.blogspot.com
Founded by Chris MaGee in 2007 The Toronto J-Film Pow-Wow is an online community dedicated to discussing and promoting Japanese cinema in Toronto, Ontario, Canada as well as around the world.

Visual Industry Promotion Organisation
http://www.vipo.or.jp
The official site of VIPO, Japan's Visual Industry Promotion Organization. The organization concentrates on the development of moving images/content industry, including Japanese films, television, animation, video games and music. The site also provides access to the VIPO-managed contents industry database (JapaCON).

TEST YOUR
KNOWLED

Questions

1. With which leading man would the director Akira Kurosawa frequently collaborate?
2. Which five-film gangster series was originated by the director Kinji Fukasaku?
3. Who played the title role in *Female Prisoner #701: Scorpion* and its two sequels?
4. Which short story by the popular novelist Haruki Murakami was adapted for the big screen by Jun Ichikawa in 2004?
5. The Hollywood western *The Magnificent Seven* was inspired by which Akira Kurosawa classic?
6. Which 1960 film by Kaneto Shindo won the Grand Prix at the Moscow International Film Festival?
7. What is the Japanese term for a period piece?
8. Which 1999 Hideo Nakata horror film spawned several sequels and an American remake?
9. What was the sequel to Akira Kurosawa's *Yojimbo*?
10. What is the Japanese term for the New Wave?
11. Who was regarded as the 'godfather of pink cinema', due to such controversial classics as *Violated Angels* and *Go Go Second Time Virgin*?
12. Which Akira Kurosawa classic concerns the hunt for a police detective's missing pistol?
13. Which cult gangster film by Seijun Suzuki led to the director's dismissal from Nikkatsu Studios?
14. Which 1954 film follows the lives of a school teacher and her first twelve students?
15. Who directed the revisionist samurai films, *The Twilight Samurai* and *The Hidden Blade*?
16. Akira Kurosawa used Shakespeare's *Macbeth* as the template for which historical epic?
17. The anime feature *The Castle of Cagliostro* was a big-screen spin-off from which popular animated television series?

18. What is the name of the regulatory board for Japanese Cinema which was established in 1949?
19. Which 1998 film deals with a group of people who find themselves in spiritual limbo following their mortal passing?
20. Which blind swordsman, who has featured in a series of samurai films, was revived recently by Takeshi Kitano?
21. Which Shōhei Imamura film was based on the exploits of a real-life serial killer?
22. Nagisa Oshima directed which infamous pink film starring Eiko Matsuda in 1976?
23. Which 1960 Mikio Naruse film dealt with a middle-aged bar hostess working in the Ginza district of Tokyo?
24. Who is the internationally-popular star of *Bright Future*, *Maborosi* and *Ichi the Killer*?
25. What is the Japanese term for a monster movie?
26. Which anime feature by Satoshi Kon concerns three homeless denizens of Tokyo who find an abandoned baby in a rubbish dump?
27. The comedian Matsumoto Hotoshi parodied the monster movie genre with which 2007 spoof?
28. What is the Japanese term for a gangster movie?
29. Which festival devoted to Japanese Cinema is held annually in Frankfurt?
30. What is the Japanese term for a contemporary drama?
31. Which studio was responsible for the *Godzilla* series?
32. Which Nagisa Oshima film was based on the true story of a Korean man who murdered two Japanese schoolgirls?
33. Which Japanese film won the 2003 Academy Award for Best Animated Feature?
34. What is the name of the director of *Tokyo Story* and *Floating Weeds*?
35. Which director of pink films ventured into the mainstream with his 2009 thriller *Pandemic*?
36. What is the Japanese term for a samurai film?
37. Which studio was responsible for the *Gamera* series?
38. What is the literal translation of the title of Takeshi Kitano's 1997 film *Hana-Bi*?
39. Which independent film company, often cited as being responsible for the Japanese New Wave, was founded in 1961?
40. Which 2008 Takeshi Kitano film found the writer-director-star exploring his obsession with painting?
41. *The Pornographers* was the first independently-financed feature by which New Wave director?
42. Which artistic movement of the 1960s formed the basis for experimental photography and video art?
43. Which popular Fuji Television series was brought to the big-screen by Toho in 2003?
44. *Sukiyaki Western Django* is the first English-language feature by which prolific Japanese director?
45. Which film by Shinya Tsukamoto concerns the repressed desire of woman who works on a mental health hotline?
46. Who directed the 1965 period espionage film *Samurai Spy*?
47. Which 2004 film was anime director Katsuhiro Otomo's long-awaited follow-up to his groundbreaking *Akira*?
48. Who starred in the classic Japanese gangster films *Branded to Kill* and *A Colt is my Passport*?
49. Who directed *The Life of Oharu*, *Osaka Elegy* and *Tales of Moonlight and Rain*?
50. Which 1959 film by Kon Ichikawa was set during the final days of World War II?

Answers

1. Toshiro Mifune
2. *Battles without Honour and Humanity*
3. Meiko Kaji
4. *Tony Takitani*
5. *The Seven Samurai*
6. *The Naked Island*
7. Jidaigeki
8. *The Ring*
9. *Sanjuro*
10. Nuberu bagu
11. Kôji Wakamatsu
12. *Stray Dog*
13. *Branded to Kill*
14. *Twenty-Four Eyes*
15. Yoji Yamada
16. *Throne of Blood*
17. *Lupin III*
18. Eirin Motion Picture Code of Ethics
19. *Afterlife*
20. Zatôichi
21. *Vengeance is mine*
22. *In the Realm of the Senses*
23. *When a Woman Ascends the Stairs*
24. Tadanobu Asano
25. Kaiju eiga
26. *Tokyo Godfathers*
27. *Big Man Japan*
28. Yakuza
29. Nippon Connection
30. Gendaigeki
31. Toho
32. *Death by Hanging*
33. *Spirited Away*
34. Yasujiro Ozu
35. Zeze Takahasa
36. Chambara
37. Daiei
38. Fireworks
39. The Art Theatre Guild
40. *Achilles and the Tortoise*
41. Shohei Imamura
42. The Neo-Dadaist movement
43. *Bayside Shakedown*
44. Takashi Miike
45. *A Snake of June*
46. Masahiro Shinoda
47. *Steamboy*
48. Jo Shishido
49. Kenji Mizoguchi
50. *Fires on the Plain*

NOTES ON CONTRIBUTORS

The Editor

John Berra is a Lecturer in Film Studies and the author of *Declarations of Independence: American Cinema and the Partiality of Independent Production* (2008). He is also a regular contributor to *Electric Sheep*, *Film International* and *Scope* and is currently researching World Cinema with regards to evolving practices in authorship, production and distribution.

The Contributors

Elest Ali is an aspiring young author and freelance writer with a degree in English literature from Kings College, London. She is currently completing her Masters in Comparative Literature, at SOAS; Japanese Literature and Cinema are among her chosen areas of study.

Colette Balmain is a Lecturer in Film Studies. Her main area of expertise is East Asian Popular Cinema, although she also has published extensively on European horror cinema. She is the author of *Introduction to the Japanese Horror Film* (2008) and is currently working on a book about Korean Horror Cinema. She is an editor for the *Electronic Journal of Japanese Studies*, and is a member of the Global Gothic Network, which examines the impact of East Asian Gothic forms on definitions of the gothic.

Amelia Cook is a postgraduate student on the MA Global Cinemas and the Transcultural course at the School of Oriental and African Studies, with a degree in Japanese Studies from the University of Sheffield. She intends to pursue a PhD in Japanese film and television.

Marc Saint-Cyr graduated from the University of Toronto with an Honours Bachelor of Arts in Cinema Studies and History. He is a regular contributor to the Toronto J-Film Pow-Wow.

Bob Davis is a Professor of Film Production and History at California State University, Fullerton and a contributor to *American Cinematographer* magazine.

Alanna Donaldson studied Film at the universities of Bath and Bristol and has written reviews for Bath Film Festival and *Imagine Animation* magazine. She currently works as part of the journals team at Intellect Books.

Matthew Hardstaff was born in Nottingham, England, in 1976, and his family emigrated to Georgetown, Ontario, Canada when he was eight. Still residing in the Central Ontario region, the Toronto-based writer, film-maker and dungeon master contributes regularly to the Toronto J-Film Pow-Wow, and is currently working on his first feature, entitled *Bluebird*.

Jim Harper is the author of *Legacy of Blood: A Comprehensive Guide to Slasher Movies* (2004) and *Flowers from Hell: The Modern Japanese Horror Film* (2008), and *Dark Dreams: The World of Anime Horror* (2009). He also continues to contribute reviews, biographies, articles and DVD-liner notes, specializing in cult and horror cinema from around the globe.

Derek Hill is a freelance film critic and author of the book *Charlie Kaufman and Hollywood's Merry Band of Pranksters, Fabulists and Dreamers* (2008). He currently resides in Athens, Georgia.

Matthew Holland is a Bachelor of Arts graduate in Film Studies and Creative Writing from Roehampton University and is currently studying for a Masters in Japanese Cultural Studies at the University of London, School of Oriental and African Studies (SOAS), majoring in Japanese Film Studies.

Christopher Howard teaches at the Centre for Media and Film Studies at SOAS, University of London, where he has recently completed a PhD in Japanese Cinema.

Justin Howe is a graduate of the Boston University film programme, and his writing on film has appeared online at Strange Horizons, the Internet Review of Science Fiction, and Tor.com. His fiction has appeared in the anthologies *Fast Ships, Black Sails* (2008) and *CinemaSpec: Tales of Hollywood and Fantasy* (2009). He currently lives in New York City.

Angus McBlane is a PhD Student at the Centre for Critical and Cultural Theory at Cardiff University. His current research focus is on critical posthumanism, technology and cyberculture.

James Mottram is a film journalist who writes regularly on the subject for, among others, *The Times*, *The Independent*, *Total Film* and *Marie Claire*. He is also the author of four books: *Public Enemies: The Gangster Movie A-Z* (1998); *Coen Brothers: The Life of the Mind* (2000); *The Making of Memento* (2002) and *The Sundance Kids: How The Mavericks Took Back Hollywood* (2006). In addition, he has contributed to numerous critical anthologies, including *Ten Bad Dates with De Niro* (2007) and *Under Fire: A Century of War Movies* (2009). He lives in London.

Ricardo de Los Rios is a screenwriter based in Santa Monica, CA and an Associate Professor with the Department of Radio-TV-Film at California State University, Fullerton.

Julian Ross is a student of Film Studies at Queen Mary University of London and a librarian at Close-Up Film Library in East London. His research interests include post-war Japanese cinema, independent cinema, and theories on national cinemas.

Brian Ruh is the author of *Stray Dog of Anime: The Films of Mamoru Oshii* (2004). He is on the editorial board of the journal *Mechademia* and has contributed chapters to a number of books on anime and Asian cinema. He is currently a PhD candidate in the Department of Communication and Culture at Indiana University.

Mark Schilling was born in Zanesville, Ohio in 1949 and arrived in Tokyo in 1975, where he has lived ever since. He has reviewed Japanese films for *The Japan Times* since 1989 and has reported on the Japanese film industry for *Variety* since 1990. Since 2000, he has been a programmer for the Udine Far East Film Festival, Europe's largest festival of Asian popular cinema. His books include *The Encyclopedia of Japanese Pop Culture* (1999) *Contemporary Japanese Film* (1999), *The Yakuza Movie Book: A Guide to Japanese Gangster Films* (2003) and *No Borders, No Limits: The World of Nikkatsu Action* (2005).

Fred Shimizu, a native New Yorker, learned to read at an early age through the subtitled Japanese films he viewed on a weekly basis. Since, he has attended NYU Film School, amassed a collection of over 300 Japanese films, written three screenplays, won six Television Arts and Science Emmy Awards and completed eight New York City Marathons. Still, he is most proud of his three beautiful daughters.

Jelena Stojković is undertaking PhD research on the transnational legacy of Surrealism in Japanese photography with the University of Westminster, following three years with the Japanese Gallery in London, and her MA in History of Art at SOAS.

Bob Turnbull is the writer and editor of *Eternal Sunshine of the Logical Mind* – a blog devoted to all things film-related. He is also a regular contributor to the J-Film Pow-Wow web site. Though a fan of a wide variety of Japanese films, he has a particular fondness for yakuza and crime films from the 1960s and 1970s as well as horror films from any time period. He lives in Toronto with his wife and son.

William M. Tsutsui is Professor of Modern Japanese History at the University of Kansas. He is the author of *Godzilla on My Mind: Fifty Years of the King of Monsters* (2004), which won the 2005 William Rockhill Nelson Award for non-fiction, and co-editor (with Michiko Ito) of *In Godzilla's Footsteps: Japanese Pop Culture Icons on the Global Stage* (2006).

Nikolaos Vryzidis has studied Film at Queen Mary, University of London and History of Art at SOAS. His academic interests include transculturalism in cinema and visual arts, cultural hybridity and museology.

Alexander Zahlten is an independent scholar in Film Studies and co-organizer of the Nippon Connection Film Festival. His PhD was undertaken at Johannes Gutenberg University Mainz and Nihon University, and discussed the role of genre in Japanese film. His current research focuses on the transnational dynamics in East Asian cinema and popular European cinema from the 1960s.